Approaches to Teaching Defoe's *Robinson Crusoe*

Approaches to Teaching
World Literature

Joseph Gibaldi, series editor

For a complete listing of titles,
see the last pages of this book.

Approaches to Teaching Defoe's *Robinson Crusoe*

Edited by

Maximillian E. Novak

and

Carl Fisher

The Modern Language Association of America
New York   2005

PR 3403
Z5
A67
2005

For information about obtaining permission to reprint material from
MLA book publications, send your request by mail (see address below),
e-mail (permissions@mla.org), or fax (646 458-0030).

Library of Congress Cataloging-in-Publication Data

Approaches to teaching Defoe's Robinson Crusoe / edited by
Maximillian E. Novak and Carl Fisher.
p. cm. — (Approaches to teaching world literature)
Includes bibliographical references and index.
ISBN 0-87352-916-2 (alk. paper) — ISBN 0-87352-917-0 (pbk. : alk. paper)
1. Defoe, Daniel, 1661?–1731. Robinson Crusoe. 2. Survival after airplane accidents,
shipwrecks, etc., in literature. 3. Defoe, Daniel, 1661?–1731—Study and teaching.
4. Crusoe, Robinson (Fictitious character)
I. Novak, Maximillian E. II. Fisher, Carl, 1958– III. Series.
PR3403.Z5A67 2005
823'.5—dc22   2005003987

ISSN 1059-1133

Cover illustration of the paperback edition: frontispiece
from the first edition of *Robinson Crusoe*, 1719

Printed on recycled paper

Published by The Modern Language Association of America
26 Broadway, New York, New York 10004-1789
www.mla.org

CONTENTS

PREFACE TO THE SERIES

In *The Art of Teaching* Gilbert Highet wrote, "Bad teaching wastes a great deal of effort, and spoils many lives which might have been full of energy and happiness." All too many teachers have failed in their work, Highet argued, simply "because they have not thought about it." We hope that the Approaches to Teaching World Literature series, sponsored by the Modern Language Association's Publications Committee, will not only improve the craft—as well as the art—of teaching but also encourage serious and continuing discussion of the aims and methods of teaching literature.

The principal objective of the series is to collect within each volume different points of view on teaching a specific literary work, a literary tradition, or a writer widely taught at the undergraduate level. The preparation of each volume begins with a wide-ranging survey of instructors, thus enabling us to include in the volume the philosophies and approaches, thoughts and methods of scores of experienced teachers. The result is a sourcebook of material, information, and ideas on teaching the subject of the volume to undergraduates.

The series is intended to serve nonspecialists as well as specialists, inexperienced as well as experienced teachers, graduate students who wish to learn effective ways of teaching as well as senior professors who wish to compare their own approaches with the approaches of colleagues in other schools. Of course, no volume in the series can ever substitute for erudition, intelligence, creativity, and sensitivity in teaching. We hope merely that each book will point readers in useful directions; at most each will offer only a first step in the long journey to successful teaching.

Joseph Gibaldi
Series Editor

THE
LIFE

John AND *Lord. 0:5:0.*

STRANGE SURPRIZING

ADVENTURES

April. OF *inig.*

ROBINSON CRUSOE,

Of *YORK*, Mariner:

Who lived Eight and Twenty Years,
all alone in an un-inhabited Island on the
Coast of AMERICA, near the Mouth of
the Great River of OROONOQUE;

Having been caft on Shore by Shipwreck, where-
in all the Men perifhed but himfelf.

WITH

An Account how he was at laft as ftrangely deliver'd by PYRATES.

Written by Himfelf.

LONDON;

Printed for W. TAYLOR at the *Ship* in *Pater-Nofter-
Row.* MDCCXIX.

Title page from the first edition of *Robinson Crusoe*, 1719

INTRODUCTION

Issues in Teaching Robinson Crusoe

The field of eighteenth-century studies has undergone serious shifts since the middle of the twentieth century. Not only has the canon been significantly revised, opened to voices that were previously considered marginal, but also critical theory has taken on the century in consequential ways, forcing us to read texts in a new light. Issues of race, class, and gender have become predominant foci, and we understand that no text is ever ahistorical. Still, with all the canon shifts and critical attention, or perhaps because of them, *Robinson Crusoe* remains a standard text for teaching the period. The character Robinson Crusoe is a mythic, international figure and a touchstone of popular culture. Daniel Defoe's novel exerted a significant influence on the fiction of its time and today continues to live outside its original context and culture. *Robinson Crusoe* has been adapted endlessly: in abridged versions, as a popular children's tale, and in many retellings. It still provides a common cinema motif; movies often utilize the Crusoe formula of coping with shipwreck, adapting to a natural environment, and fighting off an unfriendly indigenous population. Like most pop cultural icons, however—for example, *Frankenstein's* creature, which most people know better from the Boris Karloff film than from Mary Shelley's novel—Crusoe in common culture is decontextualized, misinterpreted, and adapted to each generation's use. Teaching *Robinson Crusoe* requires a multifold maneuver. First, both students and teachers need to be able to separate the popular image of Crusoe from the text itself. They need to find distance from the myth of Crusoe without losing sight of why it is powerful. Often the novel is contrasted to contemporary rewritings of the text or diagnosed using recent critical modes. The best understanding of the text not only demands a rigorous ideological questioning but also entails an appreciation of the text as a text, within the context of its production.

The essays offered here discuss the cultural milieu and contexts of the eighteenth century as well as the social, political, moral, ethical, and ideological implications of the work. The essays are intended to have practical value for teachers by providing important background and interpretive material while offering approaches and strategies that are classroom-tested. From our survey of instructors, we found that *Robinson Crusoe* is widely taught at all levels of the undergraduate curriculum, from world literature surveys to rise-of-the-novel courses; it is often included in freshman core courses as a central text of Western civilization and in courses on postcolonial literature as an example of imperialism at work. It is a novel that bridges disciplinary boundaries and finds adherents not only in English literary studies but also in history, sociology, political science, world literature, adolescent literature, and even religious studies or in topics courses in autobiography, colonial and postcolonial fiction, the literature of exploration, the myth of modern individualism, and castaway narratives.

Teaching *Robinson Crusoe*, however, remains a difficult task for a number of reasons. The reader struggles with the historical distance, which must be overcome to avoid simplifying the text. Themes central to the eighteenth-century context need illumination. The complex narrative technique demands analysis. Additionally, giving students a framework for thinking about elements of the novel that are specific to Defoe as well as those common to other works facilitates learning about the text. Our survey results show us that *Crusoe* remains an ambiguous text, complex to teach and open to many readings. The debates on *Robinson Crusoe* began with the original publication in 1719, when Charles Gildon attacked Defoe and the implications of his work, and continue to the present day. This volume presents both traditional and contemporary viewpoints and explores historical and theoretical aspects of the text and its interpretations. Defoe scholars raise issues that teachers of the novel put to practical use in the classroom. For example, one of the first concerns for any teacher involves genre and categorization. Scholars have questioned whether the narrative is an allegory, a romance, an economic tract, a travel tale, a biography, an autobiography, or a new species of fiction. Another issue is how to judge the character of Crusoe. How representative is the rebellious sensibility that leads Crusoe to reject his father's advice concerning his calling and head to sea? Is Defoe lauding or condemning an adventurous spirit? Crusoe himself gives us a choice of interpretations in referring to his island condition alternately as his "reign" or his "captivity" (100). There are continuing debates on the religious elements of the narrative. How are we to understand Crusoe's blaming his misfortunes on "original sin" and how significant are his conceptualizations of a providential order (141)? Defoe often wrote not in a vacuum but in response to other popular writing. How influential was Defoe's source material for *Robinson Crusoe*, such as contemporary narratives about Alexander Selkirk's experiences (see Steele)? Economic concerns always influence Defoe's prose. Is Crusoe, as Karl Marx suggests, an exemplar of *homo economicus* in his husbandry and hoarding?

The essays in this volume address these and myriad other issues. For example, how does a teacher generate the interest of a modern student in a text that seems distant not only in historical time but also in psychological space and narrative voice? The need to develop coping and compensatory strategies, to develop both practical and theoretical abilities, for understanding the novel is fitting for one of the West's first narratives of modernity. While these collected essays have the practical aim of offering useful material for the classroom, they also take up difficult and controversial aspects of *Robinson Crusoe* and extend our critical understanding of the novel. Most important, the essays address how to make *Robinson Crusoe* a living text and not merely a document of the past.

Robinson Crusoe: *Reader Reception and Generic Conventions*

When *The Life and Strange Surprizing Adventures of Robinson Crusoe*, known immediately as simply *Robinson Crusoe*, first appeared on 25 April 1719, what might book buyers have expected from the title page and the illustration? For those who could afford the five shillings, the title page promised exciting adventures—a story of strange lands and "An account how he was at last as strangely deliver'd by PYRATES." Robinson Crusoe is identified as a "Mariner," and all the elements of this account suggest an exciting tale of the sea. The frontispiece by John Clark and John Pine (reproduced on the cover of the paperbound edition of this book) shows a ship that seems to be sailing well enough but that has a dark cloud above it and threatening waves surrounding it. Crusoe has a rifle over each shoulder, a pistol in his belt, and a sword. He is bearded and dressed in an odd costume that might have reminded readers of images of Selkirk (whose story had been told in Woodes Rogers's *A Cruising Voyage round the World*) or of philosophers seeking to live close to nature (a resemblance that might have been stronger for those readers on the Continent who encountered a frontispiece etched by Bernard Picart in the first French edition, with Crusoe carrying a very large saw instead of a sword). The second edition, published about two weeks later on 9 May, contained the large logo of a ship, like those that frequently appeared on accounts of voyages. This logo accompanied the original novel and the two sequels, as well as all subsequent editions published by William Taylor, *The Farther Adventures of Robinson Crusoe*, first published on 20 August 1719, and *Serious Reflections during the Life and Surprizing Adventures of Robinson Crusoe, with His Vision of the Angelick World*, published on 6 August 1720.

The title page noted that the book was "*Written by Himself*," which is what would have been expected of a work whose main character's voice resembled those of William Dampier's *A New Voyage round the World* (1697) and Woodes Rogers's similar account, published in 1712. Even the popular historical narrative of Alexandre Oliver Exquemelin, *History of the Buccaneers* (1672), originally narrated in the third person, gave way to a collective first person in Basil Ringrose's continuation (1684–85). Maps accompanied many of these works, a strategy imitated in *The Farther Adventures*, which included a map showing the countries to which Crusoe traveled.

Such works offer an authenticity that few readers of any sophistication would have granted *The Surprizing Adventures* after the shipwreck on the island. For one thing, there was a general expectation that travel accounts would contain considerable fiction. Imaginary voyages such as Gabriel de Foigny's *La terre Australe connue* (*The Southern Land, Known* [1676]), provided a fairly realistic account of a shipwreck before moving on to its utopian elements. Similarly, a sense of the real was preserved throughout Tyssot de Patot's *Voyages et aventures de Jacques Massé* (1710). The strenuous insistence on authenticity at the beginning of the work was, by the time of *Crusoe*, a convention of fictions involving voyages.

Defoe never dropped his cover of anonymity. Long after Gildon's pamphlet exposing the work as a fiction by Defoe, it was as Crusoe that he spoke of the work as an allegory or what we would call a symbolic fiction. On the Continent, *Crusoe* was usually reviewed as a work of fiction. This was the case in both the *Journal des scavans* and in Jean Le Clerc's *Bibliotheque ancienne et moderne*. Le Clerc described *Crusoe* as a "sort de Roman Moral" and praised all but the last volume (15: 441); the *Journal* selected Crusoe's "O Gold" speech as an example of its excellence. And the introduction to the Leipzig edition claimed *Crusoe* not only as a fiction by "Daniel De Foe" but also as one that would last as long as literature was read.

The first French translator of *Crusoe*, however, asserted that it had to have been written by a sailor because the language was too simple for the work to be by a learned writer. The work was written in a colloquial language that became a hallmark of novels in English. Over two hundred years later, this issue was still contested. Ian Watt in his groundbreaking study *The Rise of the Novel* later dismissed works that had too elegant a style as being outside the mainstream of the novel. Watt argued that Defoe and Samuel Richardson established colloquial English as an element of realism that defined the novel genre. Toward the end of the first Crusoe novel, when Crusoe is helping to retake the ship for the English Captain, a sailor who has decided to rejoin the forces led by Crusoe and the Captain and a mutineer engage in a conversation:

> [S]o he calls out as loud as he could, to one of them, *Tom Smith*, *Tom Smith*; *Tom Smith* answered immediately, *Who's that*, Robinson? for it seems he knew his Voice: T'other answered, *Ay, ay; for God's Sake*, Tom Smith, *throw down your Arms, and yield*, or, *you are all dead Men this Moment.*
>
> *Who must we yield to? Where are they?* (says Smith again;) *Here they are*, says he, here's our Captain, and fifty Men with him, have been hunting you this two Hours; the Boatswain is kill'd, *Will Frye* is wounded, and I am a Prisoner; and if you do not yield, you are all lost.
>
> Will they give us Quarter then, (says *Tom Smith*) and we will yield? *I'll go and ask, if you promise to yield*, says *Robinson*; so he ask'd the Captain, and the Captain then calls himself out, You *Smith*, you know my Voice, if you lay down your Arms immediately, and submit, you shall have your Lives, all but *Will. Atkins.*
>
> Upon this, *Will Atkins*, cry'd out, *For God's sake, Captain, give me Quarter, what have I done? They have been all as bad as I*; which by the way was not true neither . . .   (192–93)

There is a certain irony in the situation. Will Atkins is indeed not telling the truth, but then neither is the former mutineer, also named Robinson. The capture is part of an elaborate hoax in which Crusoe poses as the "governour" of the island (193). The dialogue depicts ordinary men in a state of excitement when their lives are at stake. The mutineers are confused; Robinson is orchestrating a well-designed game. But the success of the counterplot depends on both Robinson's and Crusoe's convincing Smith and Atkins that they must give up to save their lives. Though both sides are lying, it is Atkins and Smith who are confused, lack knowledge, and thus must yield. The direct, conversational language conveys the anxiety of the situation. These are ordinary people but at a moment of high drama. This is the way people would talk under such circumstances. Allusion to classical epic would ruin the effect.

The language of *Robinson Crusoe* was not expected by eighteenth-century readers, who were steeped in classical learning. But it was not as unadorned as some later critics found it. The metaphors are few but powerful. The ocean that seems to attack Crusoe like an executioner as he is thrown on his island also acts as the bars of a prison. The frequent biblical allusions—to Jonah, Job, parables—lend a surprising richness of texture. The image of the parrot crying out, "Poor Robin Crusoe," seems to evoke much about language itself (104), and the magnificent description of the storm and shipwreck that precedes Crusoe's voyage to London has the force of a contemporary Dutch painting. In scenes of action, Defoe knows how to make verbs, often in the historical present, carry the action forward.

The reader expecting an adventure narrative of the sea would have been surprised to find out how much else there was in the text. Dampier's popular *A New Voyage* is a story in E. M. Forster's sense of the word (see pp. 25–42), which privileges the sequence of events as they unfold over causation. Defoe criticized writers similar to Dampier, such as John Narborough, John Wood, and Martin Frobisher, travel-narrative authors, in the preface to *A New Voyage round the World* (1724). *Robinson Crusoe* was to be something very different. The reader is given any number of ways of seeing the events. Is the cause of everything Crusoe's disobedience to his father's wishes, as Crusoe often suggests? Or is it Crusoe's tendency to overreach himself—the dissatisfaction of Thomas Hobbes's modern man, always striving for something new? Or perhaps, despite Crusoe's interpretation that Providence is behind every event, the cause of everything is simply the randomness that may be expected when human beings confront natural forces. The text demands that we find answers to important questions. Events not only unfold for various reasons; their unfolding is inevitable. Crusoe, for example, meditates on the wisdom of attacking the cannibals and then does it despite his misgivings. And then he is so upset by the slaughter that he has Friday sanitize the scene in a way that enables him to think it never happened (86–88). This instability, along with the continual projection into the future and vision back into the past, ties the work together the way novels, in Forster's memorable term, are supposed to "connect" (25).

The early novel blended many genres: romance, the picaresque tale of wandering, the novel in the contemporary sense, spiritual autobiography, diary, midrash, essay, economic and political allegory, dialogue, meditation, oration. In works such as Henry Fielding's *Tom Jones* and Laurence Sterne's *Tristram Shandy* the authors reveled in the mixture of forms. Defoe and Richardson were more interested in the "code" of the "real," as Roland Barthes calls it (80), produced by details that function in the text only to create in the reader a sense of the solidity and concreteness of the world in which fictional characters move. In trying to simultaneously explain and conceal what he was doing, Defoe wrote the preface to *Serious Reflections*, which blends such terms as *just, true, history, fable, allegoric, emblem,* and, over and over again, the word *real*. Defoe's claim that the entire work was what might be considered an imaginative autobiography—his affirmation that "[i]t is as reasonable to represent one kind of imprisonment by another, as it is to represent anything that really exists by that which exists not"—seems to argue that all works of fiction are essentially autobiographical (xiii). This argument is confusing because the words come from the mouth of Robinson Crusoe, which suggests Defoe's protagonist has more reality in the text than any vague Daniel Defoe who existed outside it.

Robinson Crusoe appeared at a time when there was a demand for fiction. No fortune was to be made on political pamphlets as might have been possible during the reigns of King William and Queen Anne, and Defoe, who earned a living by his writings, was always looking for financial success. Defoe had experimented with an older letter form in his *Continuations of the Letters of a Turkish Spy* (1718) and was clearly gearing up for the fictions that followed.

His fictions were published contemporaneous with those of Eliza Haywood, whose first novel, *Love in Excess*, appeared in the same year as *Robinson Crusoe*. She continued producing fiction long after Defoe had turned his interests to economic, social, and moral issues, and she was extraordinarily popular. Defoe's *Roxana* (1724) was a tribute to Haywood's popularity to the extent that the original title, *The Fortunate Mistress*, echoed one of Haywood's titles. Yet Defoe's fiction may be considered the "un-Haywood." Like so many of the "novelists" of the time, Haywood devoted herself to themes of love expressed in a style that might be considered "soft porn." The following passage from *Love in Excess* is not untypical of her style:

> The heat of the weather, and her confinement having hindered her from dressing that day, she had only a thin silk night gown on, which flying open as he caught her in his arms, he found her panting heart beat measures of consent, her heaving breast swell to be pressed by his, and every pulse confess a wish to yield; her spirits all dissolved sunk in a lethargy of love, her snowy arms unknowing grasped his neck, her lips met his halfway and trembled at the touch.   (63)

This might come out of a modern romance novel intended to draw the reader into the scene through sexual identification and to encourage arousal. Like Haywood, Defoe was not sentimental about sex, but the orgy scene in *Roxana*, in-

volving Roxana's lover, the jeweler, and her maid Amy is more than unsentimen-
tal; it is cruel and bitter. There is no real sex on Crusoe's island in *Robinson
Crusoe*, and Crusoe's paean to the virtues of the wife he finds after his return to
England is mainly directed to the ideal of the wife as companion. Haywood
could write novels concerned with current social issues, but love and sexuality
were her primary theme; Defoe tended to focus on the world about him and its
events, moral issues, and ideas. It is doubtless women read Defoe and men read
Haywood, but the appeal of their fictions to the eighteenth-century audience
tended to divide along gender lines (see Hunter, *Before Novels* 262–75).

Teaching the Text in and with Contexts

The essays in this volume have been grouped in ways that allow them not only
to speak to *Robinson Crusoe* but also to engage with one another. Although not
every essay deals directly with pedagogy, they all offer background, context,
and interpretation that can help any reader of the novel and that can be
adapted for classroom use. The essays address some of the questions raised in
this introduction and many others yet unasked. Some deal with specific textual
dilemmas, and others deal broadly with large issues. Almost all analyze specific
passages, and several present classroom experiences and exercises. Many offer
comparison texts and bibliographic material that can help expand the boundaries of a reader's knowledge. The myriad experiences of the authors in teaching *Robinson Crusoe* constitute both a resource for teaching the novel in multiple contexts and a way to see the continuing relevance of the text.

Locating the novel in a historical narrative tradition can help a teacher create a framework for student understanding. The first grouping of essays situates the novel in British narrative history, elaborating on Defoe's textual and
generic sources and audience expectations. Robert Maniquis's essay on teaching *Pilgrim's Progress* with *Robinson Crusoe* illustrates a shift in the depiction
of things in British writing that indicates Defoe is representing a new world.
John Bunyan uses allegory to reveal corruption; Defoe creates a new form of
spiritual autobiography that asks his readers to see alternative meanings in the
material world. By depicting Crusoe's love of things, Defoe becomes "our first
fictional ideologizer of the spiritualized capitalist self." It is difficult for our students, who live in a world of shopping malls, to perceive the newness of
Defoe's world, which is why Bunyan's contrasting focus on the degradation of
the material world is so important for teaching *Crusoe*. Only after students see
how little importance Bunyan grants to the things of the world in *Pilgrim's
Progress* can they fully grasp the change in attitude toward physical objects and
material possessions that Defoe wrought.

In a similar vein, Richard Braverman discusses teaching *Gulliver's Travels*
with *Robinson Crusoe*; he lays out and then compares the historical framework
of each text to show the contrasting views of English history in each. Braverman

draws out issues useful for seeing the texts in context—the themes of exile and wandering and paternal and filial devotion, debates about ancients versus moderns and Enlightenment versus counter-Enlightenment thought, and the generic conventions of novels and satires—and suggests how these issues come to the fore once the ideological underpinning of each text is established. Since the revolutionary spirit exemplified in Crusoe is critiqued and derided in the satiric figure of Gulliver (although, as Braverman points out, Jonathan Swift's targets went far beyond Defoe's), juxtaposing the texts offers students an object lesson in the engagement of literature and history, an interesting window into a specific historical period.

Voyages, imaginary and real, were a popular form of eighteenth-century narrative, but they always faced questions about authenticity; they also tended to be derivative. Within these parameters, Roxanne Kent-Drury and Gordon Sayre discuss Defoe's imitation of travel writing and other writers' imitation of *Robinson Crusoe*. They summarize some of the more famous imitations and parodies of *Robinson Crusoe*, from Gildon's doubts about the generic nature of Defoe's work to the pseudonymous Eliza Winkfield's *The Female American*, which draws extensively on Defoe's island adventure for its material, and to Derek Walcott's vision of Crusoe's island life as comparable to modern West Indian experience.

Manuel Schonhorn's essay brings together several of the themes in this section in describing seventeenth-century narrative conventions such as utopias, travel literature, and religious conduct books, as well as the intellectual traditions, particularly as delineated in Max Weber's *The Protestant Ethic and the Spirit of Capitalism*. Although Weber concludes that material goods exert an "inexorable power" over human life, Schonhorn argues Defoe advocated restraint and sees Crusoe balanced between the emergent world of economic accumulation and the older religious world of morally imposed restrictions. This tension makes Crusoe a fascinating fictional hero. He seems both to be part of our world of accumulation and to evince older attitudes toward restraint. He thus echoes ideas from long ago that nonetheless remain attractive.

The next section of essays extends the discussion of teaching backgrounds to *Robinson Crusoe*, examining the intellectual and ideological contexts of production and the effect of ideas on identity formation. Geoffrey Sill approaches Defoe from the standpoint of individualism; he wants us to see Defoe's work as an educational tool, training young students in ideals of self-reliance and inventiveness. Sill traces the ways in which Defoe's mythic work influenced Benjamin Franklin and then the ways in which Franklin influenced Walt Whitman. The combination of the three writers, Sill suggests, makes for an excellent course on ideologies of independence, survival, self-interest, creativity, and dissent.

Paula R. Backscheider investigates structure of belief in *Robinson Crusoe*, and she shows Crusoe to be a character caught between the new world of scientific investigation and the older world of spirits and demons. Backscheider compares the novel with travel narratives by Robert Knox and Penelope

Aubin; all three works involve abandonment in strange lands and demonstrate the survival instincts of the various characters, although Aubin's treatment of women as strong and courageous contrasts to Defoe's work.

George E. Haggerty dissects the masculinist quality of Crusoe's individualism, especially in his attempts at self-definition. From the very beginning of the novel, Crusoe's desire for adventure defines his masculinity, and Haggerty sees considerable comedy in Crusoe's pathetic need for dominance. Crusoe's moments of terror provide a marked contrast to his attempts at self-assertion. Although Crusoe fulfills his dream of masculine mastery, readers recognize the pitfalls of this fulfillment.

Themes of race and class, often taken for granted by Defoe's contemporaries in the period, resonate dissonantly for modern readers. Roxann Wheeler explores the issue of race in *Robinson Crusoe*, noting Crusoe's colonialist attitudes toward Xury and Friday and arguing that Defoe opens his readers to a broader vision of race than prevailed among his contemporaries. Wheeler points out that a major determinant in rejecting the peoples of the newly discovered lands was not skin color but *savagery*. *Robinson Crusoe* is in some ways a colonialist text written when attitudes toward non-European races were in flux. Crusoe's acceptance of the Christian Friday and Friday's pagan father suggests that the text does not reflect the vicious oppression practiced against the slaves in the West Indies that was to become the norm of mid-century colonialism.

Robert Markley demonstrates the value of teaching *Robinson Crusoe* and the two sequels as a trilogy. Doing so enhances our understanding of Crusoe's psychology and offers a story of survival and isolation different from the one found in the first Crusoe novel. Markley points out that his students have found a more pensive, perhaps more neurotic, Crusoe in the last two novels. Those who do not read these works cannot see that Crusoe's colony is a failure and do not encounter the continuance of contradictions that were resolved, albeit uneasily, in the original volume.

The section of essays on formal and thematic approaches to *Robinson Crusoe* offers ways to find a focus in the text. Timothy C. Blackburn concentrates on the art of *Robinson Crusoe*; he wants students to become interested in Defoe's craftsmanship and to recognize the resonance of allusions and how the narrative avoids formulas. Defoe's repetition, particularly through the retelling of experience in Crusoe's journal, allows students to make comparisons and to see how the parts of the text fit together. Close reading shows Defoe's mastery of English prose, including its poetic power.

John Barberet treats the novel as a castaway narrative, which students can discover in ancient works such as *The Arabian Nights* and in modern television programs such as *Gilligan's Island*. Barberet contrasts the castaway narrative with the utopian narrative and shows how to encourage students to think critically about the implications of such narratives.

Matthew Wickman also begins with a broad sweep of works that draw on the story of *Robinson Crusoe*, from Bugs Bunny cartoons to the movie *Cast Away*.

He asks his students to deliberately ignore how Defoe's work is consumed as an image in our modern society and to concentrate on the text. After close textual readings, Wickman assigns essays by cultural theorists such as Walter Benjamin, Michel Foucault, and François Lyotard. These theorists elucidate not only the kinds of exchanges inherent in narrative, including the socioeconomic transformations that occur, but also the way Crusoe's interpretation of his experience reflects the social fragmentation Benjamin associates with the novel.

Teaching *Robinson Crusoe* by comparing it to eighteenth-century contexts or more recent texts and films demonstrates the novel's immediacy and its resonance for the present time. Carl Fisher offers a history of the Robinsonade, the genre that takes its name from and substantiates the popularity of Defoe's novel. Fisher focuses on British and Continental appropriations and adaptations and discusses the development of the genre as important literary history and as useful background for any discussion of the novel's influence.

Laura M. Stevens examines a subgenre, the female Robinsonade, to suggest that Defoe's work made envisioning women as adventurers and survivors possible. Stevens contrasts *Robinson Crusoe* with Winkfield's *The Female American*, focusing on the resourcefulness of the heroine's behavior. Like a number of other fictional figures that Stevens discusses, the heroine of *The Female American* fulfills a role that exceeds the usual domesticity that women in life and in fiction were consigned to at the time.

The richness of approaching *Robinson Crusoe* comparatively has made it a common text in classes on postcolonial literature. Everett Zimmerman reveals the intellectual and spiritual ambiguities of the colonial enterprise evident in Defoe's work. To best provide students the tools to engage these issues, Zimmerman proposes a comparative study of other texts with related problems—Aphra Behn's *Oroonoko*, Joseph Conrad's *Heart of Darkness*, and William Golding's *Lord of the Flies*. Using these texts, students can interrogate the values of civilization in relation to the supposed darkness that challenges it at every turn.

Another comparative approach to studying postcolonialism is detailed by Charles W. Pollard, who describes using *Crusoe* in a world literature course to contrast Western and postcolonial literatures. Pollard thus establishes the "great Gulph"—Crusoe's own term for describing the distance between his island and the remote civilized world—between Enlightenment, colonial, and Puritan ideals and contemporary postmodern and postcolonial responses, such as J. M. Coetzee's *Foe* and Walcott's poetry. By reading parallel scenes—such as the varying descriptions of Crusoe's attempts to make his island habitable or the characterization of Friday—students can explore not just the clear distinctions between aesthetic, philosophical, political, and religious ideals but the significance and the power of *Crusoe* as narrative and metanarrative.

The final essay in this section shows how the novel and character have fared in the age of mechanical reproduction. Robert Mayer looks at the Crusoe myth in film and discusses how Hollywood has approached Defoe's story over the years. Any teacher might see the potential for a course that surveys film versions of *Crusoe* from 1903 to the present, from the comic to the more serious, which consider racial difference and the problems of colonialism. Mayer focuses on Robert Zemeckis's *Cast Away* (2000) as one of the richest film versions of *Robinson Crusoe* because it reveals a contemporary version of economic man and the strains of isolation. He suggests that many of the solutions created by Zemeckis's film throw light on possibilities inherent in Defoe's text.

One of the most fascinating aspects of teaching *Robinson Crusoe* is how the novel can be used in many classroom contexts and at all levels of the curriculum. The essays in the final section address both the general and specific multifaceted uses of the novel. Since students typically have little literary background and rarely read novels outside the classroom, Christina Sassi-Lehner puts the novel in the context of students' familiarity first with self-help or self-improvement books and then with romance and thrillers. Students develop their critical abilities by learning how to differentiate among a variety of critical perspectives on fiction—for example, formal realism, psychological realism, and allegorical signification. They also compare the physical journey to the spiritual quest in considering Crusoe, who embarks on a life that tests his most deeply held beliefs, ingenuity, survival skills, and will to succeed.

Anne Chandler fuses formalism and cultural studies in teaching the novel in a required methods course for English majors, emphasizing close-reading strategies. Her approach relates the labor of reading the novel to Crusoe's labors in reading the island. Students are encouraged to develop data-gathering and pattern-naming skills that help them perform close reading and contemplate broader thematic concepts.

Fisher, in his second essay in this volume, suggests including *Robinson Crusoe* in a British literature survey course, where the novel can operate as a capstone to the first part of the survey or the urtext of modernity for the second part. Since cultural studies and the culture wars have been challenging the canon and thus changing the typical reading list, Fisher argues, a novel like *Robinson Crusoe* is useful on a syllabus because it can allow a discussion of generic and thematic development yet still work for traditional courses that emphasize close reading and the study of literary history.

Maximillian E. Novak comments on the changing fortune of *Robinson Crusoe* in the academy. He discusses the emergence of the novel as a subject of study, the evolution of approaches from older forms of historicism through New Criticism and toward contemporary theories of literature, and the current status of *Robinson Crusoe* as the bedrock of a novel course, as well as the many possible ways of constructing such a course.

Few works of literature have been as influential as *Robinson Crusoe* on children's literature, which the many direct adaptations of the novel prove. Anne Lundin places the novel in the context of a class on children's literature that examines children's Robinsonades, adaptations of *Crusoe* in periodical literature, and the novel's intertextuality with other castaway stories. Lundin offers bibliographic information that demonstrates the legacy of the novel and rec-ommends children's books that deliberately or unconsciously utilize the Cru-soe myth and plot, including numerous books with female heroines.

In adult contexts, one of the standard truths of reading *Robinson Crusoe* is that the main character represents *homo economicus*, Marx's term for a West-ern man who has internalized, reified, and deified the economic aspects of life. Teaching the novel in a business school presents a special challenge, and Cheryl Nixon's essay shows how business students can be encouraged to utilize the tools they learn in business classes about supply and demand, production and consumption, and credit and debt. Using these tools, students can explore Crusoe's enterprise and entrepreneurial intentions, the individual's roles in sys-tems of exchange, the morality of applying business concerns to private aspects of life, the ethics of Crusoe's practical actions, and the connection between Crusoe's spiritual and economic self-definition. Nixon enhances class discus-sion by using excerpts from Hobbes, John Locke, Jean-Jacques Rousseau, and Adam Smith to compare Defoe with background texts.

The essays in this volume are grounded in the experience of teaching *Robin-son Crusoe*. The significance of the novel, including its controversial elements, and the continuing value of studying it should be apparent from the focused attention and enthusiasm that authors bring to their contributions. Each essay offers a distinct interpretation of *Robinson Crusoe*, often combined with a spe-cific approach to teaching the novel, and it is our hope that the volume will contribute to a continuing engagement with a text so influential to both West-ern culture and world literature.

MEN and CF

Part One

MATERIALS

Publishing History and Modern Editions

The Life and Strange Surprizing Adventures of Robinson Crusoe, of York, Mariner was first published on 25 April 1719. A second edition appeared on 9 May, a third on 4 June, a fourth on 7 August. This fourth edition was the first to include the map of the world showing Crusoe's travels. Although William Taylor and his shop at the sign of the ship in Pater-Noster Row was the publisher listed on the title page, sharers in the publishing venture included J. Graves, T. Harbin, J. Brotherton, and W. Meadows. *The Farther Adventures of Robinson Crusoe* first appeared on 20 August 1719, and *Serious Reflections during the Life and Surprizing Adventures of Robinson Crusoe, with His Vision of the Angelick World* on 6 August 1720. Taylor appears to have been the sole publisher of these continuations. The best account of these and subsequent editions may be found in Robinson Crusoe *and Its Printing*, by Henry Hutchins. In addition, Keith Maslen published two useful articles in *Library* on the printers and quantities of early editions.

The first *Robinson Crusoe* novel was a huge success. A fifth edition appeared in 1720; a sixth, with illustrations, in 1722; a seventh in 1726 under the auspices of W. Mears and T. Woodward (Taylor died in 1724). When the eighth edition appeared in 1736, the first two novels were joined together as a unit and were often published this way for the following two centuries. Only during the second half of the twentieth century, when texts of *Robinson Crusoe* were prepared for use in classrooms, did the first novel emerge as what we think of as *Robinson Crusoe*. The second novel went through five editions before it was usually merged with the first, although now they are rarely printed together. The third novel had only one printing by Taylor. Meanwhile, the first was abridged by T. Cox in August 1719, and, despite threats of legal action against Cox from Taylor, another abridgement was published shortly thereafter, the so-called O edition. In 1722 Edward Midwinter brought out an abridgement of all three Crusoe novels; other abridgements followed. Long before Midwinter's abridgement, however, the first two novels had been serialized in a newspaper, the *Original London Post*, in 1719 and 1720. By 1720, it had been translated into Dutch, French, and German.

In some ways, at a time when Shakespeare was little known outside Great Britain, *Robinson Crusoe* was the first work of English literature to make a splash on the Continent. Whereas in England Charles Gildon had attacked it as a product of the notoriously unreliable Daniel Defoe, on the Continent it was reviewed in the distinguished *Journal des scavans* and other serious journals. In England it became the quintessential adventure story and in its abridged form was constantly reprinted. Jane Austen thought it ideal reading for a young boy. In France and Germany, it was read as an allegory for human development.

A glance at the catalog of the British Library reveals that there was a great increase in editions after the 1780s, when Defoe's reputation as a writer received increasing scrutiny. During the nineteenth century, editions sometimes appeared at the rate of eight each year. Expensive editions containing the illustrations of Thomas Stothard became fairly common. George Chalmer's biography, published originally in 1785, presented Defoe in an excellent light. By 1810, when Bell's edition of Defoe's novels appeared, Defoe was beginning to enter the canon of British novelists who were regarded as deserving to have their works published in collected editions. In editions of Defoe's collected works such as that published by Thomas Tegg in 1840–41, the first two parts of *Robinson Crusoe* occupied the privileged position. Dent positioned *Robinson Crusoe* at the beginning of its fourteen-volume edition of Defoe's works in 1895, produced under the editorship of George Aitken and entitled *Romances and Narratives*, and Blackwell placed it at the front of its *Shakespeare Head Edition of the Writings of Daniel Defoe*.

Robinson Crusoe is one of those works that have an illustration as well as a print history. David Blewett's book *The Illustrations of* Robinson Crusoe suggests some of the ways in which the critical history of the work may be read through the illustrations and provides a history of those illustrations. In England, the frontispiece of *The Surprizing Adventures* was done by John Pine and John Clark, and Bernard Picart provided an influential frontispiece for the French edition. In keeping with the distinct critical approaches of both England and France to the text, one illustration stresses adventure while the other shows Crusoe with his tools for building. Over the years, many major illustrators took their turns in rendering Crusoe. These included Stothard, Jean-Ignace-Isadore Grandville, and N. C. Wyeth. Even William Blake has a drawing of Crusoe.

There are many modern editions of *Robinson Crusoe*, but no fully annotated critical edition is available. The text that the editors have chosen to use for this volume is edited by Michael Shinagel and published by Norton in a second edition in 1994. This edition preserves the original spelling and punctuation, has useful notes, and includes a selection of critical essays. Another useful edition, however, is the Oxford World Classics, which is based on the text established by Donald Crowley in his original Oxford English Novels edition, published in 1972. Also popular in the classroom is the version published by Penguin. Although Angus Ross used modernized spelling in an early Penguin edition, the editor of the 2002 Penguin reissue, John Richetti, uses the 1719 first edition, making only spelling changes culled from other early editions and lowercasing common nouns. Almost every publishing house has editions of *Robinson Crusoe* in paperback; some attempt drastic modernizations, including divisions of the text into chapters and, of course, heavy cuts in some versions intended for high schools.

Modern editions print only the first of the three novels that Defoe wrote. *The Farther Adventures of Robinson Crusoe* is available in a 1999 paperback, but *Serious Reflections* does not exist in any modern printed edition. The best available text of *The Farther Adventures* is found in the *Shakespeare Head Edition of the Writings of Daniel Defoe* (1927). An edition of *Serious Reflec-*

tions is in the 1895 collection, the *Romances and Narratives*, edited by Aitken. This is out of print but usually available in university libraries; see the section on Internet resources for online editions. Occasionally students in college courses who prefer to use a library copy of *Robinson Crusoe* will pick out a version that includes only *The Farther Adventures*, and we try to warn them that the text under discussion, usually the first novel, does not end with voyages to China and through Siberia, as *The Farther Adventures* does.

Daniel Defoe: A Brief Biography

Daniel Defoe was born toward the end of 1660, the year of the Restoration of Charles II to the throne of England. By 1662, Defoe's family, along with all those who could not accept the tenets of the Church of England, became Dissenters or Nonconformists, subject to severe penalties, sometimes imprisonment, for the practice of their beliefs. It made Defoe an outsider in his society, a position Defoe came to relish. He was raised as a Presbyterian but believed that all the dissenting sects should act as a single political body against the tyranny of the Church of England. He grew up in London (and in one of his last works, *Augusta Triumphans*, written in 1728, he suggested a variety of utopian schemes to improve his beloved city). After a brief stay at a school in Dorking, he was sent to the Dissenting Academy at Newington Green, run by Charles Morton. Unlike the universities where the system of education was antiquated, Newington Green attempted to teach the latest philosophical ideas, the new science being pioneered by the Royal Society, and English-language exercises. Defoe's English training included writing compositions in English from the point of view of a particular character, an exercise that may have helped prepare him for writing fiction.

Defoe's family considered having him trained as a minister, but he left Newington Green around 1680 for London, during the Popish Plot—a time when English Protestantism was under attack by Catholics at home and abroad. Action against enemy forces seemed called for, and Defoe turned away from the pulpit toward a life as a tradesman and merchant. Although he received a substantial dowry in 1684, when he married Mary Tuffley, he was forced to declare bankruptcy in 1692. Defoe was always an advocate of steadiness in trade, but he showed a tendency toward political and economic adventures. In 1685 he had fought with the forces of James Scott Monmouth in an uprising against James II. After Monmouth's defeat, Defoe must have gone undercover for a while. His trade ventures (after he received a pardon) were frequently in luxury goods such as wines and perfumes, and he showed an interest in such doubtful schemes as searching for buried treasure. At heart he was more of an adventurer and dreamer than a cautious businessman.

Although he wrote some poetic meditations in 1681, his bankruptcy enabled him to turn his mind to writing. A staunch supporter of William III and Mary, who had come to the throne after the Revolution of 1688, Defoe wrote a number of satiric poems and political tracts during the 1690s as well as his first book, *An Essay upon Projects* (1697). It was a book filled with imaginative schemes that he thought the government ought to support, including a literary academy and an academy for the education of women, whom he thought should be as thoroughly educated as men. In 1701 he wrote a poetic satire against the hatred of foreigners, *The True-Born Englishman*, which gave him a reputation as a political radical and witty opponent of those who disliked William III. Wit and irony, however, were to be his undoing when he parodied the violent extremists of the Church of England in their attacks against the Dissenters. For this work, *The Shortest Way with the Dissenters* (1703), he imitated the vitriol spewed forth by High Church leaders so well that everyone, including the Dissenters, were furious. He was arrested, found guilty of libel, and forced to stand in the pillory. He won the mob over, however, by having his friends sell his satire on government and the law, *A Hymn to the Pillory*, at the scene of his punishment.

In 1704, released from prison but bankrupt for a second time, Defoe embarked on a career as a political activist, journalist, and spy. His patron, Robert Harley, then secretary of state and from 1710 to 1714 the equivalent of prime minister, sent him on missions around England and to Scotland to gather information and support the actions of the English government. Defoe published the *Review*, a journal of opinion, scandal, and occasional news, from 1704 until 1714 and, in addition to scores of pamphlets and poems, wrote *The Consolidator* (1705), a story about an imaginary voyage to the moon mixing fanciful science and political satire. In 1709 he brought out the massive *History of the Union between England and Scotland*, a mixture of detailed historical recording, documents, and his personal experiences in Scotland during the time of the union of the two nations.

Because he supported Harley and his Tories from 1710 to 1714, Defoe had a difficult time convincing anyone of his Whig credentials after George I succeeded Queen Anne in 1714. Eventually he was able to use his associations with the Tories to take the sting out of newspapers intent on expressing their opposition to the new king and his ministries. During the years preceding the publication of *Robinson Crusoe* in 1719, Defoe wrote a number of memoirs blending fictional characters and events. In 1718 he decided to add a volume to a collection of letters purportedly by a Turkish spy in Paris during the seventeenth century. His addition gave not only a picture of Europe during a period he knew well but also a sense of personal isolation that the Turk felt in his long exile from his native land. It was a perfect lead-in to the story of someone stranded on an island in the Caribbean for twenty-eight years. *Robinson Crusoe* and its two sequels, *The Farther Adventures* and *Serious Reflections*, were an enormous success. The popularity of these works and the novels of Eliza Haywood showed there was a substantial audience for prose fiction both in England and on the Continent. Defoe followed with an out-pouring of novels, including *Memoirs of a Cavalier* and *Captain Singleton* (1720); *Moll Flanders*, *A Journal of the Plague Year*, and *Colonel Jack* (1722); and *Roxana* and *A New Voyage round the World* (1724). These novels differ in their emphases. Some are what we would call historical novels, and others are adventure novels, picaresque novels, or novels of society. While Haywood was exploring the psychology of sex and love, Defoe was focusing on the na-ture of British and European society and the struggles of individual charac-ters with their environments.

While writing these works of fiction, Defoe was publishing volumes in which he explored important moral issues, often in a series of dialogues. He dropped what one might call pure fiction after 1724 but continued writing volumes on economics (*The Compleat English Tradesman* [1726–27], *A Plan of the English Commerce* [1728]), the occult (*The Political History of the Devil* [1726], *An Essay on the History and Reality of Apparitions* [1727]), explorations of the ge-ography of Britain and the world (*A Tour Thro' the Whole Island of Great Britain* [1724–27], *Atlas Maritimus* [1728]), and commentaries on British soci-ety (*The Great Law of Subordination* [1724], *Conjugal Lewdness* [1727]). He composed these works from his comfortable house in Stoke Newington, but in 1730 he lost a suit to a creditor who claimed he had not paid a large bill dating back to his bankruptcies. Rather than pay a debt he felt he had already cleared, Defoe fled. He died in hiding at the end of April 1731 and was buried in Bun-hill Fields, close to John Bunyan and William Blake, two other great Dissenters.

The Critical Reputation of *Robinson Crusoe* and Its Status as a Novel

Shortly after the publication of *Robinson Crusoe*, Charles Gildon attacked it as a form of what we would call popular literature, associating it with the many chapbooks of fictions such as *Guy of Warwick* whose length varied from six-teen to several hundred pages. For Gildon *Crusoe* was another fiction from Daniel Defoe, who was considered a traitor to Whig principles in the party wars of 1710–14 and who would be willing to write for anyone who paid him. Behind *Robinson Crusoe*, then, was a seemingly sinister authorial figure. Gildon pointed out inconsistencies that revealed *Crusoe* as a work of fiction, and, in a prediction of postmodern methods, created a metanarrative in which Crusoe and Friday, in the early hours of the morning, confront Defoe in a field not far from his house in Stoke Newington and thrash him for his crimes. In England, although *Robinson Crusoe* was a popular success (Henry Baker de-scribed it as "read over the whole Kingdom, and pass'd as many Editions as, perhaps any Book now extant"), any contemporary attempt to treat it as a serious work of literature was clouded by Defoe's status as a political turncoat and by continuing contempt for the genre of prose fiction. Alexander Pope praised *Robinson Crusoe* in private conversations with Joseph Spence but continued to attack Defoe as a hack in his *Dunciad*. The British critical treatment of *Crusoe* contrasts with the admiration it received on the Continent. The anonymous writer of the introduction to the German translation of 1720 argued that it was a masterpiece that would live forever (*Das Leben* A3–A4).

The 1753 biography of Defoe by Robert Shiels and the passage of time, which helped people forget about Defoe's political career, made a revised judgment of *Crusoe* possible. Shiels defended Defoe for his "invincible integrity" (51) and *Robinson Crusoe* as an admirable work, the product of an imagination "fertile, strong, and lively" (49). In 1762, Jean-Jacques Rousseau's *Émile* gave a huge boost to the reputation of *Robinson Crusoe*, describing it as "a complete treatise on natural education" ("Treatise" 262) and the first book Rousseau would give to his ideal pupil. Although Rousseau read a French translation of *Robinson Crusoe* that presented a more idealized contact between the protagonist and nature, the concept of isolation struck Rousseau's imagination. As a study on isolation, *Robinson Crusoe* comes up in Rousseau's *Confessions* and other works.

During the 1780s, *Robinson Crusoe* began to achieve status as a work of literature. Herbert Croft gave it high praise in *Love and Madness*, but he then accused Defoe of stealing the work from Alexander Selkirk (37–38), a charge that diminished Defoe's reputation considerably. Hence it was Selkirk, not Crusoe, who announced, "I am the monarch of all I survey," in William Cowper's famous poem (line 1). Nevertheless, it was praised by the literary critics Hugh Blair and James Beattie, in 1783, for its realist rendering of experience and continual engagement of the reader's imagination. With George Chalmer's *Life of Daniel Defoe*, Defoe emerged as a staunch advocate of liberty and trade and *Robinson Crusoe* as a work that "instantly pleased and always pleased" (52). Some of the early criticism is collected in *Daniel Defoe: The Critical Heritage*, edited by Pat Rogers.

Crusoe was both a Romantic text, admired by Walter Scott, William Wordsworth, Samuel Taylor Coleridge, and Edgar Allan Poe, and a Victorian text of colonial adventure. Karl Marx used it to illustrate his labor theory of value, and Böhm Bawerk for the economic theory of marginal utility (see 101–49). Although it was always a text read by the young, it continued to be read and reread by adults. It even gained status as a magical work. The character Bettredge in Wilkie Collins's *The Moonstone* governed his life by opening a random page of Defoe's novel for advice or consolation. The illustrator and stage designer Edward Gordon Craig was haunted by images of Robinson Crusoe and Friday and maintained an inner dialogue with them for decades (11–12). And the philosopher Gaston Bachelard viewed Crusoe's cave and island as an archetype that is always with every person (69–70). Though *Crusoe* is not always treated with respect, it remains an illustrative work for postcolonial studies. Michel Tournier's

Vendredi and J. M. Coetzee's *Foe* rewrite it from a postmodern perspective. Excellent in their own right, these novels function not as replacements for *Crusoe* but as modern ways of reviewing a work that has become a classic.

Modern criticism of *Robinson Crusoe* has often focused on the genre, on whether it is a novel or not. Critics such as Ronald S. Crane argue that this is the first question we need to address in dealing with any work of literature, and generic concerns were certainly part of the critical situation in 1719 when Defoe's work was published (20, 38–39). What is true about the period, however, is that the best writing tended to break the bounds of traditional genres. Prose fiction that created a degree of verisimilitude was by no means recognized as a respectable form. The novel, a work of prose fiction that ran anywhere from twenty-five to two hundred pages, had replaced the long romances of the mid-seventeenth century and was extremely popular. As William Congreve noted in the preface to his *Incognita* (1692), the novel differed from the romance in being "of a more familiar nature," which "not being so distant from our Belief bring also the pleasure nearer us" (6). Congreve thought of the distinction not in terms of the subject of love, for both were about that, but in terms of the degree of reality each portrayed. Mme de La Fayette's *Princess de Clèves* (1678) and Aphra Behn's *Love Letters* (1684–87) depicted a sensual instead of idealized love, had real historical instead of fantasy settings, and avoided the supernatural. Such antiromance features characterized the novel even in Clara Reeve's *Progress of Romance* (1785).

Insofar as *Robinson Crusoe* avoided the miraculous, it was not a romance, but in its concern with matters that had nothing to do with love—isolation, survival, meditations on religion and the human condition—it was very different from any novel that preceded or followed it. In defending his work, Defoe in *Serious Reflections* associated it with Cervantes's *Don Quixote* (1605) as a serious work of fiction, but he also suggested that it had elements of allegory (what we would probably call symbolism) and fudged on whether it was literally true as a narrative or true because it dealt with serious subjects. Defoe was the first to write prose fiction that seemed real and gripped the imagination.

Because of the novel's appeal to larger truths, Anna Letitia Barbauld included *Robinson Crusoe* in her collection *The British Novelists* (1810). It had already been included in the *Novelist's Magazine*, published between 1780 and 1788, along with Samuel Richardson, Henry Fielding, Tobias Smollett, and Laurence Sterne. Jonathan Swift's *Gulliver's Travels* and Samuel Johnson's *Rasselas* found their way into this miscellaneous collection. Barbauld's list of twenty-eight works argued for the inclusion of *Robinson Crusoe* on the grounds that it "yields to few in the truth of its descriptions and its powers of interesting the mind" (i). The two rationales for inclusion, then, were its realism and its ability to engage the reader. Since Barbauld argued for the novel as a species of entertainment, *Robinson Crusoe* might be seen as a novel, and her insistence that novels, as opposed to romances, be rooted in "truth and nature" also enabled her to include Defoe's work in the genre (i).

Michael McKeon, in *Origins of the English Novel*, is correct to argue that many of the questions of the status of prose fiction were worked out in the conflict between Richardson and Fielding, but there was no agreement on a term to describe fictions that created a degree of reality. A glance at title pages shows that the word *novel*, although used throughout the eighteenth century, was only in vogue for a few years in mid-century. There were attempts to classify prose fiction later in the century, including one in a French collection that put *Robinson Crusoe* in the category of utopias and imaginary voyages. Reeve suggested it was neither novel nor romance but "of a different species . . . singular and original" (127). When John Dunlop published his *History of Fiction* in 1814, he did not worry about classification but after placing *Crusoe* among "voyage imaginaires," he pronounced it "of all the works of fiction . . . perhaps the most interesting and instructive" (401). In fact, it was not until the middle of the nineteenth century that the term *novel* became an established term. And it was not long before evolutionary theories of criticism influenced novel criticism. Long after evolutionary criticism, which at its most reductive believed that modern works are superior to works of the past, had been discredited, critics as disparate as Eric Auerbach, Ian Watt, and Mikhail Bakhtin show some of its influences. Auerbach, for example, sees the novel gradually developing toward psychological depth. But the postwar novels of the 1950s and 1960s moved in a very different direction, and the postmodern novel generally avoids psychological explorations of character. In short, prose fiction has developed in various directions over the years, but there is no sign of what might be considered a growth toward a superior form.

It should be obvious by now that we use *novel* in a neutral way, similar to the definition E. M. Forster borrowed from Abel Chevalley: "a fiction in prose of a certain extent" (5–6). And once we examine Defoe for what he accomplished in *Robinson Crusoe* instead of worrying about whether he was a primitive novelist, it is easier to judge his work for its strengths and weaknesses. For example, Virginia Woolf found its status as a "masterpiece" to lie in its "sense of reality" (*Essays* 333; 334), although she also observed that it lacked any "introspection" or "feeling for . . . Nature" (334). This is a very different view from that of her father, Leslie Stephen, who had argued that Defoe's realism was simply a bag of tricks (12). Such different viewpoints are typical. Stephen wants to distinguish between the art of the novels written in his period and what he saw as the crude attempts at "low order of amusement" in *Robinson Crusoe* (56), but the spare and exact realism of Defoe appealed to his daughter. Woolf, however, accustomed to vivid descriptions of nature as an ideal, misses the admiration for nature that appears in Defoe's description of the sea in storm as well as in the paradisical account of the countryside, where he builds what he calls his "Country House" (Defoe, *Robinson* 115).

Although several Marxist critics of the novel continued to praise Defoe's work, F. R. Leavis, in *The Great Tradition*, a work of enormous influence on the teaching of the novel in the academy, dismisses Defoe in a footnote with the comment that Stephen had said all that was necessary (2n2). The great modern revival of Defoe and *Robinson Crusoe* came in 1957 with the publication of Watt's *The Rise of the Novel*. Watt's analysis of *Robinson Crusoe* as a text that participates in many of the developments of the modern world, from the rise of capitalism driven by the "Protestant ethic" identified by Max Weber to modern alienation, made it into a central work for our time. Although Watt tended to treat *Crusoe* as a somewhat primitive work that was only concerned with "formal" or "circumstantial" realism (32), he also made it a crucial work—the point of origin for any discussion of the novel. Oddly enough, Watt argued that the novel genre evinces no tradition that incorporates Defoe, despite the fact that it was imitated immediately in England, inaugurated an entire school of novels in Germany known as *Robinsonaden*, and continues to influence adventure novels.

Since 1957, studies of Defoe and *Robinson Crusoe* have tended to expand the boundaries of Defoe's influences on the novel's generic development. Maximillian E. Novak, in *Economics and the Fiction of Daniel Defoe*, expanded on Watt's discussion to show that Defoe was fully aware of and wrote about the problems of broad economic movements throughout his career. Novak also wrote about Defoe's adherence to contemporary theories of the state of nature and natural law (*Defoe and the Nature of Man*). George Starr, in *Defoe and Spiritual Autobiography*, first suggested that *Robinson Crusoe*, along with Defoe's other confessional novels, followed the outlines of contemporary spiritual autobiography. Starr then, in his *Defoe and Casuistry*, showed how the various excuses and palliatives for seemingly immoral actions might be read as examples of casuistry. At almost the same time, J. Paul Hunter's *The Reluctant Pilgrim* explored the presence of a variety of genres associated with writings on religion in *Robinson Crusoe*, demonstrating the way certain typological patterns function in Defoe's work.

These explorations of *Robinson Crusoe* showed that Defoe was a more complex writer and thinker than earlier critics had imagined. They were followed by a rash of studies throughout the remaining decades of the twentieth century and into the twenty-first. Defoe's political writings and their relation to *Robinson Crusoe* were the subject of a number of important studies. Manuel Schonhorn explored the complex political implications of *Robinson Crusoe* in *Defoe's Politics: Parliament, Power, Kingship and* Robinson Crusoe. Carol Kay theorized about the larger political implications of life on the island in *Political Constructions*, and Geoffrey Sill's *Defoe and the Idea of Fiction* explored the relation between *Robinson Crusoe* and the many tracts Defoe wrote in the years preceding its publication. Defoe's social and economic thought and its influence on *Robinson Crusoe* was considered further in Michael Shinagel's *Defoe and Gentility*, Peter Earle's *The World of Defoe*, and Sandra Sherman's *Finance and Fictionality in the Early Eighteenth Century*. Defoe's interest in science has been examined in Ilsa Vickers's *Defoe and the New Sciences*.

One aspect of *Robinson Crusoe* that has always attracted critics has been the protagonist's ability to overcome his solitude and the island experience—

including savages, colonialism, cannibalism. Jean Giraudoux ventured on this subject in his *Suzanne et la pacifique*, and, close to a decade later, Walter de la Mare contemplated it in his *Desert Islands and Robinson Crusoe*. Michael Seidel has written on isolation and exile in his *Robinson Crusoe: Island Myths and the Novel*, and John Bender (*Imagining the Penitentiary*) has delineated how Crusoe's reformation through isolation influenced the concept of imprisonment. The continual fascination with isolation is the main reason for the popularity of the 2000 movie *Cast Away*.

A number of important articles and chapters from books have been devoted to the issues of colonialism, cannibalism, and the question of Crusoe's relationship with Friday. Among them are Novak's "Friday; or, The Power of Naming" and sections of Peter Hulme's *Colonial Encounters*, Carol Houlihan Flynn's *The Body in Swift and Defoe*, and Roxann Wheeler's *The Complexion of Race*.

Perhaps the greatest critical interest has been in the aesthetic problems of Defoe's novels in general, including *Robinson Crusoe*. John Richetti's *Defoe's Narratives* examined the complexity of thinking in Defoe's fiction with extraordinary subtlety, and Everett Zimmerman embedded *Robinson Crusoe* in relation to the novel as a genre. David Blewett, in *Defoe and the Art of Fiction*, treated *Robinson Crusoe* and other fictional works from the standpoint of craft. Paul Alkon, using Gérard Genette's complex concept of the variety of voices in narrative, examined the chronological structures in Defoe's works in *Defoe and Fictional Time*. Ian Bell, in *Defoe's Fiction*, took up the form of "popular fiction"; Sill studied the fictions as explorations of the passions in his *The Cure of the Passions and the Origins of the English Novel*. Although it is now somewhat out of date, Pat Rogers published an excellent general book on *Robinson Crusoe*, treating both critical and scholarly problems in Defoe's works (*Robinson Crusoe*).

All these discussions have implications for the critical understanding of the development of the novel. McKeon's ingenious study, *The Origins of the English Novel*, begins with Cervantes's *Don Quixote*, but, following Bakhtin, McKeon argues (4) that before the debate between Richardson and Fielding over the nature of fiction, most texts, including *Robinson Crusoe*, suffered from a degree of indeterminacy (13). Nevertheless, McKeon's argument that the novel as a form was firmly established after the middle of the eighteenth century has not convinced many. A number of critics, such as Geoffrey Day in his *From Novel to Novel*, have suggested that it was not until the end of the eighteenth century that the novel was fully established as a form. Others have argued that this did not occur in Britain until Jane Austen and Scott, when the different rhetorical types contained in fiction—dialogues, descriptions, essays—were given an even texture.

Considering all the ink spilled on the question, it might seem frivolous to say that determining when the novel genre first appeared may not really matter very much. Dunlop's *History of Fiction*, which first appeared in 1814, was frequently reprinted during the nineteenth and twentieth centuries, and for Dunlop it was not an important issue (45). McKeon asks his readers to be wary of origins, and indeed the editors feel that although it is important to make distinctions among genres, it is also necessary to realize how artificial the boundaries are between the various subgenres of prose fiction.

Some useful books for tracing publication information and criticism are Spiro Peterson, *Daniel Defoe: A Reference Guide, 1719–1724*; John Stoler, *Daniel Defoe: An Annotated Bibliography of Modern Criticism, 1900–1980*; Robert Lovett and Charles Lovett, Robinson Crusoe: *A Bibliographical Checklist of English Long Editions, 1719–1979*; Henry Hutchins, Robinson Crusoe *and Its Printing, 1719–1731: A Bibliographical Study*. Also valuable are Rogers, *Robinson Crusoe*, and his collection of criticism in *Daniel Defoe: The Critical Heritage*. Books dealing with the Defoe canon include John Robert Moore's *Checklist of the Writings of Daniel Defoe*, which is the most complete, although it is not entirely reliable. The section "Defoe" by Novak in the *New Cambridge Bibliography of English Literature* questions some of Moore's listings. Most recently, in their *Defoe De-Attributions* and *A Critical Bibliography of Daniel Defoe*, P. N. Furbank and W. R. Owens have brought together a number of important facts, but in the process they have attempted to excise from the canon many works that are likely by Defoe.

Scholarly Biographies

All the early biographies of Defoe—those written during the eighteenth and nineteenth centuries—have their uses, but they are often inaccurate about the details of his life and writings. Maximillian E. Novak's *Daniel Defoe: Master of Fictions* is the most recent account of Defoe's life. It attempts to see Defoe in his political, social, and aesthetic milieu and to trace his career as a writer from his earliest manuscripts to his final tracts. Paula R. Backscheider's *Daniel Defoe: His Life* is a meticulously documented account of Defoe's life with extended analyses of his writings. Defoe's possible adventures are analyzed through particular historical and geographical references in Frank Bastian's *Defoe's Early Life*, which should be used with caution because Bastian reports on events and ascribes works to Defoe in a speculative manner, but his book is nonetheless extremely suggestive in covering a period we know little about. John Robert Moore's *Daniel Defoe: Citizen of the Modern World* is not so much a traditional biography as an attempt to follow Defoe's various interests throughout his life. Like some of Defoe's early biographers (William Lee, Walter Wilson), Moore tends to be a somewhat uncritical hero-worshipper of Defoe. Although James Sutherland's *Defoe* gives short shrift to many of Defoe's important works, it is very readable, and its judgments on Defoe's character are often perceptive.

Crusoe's Fictional Predecessors

Defoe does not create *Robinson Crusoe* in a vacuum, and to understand the novel's genre, one should situate the Robinsonade along with its fictional forerunners. In discussions of narrative tradition, the concept of the Robinsonade is often applied retroactively to describe shipwreck and castaway stories back to the Philoctetes section of the *Odyssey*. Just as the novel's originality is not diminished by its many imitators, suggesting that Defoe had many influences and predecessors does not detract from his achievement; in fact, that earlier narratives are categorized as Robinsonades shows the impact of the novel, as if the genre were waiting to be named (for a history of the post-*Crusoe* Robinsonade, see the essay by Fisher in this volume).

The Robinsonade is characterized most basically as a story with a voyage of exploration. The term is helpful for understanding and categorizing works with generic similarities to *Robinson Crusoe* and is used not only by critics but self-consciously by authors. Defoe follows a long tradition of travel and adventure stories, complete with shipwrecked isolation and uneasy interaction with native peoples. Defoe probably knew many of these works, including *Hayy Ibn Yaqzan*, a popular twelfth-century Arabic text from Granada, which had many English translations (see Tufail). In it, the main character lives entirely alone on an island from infancy to adulthood, only learning speech late in life from a passing mariner. When he finally experiences civilization, it disappoints him. Direct influence is hard to gauge; some critics claim that Defoe clearly knew this text, but others think it unlikely. "Parallels with the life of Crusoe are remarkable," according to Novak. "The hero is completely isolated for over twenty years, dresses in animal skins, and indulges in religious speculation. . . . Yet so far from being the 'idea' of *Robinson Crusoe* as one writer has suggested, it is almost the complete reverse" (*Defoe and the Nature of Man* 25). This is a chastening reminder to be cautious about misinterpretation and to not mistake formal similarities with ideological aspects of narrative. Many texts have important elements of what becomes *Crusoe*—Thomas More's *Utopia*; Henry Neville's *The Isle of Pines*, a risque tale of a man and three women shipwrecked on a Pacific island; the shipwreck and desert-island episode of Hans Grimmelshausen's *Simplicius Simplicissimus* (1669); and even Pierre Marivaux's *Les effets surprenants de la sympathie* (The Surprising Effects of Sympathy [1713]). It is less necessary to ascribe direct influence than to suggest a paradigm of common plots and themes.

Some of the most prominent pre-*Crusoe* Robinsonades are French. Geoffroy Atkinson, in his two volumes on the genre of the French imaginary voyage before 1720, argues that one reason *Crusoe* made such an impact in France was that there had been at least a half century of similar narratives (he also argues that even though before 1720 there is little evidence that the French imaginary voyage had been influenced by the English, after 1720 it is impossible not to see the influence of *Robinson Crusoe* on French examples). The French could easily classify Defoe's work and fit it into their frame of reference, as a French critic in 1719 could claim *Robinson Crusoe* was a novel "dans le gout de l'Histoire des Sevarambes et de Jacques Sadeur" ("in the style of *The History of Sevarites* and of *Jacques Sadeur*," our trans.; Atkinson 1: 165). These works both had English translations (*The History of the Sevarites* [1675] and *A New Discovery of Terra Incognita Australis by Mr. Sadeur* [1693]). Although neither of their plots has sustained similarities to the *Crusoe* plot, Atkinson notes a point in *The History of the Sevarites* in which a character, fearful of wild animals, builds shelters for protection. Gabriel de Foigny's *Terra Incognita Australis* (originally published in 1676) also tries to gain authenticity with minute, realistic descriptions of animal and plant life in an attempt to make them convincing for contemporary readers—at least if they were willing to allow some of the narrative's fantastic qualities (for instance, the main character, a hermaphrodite, conveniently finds a hermaphrodite tribe in western Australia). There is a desert-island plot to *Les voyages et aventures de Francois Leguat et des ses compagnons en deux iles desertes des Indes Orientales*, which was published in France in 1707 and translated into English and published in London in the same year. Another French precursor is Tyssot de Patot's *Voyage et aventures de Jacques Massé* (1710), notable primarily because it depicts extreme adventurous action and because the main character, after finally returning to civilization and being forced into slavery in Algeria, is saved by the British consul.

A number of other works may not have had a direct influence on *Crusoe* but fit the Robinsonade type, particularly the features of voyage and shipwreck. Baltasar Gracián's *Criticon* (1696), in which a shipwrecked man finds an uncivilized youth on an island, teaches him language, and finds that the youth worships a deity, constitutes "a vindication of the inherent virtue and wisdom of uncorrupted man" and "has long been recognized as having an influence on the character of Man Friday in the *Robinson Crusoe*" (Atkinson 1: 142). One work that bears similarities to *Robinson Crusoe* is the Dutch novel *Krinke Kesmes* (1708), by Hendrik Smeeks. In one episode of this work, a grounded sailor comes upon an unknown but advanced civilization and meets a castaway who had many experiences similar to those later plotted in *Robinson Crusoe*. Whether Defoe had any knowledge of this text has been a matter of debate among critics (see Fausett, Introduction [xxxv-xliii] and *Sources* [97–108]). Some of these fictional precursors to *Crusoe* show a remarkable knowledge of and a great deal of borrowing from other similar texts. They have both specific parallels and a number of generic similarities. Atkinson points out three important narrative elements that foreshadow Defoe's accomplishment and that are characteristic of many of the above-mentioned precursors: realistic, detailed descriptions of everything from ships and storms to topography and nature; sophisticated literary devices, such as briefly mentioning an event, an experience, or a figure and returning to it for broader exposition, definition, and explanation; emotional realism, from depictions of despair to laughter. Other aspects of narrative similarity include the immediate appeal due to adventure, acknowledged in the original title, *The Life and Strange Surprizing Adventures of Robinson Crusoe of York, Mariner*; images of travel; and ideas of the individual against the elements.

Another narrative aspect that precedes *Robinson Crusoe* is the idealization of a space apart from civilization. The utopian element was almost immediately championed, more so abroad than in Britain. However, critics debate whether *Robinson Crusoe* can be understood as utopic or dystopic (see Blaim, *Early English Utopian Fiction*; Claeys and Sargent). As Robert C. Elliot notes, a utopia is essentially a static form, a place where the living conditions are stable and presumably ideal (or in dystopia, stable yet problematic). By contrast, the Robinsonade is a dynamic form; Crusoe is a wanderer figure, and he builds his island life because he has no choice. Although we might be interested in what he builds and how he builds it, the character is a reluctant utopianist. The island provides food and water; Crusoe has work to keep him active and time for contemplation and meditation. Still, he thinks often about escaping from the island. He sees civilization neither as ideal nor as an evil force. When the opportunity arises to leave the island, he jumps at it. Since the novel as a genre is a hybrid, dynamic form, it is surprising neither that Defoe integrated utopian elements nor that imitators focused on those elements. In fact, *Robinson Crusoe* stands as an interesting comparison to the utopian tradition and as a signpost to changes in representation. The idealized utopia of the seventeenth century, of parallel, alternative worlds, gives way in the eighteenth century to the representation of ideal political states and economic utopias. Defoe's realism creates a world for Crusoe, but a world in which one must always see oneself as part of a larger community. While many Robinsonades try to be true to the motif of the individual struggling against the elements, more often the variations, especially if they have utopian qualities, misapprehended the novel in emphasizing the creation of alternative communities. The adventure story and the spiritual autobiography, not an idealizing force, were the features that appealed to eighteenth-century readers. Still, just as Defoe had almost innumerable sources that led to the creation of *Robinson Crusoe*, authors who are working in the Robinsonade tradition consciously appropriate the story and adapt it in innumerable, often very surprising ways.

Robinson Crusoe as International Text: Translation, Circulation, and Adaptation

To say that the world embraced *Robinson Crusoe* underestimates the novel's impact and popularity. Although the novel can be taught without referencing national and historical context but emphasizing instead theme, plot, and character, the more background that a teacher can offer a student about the novel as a world book, the better the novel can be understood as a cultural phenomenon.

The novel's influence extends to Europe and beyond, and the most obvious sign of popularity is that translations of the novel were immediate and continuous. The first translation came within a year of the original 1719 publication. French translations appeared fourteen times between 1720 and 1799. The dates of publication show that the novel was particularly in vogue during three distinct periods: in the decade after Defoe's original, buoyed by novelty and the tradition of imaginary voyages in French literature; in the period after the publication of *Émile* in 1762, when Jean-Jacques Rousseau lauded the novel as ideal for natural education; and during the French Revolution, when Robinson's rebellion struck a chord with a revolutionary society having to live with its choices. France was far from alone in embracing *Robinson Crusoe* in the eighteenth century. There were nine editions of a German translation between 1720 and 1783; five editions of Dutch translations between 1720 and 1791; and five editions of Italian translations between 1731 and 1791. Translations of the novel into other languages were not as immediate or as copious—and it should be remembered that members of the educated classes could often read in English, French, or German. Nonetheless, before the end of the century the novel was also translated into Swedish, Danish, Russian, Bohemian, and Serbian. Before the end of the nineteenth century, there were translations into Gaelic, Spanish, Portuguese, Finnish, Maltese, Polish, Hungarian, Armenian, Estonian, Arabic, Turkish, Yiddish, Hebrew, Persian, Maori, Latin, and classical Greek. More recent translations can be found in Coptic, Sudanese, Eskimo, and Esperanto. *Farther Adventures* and *Serious Reflections* were also translated, although not as often as the original volume.

It would probably not be an exaggeration to suggest that there are few world languages that do not have at least one translation of *Robinson Crusoe*, known variously as *Robinzon Kruzo* (Russian), *Robinsona Cruso* (Hindi), *Robinsun K'urvso* (Korean), and *Lubinxun piao liuji* (Chinese). Translations were often reprinted and sometimes became the basis for other translations. The first Italian *Robinson Crusoe*, for example, was a translation not from the English but from the French. Aside from changes made in translations because of marketing and commercial considerations, non-English editions also allowed the translator to make changes for ideological and nationalist reasons. Many of the translations are in reality adaptations, such as the 1772 Swedish translation that gives Crusoe the birthdate of 6 November because that is the date on which King Gustav Adolf dies in battle (see Hoffman 145). Almost every nationality has a Robinson tale that adapts or at least plays on the popularity of the original. There were not only many German editions but also versions of other national Robinsons in German; for example, *Der französische Robinson* ("The French Robinson"). Allusions to *Robinson Crusoe* abound, but novels that authors consciously construct on Defoe's model are a complete genre category (see Fisher's essay on the Robinsonade in this volume).

The novel's international appeal can be measured in translations and adaptations, but the novel is differently interpreted in each cultural context. German readers found the image of hard work leading to prosperity and of a careless, rebellious young man who learns his duty the foremost value of the novel. American audiences found the story of rugged individualism particularly appealing for a new country starting from scratch, and there were over a hundred editions of *Crusoe* published in America between 1774 and 1830 (see Brigham). And the changing French reception shows that the novel is not static but reinterpreted according to cultural contexts. Of course, the myths, archetypes, and tropes of the Western literary tradition mean very different things in different cultures. How the novel is interpreted in lesser-known literatures and cultures is sometimes hard to determine, but a brief foray into the *MLA International Bibliography* shows there is a great deal of scholarship on this issue. Just to take one example, Leah Garrett writes on a Yiddish version of *Robinson Crusoe*, Yosef Vitlin's *Robinzon di geshikte fun Alter-Leb* (1820), that is based not on the original but on Joachim Campe's 1780 German adaptation. Garrett says that the Yiddish *Crusoe* "keeps much of the plot intact yet Judaizes the story; Robinson Crusoe is renamed Reb Alter-Leb and is a practicing Jew from Hamburg; Friday is renamed Shabes (or Sabbath) and becomes a practicing Jew; and the island is Judaized by recourse to Jewish iconography" (215). Garrett also points out that Vitlin's ideological choice to adapt and translate *Robinson Crusoe* was assimilationist; in this context, Crusoe's travels become a metaphor for the Jewish diaspora. The assimilationist interpretation of the story is not unique. Jean-Richard Bloch, a century later, would write *Le Robinson juif* ("The Jewish Robinson"): "Transport him to Palestine and you have a Robinson who has found his island" (qtd. in Figuerola 162).

Clearly, minority cultures adapt and reinterpret the story for their own purposes and audiences, and student research on such adaptations could yield intercultural insights. For example, how does one understand Henno Martin's Namibian Robinsonade (*Wenn es Krieg gibt, gehen wir in die Wüste, eine Robinsonade in der Namib*), originally published in German in 1956, translated into English in 1957 as *The Sheltering Desert*, translated into Afrikaans in 1959 (*Vlug in die Namib: 'n robinsonade in die woestyn*), and made into a movie in 1992? In this tale, two German geologists escape the rise of Nazism by traveling to southwest Africa, only to find themselves threatened with internment by the British at the outbreak of World War II. The original German title literally translated is, "When the war comes, we will go into the desert." This Robinsonade allows readers to compare the experience of the geologists during the Nazi era, as well as the vexed politics of colonial-postcolonial history, to *Robinson Crusoe* and the eighteenth century. While it might seem esoteric for the average classroom, it shows how the novel has been disseminated and adapted. *Robinson Crusoe* is a story that has literally traveled around the world, and we can continue to marvel at the far reach of Defoe's invention.

Internet Resources

There is more than a little irony in searching for *Robinson Crusoe* on the Web, and much could be said about the isolating quality of the modern experience (of being stuck on an island or of staring at a computer screen). Still, a simple key word search on the Web yields massive quantities of material, and the Web will often be the first stop for students trying to find information about *Robinson Crusoe*. Online resources are not always consistent or dependable in quality or relevance, however, so the World Wide Web is something that any teacher must regard cautiously. Predictably, there are numerous summaries of the novel, à la *CliffsNotes*, as well as myriad student papers available for free and for a fee. Caveat emptor. Teachers should warn students of the dangers of using the Internet too heavily as a resource. Sometimes potentially useful sites simply disappear; for example, numerous *Crusoe* sites offer links to a *Friday* page, yet no links to it were functioning at the time this "Materials" section was written. However, along with the bad there is a great deal of good. There are numerous invaluable Web sites on the eighteenth-century context of the novel for interested students. The most well known sites, such as *The Voice of the Shuttle* from Alan Liu at the University of California, Santa Barbara, and the *Eighteenth-Century Resources* site run by Jack Lynch at Rutgers, have massive quantities of information and, perhaps most important, extensive links to numerous resources, including online articles. These sites are easy to find with any search engine, continue to add material, and are useful for both students and instructors. For teachers of the novel, there is a thriving online Listserv, C-18L, which often has discussions of pedagogy and eighteenth-century texts and courses. There is a searchable archive and a link to a *Selected Readings* site, which has extensive and recent bibliographies on Defoe and eighteenth-century authors, texts, and topics.

There are full-text, searchable versions of *Robinson Crusoe* available (along with the two sequels, *Farther Adventures* and *Serious Reflections*). It is assumed students will not want to read the entire text online, which is just as well since most of the versions on the Web are not editorially sound; they standardize capitalization and punctuation and break the text into chapters. Still, the search function that an online edition permits can prove valuable for research purposes. Probably the best versions available are from academic databases, such as *The Project Gutenberg E-Texts*, the University of Oregon's online library, and the University of Virginia Library's *Electronic Text Center* (which acknowledges that in their version "the text has been separated into arbitrary chapters for electronic manageability" [see *Electronic Text Center*]). The most dependable text is available on the Chadwyck-Healey database, which is accessible at university libraries that have subscriptions. Some journalism of the period can now be found online, and standard research databases can provide records and information about contemporaneous texts.

The Web offers other readily accessible research material. Searching for background to or details from the novel that might seem opaque to students—about Alexander Selkirk, for example, or the Juan Fernández islands—yields a seemingly endless amount of material. The Web also affirms *Robinson Crusoe*'s international appeal. In addition to American and British sites, Dutch, German, and French sites, and those in many other languages, show up as a result of any Robinson-related search. Many commercial sites, such as advertising for shipping, travel, and various products that exploit Crusoe's worldwide recognition also appear. A German site (*www.robinsone.de*) offers opportunities for other connections to *Robinson Crusoe*, including lists of Robinsonades from different periods (eighteenth century, nineteenth century, before and after 1945), different genres (such as opera and science fiction), and other media (e.g., comics). Although the site is in German, it is easy to navigate to images. One of the more interesting aspects of the site is that visitors can click on and view images of title pages and illustrations of *Crusoe* editions, as well as those of several Robinsonades.

Note   Unless otherwise noted, all quotations from Defoe's *Robinson Crusoe* are from the Norton Critical Edition, edited by Michael Shinagel.

Part Two

APPROACHES

Teaching *The Pilgrim's Progress* and *Robinson Crusoe*; or, From Filthy Mire to the Glory of Things

Robert Maniquis

Studies of Defoe since the 1960s have dissolved the assumption that *Robinson Crusoe* is mostly a brilliant variation on stories of travel and shipwreck. Narrative conventions obviously link *Robinson Crusoe* to such stories and memoirs, as well as to episodes in the *Odyssey*, the *Aeneid*, and even to such sea voyages as Paul's in the Acts of the Apostles; but today the adventure story in the novel is read commonly as entwined with both Puritan spiritual autobiography and early capitalist ideology.[1] It is, of course, very old news that *The Pilgrim's Progress* and *Robinson Crusoe* go together as Protestant classics. Shortly after the publication of *Robinson Crusoe*, in 1719, Charles Gildon claimed, in his attack on Defoe, that "there is not an old Woman that can go to the Price of it, but buys the Life and Adventures, and leaves it as a Legacy, with *The Pilgrims Progress*, the *Practice of Piety*, and *God's Revenge against Murther*" (Excerpt 260). The culture of old women, however, has changed in the last three hundred years; it is not students' grandmothers but their teachers who will have to explain to them why these texts go together.

As Crusoe is led through his spiritual biography, the new capitalist man in him is driven backward into received Puritan ways of relating the self to God. Yet Puritan autobiography is itself affected by the new *homo economicus* in Crusoe. Defoe transforms allegorical signifying with imitated primordial moments in the perception of the world and in ways not seen before in secular Christian writing. Scholars and critics, from George Starr, J. Paul Hunter, and Maximillian Novak, almost half a century ago, to John J. Richetti and Michael

McKeon more recently, have done much of the work that helps us appreciate this imaginative shift. Many years before these critics, in one of the best essays ever written on *Robinson Crusoe*, Virginia Woolf emphasizes everything that is concrete in the story; surely she is right to say of Defoe that "by being a great artist and forgoing this and daring that in order to give effect to his prime quality, a sense of reality—he comes in the end to make common actions dignified and common objects beautiful" (Excerpt 287).

In teaching these prose classics, we need to get, like Woolf, much more physical than we can as historical critics. Eyes need to be directed and ears attuned to Defoe's rhetoric of enumerated things. Yet we must also be more historically conscious than Woolf, for her essay, good as it is, does not venture into the implications of Defoe's emphasis on things. Focusing on the different manifestations of the sensorial and the symbolic in *Robinson Crusoe* and *The Pilgrim's Progress* helps us grasp the eighteenth century's newly imagined perception of things as a momentous shift in the cultural sign system.

Just as we try with Christian to understand both allegorical signs and interpretations of them as Christian journeys to the Celestial City, so we try with Crusoe to sort out the meanings of gold, corn, salvaged tools, and guns in his badly planned making of a boat or his shaping of a tool. Since *Robinson Crusoe* proceeds as if it were simply in the tradition of Puritan allegory, Defoe, like John Bunyan, allows the protagonist always to see double or alternative meanings. Indeed, the same traditional contrary meanings in things as signs can occur to Crusoe as they do to Christian. But Defoe also grants Crusoe a new signifying duality not available to Christian. Gold can stand, for Christian, as filthy lucre or as an image of the sublime spiritual laws of God. In contrast, Crusoe can read gold or silver or any form of money in Bunyan's way, as he does when he comes upon the chest of English and European coins in the wrecked ship. There he reads gold and silver outside the signifying extremes of degraded desire or heavenly colors. Gold, silver—indeed all coins of exchange become the working presence of God's grace in the actual thing. Gold as money is for Crusoe a gift for possible survival and a clue to the idea that God guides Crusoe with things that are both signs and real things. It is this duality that amuses the modern reader when Crusoe, in the purple passage on money as filthy lucre (43), has his important second thought, and, no matter how much he has fetishized what is, after all, only a commodity, carries the money back to his island together with all his other useful things. Crusoe and Bunyan both query the state of the soul through signs in the form of events or natural and made things. Bunyan is brought before these signs and taught, sometimes correctly, sometimes falsely, to interpret them. Christian is made to apprehend the interpretations as if for the first time, but he is never surprised by the natural things or the artifacts themselves. Crusoe, however, is made to see those things that become signs as if for the first time, a process repeated and reemphasized when Friday truly has new, elementary experiences of sight, taste, and sound. This imitation of perceptual beginnings comes with a surface doubleness in Crusoe's stuff and things, especially when he stockpiles them for the future. Most of his manufactured objects or loose stuff (lead, flour, grain, iron-work, sails, etc.) are already transformed from something else and are trans-formable into something else again. They are thus signs of transformability and potentiality and are ingredients in Crusoe's bricolage. Transformation and po-tential are crucial factors in Crusoe's seeing the world magically, a view that precedes his seeing the world through the analytic categories of use or ex-change value. Seeing for the first time, even before interpreting, is part of the modern Edenic experience.

The Edenic island kingdom over which Crusoe reigns in what he calls his "State of Nature" (86) only partially extracts its stuff and things from a world of exchange. Things and stuff can still bear the memory of what they signify in the world's commerce—the inevitable perversion of the soul by things. Hence the island kingdom only partly clears away the stains of sin in degraded human desire. And yet the novel works to push the reader back to that common En-lightenment hermeneutic model of the imagined place beyond memory. This is the place we know as John Locke's tabula rasa in his "Essay concerning Human Understanding" or Thomas Hobbes's state of nature in *Leviathan* and Jean-Jacques Rousseau's in his essay "On the Origin of Inequality." All these imagined hermeneutic models of psychological and social origin are both imaginary and necessary to our understanding of things, property, and desire.[2]

Amongst such models Defoe's is the most obviously fictional and yet the most easily believable. He of course did not invent the perceptions necessary to reimagining the physical world. John Calvin had begun to do that in the six-teenth century. Crusoe's is, to be sure, a fantasy island of pure use value. But use value, before it was a category of modern economic thought, was also at the heart of Calvin's awareness that much in worldly things would have to be authorized as wonderful.

Calvin, the most subtle of all Reformation theologians, knew that the in-creasing influx of wealth into Europe from the fifteenth century on posed a challenge to the Christian dualism of material vanity and spiritual eternity. Everything in this accumulating wealth spoke against the simplest lessons of Christ about rich men, camels, and the eyes of needles. Though Calvin speaks often enough of the filthy mire of materiality, he also exhorts the believer to enjoy and use the things of the world. Nothing in this is surprising, since enjoy-ing oneself in a world of material vanity was one of the teachings absorbed into Judeo-Greco wisdom literature such as Ecclesiastes. But Judeo-Christian resig-nation in humble enjoyment begins also to be modeled by Calvin into a com-plex accommodation to and even joyfulness in wealth and property. This grad-ual Calvinistic shift had to be delicately manipulated in religious consciousness, as it is in Bunyan's celebrations of bodily refreshment along the way to the Ce-lestial City. Ultimately, as in all examples of the interplay of capitalism and the Protestant ethic, Calvinist accommodation of Christian piety to wealth, like the physical pleasures in Christian's rest stops, is always to be apprehended in a sys-tem of spiritual signs—signs that call for grateful submission and a fearful awe of God.

Defoe's Calvinism, however, is of the kind that takes much more pointed pleasure than Calvin himself did in God's bounty. This newly authorized pleasure can be sensed in the fascination and the respect for the things themselves. *Robinson Crusoe* evinces the life-giving necessity of and a love for the material, the natural, thingness of—the articulated, shaped, and produced objects of—sensory reality. Twentieth-century critics, often citing Karl Marx's famous passages on *Robinson Crusoe* in *Capital*, have helped us understand the enormous ideological elaboration of capitalism in *Robinson Crusoe*. The novel contains long passages on the intricacy of the labor process, the ambivalent attitude toward money as unspendable but still useful, and the irony of the isolated spiritual hero who manages to become rich beyond all expectation. All these and other themes fuse the ancient Mesopotamian story of Job's suffering and reward with capitalist versions of restraint, Puritan discipline, spiritual humility, and the signs of one's connection to God. McKeon, for instance, helpfully explains Defoe's "naturalization of desire." But we can also come toward the symbolizing process in the novel from another direction and emphasize how this text, in bridging traditional Puritan and new capitalist values, cannot naturalize desire before it humanizes things. Both processes, it could be said, bring us to the same result—and yet not quite. Neither *Robinson Crusoe* nor texts like it could change the naturalizing mentality of desire in the eighteenth century unless writers allowed the imagination to work, as if in complete innocence, on the nature of things themselves. No reader in London in 1719 had any less use for a stool than Crusoe did. And if the Londoner did not have a stool, he or she surely had no less desire than Crusoe for one. But desire on Crusoe's island imparts a psychological magic to things. Crusoe, only after needing and often before even using an object, comes to know it in extraordinary detail. He not only appreciates what he does not have, for he indeed lacks many things, but he also synthesizes his need, his possession, and his use of things in a way that forges new intimacy with them. If Defoe is our first fictional ideologizer of the spiritualized capitalist self, he is so because he knew that the things of the world had to be embraced in constructing a new fictional perception of them. Without this perceptual adjustment, there would have been no naturalized desire, no spiritual and materialist alliance in eighteenth-century capitalist imagination.

Consider the sense of excited discovery that Crusoe has when retrieving stuff from the wrecked ship. He greatly values nearly every discovered object because value is premised on the survival of his body. The ropes, the sails, the ironwork, the cables, the gunpowder—all these we remember in Crusoe's enumerations, which can be read as litanies of blessings. Yet the emphasis is never, at first, on God's miraculous provision. That comes later when Crusoe the narrator, as McKeon demonstrates ("Defoe" 403–05), incorporates Crusoe the castaway into meditation on the meaning of providential signs. Before that meditative summing up, his prose, often like a camera eye, directs us to understand the corporeality of things and thus empowers them. Crusoe grabs onto things before he can possibly know of what use they can be to him, because everything, for his desperately isolated psyche, has a potential usefulness, a possibility of development, to use a modern sacred word, or elevation, to use an early Puritan one. Defoe incrementally elevates Crusoe from the irresponsible rambler to the penitent sinner by offering hints of Crusoe's internal life, in which providence realizes itself as thought (humbling and elevating always go together in the Puritan mind). In that elevation, Crusoe is transformed from a punished object to a Godly agent. This elevation begins, imagistically and narratively, at the surface of the kinesthetic, plastic nature of the world, in the presentation of things and stuff as innumerable potentialities. Take, for example, the long passages on Crusoe's attempting to make earthenware pots (87–89). Much of this is usefully commented on by those who emphasize the values of labor and of use in the text. Woolf focuses instead on the wonder that Crusoe has for the object. She in fact takes the pot as an image for the wonder for objects in the entire text: "There are no sunsets and no sunrises; there is no solitude and no soul. There is, on the contrary, staring us full in the face nothing but a large earthenware pot" (Excerpt 285). Yet in those passages on the making of pots the wonder is neither exclusively in the labor and the pleasure Crusoe has in making one nor in Woolf's sense of concrete aesthetic pleasure. The wonder begins in Crusoe's observing clay, fire, and embers and in seeing how in natural processes, one thing becomes another. This is where the dialectic of a new signifying in Western culture begins: in having the desire for an object simultaneous with or even before actually needing to use it and in the fetishism that Marx demonstrates in the sign system of commodities. In pointing to the new and modern wonder for and metamorphoses of things, Defoe's novels leave behind medieval and Christian obsessions with transformation as either purely spiritual or alchemical. In Crusoe's world everything is transformable not simply into gold but, more important, into what gold stands for; and the wealth that it stands for, in its magically real materiality, figures the presence of the spiritual. This intensified blending of spiritual and material transformation graces things with a status of a kind that they had never quite had before in Christian culture. Crusoe's wonder in the object and pleasure in its making and use are compacted with Defoe's fictional discovery that all stuff and things have the potential to transform. *Crusoe* marks the beginning of the modern alchemy not of magic but of production.

Consider also the social consequences of this new consciousness of things in Crusoe's tendentious list of the credit and debit sides of his existence. His account book culminates in a comparison between the absence of other human beings and the presence of those things that allow self-sufficiency:

> Have no Soul to speak to, or relieve me, but God wonderfully sent the Ship in near enough to the Shore that I have gotten out so many necessary things as will either supply my Wants, or enable me to supply my self even as long as I live.   (50)

Fig. 1. The "person" of Robinson Crusoe shadowed in consumable things.

Fig. 2. Commodities as things used in the elemental reshaping of Robinson Crusoe's life. (Figs. 1 and 2 are from *Aventures de Robinson Crusoe*, by Daniel Defoe; illustrated by Grandville. Paris: H. Fournier Aîné, 1841, pp, 39, 53.)

Crusoe does not claim that things are the same as human companions but grants things a balance sheet's equivalency. Like the allegorical sign structure, the balance sheet suggests only a binary opposition with the soul and things, on the one hand, or God and the self, on the other. But this is far more than simple twoness, sign and signified, or credit and debit. Crusoe's opposing isolation to the fact that "God wonderfully sent the Ship" invokes Calvin and Bunyan and the gift of the use of all things as God delivers them and demonstrates Crusoe's traditional Calvinism. But the things are there to counter the evil situation of having no one to speak to. Here the things take on their inevitable social aspect. In the absence of human company, the things not only connect Crusoe to God but also become familiar objects that aid his mental survival. Things for Crusoe are much more than signs or instruments because they become both intimate quotidian companions and extensions of him. Things can only become this amalgam of material stuff and outward presence of the self by first becoming things in and of themselves, after which they can continue to signify transcendence, since God arranged for their delivery to Crusoe and for his immediate deliverance in turn. What is striking, however, is that both the spiritual grace of gifted things and the isolatable power in thingness itself are allowed to share the same symbolic space, which allows things to be intimately humanized and socialized.

Consider another example of how Crusoe perceives objects: Crusoe, menaced by illness, recovers as he reads a passage in the Bible (68–70). The novelty in this bodily and spiritual healing is that it occurs in a symbiotic process by which the word of God is married to the sensations of tobacco. Smoke from the combustion of the plant is joined to the inspiration of God's word. Breathing in of stuff and elevation of the spirit become inseparable. As we have seen, Crusoe's accounting of the good and evil in his situation establishes the incipient humanization of things that comes with the spiritualization of his consciousness. In this passage on reading the Bible, it is the tobacco that seems to be both a physical and spiritual link between scripture and the body. Both more and less than a sign standing for something else, tobacco is here both instrument and instrumentalizer. We have come to describe Crusoe's accounting and imaging of things as reification or, as I prefer, the thingifying of the human. But again, in the seventeenth and eighteenth centuries, before Western culture could spiritualize things, things had to be given their own power and to be liberated from the monopolistic world of the allegorical sign. Once things were humanized, human beings were reified or thingified. In little more than a century, European imperial imagination would take this amalgam of humanness and thingness for granted. One French illustrator, in 1836, shows as much in portraying Crusoe only through his possessions. The materials Crusoe had shipped to him in the "Brasils" are portrayed in a pile, with the initials R. C. on them. The initials are not there simply as a giant luggage tag; they identify the objects as his, but then the objects seem even more insistently to represent his person. Crusoe's hat is posed on top of the pile, a covering of some kind is draped behind, and two plants stick out, almost like arms, from sacks. The pile of stuff and things seems almost like a body (fig. 1). In another illustration, the weapons, powder, rope, and tools recovered from the wrecked ship appear alone—no initials are necessary now. We know that these are the elements of Crusoe's reconstitution as a person (fig. 2). This is at least one reason why the second half of *Robinson Crusoe*, with its story of Friday, has such sinister power. Crusoe's attachment to Friday is made to seem deep because Friday is both a human being and a thing. Only after experiencing the text's new presentation of things and Crusoe's relation to them can we see that there is nothing surprising in his attachment to someone he both rescues and turns into an obedient servant. Crusoe's affection for Friday is as authentic as that for his cherished familial objects. Love, joy, and exploitation become one. Compare the passages on Crusoe's pleasure in his earthenware pot and his pleasure in being Friday's master; they are quite the same, both filled with a sense of genuine enjoyment and connection.

Emphasis on this elementary discovery in *Robinson Crusoe* runs the risk of evoking an experience that students may at first find difficult to understand. My reading of this aspect of the novel asks students to explore the history of connections between physical and social perception. But they usually find it surprising that it was ever necessary in Western culture to authorize what seems today instinctive. How can our students, indeed, how even can we their teachers, sense any novelty here? We trudge down the crisscrossing alleyways of shopping malls not quite like the pilgrim Christian, since malls have no straight and narrow paths. We carry our shopping bags or push our carts, filled now not with sin but with our things and their packaging. Or we may see ourselves as Crusoe, moving stuff from one protected place to another, from the sheltered mall to our car, to our abode. We like to touch, even fondle, our purchases. But we are also cyberspatial agents, who can turn value into electronic signals. By tapping on a computer key we can make things fly through the air or dart along the ground to arrive, all paid for, at our small or large cocoon, wherever we have hollowed it out in order to live far from the messiness of labor and production. How can creatures such as we ever recover anything like an original fictional sense of what is new about a human being's relation to things in *Robinson Crusoe*? Furthermore, how can our students, no longer intimately acquainted with the Bible's grotesque and delightful mythologies, come to see the novelty of thingness in a culture once dominated by a religion designed to lead the soul far from the material world? This is where *The Pilgrim's Progress*, with its own psychological brilliance and subtle amalgamation of allegory and realism, can provide us with useful comparisons.

As I have suggested, it is important to rub students' noses against and amuse their imaginative eye and ear with the sounds and sights of Crusoe's discovering all his good stuff. It is just as important to direct them in *The Pilgrim's Progress* to Bunyan's sense of things and nature that are not for but against us. Bunyan's allegory thrives on an acute sense of the concrete, but his material world is first to be conceived as muck and mire, an oozy place drawing us down into a bottomless pit. The list of examples is easily compiled: the Slough of Despond, made of "scum and filth," is the despairing mind dissolving into what is most feared—the dissolving formlessness of the material world.[3] Falling into the Slough of Despond is inevitable in Bunyan's world of Carnal Policy and

Carnal Desire. And if it is ever thought that the deathliness of the desiring body can be fought off by the limited imagination of the Law (as opposed to Protestant grace), the Law can be imaged, as the Dark Interpreter does, as mere dust swept up from a dirty floor. The world as filth in Bunyan compares with what I refer to as Calvin's theological accommodation of prosperity, the godly setting of all good things before us—a necessary accommodation at a time when Europe was growing rich. It is not then surprising that Christian can enjoy eating fat things and drinking refined wine. And in the image of the Delectable Mountains there is pleasure in the idea of Edenic bounty imagined as sensual delight. We sense Bunyan's own enjoyment in thingness in his constant homely similes, such as that of composition to the hooks and lines of fishing. He is, along with Dante, a powerful writer of allegory because he is so imagistically and linguistically concrete. How could Bunyan, a working tinker and mechanic preacher, not be fond of things? But no things can be imagined as they are meant to be—as signs of God's ultimate grace or the bounty of Jesus's sacrificed body—until the actual condition of our minds is changed from fascination for this world into our realization that we must escape it. As Bunyan likes to remind us—our nature, however subject to grace, is usually led by stuff and things directly into the dunghill. Coming upon Vanity Fair, Faithful and Christian show themselves to be reluctant consumers of the goods avidly hawked by merchants. Shocked by this rare breed of nonconsumers, the merchants drop all pretense of civility and reveal their base nature. Since Faithful and Christian will not purchase, all the merchants can think to do is smear them with dirt. Along Christian's pilgrimage we are shown how easy it is to be fouled by the dunghill, to trip into ditches, to fall into sloughs. Christian and we who dream him up are creatures who, whatever the celestial glory we hope for, are always only a step away from the place where our smelly bodies rise from excremental, primordial ooze.

Most of Crusoe's autobiography is also about never-ending physical menace, and yet how differently things, stuff, and the earth are related to him. Although the furious elements have nearly destroyed him, the earth is also his salvational refuge. Geological images of stuff and holes and material envelopment are reversed from Bunyan to Defoe. There is the moment when Crusoe realizes that he has hollowed out his shelter too deeply into his mountain, and earthquakes threaten his safety. But that warning of danger merely calls for a change of abode. Sometime after he has become aware of the savages that visit his island, he discovers a cave and in its mouth that famous dying he-goat, whose shining eyes startle him, as though they were of a man or the devil. Steeling himself, Crusoe is drawn back to the cave and explores it further, crawling on all fours deeper into it as if into the bowels of the earth, where he comes upon a glorious grotto of glittering stones. Here is where he decides to store precious possessions, such as his arms and gunpowder. At the end of this episode, he reminds us of the goat that has died. The narrative detail is important; he buries the goat in the cave to quell the stench of its dying body. The earth, even its dark elemental processes that transform the body of the buried goat back into dirt, is for Crusoe a warm, welcoming place of safety—never a place of earthly pollution or a sign of what is destructive in Crusoe's desires or in his attachment to the world (128–30).[4]

My own experience is that students enjoy discussing Defoe's fictionally primitive moments of coming to see and revere things and stuff. They also move easily from Crusoe's discovery of things to discussion of the consequences of such reverence in Defoe's themes of cannibalism, sacrificial rituals, religious transformation, and even the battle with the wolves at the end of the book. In this brief essay I cannot discuss how a new perception of things is connected to all these themes. But I must point to at least one connected question that always interests students—the sexlessness of *Robinson Crusoe*.

The novel is not completely without sex. There is perhaps a coded subtext in Crusoe's capture and enslavement in Morocco—any eighteenth-century reader could give free rein to sexual fantasies and fears in thinking of serving heathen Turks and Moors. After his escape, Crusoe, on the west coast of Africa, is particularly struck by the stark nakedness of the Africans, whom he impresses by shooting one of two leopards, which he imagines to be a male chasing a female, "either in Sport or in Rage" (23). Animal husbandry must be addressed when Crusoe works at raising his flock of goats. And then there is the problem of Crusoe's feline population explosion, which allows us to imagine catcalls cracking the silence of Crusoe's lonely evenings. Still, we can say that, as far as sex is concerned, *Robinson Crusoe* is, compared with most eighteenth-century novels, an innocent boy's story. Its sexlessness can give rise to interesting discussions, especially if students are also reading *Moll Flanders* or *Pamela* or *Clarissa*, thriving hothouses of sex. There is one connection I usually emphasize, however, in relation to a new perception of things. For delight in the material world to take place in this spiritual autobiography, it was appropriate for Defoe to avoid mentioning human sexual desire. Allowing it in the text would have contaminated Crusoe's new acquaintance with the material world and by eliciting the common Puritan connection between desire and the excremental—lusts of the flesh never being possible without filth. One carnal thought, dream, or image in Crusoe's loneliness, one masturbational hint, would have caused the text to tumble backward into the kinds of pits, ditches, and snares that Bunyan specializes in. To imagine anything reminiscent of Bunyan's allegorical Harlot is to imagine the filthy mire of the material.

It is time to end this essay with another question commonly asked by my students when we end our comparisons of *The Pilgrim's Progress* and *Robinson Crusoe*. If Defoe's imagination of the material world was so different from that in traditional Puritan culture, they ask, then why did both Bunyan's and Defoe's narratives remain two of the most popular in anglophone culture from the eighteenth century on? My short answer is that just as Rome was not built in a day, cultural imagination does not transform itself overnight. These texts go neatly together because the dominant culture needed both texts at the same time. The cultural work that ideology does is to hold in tense balance contradictory values and forms of imagination even as they change. *The Pilgrim's Progress* was a text that we can now see leading, as if inevitably, to *Robinson Crusoe*. Readers over the centuries have taken to Bunyan's great allegory for many reasons. But surely much of its attractive intellectual brilliance lies in its striking self-consciousness of the interpretation of things as signs along with a sense that signs may only be things perverted into false interpretations. This emerging modern form of Calvinist semiotic uncertainty, with all its attention to the things of the world, nevertheless assigns the most repellent images of the degraded material origin of humankind to the world. We see these contradictory values in the text of *Robinson Crusoe*. And we see the connected contraries of purely Puritan and developing capitalist perceptions as we look from Bunyan's allegory to Defoe's newly symbolized world. These texts go together because they are like and unlike, and both were necessary to the process of cultural change.

Perhaps *Robinson Crusoe* should always be taught alongside *The Pilgrim's Progress* with emphasis on how Bunyan's allegorical yet strikingly concrete text, a text that emerges from the seventeenth-century class of the working poor, can be said to find its competition and its complement in Defoe's middle-class, descriptively realist, and new symbolical work. In doing so, the teacher brings students back, not to one but to two of the most important texts in anglophone culture. Each text can be made easier to understand through the other. Examining a changing imagination of stuff and things is a good way to study the linguistic brilliance in both texts, the cultural implications of allegory, emerging modern symbolism, and shifting ideological values. Both texts display something of the cultural tension in our origins as modern creatures. For a few hundred years readers had a need for Bunyan's text of 1678, which in its Calvinistic mode both materialized their psyches and humbled their material nature. Readers needed it no less than Defoe's exciting narrative of 1719, which, for all its semiotic uncertainties, newly authorized the dangerous love that human beings have always had for their material part and for things of the world. In explaining the great accomplishment that lies in the making of bread, Crusoe tells us that he believes "few People have thought much upon (*viz.*) the strange multitude of little Things necessary in the Providing, Producing, Curing, Dressing, Making and Finishing this one Article of Bread" (86). But as one of the first modern novelists, Defoe made certain that the multitude of little things, even those present in any one thing, would never quite escape the attention of modern readers in describing who and what we are.

NOTES

[1]For a brief and useful summary of Max Weber's and R. H. Tawney's famous theses on Protestantism and capitalism and their effect on obscuring religious content in the narrative, along with the recovery of content by Starr, Hunter, and others, see Rogers, *Robinson Crusoe*.

²Students should read longer selections from *Émile* than those provided in the Norton Critical Edition of *Robinson Crusoe* ("Treatise" 262–64). Rousseau's praise and criticism of *Robinson Crusoe* help explain the importance of the historical laboratory model of human experience that was common in seventeenth- and eighteenth-century philosophical, political, and psychological writings and that Defoe's novel reflects. These models of first human experiences are all heuristic and fictional scenes designed to isolate in order to explain real things and processes. They are obvious secular equivalents of religious myths of origin. Rousseau is especially interesting in this regard, since he would have liked Defoe's novel to have portrayed Crusoe in even more artificially elaborated isolation from human production in order to emphasize this original, innocent discovery of the "natural" world of things and processes. The challenge to do this was taken up in more than one nineteenth-century French version of *Robinson Crusoe*, modified or "rousseauized," to emphasize unmediated first perceptions.

³ Wharey and Sharrock's edition has a detailed index in which all the passages I refer to can easily be found. For classroom use, the editions published in the Oxford World Classics series (ed. Keeble) and by Penguin (ed. Sharrock) have good introductions and helpful notes.

⁴Compare the scene in *The Journal of the Plague Year*, where the narrator describes a coin purse lifted up from the street with, of course, great care. Since the purse may have been polluted by the plague, it must be carefully removed, extracted, even purified: "[a man] fetched a pail of Water, and set it down hard by the Purse; then went again, and fetch'd some Gun-powder, and cast a good deal of Powder upon the Purse, and then made a Train from that which he had thrown loose upon the Purse; the train reached about two Yards; after this he goes in a third Time, and fetches out a pair of Tongues red hot, and which he had prepar'd, I suppose on purpose; and first setting Fire to the Train of Powder, that sing'd the Purse and also smoak'd the Air sufficiently: But he was not content with that; but he then takes up the Purse with the Tongs, holding it so long till the Tongs burnt thro' the Purse, and then he shook the Money out into the Pail of Water, so he carried it in. The Money, as I remember, was about thirteen Shillings, and some smooth Groats, and Brass Farthings" (87). There is no more obvious example of the status accorded in the early eighteenth century to commodities or things in the traditional symbolism of material pollution. The narrative action of the retrieval of the money focuses attention not on the obviously persistent desire for the money but on its material transformation from a polluted to a usable state. This is the new kind of doubled reading I have referred to in the example of Crusoe's "second thought" about carrying away the filthy lucre of gold found in the ship. Crusoe first apprehends the cave of the dying goat as a place of decay and death, but ultimately for Crusoe it is a protective, salvational place. The degraded material substrate of existence, like the plague in London, fills Crusoe's imagination, and yet he can also set it aside. The material is not simply doubled symbolically as in all allegory, when, for instance, gold can signify filth or, in its most beautiful allegorical form, spiritual glory. The narrative description of the dying goat or money snatched from streets of disease does not simply symbolize the material in a new, positive way. The imaginative goal in such descriptions is primarily to remind us of the association between money and pollution and also to relieve the thing itself from the exclusive weight of accumulated allegorical meanings, just as the money is relieved of disease or as the goat's body, with its stench, is returned to the ground of Crusoe's protective cave.

Robinson Crusoe and *Gulliver's Travels*: Some Pedagogical Frameworks

Richard Braverman

A number of years ago, in the midst of a year abroad in France, I happened to be in the city of Tours on Bastille Day. Eager to witness the festivities, I made my way to the town center, expecting to be swept up in a boisterous crowd. To my surprise, there was no crowd to speak of, just a modest gathering of Tourangeau who, after a few dreary speeches and a less than electric "La Marseillaise," dispersed in orderly fashion. Perplexed by this nonevent, I grappled for an explanation and, on my return to Paris, sought out one of my French professors. Her terse response—delivered in jest but meant in earnest—was a brief but indelible lesson in historical revisionism: "Perhaps the people of Tours have never thought the Revolution was a good idea."

That lesson resurfaced many years later when I was teaching *Gulliver's Travels* in an undergraduate survey of eighteenth-century English literature. The immediate context was an assignment that called for students to compare Gulliver's ethnographies of the Lilliputians in part 1 and the Brobdingnagians in part 2. The accounts never fail to pique student interest, and on this occasion most were quick to spot the telling differences between them. But a few also noted that the two had something significant in common, namely an evident sympathy, as one put it, for "the good old days." To support her assertion, this student pointed first to Gulliver's qualified admiration for Lilliputian institutions: "In relating these and the following Laws, I would only be understood to mean the original Institutions, and not the most scandalous Corruptions into which these People are fallen by the degenerate Nature of Man" (50); she then pointed to the litany of the horrors Gulliver narrates for the king of Brobdingnag: "And I finished all with a brief historical account of affairs and events in England for about an hundred years past" (107). It was then that I recalled my long-buried lesson in historical revisionism, which prompted me to ask why Gulliver's "brief historical account" covered events for "about an hundred years past." The question was rhetorical, since I went on without pause to add, because he didn't think the Revolution was a good idea. Continuing, I explained that "about an hundred years past," calculated from the book's publication in 1726, coincided with the reign of Charles I, who ruled as God's anointed before religious and political divisions erupted in the Puritan Revolution.[1] Furthermore, to Swift, the conflict that culminated in the martyrdom of Charles I turned English history into a narrative of decline and fall—decline and fall because, as he saw it, the divisions of the 1640s did not vanish with the Restoration but resurfaced with renewed vigor under the cover of the Revolution of 1688 and the dynastic change of 1714.

I must confess that I had already guided my students over much of this historical terrain earlier in the semester, but met as I now was with some puzzled looks, I proceeded to part 2 of my brief, beginning with the question, When do Gulliver's four voyages take place? After a minute or so of page shuffling, a hand went up from the back and a student listed Gulliver's departures: the first voyage begins on 4 May 1699; the second on 20 June 1702; the third on 5 August 1706; and the fourth on 7 September 1710; on the way back, he leaves Houyhnhnmland for England on 15 February 1714/15, finally reaching his home at Redriff on 5 December 1715. I then followed up with a second question, Why do you think Gulliver comes home in 1715, that is, why do you think the book concludes in 1715?, hinting at the chronology of Swift's life. In 1715, the answer soon came, Swift was in Ireland, a political out when the new dynasty came to power. Following further discussion, we came to the conclusion that Swift had linked his exile with Gulliver's homecoming because for Swift 1714/15 was the changing of the guard. Swift and all he believed in was out, while Gulliver and the revolutionary madness he represented was in.

This historical framework is particularly resonant when I teach the *Travels* in the immediate wake of *Robinson Crusoe*. Students who have already been primed with Defoe's spin on English history come to see how the works make very different use of the past century and its impact on the present. Defoe had a much different take than Swift on the recent past, and for that reason he situates Crusoe's story in the later seventeenth century as a run-up to what he saw as the defining political event of his lifetime, the Revolution of 1688. More specifically, Defoe places Crusoe's exile in the years 1659 to 1687, timing them to coincide with the Stuart Restoration. As Michael Seidel has observed:

> Defoe felt that the important gap in the continuity of English history was not the dramatic parliamentary revolution from 1641 to the Protectorate but those lost years from 1660 to 1688, coincidental also with the first twenty-eight years of his own life, when the Stuarts returned to a land whose best interests Defoe was convinced they did not represent.
>
> ("Crusoe" 366)

The years on the island also serve as a prelude to 1688, as Crusoe builds in the state of nature an alternative to the England of the Stuarts he has left behind. Defoe, then, thought the revolution was a good idea, and its preservation through the dynastic change in 1714 was confirmation of the new order that Swift abhorred.

The historical framework sketched above is just one of several for teaching *Robinson Crusoe* and *Gulliver's Travels* together in an undergraduate survey. I draw on other historical frameworks in due course—ancients versus moderns, Enlightenment versus counter-Enlightenment, novel versus satire—but I begin with the revolutionary framework because in my experience the others resonate more fully when students come to see the texts as rivals in a protracted struggle over bitterly contested ground that produced clear winners and losers. I turn next to the narrative framework, drawing on the historical

ground already established to show how Defoe and Swift exploit literary form
for ideological ends. There are relatively few instances where the *Travels* directly addresses or parodies *Crusoe*, because Swift's target is broader than
Defoe's, making it difficult to sustain a dialogue between the works through a
series of parallel passages. I thus find it useful to link the two through a common narrative framework, one that is grounded in their roots in travel literature: the travails of the wandering hero.

In a lecture James Joyce delivered in Trieste in 1912, he wrote that "the
whole Anglo-Saxon spirit is in Crusoe: the manly independence, the uncon-
scious cruelty, the persistence; the slow yet efficient intelligence; the sexual apathy; the practical, well-balanced religiousness; the calculating taciturnity"—
and, it might be added, the spirit of adventure, for Joyce saw Crusoe as the
English Ulysses (323).[2] In the tradition of the wandering hero, Crusoe, like
Ulysses, is a boundary figure, for he defines—or rather redefines—the limits of
the known world. Likewise, Gulliver is a boundary figure, because his four voyages take him to the ends of the earth. Students often note, in addition, that
Crusoe and Gulliver are not homebodies but all too willing exiles. In this light,
some of them have even seen in Crusoe a kinship with the Homeric legend of
the winnowing oars, since his return to domestic life lasts a single sentence: "I
marry'd . . . and had three Children, two Sons and one Daughter: But my Wife
dying . . ." (219). They tend to view Gulliver, however, as a reluctant Ulysses,
since, as one student aptly put it, he returns to England only after being voted
off the island.

The main reason Crusoe and Gulliver are wandering heroes is that both are
younger sons. Students already familiar with *Crusoe* recognize from the opening of the *Travels* that Gulliver is not the inheriting son and so must pursue an
education to make his way in the world:

> My Father had a small Estate in *Nottinghamshire*; I was the Third of five
> Sons. He sent me to *Emanuel College* in *Cambridge*, at Fourteen Years
> old, where I resided three Years, and applied myself close to my Studies:
> But the Charge of maintaining me (although I had a very scanty Al-
> lowance) being too great for a narrow Fortune; I was bound Apprentice
> to Mr. *James Bates*, an eminent Surgeon in *London*, with whom I contin-
> ued four Years; and my Father now and then sending me small Sums of
> Money, I laid them out in learning Navigation, and other Parts of the
> Mathematicks, useful to those who intend to travel, as I always believed
> it would be some time or other my Fortune to do.   (15)

Although Crusoe too is a victim of birth order, Defoe offers up a variation on
the theme, as circumstances make Crusoe the inheriting son, even though he
is the youngest of three brothers: "I had two elder Brothers, one of which was
Lieutenant Collonel to an *English* Regiment of Foot in *Flanders*, formerly
commanded by the famous Coll. *Lockhart*, and was killed at the Battle near

Dunkirk against the *Spaniards*: What became of my second Brother I never knew any more than my Father or Mother." Crusoe becomes heir to the family estate, but he cannot accept the future inscribed in the paternal legacy. Neither can he pursue the career for which his father has prepared him: "My Father, who was very ancient, had given me a competent Share of Learning, as far as House-Education, and a Country Free-School generally goes, and design'd me for the Law" (4). Satisfied with "nothing but going to Sea," he rejects the "middle station" in life, a station "not embarrass'd with the Labours of the Hands or of the Head, nor sold to the Life of Slavery for daily Bread" (5). The impulse is not directed against his father so much as against the filial narrative that defines the inheritance. But that patrimony, like the "competent Share of Learning" provided him, is not enough to sway his spirit as a younger son, and so he chooses to seek his fortune elsewhere.

Crusoe's desire to seek his fortune elsewhere is also inscribed in his name. As the novel opens, Crusoe explains that his full name is a combination of parental surnames. His Christian name comes from his mother, who is English, and his surname from his father, an immigrant from Bremen. Crusoe, however, was not the original family surname: when his father emigrated he was still "Kreutznaer," but in time that changed to its present form "by the usual Corruption of Words in England" (4).[3] The revised form preserves the original sense of the German—Crusoe means "cross," Kreutznaer "near the cross" (my trans.). Their difference is more important than their resemblance because the change over time undermines inheritance as the yardstick of value. In *Robinson Crusoe*, name is not the mark of inherent value but the sign of virtue achieved, and for that reason it is subject to change. It changed for another, related reason: Crusoe is a younger son who rejects his inheritance—the name, estate, and narrative offered to him—for a legacy of his own devising. In the process, Crusoe, not Kreutznaer, is the name he must redeem, and as he does so he creates an imaginative world in which he metaphorically fathers himself.

In sharp contrast to *Robinson Crusoe*, *Gulliver's Travels* lacks the pervasive paternal-filial tension of Defoe's narrative. Gulliver and Crusoe may both be younger sons, but there is a marked difference in the ways they play out their roles as boundary figures. Whereas Crusoe's crossings sanction an alternative society, one in which the law of the son (the revolutionary legacy) displaces the law of the father (the Stuart legacy), Gulliver's transgress traditional limits by virtue of his unexamined assumption that the human being is the measure of all things.[4] The respective crossings of each character are inscribed in literary form too, for whereas the novel is Defoe's vehicle for a new dispensation that legitimizes the self-made man, Swift's satiric antinovel taps the dark side of that dispensation, turning Crusoe's brave new world into Gulliver's grand illusion, his homecoming a descent into the perpetual exile of madness.

The familial and political implications of Crusoe's disobedience are signaled in his early misadventures.[5] Paternal-filial tension resonates in each episode, from Crusoe's meeting with his stern but forgiving father to the sea captain who admonishes Crusoe after his first disastrous voyage and the Turk who keeps him on a short leash following his capture: "when he went to Sea, he left me on Shoar to look after his little Garden, and to do the common Drudgery of Slaves about his House" (19). Had Crusoe accepted the middle station of life, a life "not embarass'd with the Labours of the Hands or of the Head, not sold to the Life of Slavery for daily Bread," he would not now be tending another's garden. But his fall is more than a poignant reminder of an earlier choice; it is also a harbinger of things to come. It will not be until he escapes the Turk that he will be able to tend his own garden, beginning with his Brazilian plantation. Yet even that episode serves as a prelude to his island exile, because it is only in the state of nature that Crusoe will be able to build the society that will permit him to escape his personal and political past.

Shortly before we start to discuss Crusoe's island, I ask students to reflect on the garden as a recurring image that mediates the text's pervasive paternal-filial tension. Most students are quick to see variations of the image in the middle-class life initially offered Crusoe, in the Turkish captain's little garden, and in Crusoe's Brazilian plantation—all of which are left behind because, for Crusoe, as one student succinctly put it, the law of the son is to the law of the father as the made Eden is to the found Eden. And so Crusoe lands on a barren island, the sole survivor of a sinking ship that symbolizes the old regime he has left behind. Students who see in the shipwreck a metaphor of Crusoe's rebirth nevertheless recognize that Crusoe is reborn in the state of nature not quite the Adam he at first appears. He soon rafts back to the ship to salvage whatever he can, in particular the carpenter's chest: "it was after long searching that I found out the Carpenter's Chest, which was indeed a very useful Prize to me, and much more valuable than a Ship Loading of Gold would have been at that time" (38). The tools, the most useful items from the world he has left behind, are the instruments that will permit him to domesticate nature, create wealth, and establish dominion. Moreover, he will create his brave new world in historical time, for shortly after his first return from the shipwreck, Crusoe reflects after shooting at a wild fowl: "I believe it was the first Gun that had been fir'd there since the Creation of the World" (40). By this action, Defoe inserts the state of nature into history, the temporal dimension underscoring that the island is not the estate available to the son through inheritance—or the lost paradise of fiction—but a utopia that must be made.

And make Crusoe does, illustrating John Locke's ideas on labor and value in the process. Yet even as his accumulations grow, he is still vulnerable: like Ulysses, who was faced with the temptations of Kalypso, Circe, and Nausikaa, Crusoe meets a comparable temptation when, after about a year in exile, he discovers a lush spot in the interior of the island. After noting the natural abundance of the place, he makes an astonishing discovery:

> At the End of this March I came to an Opening, where the Country seem'd to descend to the West, and a little Spring of fresh Water which

> issued out of the Side of the Hill by me, run the other Way, that is due
> East; and the country appear'd so fresh, so green, so flourishing, every
> thing being in a constant Verdure, or Flourish of *Spring*, that it looked
> like a planted Garden.   (73)

Before he leaves the spot, Crusoe weighs the ease it offers against the labor required elsewhere. But leave he does, and in doing so passes the test because
the planted garden, an emblem of Eden, is the femme fatale he must resist to
establish his new order.

While Crusoe resists temptation, he does so not for a mortal wife but for a
mortal son. Students who recognize in Crusoe's brave new world values of Enlightenment idealism are quick to point out a darker side of the novel when it
comes to the question of Friday. There is little question about Defoe's belief in
colonial expansion or about Friday's role as the subaltern. But students also
note that his physical features bring him closer to Crusoe: "He had a very good
Countenance, not a fierce and surly Aspect; but seem'd to have something very
manly in his Face, and yet he had all the Sweetness and Softness of an *European* in his Countenance too, especially when he smil'd" (148). And so it is
with the bond that develops between them: "his very Affections were ty'd to
me, like those of a Child to a Father" (151). This passage shows that, although
Friday may be Crusoe's colonial prize, he appears to solve another problem
too: Crusoe needs an heir as well as a companion. And so, I argue, Friday is the
solution, foreshadowed first in Crusoe's grief over the dead child who washes
up in a shipwreck, then in his dream about Friday, and finally in the actual rescue. The paternal-filial thread that runs throughout the narrative is thus carried forward, because Friday—the tabula rasa who is heir to Crusoe's accumulated knowledge—becomes his metaphoric son, their bond abrogating the
metaphorics of blood.[6] In time, Friday's biological father materializes, but Crusoe loses a son to gain a family in the form of the English and Spanish seamen
who eventually come under his civil authority and who receive a similar legacy,
which they pledge to honor in Crusoe's absence.

Although in the preceding pages I've sketched several frameworks I find
useful when pairing *Gulliver's Travels* and *Robinson Crusoe*, I must confess
that I begin discussion of the *Travels* like everyone else, by asking students
what in the text caught their attention. Over the years, their responses have become predictable: Gulliver's bodily functions, his lack of interiority, his knack
for languages, and so on. For that reason, I usher them as quickly as possible to
a passage in book 2 in order to redirect our discussion to the philosophical differences between the works. The passage in question comes on the heels of
Gulliver's capture by a Brobdingnagian farmer who is unsure of just what he
has found but hopeful he might exploit it for material gain. Soon enough the
discovery is the talk of the neighborhood:

> It now began to be known and talked of in the Neighborhood, that my
> Master had found a strange Animal in the Fields, about the Bigness of a

Splacknuck, but exactly shaped in every Part like a human Creature; which it likewise imitated in all its Actions; seemed to speak in a little language of its own, had already learned several Words of theirs, was tame and gentle, would come when it was called, do whatever it was bid, had the finest Limbs in the World, and a complexion fairer than a Nobleman's Daughter of three Years old.   (80)

The passage goes on about the farmer's plans to display Gulliver for profit on market day, but I stop here to ask students if it summons up anything from *Robinson Crusoe*. After a brief pause, several hands usually go up, at least one of them zeroing in on the colonial encounter of Crusoe and Friday. In the *Travels*, as in *Crusoe*, the other is portrayed through the eyes of the master. But the earlier equation—Friday as nature to Crusoe's reason—is inverted, for it is Gulliver who must prove he is a rational animal. And to do that, he is put on display, first in the marketplace where his performance has the air of a freak show:

I turned about several Times to the Company, paid my humble Respects, said they were welcome; and used some other Speeches I had been taught. I took up a Thimble filled with Liquor, which *Glumdalclitch* had given me for a Cup, and drank their Health. I drew out my Hanger, and flourished with it after the Manner of Fencers in *England*. My Nurse gave me Part of a Straw, which I exercised as a Pike, having learned the Art in my Youth. I was that Day shewn to twelve Sets of Company; and as often forced to go over again with the same Fopperies, till I was half dead with Weariness and Vexation.   (82)

A monster in the original sense of the word, derived from *monstrare* ("to display"), Gulliver is a freak of nature, a one of a kind who violates the laws of reproduction. And while he is the brunt of lowbrow humor in this passage, a much darker message materializes following his command performance for the king, whose assertion that Gulliver represents a race of odious vermin insinuates that the rational animal is nothing more than a delusion.

While Gulliver's desire to prove himself a rational animal is set up in the second voyage, it is not until the third voyage that Swift unveils the metaphorics of Gulliver's quest. This unveiling occurs during the visit to the flying island, the paradise of speculative thought where natural philosophers, seduced by the pursuit of knowledge, neglect their conjugal duties, leaving their wives no choice but to seek fulfillment in the world below. Ever the inquisitive linguist, Gulliver is careful to note the etymology of the place:

The word, which I interpret the *Flying* or *Floating Island*, is in the Original *Laputa*; whereof I could never learn the true Etymology, *Lap* in the old obsolete Language signifieth *High*, and *Untuh* a *Governor*; from which they say by Corruption was derived *Laputa* from *Lapuntuh*. But I do not approve of this Derivation, which seems to be a little strained. I

> ventured to offer to the Learned among them a Conjecture of my own,
> that *Laputa* was *quasi Lap outed*; *Lap* signifying properly the dancing of
> the Sun Beams in the Sea; and *outed* a Wing, which however I shall not
> obtrude, but submit to the judicious Reader.   (136)

The tortured derivation is of course a thin veneer for *la puta*, the whore—so
named because she is Gulliver's femme fatale, seduced as he is by the new science and its ideology of progress. Gulliver's seduction leads him to observe
with uncritical fascination the improbable projects of contemporary scien-
tists—projects that have recently prompted me to solicit students' thoughts on
some of the stranger ventures of the now defunct dot-com frenzy. Satire aside,
Gulliver's enterprise takes a much darker turn in the final voyage, as the de-
luded hero comes to believe in nature as the way to grace.[7]

Laputa may be her most provocative in part 3, but Gulliver's fatal attraction
materializes in part 4, and not in the guise of a seductress but in the form of
the rational animals, the Houyhnhnms. Gulliver's first contact with the Houyhnhnms follows his hazing by the Yahoos, after which two horses—like the
Brobdingnagians before them—probe this apparent freak of nature. This latter
encounter ends a bit differently, with Gulliver spinning out a theory of the
Houyhnhnms' peculiar appearance: "Upon the whole, the Behaviour of these
Animals was so orderly and rational, so acute and judicious, that I at last concluded, they must needs be Magicians, who had thus metamorphosed themselves upon some design" (191). I am sometimes tempted to supplement these
lines with the famous passage from *Don Quixote* in which the knight errant explains his theory of enchantment to the skeptical Sancho: "there is a crew of
enchanters always amongst us who change and alter all our deeds, and transform them according to their pleasure and desire either to favour us or injure
us" (Cervantes 204). In Quixote's world, enchantment is much more than delusion; it bespeaks the demise of scribal culture with the arrival of print culture.
With that loss, moreover, goes the coherence of a world encoded by resemblance rather than difference, a world, that is, in which nature could be read
through a theory of enchantment. Students point out that *Robinson Crusoe*
can still be read, in part, according to the remnants of that code, yet they are
quite firm in their conviction that the novel's narrative of worldly success
trumps the spiritual autobiography. They note, for example, Crusoe's initial belief in the providential origin of agriculture, which is no sooner expressed than
it is immediately undercut by his recollection of having "shook a Bag of Chick-
ens Meat out in that Place," so that "the Wonder began to cease" (58). And
they point to Crusoe's personal success, which is measured in material rather
than spiritual coin, for when he returns to England he finds himself a rich man.
The money may come from his success in Brazil, not the island, but despite the
source it would seem to legitimize Crusoe's economic self-interest and to intimate that the narrative of worldly success (the novel) eclipses the narrative of
spiritual redemption (the spiritual autobiography).

Let me add that I caution students against doubting Defoe's own deep religious convictions. Yet *Crusoe* surely endorses the less than enchanted world of commerce and in that context finds its satiric antidote in Gulliver's final voyage. Gulliver, who never shares Crusoe's desire to create a utopia, seeks instead to recover one, giving the final voyage the trappings of *nostos* (homecoming)—not, however, for a mortal wife but for an imagined world. No longer enthralled by experimental science, he now seeks to recover a classical ideal, the life according to nature. There is much to admire about his pursuit, and students are intrigued to see Gulliver seduced by the simple life freed from ambition, a sharp contrast to Crusoe's constant striving. It is a world that to some students sounds vaguely familiar to the Marxist dictum, To each according to his needs. Yet at the same time it is clearly a stratified society in which birth confirms worth, as the classes are not "born with equal Talents of Mind, or a Capacity to improve them" (216). Nevertheless, all Houyhnhnms are brought up to practice the utilitarian virtues of *"Temperance, Industry, Exercise,* and *Cleanliness"* (235), virtues fitting for Crusoe, who might view the rational animals much the way he does Friday, the natural man with an innate capacity for reason. But we know that Gulliver's infatuation is a delusion because of the misguided nature of his quest. Nature, to Swift, is not the way to grace but the road to perdition, the secular paradise seemingly within Gulliver's grasp the purgatory he re-creates in exile.

Before his expulsion, Gulliver proves more sympathetic to the Houyhnhnms than to the Brobdingnagians in his attempt to prove that he is a rational animal. But in the end he is the thing that is not, undone by physical evidence of a female Yahoo (and not even a redhead, meaning Irish) in heat: "For now I could no longer deny, that I was a real *Yahoo*, in every Limb and Feature, since the Females had a natural Propensity to me as one of their own Species: Neither was the Hair of this Brute of a Red Colour" (225). Biology, it seems, is destiny, and Gulliver, the "gentle Yahoo," accepts the verdict of the Houyhnhnm elite and departs with deep regret.

But his exile is his homecoming, and it has consequences beyond his descent into madness. To Swift, Gulliver's homecoming marks the passing of an era, a view that he sounds with deep resonance in the final chapter in a passage that connects the *Travels* and the ruse of the Trojan horse (256). The passage cited is from the *Aeneid*, book 2: "Nec si miserum Fortuna Sinonem / Finxit, vanum etiam, mendacemque improba finget" (79–80), which Robert Fitzgerald translates as, "Fortune has made a derelict / Of Sinon, but the bitch / Won't make an empty liar of him, too" (36; lines 109–11). Like Sinon, Gulliver is a liar, but the deeper irony of the allusion is that the *Travels* reprises the fall of Troy because the tragic history the horse contains has already escaped the belly of the beast and penetrated the walls of the city in the form of a madman who thinks he is a horse. Moreover, if tragic history is repeated here as farce, there is little joy in the repetition for Swift. After all, his own exile was bound up with that history, so that the figure of Gulliver as the Trojan horse is the envoy of a broader historical fait accompli. That is why the book concludes in 1715: the year of Swift's exile, it was also the year of Gulliver's homecoming, and it coincides with the recent dynastic succession because to Swift that event was the historical culmination of the long, and irreversible, descent that began with the Puritan Revolution.

If Gulliver's legacy is Swift's conviction that the historical clock cannot be turned back—and the consequences of the Puritan Revolution held back—Crusoe sees his legacy as the blueprint for the Glorious Revolution and its aftermath. Defoe conveys as much in the scene that precedes Crusoe's departure, the scene in which Crusoe sets out the terms under which he will leave the island in the hands of the Spaniards, who will manage his estate during his absence. He begins with the property settlement: "I shared the island into parts with 'em, reserved to my self the property of the whole, but gave them such parts respectively as they agreed on." Next comes what amounts to their intellectual legacy, conveyed in the form of Crusoe's narrative: "In a Word, I gave them every Part of my own Story . . ." (199). Crusoe's legacy to the Spaniards is, in effect, the text of *Robinson Crusoe*, which, as the blueprint for the revolution achieved, contains what is necessary to carry it forward.

It almost goes without saying that Crusoe's legacy is the more appealing to students, for whom *Robinson Crusoe* is still very much alive as a cultural myth.[8] Even before we begin our discussion of the book, I ask students where they have previously encountered the Crusoe story, and I always get a wide range of responses, from the occasional student who has read the novel in high school (though it doesn't seem to be a very widely assigned book) and the many who read it long ago in versions for young readers, to those who have encountered it more recently in the movies—in the adaptations with Aidan Quinn (*Crusoe*, 1988), Pierce Brosnan (*Robinson Crusoe*, 1996), and Tom Hanks (*Cast Away*, 2000)—and the rare few who have read J. M. Coetzee's *Foe*. Interested as I am in *Crusoe*'s staying power, I ask students after they've finished the novel to write a brief reaction piece about why they think the story has retained its power as a cultural myth. I must admit that to date no student has written that Crusoe embodies the Anglo-Saxon spirit. Quite a few, however, see in Crusoe a central component of what might be called the Anglo-American spirit, for even while they may not admire Crusoe the recluse and colonialist, they find that his narrative resonates deeply with a cultural myth of their own, self-reliance.

It has been my experience, as I'm sure it has been the experience of others, that *Gulliver's Travels* doesn't resonate with students in the ways that *Robinson Crusoe* invariably does. Nevertheless, there is one part of the *Travels* that never fails to intrigue them—Gulliver's descent into madness—and for that reason I round out our discussion with a short reaction paper in which I ask them to consider how Swift might take Crusoe's self-reliance as a recipe for madness. Their responses range widely—some avoid the question altogether, preferring instead to attack Swift as a bitter victim of politics or as a conservative ideologue—but most address the question head on. Even while students might be less sympathetic to Swift than Defoe, they acknowledge that Swift may have a point when he takes self-reliance to be the dark side of Crusoe's brave new world. Crusoe, they see, not only cuts himself off from the past but in doing so transforms himself into a wanderer who finds the impulse to travel irresistible and discovers in that experience a kind of redemption that, to Swift, was achievable only through grace.

NOTES

[1] I've used Puritan Revolution here to stress Swift's dread of dissent, even though it was the Great Rebellion to contemporary historians and has become the Civil War to most recent historians, who have revised the views of an earlier generation that included, most prominently, Christopher Hill and Michael Walzer.

[2] Contending that Crusoe instead of John Bull was the appropriate emblem of the English character, Joyce noted that the novel "reveals, as perhaps no other book throughout the long history of English literature does, the wary and heroic instinct of the rational animal and the prophecy of the empire" (322).

[3] Ayers suggests several possibilities: *Kreutz* means either "to cross" or "to cruise," and it is related to *Kreutzzug*, meaning "crusade"; *naer* means "near," and its variant, *naher*, means "to journey or approach" (402). The variants situate Crusoe squarely in the tradition of the wandering hero.

[4] For a comprehensive discussion, see McKeon, *Origins* 315–56.

[5] On patterns of filial disobedience, see Novak, *Economics* 32–48.

[6] For a fuller discussion, see my *Plots and Counterplots* 263–71.

[7] For a full account of Swift's counter-Enlightenment attitudes, see Boyle.

[8] On adaptations of the myth, see Green, *The Robinson Crusoe Story*.

Robinson Crusoe's Parodic Intertextuality

Roxanne Kent-Drury and Gordon Sayre

Throughout Unca Eliza Winkfield's 1767 novel, *The Female American*, the pseudonymous author and female protagonist tries to establish the authority of her text as a colonial exploration narrative. Early in volume 1 of the novel, the heroine, a mixed-race Amerindian princess who has been recently stranded on an island, discovers an earlier castaway's journal, which she quotes at length in her account. Just as an eighteenth-century reader would expect of a reputable, accurate travel narrative, the journal describes in detail the geographic, meteo-rologic, botanical, and zoological features of the island the heroine inhabits (70 [1974]). Readers of *Robinson Crusoe* would recognize the especially detailed account of dairy-goat husbandry, which Unca puts to such good use that she is able to nurse from one of the goats during an illness (97). Any expectation that the journal Unca finds is the work of Robinson Crusoe himself, however, is frustrated when the journal's author appears briefly before dying (122). Subse-quently, Unca explicitly claims that her narrative preceded *Robinson Crusoe*: she suggests that her story inspired a later "adventurer" to "form a fictitious story of one of his own sex, the solitary inhabitant of a desolate island" (15). The book's editor adds the authority of a footnote, which points out the prophetic accuracy of Unca's prediction, since Defoe's *Robinson Crusoe* fol-lowed it. At the same time, the editor claims Defoe's work is inferior because it is a work of fiction (16), which, according to the logic of the travel narrative genre, therefore must be less respectable than Unca's "true" (though prepos-terous) story.

The narrator's attempt to establish textual authority in *The Female American* illustrates the multivalent complexity of the travel narrator's claim to the verisimilitude of his or her text. A travel narrative's value and significance were established through intertextual and parodic references that evoked other works of the same genre. Through frequent repetition certain details, events, and devices become tropes (e.g., the many permutations in *Robinson Crusoe* and its variants of the island's cultivation, the domestication of its wild animals, and the racial composition of its human inhabitants). Because *Robinson Cru-soe* accrues some of its meaning through intertextuality and parodic references to exploration texts, students must understand the context of a travel narrative's production before they can appreciate the work's significance. Imparting the complexity of such relations to students today, however, is a significant peda-gogical challenge. Such students may not be equipped to consider the histori-cal and intertextual relations among eighteenth-century travel narratives.

One way to help students understand this complex intertextuality is to en-courage them to read *Robinson Crusoe* parodied and as parody alongside other texts that can be seen as preceding, succeeding, or coexisting with the text. Linda Hutcheon offers a particularly useful definition of *parody* as "textual or discursive" in nature. Hutcheon explains that the term *parody* is derived from the Greek *odos*, which implies song, and *para*, which means both *with* and *against*; consequently, Hutcheon's definition implies that reading parodically requires reading both with and against the grain of the parodied text. A text can be seen as parodic not only if it satirizes or criticizes another text (the more common critical definition of *parody*) and also if the parodied text represents an adaptation or response but not necessarily a satire or critique (*Modelling* 32). This expanded definition of parody invites the reader to identify how works not only critique but also participate in dialogue with one another and create meaning in combination. For instance, *The Female American* asserts its truth by assimilating itself to a best-selling novel that had also falsely claimed veracity.

Encouraging students to understand how works such as *Robinson Crusoe* and *The Female American* interact in historical-generic contexts helps them develop critical skills they can then use to identify and analyze the parodic nature of both past and contemporary artistic production. Consequently, the remainder of this essay analyzes several exploration narratives of the hundreds that inspired Defoe's *Robinson Crusoe* and a number of overt parodies of *Crusoe* that are pedagogically useful in helping students understand *Robinson Crusoe* and its evolving place in literary history.

Reading Robinson Crusoe *against Earlier Exploration Texts*

For many educated people in the eighteenth century, novels were morally suspect; because the stories they told were untrue, reading them was seen as frivolous compared with reading histories and religious tracts, which provided sober edification. But Defoe, a Protestant dissenter, saw his *Robinson Crusoe* and its two sequels as offering important lessons in the powers of divine providence. A similar tension between truth and fiction, between the didactic and the deceptive, operated in the genre of travel narrative, which could be informative and practical. Richard Hakluyt's collection, *The Principal Navigations, Voyages, Traffiques and Discoveries of the English Nation* (1598–1600), promoted the heroic and often profitable successes of English imperialism and made available the writings of explorers and merchants as guides for subsequent voyagers. As the new science developed during the seventeenth century, and especially after the Royal Society was founded, much importance was placed on careful observation of geography and natural history. The *Transactions of the Royal Society* published primers for explorers on how properly to collect such observations. Travel texts were valuable if they were accurate and serious.

Conversely, a common aphorism cautioned that travelers "may lie by authority, because none can control them" (Wood, sig. A3). In an age when large parts of the globe remained unknown to Europeans and new descriptions of the flora, fauna, and cultures of remote lands were as astonishing as old myths and monsters, the true accounts of exploration were hard to discern from the fabricated. Imaginary voyages became very popular, and a few were widely received as fact (see Atkinson; Adams, *Travelers* and *Travel Literature*).

How could the first published account of a certain place be trusted or rejected? Judgments of the truth value of an account had to be based on the text's rhetorical or stylistic features, which bore no necessary relation to place or truth. Hence exploration narratives, like parodies, focused readers' attention on exaggerated rhetorical and stylistic features. Authors' prefaces did not simply state that the texts were written by the authors themselves and that the authors were eyewitnesses of all that the texts related; the prefaces had to emphasize these points ever more strongly, inevitably undermining the very claims their authors wished to support. For example, William Wood in his preface to *New Englands Prospect* (1634) quoted the proverb about travel liars and then challenged the skepticism of the reader: "because anything stranger than ordinary, is too large for the straight hoops of his apprehension, he peremptorily concludes it is a lie" (sig. A3). A comparison of *Robinson Crusoe* to earlier travel texts reveals how Defoe parodied not only the accounts of Alexander Selkirk that served as his primary source but also the truth claims that supported travel texts.

The Selkirk story was a newsworthy sensation in 1712, and the brief reports by Richard Steele and Woodes Rogers provided Defoe with basic elements of his novel, whether he met Selkirk, as is likely, or not. From the attention paid to the list of items Selkirk had when he was stranded to the domestication of goats to his fits of melancholy assuaged by Christian faith—Defoe writes alongside these details in constructing *Robinson Crusoe*. But Selkirk was an ideal travel narrator, one whose veracity was ironclad. Juan Fernandez Island was tiny, was already well known to privateers like William Dampier and Rogers, and had no native population. Since Selkirk was abandoned by Dampier and rescued by Rogers, and since all three men returned to England, Selkirk's story rang true. Yet for his four years and four months there, he was the only witness. Many authors of travel narratives attested to what Michael McKeon has called the "quantitative completeness" of their texts (*Origins* 93) by asserting, as Dampier himself did, that his "mixt relation of Places, and Actions, [is] in the same order of time in which they occurred: for which end I kept a Journal of every days Observations" (qtd. in McKeon, *Origins* 103). Ship captains all kept logs, and exploration texts often mimicked this form, even though they were extensively edited and embellished for publication. The journal that Crusoe began to keep on his birthday parodies this form (52–76), providing a sense of immediacy for the scene of his religious awakening but maintaining the retrospective point of view and past tense of the rest of the narrative.

The original title page proclaims that the "strange surprizing Adventures of Robinson Crusoe" are "written by Himself" and does not give Defoe's name, but the brief preface asserts the voice of an "editor" (3) who, somewhat as Wood did, makes a claim for its factuality based on the paradoxical logic that McKeon calls "Strange, therefore true" (*Origins* 47). By writing that "the Wonders of this Man's Life exceed all that (he thinks) is to be found extant," the editor forestalls the reader's skepticism. Yet the last paragraph of the preface retreats to a cagey half defense of the book's truth and improvement or didactic value (Defoe, *Crusoe* 3). Reading these lines alongside Crusoe's reproof "[o]f talking falsely" in the *Serious Reflections* (103), Defoe seems to parody the challenges and the defenses of both novels and first-person travel narratives. Crusoe attacks "[t]he liberty of telling stories, a common vice in discourse" (*Reflections* 103), but then defends "[t]he selling or writing a parable, or an illusive allegoric history . . . designed and effectually turned for instructive and upright ends . . . . Such are the historical parables in the Holy Scripture, such as 'The Pilgrim's Progress,' and such, in a word, the adventures of your fugitive friend, 'Robinson Crusoe'" (*Reflections* 107). That Crusoe can in his sequel refer to his own narrative in quotation marks, eliding his name with his title, undercuts the rhetorical devices used in the first volume to attest to his real existence. When Charles Gildon in his parody wrote scenes involving Defoe, Crusoe, and Friday, he was only following the lead of Defoe's texts, which parody the methods that travel narratives employed to appropriate the claims of factual eyewitness testimony.

Reading Robinson Crusoe *alongside Its Successors*

In *Émile*, Jean-Jacques Rousseau asserted that *Robinson Crusoe* was the only book required for a proper education (176–77). Perhaps because *Robinson Crusoe* comprehensively treats issues that have greatly concerned readers, it has spawned hundreds of editions, translations, abridgments, Robinsonades, and parodies. In the process, the novel has been read parodically against the grain, with the grain, and ambivalently from Defoe's time to the present day. When students read *Robinson Crusoe* alongside works that parody or critique it, they gain insight into the issues in play at various historical moments and are encouraged to develop the critical skills necessary to analyze and compare texts.

Although addressing the bulk of these works is beyond the scope of this essay, the following are particularly worthy of mention for their potential pedagogical usefulness:

Gildon, Charles. *The Life and Strange Surprising Adventures of Mr. D— De F—, of London, Hosier, in a Dialogue between Him, Robinson Crusoe, and His Man Friday*. 1719.

This pamphlet, written by a contemporary of Defoe, analyzes *Robinson Crusoe* for its inconsistencies and its fragmented view of religion. It culminates in a dialogue that dramatizes an imagined encounter on a dark road (reminiscent of a highway robbery), in which Robinson Crusoe and Friday confront Defoe for his unflattering characterizations. Crusoe and Friday force Defoe literally to eat his words (i.e., the novel). Analyzing this exchange encourages students to develop an awareness of the eighteenth century's construction of other races: Friday in particular takes Defoe to task for characterizing him as perpetually speaking pidgin English.

Longueville, Peter. *The Hermit; or, The Unparalle[le]d Sufferings and Surprising Adventures of Mr. Philip Quarll.* 1727.
Book 3 of this work, a misanthropic version of *Robinson Crusoe*, recounts Philip Quarll's mental state (his dream life, reliance on providence, alternating despair and euphoria, and propensity to write) and his physical activities (he builds a house, initiates agriculture, and domesticates goats and antelope). Quarll also establishes political sovereignty over the island, settling wars among the monkeys, mapping his estate, and creating a will. Four sets of visitors fail to rescue him because they are repelled by the geography of the island, encouraged by their own greed and selfishness to abandon him, and put off at last by Quarll's final reluctance to be rescued. Quarll is so disaffected from people that his monkey, Beaufidell, is his Friday.

Winkfield, Unca Eliza [pseudo.]. *The Female American.* 1767.
This parody claims to be antecedent to *Robinson Crusoe* and provides a useful exploration of mid- to late-eighteenth-century religious and racial politics (see Wheeler, *Complexion* 313). Its mixed-race, bilingual heroine is equally at home with Europeans and indigenous peoples, though she remains true to her Christian beliefs by impersonating an oracle to convert the local population of sun worshippers.

Séguin, Alfred. *The Black Crusoe.* Trans. of *Robinson Noir.* 1877.
In separate shipwrecks, Charlot, a young slave, and George, the cruel son of a kind master, end up on the same island, where Charlot's natural superiority makes him a "black Crusoe" and George a "white Friday." George and Charlot jointly write a journal before they are rescued by Charlot's former shipmate, now ruler of a native population. These natives, supposed cannibals, are critiqued by all the characters; their inferiority makes even Charlot welcome return to Peru. Failed attempts to establish authority through natural history and anthropological details include tortoises presented as crustaceans, penguins that fly, and ethnically ambiguous (Maori-Carib) natives who live in Plains-style tepees.

Michel Tournier. *Friday; or, The Other Island.* Trans. of *Vendredi: ou, Les limbes du Pacifique.* 1967.
This parody of *Robinson Crusoe* imagines Crusoe's transformation from westernized imperialist to islander coexisting peacefully on the island with Friday. From his initial fixation on the sea to his rescue, Crusoe turns erotically toward the island Speranza, descending into and emerging from a womblike cave. During his phase as planter, governor, and lawmaker, he figuratively marries the island, copulating with a meadow and producing mangrove offspring.

When Friday accidentally ignites Crusoe's gunpowder and grain stores, Crusoe surrenders his material pursuits and enters Friday's realm, living in the moment and abandoning time and structure.

Coetzee, J. M. *Foe*. 1987.
This parody critiques the politics surrounding how and by whom narratives are constructed and appropriated. The novel is told from the perspective of Susan Barton, who is cast adrift by mutineers and washes up on Crusoe's island. She spends a dull year watching Crusoe and Friday engage in fruitless activities (they clear land for crops but have no seeds) and learning little about their earlier lives on the island (Crusoe refuses to keep a journal, while Friday is mute after losing his tongue to a slaver). All three are rescued, but Crusoe dies on the return trip, and Barton asks Foe (aka Defoe) to write their story, whereupon he disappears, pursued by creditors. Reunited, Barton and Foe argue inconclusively about how the story should be constructed. They finally teach Friday to write so that he can complete the story, but he resists, and the novel ends without resolution.

Carter, Angela. "Master." 1981.
In this parody, Friday is a young, gentle, female South American Indian who is purchased by Crusoe, a sadistic jaguar hunter. Ironically, Crusoe becomes the cannibal as he masticates her neck during lovemaking. Gradually, she abandons her spiritual pacificism, and, growing to resemble Crusoe, she shoots him.

Bishop, Elizabeth. "Crusoe in England."
This brief poem describes a nostalgic Crusoe looking back at life on the island after rescue and repatriation. The island, the artifacts of his exile, and even Crusoe himself, vivid and memorable on the island, appear insignificant in their new surroundings. His companion, "dear Friday," has died of measles.

Martin, Charles. *Passages from Friday*. 1983.
This poem is supposed to have been written after Crusoe's demise by Friday, whose voice, diction, and style mimic those of Crusoe-Defoe (including appropriate references to providence and the implements of writing). The narrator, Friday, offers his own interpretation of captivity, servitude, and liberation, including Crusoe's brutality, impracticality, and drunkenness. Friday's imperfect assimilation of Crusoe's teaching is revealed when Friday murders the paralyzed Crusoe to liberate the spirit trapped in Crusoe's body. The narrator implies that the paper on which the poetry is written may actually be Crusoe's skin, cured like vellum.

Walcott, Derek. "Crusoe's Island" and "Crusoe's Journal."
These poems explore the affinities between the shipwrecked Crusoe and the poet as creator of texts and world through writing. They also explore how

the postcolonial poet ventriloquizes the voice of the colonist through language and poetic form. In "Crusoe's Island," Crusoe and the poet are connected and thus separated from God and other people. Ironically, this connection and separation align the postcolonial black poet with the white colonist, distancing the poet from "Friday's children," his own countrymen. "Crusoe's Journal" shows the allure of Crusoe's island life while considering the extent to which the postcolonial poet's symbols, images, and figures of speech are borrowed from the colonizing language.

Preston, Michael J. "Rethinking Folklore, Rethinking Literature: Looking at *Robinson Crusoe* and *Gulliver's Travels* as Folktales, a Chapbook-Inspired Inquiry." Preston and Preston 19–73.

This essay contextualizes *Robinson Crusoe* and *Gulliver's Travels* in the popular print tradition and reproduces complete chapbooks of both works in facsimile. The essay also analyzes the engravings accompanying the texts, which at times interpret, augment, or contradict the narratives.

Weber, Watt, and Restraint: *Robinson Crusoe* and the Critical Tradition

Manuel Schonhorn

On 13 September 1959, Arthur Scouten convened an English seminar of one dozen selected students of the British eighteenth century at the University of Pennsylvania. It was a special occasion, he immediately informed us. Not only was this the first graduate seminar, he believed, dedicated solely to the writings of Daniel Defoe taught at an Ivy League institution, it also auspiciously marked the three-hundredth anniversary of Robinson Crusoe's landing on his island of salvation and despair and his ascent to immortality. For many of us— at least for me—it was to be a stimulating seminar, for we too were on our own voyage into history. We were coming from our Yale-dominated study of Alexander Pope and chiasmus and zeugma and from Norman O. Brown's still memorable lecture on Swift's excremental vision, in which Brown praised Swift's scatological poetry for what it was, a Freudian recognition of the obsessional and the prurient that results from an unhealthy, unrealistic, and destructive denial of human sexuality, but in which Brown found himself unable to conclude, as Swift did, that "Celia, Celia, Celia shits!" Instead, we were to spend that semester enmeshed in the recognizably early modern reigns of William III and Anne and George I, with readings in political diplomacy, pirate narratives, and plague tracts, learning about the wars of the duke of Marlborough and the earl of Godolphin and becoming surprisingly comfortable with the raucous journalism of the *Review*, the *Observator*, and the *Rehearsal*. Two subjects caught my interest then and have continued to be a great part of my teaching of *Robinson Crusoe* over the years.

Without a doubt, the adherents of New Criticism in Scouten's seminar contributed to the richer, more complex readings of Defoe's fictions (see Columbus; Koonce; and James). My colleagues were in the vanguard of successive voices who propounded the arguments for Defoe's conscious artistry and deliberate irony. But since one had to edge Defoe and *Robinson Crusoe* into a simplistic history of the evolution of the novel and since Defoe's fictions bore little similarity to the fictions of our tradition—to Dickens, Flaubert, and Conrad, for example—Defoe could only enter the pantheon by becoming a citizen of the modern world. Crusoe then became a fit example of an age of anxiety, a true agent of, a voice for, secular and commercial modernity. Once "a triumph of human achievement and enterprise," as Ian Watt resoundingly asserted, *Robinson Crusoe* had become "the wishful affirmation of a flagrant economic naivety," the "menacing symbol" of the less admirable aspects of the human condition (*Myths* 159, 168).

Robinson Crusoe was not then, and does not now continue to be, a satisfying text for New Critical analysis. What New Criticism overlooked in Defoe's novel was the inheritance of fiction. Seventeenth-century narrative offered a torrent of narrative strategies. Jestbook, song, proverb, ballad, romance, prophecy, epistle, biography—all jostled one another on the page, mingled and associated, not like a melting pot inducing form and coherence, but rather, like a salad bowl. Early fiction embraced all the classical and contemporary forms; each text was a composite of genres or forms, each easily recognizable but mutually exclusive and distinct. Differences in genre were almost always signaled by chapter headings or typography or clearly demarcated by tone or style. Generic hierarchies were observed, but they nestled individually and comfortably between the covers of one text. By the end of the seventeenth century, storytelling strategies that presented either fiction or fact had been augmented by the newspaper and the periodical. I noted for my students both the messy titles in Charles C. Mish's *English Prose Fiction, 1661–1700*, which promoted fiction as fact or fact as fiction, and the contents of if not the titles in Donald A. Stauffer's *The Art of Biography in Eighteenth-Century England*. I cited the nebulous distinctions between factual and fictional narratives in William Harlin McBurney's *Check List of English Prose Fiction, 1700–1739*:

> If title pages are almost universally untrustworthy guides, the actual contents of many publications are such a mixture of invention and fact, that, without contemporary evidence, it is virtually impossible to distinguish between the fictional and the non-fictional.   (viii–ix)

"Modern" Defoe thus appeared closer, in Joseph Levine's words, to those "fifteenth-century writers [who] were usually unwilling and largely unable to make a clear distinction between fact and fiction, either in theory or in practice." Neither did they "seek to differentiate between romance and chronicle or between past and present" (11).

Thus New Critical readings or an understanding of the novel not grounded in wide-ranging genre history did not seem to me to contain or do justice to *Robinson Crusoe*. By Defoe's time novels absorbed the fictional and the non-fictional, travel narratives, utopian literature, annals of exploration, the Puritan tradition of conduct and providence books, captivity narratives, propaganda for trade and empire, prospects for colonization, even voyages to the moon. Thoughtful source studies would then minimize the developing readings of Crusoe's psychological and economic peculiarities. Many of the beauties and "sublimities of nature" that Virginia Woolf would have liked Crusoe to respond to are also distant from the experiences of his fictional forebearers (Excerpt 286). Island life provided few occasions for romantic exhilaration or glory. Still, in some such occasions the pleasantries of living are not lost in isolation. There is no total reversion to primitivism.

To indict Crusoe for what we have taken from his political economy is also somewhat wide of the mark. Plucky seventeenth-century Englishmen of every persuasion, set adrift voluntarily or involuntarily on alien shores, attempted to secure the maximum utility from their environments. For example, much criticism of Defoe's Puritan imagination could have been tempered with readings in Robert Knox's *Ceylon* or Henry Pitman's *Relation*. Knox, who remained unlike his captured mates an adamant bachelor during his incarceration of nineteen years, peddled knitted caps. His entrepreneurial activities and trading ventures, while he was held captive by Ceylon's natives concluded in his lending out his corn crop at the exorbitant interest rate of fifty percent per annum (207, 240 [ed. Ryan]). Although Knox is thrilled with the purchase of a Bible in his native language, its teachings do not interfere with his pursuit of rational self-interest (Watt, *Myths* 173).

Watt in 1951 exposed to us the demons that were masked by our myth of *Robinson Crusoe*. It does not diminish his insights to suggest that the students of the 1960s were to rediscover the story's bifocal themes on their own. Conservatives of the incipient culture skirmishes saw in Defoe's hero their exemplar of the American dream. His success proved the crowning achievement of that dream and reaffirmed its vision of freedom and independence. His westward voyaging paralleled the expansive energy of the United States, his flight from a stilted and stultifying home echoed the social mobility that had brought many of the nation's cultural conservatives to the university. To better oneself, one had to break with tradition. Crusoe had pulled himself up by his bootstraps. For conservative students in the 1960s, the mantras of the moment were self-actualization, self-realization, self-revelation, and an arid self-reliance that endorsed their new worldview, so drastically unlike Emerson's, pronounced more than a century earlier. Crusoe had gotten in touch with his true self. These students endorsed his private enterprises with vigor and vim. Extremism in the pursuit of self and wealth was a virtue.

Whereas these true believers were indifferent to the anarchic excesses and cultural myopia that pervaded the narrative, the anti-institutional, anti-American rants of their radical opposites caught the developing mood of the moment. The bourgeois values of their student contemporaries, even of their parents, and the American values preached incessantly in school, church, and the media disgusted these radicals. Crusoe's egoistic efforts were destructive, his dreams of empire nightmares. These students' insights into the strictures of a hegemonic America attempting to create the world in its own image were deflected onto Crusoe's activist pronouncements and actions. His capitalist drama was a lie, a great and monstrous lie. This true epitome of Western civilization exploited the universe; the suffering of humankind and the environment were the conditions of Crusoe's savage success.

All such students of the 1960s, of the left and the right, like some of my graduate colleagues, had forgotten history. For what seems to me to have been the most insightful answer to the collapse of a fuller understanding of the true myth of *Robinson Crusoe* had been sadly intuited but overlooked in a book that with hardly a mention of Defoe resonated in all the economic, capitalist interpretations of *Robinson Crusoe* in the twentieth century: Max Weber's *The Protestant Epic and the Spirit of Capitalism*. To Weber we stand indebted for the historical concept that attempted to explain the specific religious idea, seventeenth-century Protestant-Puritanism, which influenced the material culture of western Europe and brought about the phenomenon of the spirit of capitalism. His construct cohered a new asceticism, the peculiar rationalism of Western culture, the moral justification of worldly activity, and the concept of a calling, which sanctioned systematic human efforts and became for some the equivalent of faith and salvation. Only momentarily, at the somber conclusion of his study, did Weber stray from his purely historical discussion to the world of judgments of value and of faith:

> Since asceticism undertook to remodel the world and to work out its ideals in the world, material goods have gained an increasing and finally an inexorable power over the lives of men as at no previous period in history. . . . But victorious capitalism, since it rests on mechanical foundations, needs its support no longer. . . . [T]he idea of duty in one's calling prowls about our lives like the ghost of dead religious beliefs. In the field of [the calling's] highest development, in the United States, the pursuit of wealth, stripped of its religious and ethical meaning, tends to become associated with purely mundane passions, which often actually give it the character of sport.   (181–82)

Weber's most significant insight is only a passing thought, which he chose not to pursue in his historical study: "Capitalism *may* even be identical with the restraint, or at least a rational tempering, of this irrational impulse . . . unlimited greed for gain" (17). His aside becomes an insistent refrain coursing through Daniel Bell's early essays on the cultural contradictions of capitalism. For Bell, these contradictions, or disjunctions or discordances, result from the tensions between a traditionalist capitalist economy and capitalism's modern culture. Modernity has given us "a social structure which is bureaucratic and hierarchical . . . that is organized fundamentally in terms of roles and specialization, and a culture which is concerned with the enhancement and fulfillment of the self and the 'whole' person" (14). Restraint, only a passing comment in Weber, in Bell explains the many differences—political, social, and psychological—between Defoe's time and ours. Bell makes no mention of Defoe or *Robinson Crusoe*, yet he and Watt join company in their dissections of modernity and use the same language. Both twentieth-century scholars mire us in a dystopia. Bell's is a capitalism where the center cannot hold because there is no center, where capitalism's status personalities could no longer sustain a social and civil community; Watt's is the cash nexus and the instrumental utilitarianism of the Protestant ethic. Bell's insistence on and repetition of aggressiveness, incoherence, disorientation, fragmentation, and the like and his relentless accumulation of discordant and deviant examples ratify the last, sad, and prescient pages of Weber's work.

What Bell and Weber make clear is that the acquisitiveness, the boundlessness, the radical and disruptive individualism, the commodification of humanity and the world, the demystified dystopic myth of Watt's Protestant ethic are moderated in Crusoe's utopia because of the constraint that Crusoe's Protestant Christianity imposed on the incipient corrupting forces of modernity. Defoe himself recognized the importance of restraint. As he wrote in *The True-Born Englishman* (1700), "Restraint from Ill is Freedom to the Wise" (662). Much later, in Crusoe's voice, the restraint internalized by his dissenting heritage follows, significantly, his readings in both the Old and New Testaments and his scriptural recovery of God. He discovers his island's Eden, "that delicious Vale . . . a planted Garden" (80). Though tempted by its pleasure and abundance, he rejects the paradisaical splendor of his bower and stabilizes himself in his old abode. It is the first and most important sequence in which Crusoe's "Religion joyn'd in with this Prudential" (135), limiting his acquisitive endeavors. Bell later was to examine "the sober, prudential, delayed gratification of the Protestant ethic" (295).

Defoe and his dissenting sect were aware of the dangers in the pursuit and temptation of wealth. An unregulated acquisitive spirit was suspect. Thus we trivialize Defoe's story by overlooking the inherently religious foundation of *Robinson Crusoe*. Defoe's narrative is subordinated to the larger perspective of a whole life, and this perspective in turn is integrated into an evangelical frame that gives meaning and order to that experience. Crusoe's religion has allowed him to internalize the limits of permissable accumulation, as we see in his rejection of his island's Eden, where Crusoe could live without working. His later casuistic dialogues with the self, which restrain his impulses to eradicate the savages, seem to me to be of the same order. It is his religious impulse, attenuated though it may be, that morally legitimates his transformative capitalist endeavors; that impulse also holds in check those self-indulgent concerns of the individual that can hardly be imagined by his twentieth-century readers. His moorings are religious, providing transcendental justification for his work and wealth and preventing him from going off the deep end.

What thus limits a full reading of Defoe's text is modernity's modal separation between the sacred and the secular. It is the continued "erosion of the religious ethic" (Bell xxv) that Weber foresaw a century earlier. Undeniably, Defoe has given us our archetype, asserting a work ethic with values of individualism, self-discipline, and acquisitiveness that in the novel is anchored in sanctified labor countenancing restraint, a restraint that contains the ultimate check on the emerging undisciplined forces of modernity. Coupling religion and prudence, Crusoe appears balanced between a disappearing world that imposed restrictions on economic activity and the present one, in which economic accumulation allows free rein in the pursuit of economic ends. His religious anchor prevents him from drifting beyond safe economic and psychological shores and into our modern world.

In Joseph Conrad's *Heart of Darkness*, as Marlow steams upriver to Kurtz's station, he reflects on the cannibals on board, outnumbering his tiny white crew and stoically existing on their limited rations of rotten hippo meat. Why their passivity? Why their acceptance of seeming starvation in the midst of white human plenty? "Restraint," he exclaims (43). Again we have the word "restraint." Like many of Conrad's heroic protagonists, and like all the epic heroes of myths old and new, Robinson Crusoe is one of us and yet also not one of us, and in that paradox lies the enduring greatness of Defoe's creation.

Myths of Modern Individualism: Defoe, Franklin, and Whitman

Geoffrey Sill

Readers of the biographies of famous persons, such as the anatomist Alexander Monro Secundus, a professor of medicine at the University of Edinburgh, can probably recall anecdotes that describe the moment in which the subject of the biography, as a youth, receives a copy of *Robinson Crusoe* from a parent who hopes by this "strategem" to interest the child in stories of history and travel, leading eventually to "more useful studies." Similarly, collectors of old editions of *Robinson Crusoe* are used to seeing inscriptions such as "To Jesse W. Fallon. Compliments of Your Mother & Father. Christmas 1831" on the flyleaves of their books.[1] If *Robinson Crusoe* has come to be known as a boy's book or a children's classic, the reason is not that the novel panders to childhood amusements but that it has been for many years regarded by adults as a way to inspire young people to begin building their own lives. Written in the first person, without most of the artistic trappings of more conventional novels' extensive scene setting, dialogue, and layers of irony and ambiguity, the narrative of Robinson's adventures seems to have been designed as a blueprint for the construction of an individualized, adult self. In this essay, I argue that *Robinson Crusoe* has remained a central work in our literature because it has a mythic power to transform young lives. If we have stopped putting the book into the hands of our children, perhaps it is because Defoe's original Robinson-ade has been superseded by more-modern autobiographies of the self-made individual or more-sophisticated songs of the self, such as Benjamin Franklin's *Autobiography* or Walt Whitman's "Song of Myself." But, although they may be more modern or sophisticated, Franklin's and Whitman's songs of the self are in essence imitations of their famous ancestor, and the three works must be taken together for a full understanding of the myth of modern individualism in the mainstream of Anglo-American literature.

Ian Watt describes the foundations of this myth in his book *Myths of Modern Individualism*. He argues that Robinson Crusoe was the first individualist hero to rebel against the powerful religious and secular structures of the Counter-Reformation without suffering punishment. In Watt's view, "individualism" was defined before the eighteenth century by such figures as Faust, Don Quixote, and Don Juan, all of whom have "exorbitant egos" (120). They are all travelers who leave home on some irrational or monomaniacal quest; they are solitary, having only a single male servant for a companion; they experience hardship and difficulty in the single-minded pursuit of personal fame or glory; and they suffer deaths that underscore the futility of their rebellions. Robinson Crusoe is like these men in all respects except the last: he returns home from his travels a rich and honored citizen who, in the third volume of his trilogy, shares with us his visions of the angelic world. Despite the mockery of some of Defoe's contemporaries, Robinson's story was exceptionally well received by the reading public, suggesting that by 1719 the power of the anti-individualist ideology of the Counter-Reformation was finally broken. As Watt further shows, the stories of Faust, Don Quixote, and Don Juan were all rewritten during the course of a "Romantic apotheosis" at the end of the eighteenth and the beginning of the nineteenth century, in which versions of their deaths were softened, their excesses redeemed, and their endings made to accord with the more optimistic conclusion of *Robinson Crusoe* and the ideology of "capitalist individualism" (*Myths* 236).

The term *individualism*, first used during the French Revolution in a derogatory sense to describe extreme forms of political and religious protestantism, was used by Alexis de Tocqueville in the second volume of *Democracy in America* (1840) to designate "a mature and calm feeling" that disposes a person "to sever himself from the mass of his fellows and to draw apart with his family and friends" (2: 98). Although Tocqueville allowed that individualism differed from *égoïsme* (selfishness), he was still ambivalent about the effects of such a separation. Men who withdraw from society "are apt to imagine that their whole destiny is in their own hands," he said. This illusion of independence makes a man forget his ancestors and his obligations to his contemporaries; "it throws him back forever upon himself alone, and threatens in the end to confine him entirely within the solitude of his own heart" (2: 99).

Some authors have supposed that Tocqueville's ambivalence about individualism may be due to his aristocratic origins, but his description of the isolated individual seems to echo the condition of Robinson Crusoe on the island. Robinson's isolation came about as the indirect result of his rejection of his father's advice:

> My Father, who was very ancient, had given me a competent share of learning . . . and design'd me for the Law; but I would be satisfied with

nothing but going to Sea, and my Inclination to this led me so strongly
against the Will, nay the Commands of my Father . . . that there seem'd
to be something fatal in the Propension of Nature tending directly to the
Life of Misery that was to befal me.   (4)

Robinson's "inclination" is never satisfactorily explained, although he describes
it several times as a "sin," for which his confinement on the island is a punishment; yet at other times he reflects that "it was possible I might be more happy
in this Solitary Condition, than I should have been in a Liberty of Society, and
in all the Pleasures of the World" (82) and gives thanks to God. What appears
sinful in social terms seems instead to be a blessing to Robinson when he considers his true interests. Tocqueville's reservations about individualism, written
in the wake of both the American and the French Revolutions, reflect this
same ambivalence over the guilty pleasure that the individualist takes in solitude and freedom from social obligations.

Of the many incidents in *Robinson Crusoe* that betray this ambivalence, I
examine just one: Robinson's relation with the boy Xury. Early in the narrative,
Xury helps Robinson escape in a boat from the pirate at Sallee who has made
Robinson his slave. After throwing overboard a Moor whom he does not trust,
Robinson extracts an oath of loyalty from Xury by promising that "if you will be
faithful to me I'll make you a great Man." In response, the boy "innocently . . .
swore to be faithful to [Robinson], and to go all over the world" with him (19).
In a voyage of several hundred miles along the coast of Africa, Robinson and
Xury become close friends, sharing their fears of the animals and human beings who inhabit the land and their "great Joy" at the discovery of fresh water
or meat (21). When, however, they are picked up by a Portuguese ship, the
bond of trust and friendship between them is dissolved. Robinson remarks on
his joy "that I was thus deliver'd," not that "we" were delivered; he insists that
it was "my Deliverance" and exults that the captain of the ship promises that
"all I had should be deliver'd safe to me when I came to the Brazils" (25, 26).
The captain offers Robinson "80 Pieces of Eight" for his boat and another sixty
"for my boy Xury." Robinson is "loath to sell the poor Boy's Liberty, who had
assisted me so faithfully in procuring my own," but he does so on the promise
that the captain would free Xury in ten years "if he turn'd Christian" (26).
Through the sale of both the boat and the boy, Robinson obtains the captain's
good will and ensures his individual prosperity while negating his promise to
make Xury a "great Man" and obliging Xury to give up his religion, if he survives ten years of servitude. As is often the case with Defoe, it is difficult to say
whether the narrator is aware of the irony of the situation, although Robinson
clearly feels a need to extenuate his guilt by emphasizing Xury's willingness to
go with the Portuguese captain. Whether ironic or not, the incident conveys
the ambivalence of the individualist hero, who often must deny or disguise his
awareness of how cruelly he has severed himself from his fellows.

Robinson's subsequent adventures complete, for better or worse, the formation of his individualist self and the ideology that sustains it. His sole survivorship

of the shipwreck arouses the ambivalent feelings I remark on above: on the one hand, he feels dreadful guilt and sorrow, reflected in his discovery that all that remains of his companions is "three of their Hats, one Cap, and two Shoes that were not Fellows"; on the other, he feels the "Extasies and Transports" of a felon who has escaped execution (35). His guilt expresses itself in a punishment dream, while his deliverance onto the island brings him "a secret Kind of Pleasure (tho' mixt with my other afflicting Thoughts) to think that this was all my own, that I was King and Lord of all this Country indefeasibly" (73). He reinscribes the events of his life, including his being "deliver'd and taken up at Sea by the *Portugal* Captain" and his singular escape from the wreck, in a religious framework that enables him to interpret them as acts of providence, or the "Hand of God" (65, 66). At the same time, he "cures" the passions that have "hurried" him on through life, reflecting on them and discarding those that (like his fear of the Devil, aroused by the dying goat in the cave) prove to be baseless. Robinson's rescue of and subsequent friendship with Friday, although it appears patronizing and even racist to modern eyes, complements and in part redeems his previous sacrifice of Xury. His story is mythic because it constructs an ideology, or a theoretical framework, according to which an individual's pursuit of his or her own interests is, on the whole, not a bad thing.

Because neither the term nor the concept was in use in 1719, it is doubtful that Defoe self-consciously promoted individualism, capitalist or otherwise, in *Robinson Crusoe*. Later readers, however, influenced perhaps by the Romantic movement, political or economic events, or their own experience, have found in the novel a justification for such feelings in themselves. One such reader was Benjamin Franklin, who lived in London for eighteen months in 1724–26, at a time when, as Charles Gildon complained, there was "not an old Woman that can go to the Price of it, but buys thy Life and Adventures" (Gildon, Excerpt 260). It is doubtful that Franklin ever met Defoe, but he certainly knew Defoe's works: in his *Autobiography*, begun in 1771, Franklin acknowledges that "De foe in his Crusoe, his Moll Flanders, Religious Courtship, Family Instructor & other Pieces" furnished him with his prose style, and he praises Defoe's *An Essay upon Projects* for giving him "a Turn of Thinking" that influenced the course of his life (*Autobiography* 1326, 1317). Like young Crusoe (and like Defoe), Franklin admits that he exhibited "an early projecting public Spirit, tho' not then justly conducted" (1314), which eventually led him to write and print some "little pieces" that gave him the reputation of "a young Genius that had a Turn for Libelling and Satyr" (1323–24). As a printer in Philadelphia both before and after his sojourn in London, Franklin worked for Samuel Keimer, who had printed perhaps a dozen pamphlets for Defoe and "seems to have introduced Defoe to the Quaker persona" (Backscheider, *Daniel Defoe* 377), which Franklin would also come to adopt.

In his *Autobiography*, written for the benefit of his son William, Franklin reenvisions his origins in terms that closely mimic those used by young Robinson. He begins by mythologizing the name Franklin, tracing it back to its generic origin as "the Name of an Order of People" (1308), and recounts with pride the nonconformity of his forebearers, who hid a Bible in a closestool to study the Scripture in secret. He recounts the migration of his father to America in 1682 to enjoy religious liberty, much as Robinson suggests that his father, "a Foreigner of *Bremen*," left that German province for either religious or economic freedom in England (4). Franklin eulogizes his mother, Abiah Folger, as "a Daughter of Peter Folger, one of the first Settlers of New England" (1312), just as Robinson identifies himself as the son of an English mother "whose relations were named Robinson, a very good Family in that Country" (4). Young Franklin's family apprentices him to the trade of candle making, but he, again like Crusoe, has his own ideas about his future: "I dislik'd the Trade and had a strong Inclination for the Sea; but my Father declar'd against it" (1314). Through working on his brother's newspaper, Franklin acquires the skills of a printer and soon determines to leave Boston for New York. In this plan he is opposed by both his father and brother, but he secretively boards a ship and soon "found my self in New York near 300 Miles from home, a Boy of but 17, without the least Recommendations to or Knowledge of any Person in the Place, and with very little Money in my Pocket" (1326).

Like young Robinson in London, Franklin relishes the guilty pleasure of his independence while pretending to recall his pleasure with disapproval. Franklin finds no work in New York and thus sets out again, this time for Philadelphia. Just as Robinson experiences a dreadful storm, so Franklin's boat meets with "a Squall that tore our rotten sail to pieces" (1326), and Franklin rescues a man from drowning. Through a series of adventures that include a fever and an encounter with a rather satanic "Dr. Brown," Franklin eventually washes up on an unknown shore of the Delaware: "the others knew not where we were, so we put towards the Shore, got into a Creek, landed near an old Fence with the Rails of which we made a Fire, the Night being cold, in October, and there we remain'd until Daylight" (1328). If this language is not a conscious imitation of Robinson's arrival on his island, it at least takes advantage of the same mythologizing effects to present Franklin as a castaway who has, as Tocqueville would later put it, "sever[ed] himself from the mass of his fellows" (2: 98). At length, by dint of ingenuity and hard work that mimic Robinson's labors on the island, Franklin makes a success of himself in Philadelphia and impresses the governor of the province, who smooths the way for Franklin's return to his father's house in Boston. Franklin's return is even more triumphant than Crusoe's, whose family is all dead by the time he comes back; Franklin's "unexpected Appearance surpriz'd the Family; all were however very glad to see me and made me Welcome, except my Brother" (1333). The brother is offended at Franklin's display of his wealth, but Franklin's father—like Crusoe's God—forgives his rebellion and blesses his success.

Franklin does not suffer (as Crusoe claims he does) a "Life of Misery" for his rebellion, but he does recriminate himself for his headstrong youth. In particular, he renounces as an "Erratum" (1346) the philosophical essay, "A Dissertation on Liberty and Necessity, Pleasure and Pain," which he wrote in London in 1725 under the influence of the libertine James Ralph, to whom it was inscribed (Battestin 152). The "Dissertation" advanced the notions that self-interest and the pursuit of pleasure are natural virtues and that we must pursue our desires without restraint. Franklin replaced, or at least softened, this individualist doctrine in the years following his return to Philadelphia with a moral system based on a list of thirteen virtues that he defined for himself, based on his reading of "various Enumerations" of the principles of virtue (1384). What texts these were he does not say, but we know that during this period Franklin published the first American editions of Defoe's *Compleat English Tradesman* (1732) and *Family Instructor* (1740). Franklin's moral system, like the one Crusoe invents for himself on the island, is a practical guide to conduct that emphasizes utilitarian values and that recognizes the connection between public and private virtues.

If it is fairly evident that Franklin's *Autobiography* is a literary descendant of *Robinson Crusoe*, it is less easy to show that there is common ground between Defoe and Walt Whitman. Defoe was a tradesman, an economist, a historian, and a journalist whose art was generally subsumed under some political, religious, or moral agenda; Whitman was a bohemian, a dropout, an aesthete, and a prophet of the world of things unknown to the bourgeois imagination. But below the surface, there are similarities: both believed in the progress, if not the perfectability, of humankind through science and technology; both believed in a constitutional form of government with an elected body of representatives of the people at its center; both believed in freedom of expression, particularly in the right of a minority to dissent and divide from the majority without punishment; both professed admiration for such Nonconformist sects as the Quakers, though neither joined them; and both looked on and wrote of America as a new Eden, a second chance for humankind to put democratic, improving principles into practice. The missing link that connects Defoe with Whitman and reconciles their differences is Franklin.

Whitman admired Franklin for the very qualities that Franklin shared with Defoe. Like Franklin, Whitman learned the craft of printing by the age of twelve and soon moved on to journalism, acquiring the tools for shaping public opinion through print that Defoe had forged in the pages of his *Review*. Whitman certainly had Franklin in mind when he described the United States Constitution as "the grandest piece of moral building ever constructed; I believe its architects were some mighty prophets and gods" (1318). He listed Franklin among the "many flashing lists of names" that illuminated the period from 1750 to 1830 in Whitman's biography of Elias Hicks, the Quaker reformer whom Whitman heard preach when he was a child (1223). Whitman praised Hicks as one who, like Franklin and Defoe, followed "the inward Deity-planted law of the emotional soul" rather than the dictates of an established church ("Constitution" 1235). Whitman considered his *Leaves of Grass* to be, variously, a "New Bible" or a "Bible of the New Religion"—a nonsectarian "translation" of the Quaker beliefs he had absorbed from Hicks and George Fox (Harris 172) and of the deistical convictions he took from Franklin, Tom Paine, and Thomas Jefferson and made into a new ethos for the individual self (Reynolds 36).

In some ways, "Song of Myself" improves on the self-fashioning voyage of Robinson Crusoe. Whereas *Robinson Crusoe* espouses a liberal yet still colonialist attitude toward the peoples of Africa and the New World, "Song of Myself" requires equality and freedom in the self regardless of nationality or race ("Of every hue and trade and rank, of every caste and religion, / Not merely of the New World but of Africa Europe or Asia" [43]). Whereas *Robinson Crusoe* privileges male autonomy, the voice of "Song of Myself" declares itself to be "the poet of the woman the same as the man" (46). Whereas *Robinson Crusoe* dodges questions about sexuality and death, "Song of Myself" embraces these aspects of the self and insists on including them in the new person fashioned by the poem ("Copulation is no more rank to me than death is" [51]). Whitman's prose works also emphasize the primacy of the individual: the 1855 preface envisions the poet as "an individual . . . complete in himself . . . not one of the chorus" (10), while "Democratic Vistas" develops the idea of "perfect individualism," which "deepest tinges and gives character to the idea of the aggregate" (942). But in this very perfection, perhaps, Whitman overshoots the mark. There is in "Song of Myself" little of the ambivalence, the irony, or the self-doubt that tempers *Robinson Crusoe* and Franklin's *Autobiography*. The poet's soul, says Whitman in the preface, "has that measureless pride which consists in never acknowledging any lessons but its own" (13). "And I call to mankind," says the voice of the poem, "Be not curious about God, / For I who am curious about each am not curious about God, / . . . I hear and behold God in every object, yet I understand God not in the least, / Nor do I understand who there can be more wonderful than myself" (85). Finally, in "Democratic Vistas," Whitman defines "individuality" as "the pride and centripetal isolation of a human being in himself" (958). One could hardly ask for a better evocation of the tendencies implicit in *Robinson Crusoe*, from which (for better or worse) all the constraints of humility and ambivalence have been removed.

In the fall of 1998, I taught a course, Myths of Modern Individualism, based on Watt's book of the same title, in the graduate program at Rutgers University. Instead of beginning with the precursors of individualism as Watt did, I began with *Crusoe* and proceeded to the two texts discussed above—Franklin's *Autobiography* and Whitman's *Leaves of Grass*. Although dissimilar in their formal characteristics, these works share roots in the tradition of Protestant dissent, that seventeenth-century response to the doctrines of both the Roman Catholic and the established Protestant churches—thus the subtitle of the course, Three Protestant Dissenters: Defoe, Franklin, and Whitman.[2] In addition to the three primary texts and Watt's study, the students read several short works by Defoe in a collection edited by P. N. Furbank and W. R. Owens, *The True-Born Englishman and Other Writings*; selections from the Library of

America edition of Franklin's *Writings*; and selections of poetry and prose in the Library of America edition of Whitman's *Complete Poetry and Collected Prose*. The purpose of the course was to show that *Robinson Crusoe* is the source not only of the many Robinsonades having to do with epic journeys or castaway sailors in Anglophone literature but also of a tradition of dissent and individualism that helped shape the Constitution and the mainstream of American literature.

NOTES

[1]The anecdote about Alexander Monro secundus is in Benjamin Rush's "Journal, commencing Aug. 31, 1766," in the collection of the Indiana University Library. The anecdote is quoted in Rex E. Wright-St. Clair, *Doctors Monro: A Medical Saga* (69). The copy inscribed to Jesse Fallon is from this writer's personal collection.

[2]In developing this course, I benefited from the experience of having organized a symposium on this theme at a meeting of the Northeast Modern Language Association in spring 1998. The papers from this seminar, written by Glenn N. Cummings, Michael J. Drexler, Carla Mulford, Joseph Murphy, and David S. Reynolds, were published as an issue of *Modern Language Studies*.

Crusoe among the Travelers

Paula R. Backscheider

> It happen'd one Day about Noon going towards my Boat,
> I was exceedingly surpriz'd with the Print of a Man's
> naked Foot on the Shore, which was very plain to be seen
> in the Sand: I stood like one Thunderstruck, or as if I had
> seen an Apparition; I listen'd, I look'd round me, I could
> hear nothing, nor see any Thing; I went up to a rising
> Ground to look farther; I went up the Shore and down the
> Shore, but it was all one, I could see no other Impression
> but that one, I went to it again to see if there were any
> more, and to observe if it might not be my Fancy; but
> there was no Room for that, for there was exactly the very
> Print of a Foot, Toes, Heel, and every Part of a Foot. . . .
> . . . Sometimes I fancy'd it must be the Devil. . . .
> . . . . And I presently concluded then, that it must be
> some more dangerous Creature. (*viz.*) That it must be
> some of the Savages of the main Land. . . .
> —*Robinson Crusoe* 112–13

I always begin teaching *Robinson Crusoe* here, at this beautifully spun-out incident. This passage opens into every major theme in the book and is typical of Daniel Defoe's leisurely, superbly imaginative writing. Crusoe, "terrify'd to the last Degree," returns to his obsessively fortified "castle" "like one pursued" (112). Lying awake, mind racing, Crusoe is revealed to be more afraid of humankind than of the devil. He imagines being devoured or, perhaps worse, men destroying his corn, taking his goats, and leaving him to "perish at last for meer Want" (113). The five pages in the Norton edition that this incident occupies (112–17) trace Crusoe's efforts to cling to a wavering faith: "all that former Confidence in God . . . now vanished" (113); "as I was his Creature, [he] had an undoubted Right by Creation to govern and dispose of me"; "the Scripture came into my Thoughts, *Call upon me in the Day of Trouble, and I will deliver*" (114).

Defoe is an important writer partly because his fictions capture a fascinating, critical moment—the point in history during which humankind was balanced between the older religious, almost fideistic perspective and the modern, secular, even scientific viewpoint. Therefore "one Day" Crusoe thinks "that all this might be a meer Chimera of my own; and that this Foot might be the Print of my own Foot." He goes to see and, of course, finds not only that the footprint is still improbably clear in the sand but also that his own foot is "not so large by a great deal" (115). This creature, then, is a much larger being than he. "O what ridiculous Resolution Men take, when possess'd with Fear! It deprives them of the Use of those Means which Reason offers for their Relief" Crusoe reflects (115–16).

This incident allows discussion to spiral through the novel's religious, economic, and political themes and to explore the psychological being that Defoe makes Crusoe. It enables students to see how Defoe made Crusoe think and, therefore, how many people living in the early eighteenth century thought. They see a character applying probabalistic reasoning (Alkon) at the very moment he is trying to summon an unquestioning, secure faith. Comforting calculations ("it was probable they went away again as soon as ever they could" [116]) compete with puzzling, unsettling ones ("'twas Ten Thousand to one whether I should ever see it or not, and in the Sand too" [113]). Crusoe responds to the experience by increasing his fortifications and protecting his possessions more carefully. Two years later and then five years later he measures his improved security. "No Man living could come down to me without mischieving himself," he reflects (117). Crusoe's fear and distrust of other men create another pattern of wavering faith and confidence. At one moment he is desperately afraid, and at another he feels he is one of the political titles he assumes, "King," "absolute Lord and Lawgiver" (174), "Prince" (186), "Generalissimo" (192), "Governor" (193). These titles are indexes of the time's changing perceptions of the role of government and the broader possibilities for leadership. Crusoe's conceptions are, first, revealed to be fantasies dependent on those willing to play the role of the governed. Obviously not part of the traditional, honor-bound society that relies on collective relationships, he insists on written contracts from those who join him. Second, these titles reveal Defoe's skepticism about positions of authority. As I wrote in *A Being More Intense*, that Crusoe is finally a colonial governor and treats his colony with the neglect and haughty attitudes of most real colonial governors is one of Defoe's little noticed but deeply ironic comments (170).

The footprint passage is a good introduction to Defoe's style and character creation. Incidentally, it is also a good schooling in how to read eighteenth-century novels, where emphasis should be on recognizing subtleties and the maneuverings of authors and characters rather than on concentrating on the plot and its resolution, which leads to the modern practice of "consuming" books. The detail for which Defoe and the realist novel are famous and sometimes ridiculed is present in the footprint passage. Students can see that it goes beyond the material world to detailed descriptions of physical movement and thoughts. This incident, which shows how speculative and obsessive Crusoe is, how busy his brain, is a more intense example of most of the portrayals of Crusoe. In this time of active study of the human mind, Defoe was a leader. He posits firm and varied ways that the brain affects external behavior, and he draws connections between thoughts and health. Yet the mind of the century before Defoe wrote is always present, as represented by Crusoe's continual return to the possibilities of the supernatural whether in dreams, fears of the devil, or interpretations based on typology and Providence. *Robinson Crusoe*, after all, is the first of several fiction and nonfiction books in which Defoe attempted to separate superstition from religion for himself and his contemporaries.[1]

This approach offers a dramatic entrée into *Robinson Crusoe* and engages the students immediately and dynamically, and I follow the study of this novel with two short travel narratives: part 4, chapters 1–11, of Robert Knox's *An Historical Relation of Ceylon* (1681)[2] and Penelope Aubin's *The Strange Adventures of the Count de Vinevil and His Family* (1721). In *Ceylon*, Knox, then seventeen years old, goes ashore with a party when his father's ship docks in a Ceylonese bay to make repairs. Sixteen men are left captive, and the king divides them throughout the kingdom. Knox and his father are together, but his father soon dies of a fever. Knox survives by careful negotiation, skillful avoidance of close association with politicians, and the very English ability to develop trade, for example, in caps and corn. He eventually escapes in a suspenseful journey of about one hundred miles.

In *Count de Vinevil*, the count de Vinevil, "finding his estate impoverished by continued taxations, and himself neglected by his sovereign and no way advanced," decides to move from France to Constantinople to trade (115). His only child, Ardelisa, and the count of Longueville, for whom he was guardian, accompany him. A Turk falls in love with Ardelisa, which puts the family in mortal danger. Ardelisa hastily marries Longueville, and the family tries to escape, but a storm drives Longueville's ship away and the Turk slaughters her father. Ardelisa begins a life of hiding and disguise. Among her adventures are hiding with a mendicant missionary, nearly starving on an island, and conspiring to burn down a harem in which she has been imprisoned.

Both works are short enough to be prepared for a single class (at least in a course that is probably gulping down *Tom Jones* and *Tristram Shandy*), and I assign them without introduction or comment. At the beginning of the next class, I explain that, after sermons and religious literature, travel books were the best sellers and that the English excelled all other nations in numbers and varieties of travel narratives. For instance, 274 collections of travels were published between 1550 and 1625, and Defoe, Knox, and Aubin were part of a second great wave beginning around 1680.

What was (and is) the appeal of these books? What did you notice? What is worth discussing? I ask, and we generate a list of responses from which we will work. The answers to the first question and, to some extent, the third develop an understanding of the "work" that fiction does at various times and in different cultures. I try to gauge the degree of interest in various topics and begin where the engagement is greatest. Surprisingly, that is often in the contrasts in the representation of the relationship between God and humankind. Religion is not always an easy topic to discuss in classes today, whether the students are largely secular, extremely diverse in their religious backgrounds, or inclined toward fundamentalism. These three texts break down these barriers by demanding that students analyze contrasts and recognize them as representations of God and of a religious person that they may or may not agree with. Knox's secure faith, his easy repetition of "by the blessing of God" and "by the Providence of God" (117, 127), and Aubin's good characters who are invariably rescued by God's providence and reflect confidently on "the goodness of God" highlight Crusoe's fraught, contentious relationship with God.

Faith is rewarded in *Ceylon* and *Count de Vinevil*, but it is the Job-like interrogation of God, the obsessive desire to understand God's relationship to his creatures, that characterizes *Robinson Crusoe*. Whether or not Crusoe is delivered from the island as a reward for his faith will never be more than one interpretation among many. In the modern world, a god who violates the laws of physics, astronomy, psychology, and other sciences is frightening, and there are no miracles in these texts. Defoe debunks miracles, as he does with the barley (58), but he is aware of the typological possibilities and never entirely dismisses God's care. The arrival of each group of men on the island can be explained without appeal to the supernatural, but Friday and the moral and ethical character of the sea captain keep open the possibility of a benign God watching over his creatures. For Aubin, a younger person and writing from a Catholic perspective, "Providence" is not a particularly interesting term, and she often appears to use it as a synonym for luck, fate, or "it just happened." For example, Aubin writes, "[I]t was a great Providence for her and the family, she was not there" (125). Knox takes for granted a mainstream Protestant view of providence as God's daily care and oversight, which is exactly what Crusoe questions. Latent in *Robinson Crusoe* are Defoe's suspicions that God's plans may wipe out the hopes and aspirations of individuals, like the "unseen mines" of Moll Flanders (250) and Colonel Jack (264) and, perhaps, of Defoe himself, who wanted to be a success in trade but was repeatedly diverted by "callings" to take a stand in political-religious crises.[3]

Sometimes the economic aspects of the texts evoke the most exploratory discussions. Students who may have missed just how representative an Englishman Crusoe is often are struck by his values and practices in the light of Knox's. Knox and Crusoe try to build modest English country houses, not the great retreats of mid-century but the comfortable spaces amid nature's bounty of the early century. Both characters try to protect themselves from want with corn, other grains, and goats. The distinctive trading-nation, commercial, industrious spirit is obvious in both, and the trade in caps and other goods in *Ceylon* is quintessentially English. Knox writes that his countrymen "betook themselves" to employment:

> some to Husbandry, Plowing Ground, and sowing Rice, and keeping Cattle, other stilled *Rack* to sell, others went about the Countrey a Trading. For that which one part of the Land affords is a good Commodity to carry to another that wants it. . . . After this manner by the blessing of God our Nation hath lived and still doth.   (146)

This conception of the world as a vast market in need of trade from other regions would later be famously expressed in Joseph Addison's essay on Exchange Alley (Bond 1: 292–96) and in Defoe's *Tour through the Whole Island of Great Britain*. At every point in *Robinson Crusoe* this same trading and opportunistic mind-set is apparent, and when Crusoe needs to he can increase production. Things are always potential commodities. Ardelisa in *Count de Vinevil* turns her goat into a pet, a feminine touch that stands in contrast to Knox's and Crusoe's view of goats as useful but entirely disposable. Knox owns a servant boy, and, later in the narrative, because he does not want to marry an island woman, he contracts to adopt a child to take care of him in his old age (152–53). This child disappears in the narrative. Crusoe talks of *possessing* a savage (144), and he sells Xury.

In all three books, the characters are engaged in international trade and experience the hazards of sea travel. Storms, pirates, thieves, unscrupulous governors, and the uncertainty of safe harbors affect them all; these characters occupy the same world and are willing to take risks for gain. Despite Crusoe's and Ardelisa's observations that money is worthless on their islands (*Count de Vinevil* 142; *Crusoe* 43), gold and commodities are always present, and in each book what they buy is enjoyed in what can only be called a sensuous way.

All three texts problematize the questing, restless spirit that led Crusoe and the count to leave home and safety. Ardelisa and her husband-to-be, the count of Longueville, ask in dread as they undertake the voyage, "[W]hat will our father's ambition and resentments cost both him and us?" (118). Crusoe's and Knox's fathers resist their sons' desire to go to sea. Knox will come to reflect on his nineteen years of captivity (and four more years outside England) and conclude that he lost "the prime of my time for business and preferment" (Knox "Autobiography" xxxv). Crusoe spends this same period of life on the island. In all these texts, however, the whole world seems to be in motion, and the characters in each book encounter people from almost every European nation and from many non-Western cultures. Although there are good people and bad people from these places, overall the non-Westerners are decidedly the Other.

That religion is the great barrier for Knox and Aubin opens a new line of discussion about *Robinson Crusoe*. Knox finds the idea of marrying one of the Ceylonese completely unacceptable, and the strong statements Aubin's characters make to express their abhorrence of the Turks are usually based on religion. Defoe's attitudes to nationality and race are significantly different and comparatively complex. Although Crusoe's aversion to Catholicism is the primary reason he sells his Brazilian holdings, the people he meets are not immediately and permanently categorized by nation or race. He decides he has no right to be the cannibals' "judge" and "executioner" (168) and reflects, "[God] has bestow'd upon them the same Powers, the same Reason, the same Affections, the same Sentiments of Kindness and Oligation, . . . the same Sense of Gratitude, Sincerity, Fidelity . . . that he has given to us" (151). The Spanish and Portuguese peacefully become part of his colony, and it is Englishmen who have mutinied and must be attacked.

These texts also open discussion about sex and gender. That Knox concludes that he can't succeed at husbandry because so much of the work is "properly" that of the female sex is striking (149), and he bans women from his household to "prevent all strife and dissention" (145). Aubin's book, the first Robinsonade and the first by a woman, is rich in its own right and in comparison to *Crusoe*. The different threats and physical and social weaknesses that women are subject to add new elements. In one incident, a Turk cannot tell if the disguised Ardelisa is a boy or a woman, and he unceremoniously rips open her shirt to find out. Although Aubin includes some statements about women's weakness, she is in fact demonstrating how many strengths women have in common with men. Certainly Ardelisa's courage equals that of men. And where Knox assumes women's strengths and weaknesses unproblematically, Aubin definitely problematizes them. As Karen Zagrodnik and Elizabeth Bohls have argued, these fictions create women characters who recognize and exercise qualities that allow them to survive catastrophes and danger. Zagrodnik, who writes specifically about this time period, concludes that women travelers created by the early women writers, including Aubin, possess "innate qualities such as courage, resilience, and devotion to self" (iv). Aubin makes a strong case against traditional conceptions of women's weaknesses and contributes to the eighteenth-century debate over custom versus nature. Another contrast is that neither Crusoe nor Knox establishes meaningful, equal relationships, but Ardelisa is always in mutually supportive friendships. These three narratives, thus, remind us of the tradition of fictional male loners in texts such as *Pilgrim's Progress* and how, when women are introduced, as in *The Pilgrim's Progress, from This World to That Which Is to Come: The Second Part*, solitary men are replaced with traveling groups.

Much has been made of the fact that Crusoe never thinks about women, and the juxtaposition of these texts affirms how attitudes toward sex in the early eighteenth century differ from our own. Knox does not "need" a woman any more than Crusoe did and at one point won't even tell a married man the real purpose of a trip because he is afraid the wife would betray them. Certainly Aubin's text opens the topic of cultural pressures on individuals. Written at the time when individual identity, self-actualization (vocational, economic), and autonomy were controversial because they could work against community and family stability, harmony, and even wealth, these texts offer contrasting views of and responses to cultural expectations. The count says to Ardelisa, "Permit not a vile infidel to dishonor you, resist to death, and let me not be so completely cursed to hear you live and are debauched" (121). Ardelisa seems to accept without question the injunction that she die rather than submit to rape; modern students notice how completely she agrees with her fiancé's opinion and the desperate determination she expresses when delivered to a seraglio. As part of Aubin's philosophy that women are capable of more than most people think, Ardelisa does not hesitate to "admire" a plan to set buildings on fire (133). Other eighteenth-century women writers, like the modern feminist critic Claudine Herrmann, problematize or even ridicule the Lucretia plot (101–05), but not only does Aubin endorse it here, but in later fictions some of her heroines will commit extravagant acts in self-defense. Ardelisa, the monk, and others often discuss how behaving as society expects protects them. The sacrifices of male characters when a group of them face starvation are as taken for granted as Knox's comment about gendered roles in husbandry. Throughout, however, Aubin endorses reason, and all of her women characters display it. They "summon up" their "faith and reason," do not despair, and develop a plan to survive or escape (140).

Crusoe and Knox, however, feel the full force of historical and social forces. Both want to go to sea, and both are opposed by their fathers. Crusoe was marooned on his island in 1659, and Knox went on his voyage to Ceylon in 1658. Crusoe's father gives the famous speech on the middle station of life and threatens that God will not bless Crusoe if he goes to sea (4–6). Similarly, a delegation of sea captains calls on Knox's father and reminds him that a ship is "as good as estate" and "younge men doe best in that Calling, they have most in mind to be in" (Knox qtd. in Ryan xi). Although Crusoe's story can be interpreted as punishment for disobeying his parents, the advice his father gives would have sounded dated, tiresome, and even impractical, and both Knox and Defoe would have known that England was not a promising place in which to make a fortune—or even live—in 1658. It was a time of civil war, confiscation of estates, and high taxes, and few, especially of the middle and upper classes, were free of the consequences of factions that alternately rewarded and penalized landowners and imposed or lifted arbitrary restrictions on religious sects. At the same time, the temptations caused by new money, new material goods, and stories of men who became fabulously wealthy in the new economy contrasted with the slogging misery of war-torn England.

Aubin's text often sparks a recognition of how much violence occurs in all of these fictions. Mahomet orders his servants, "Bring her naked from her bed that I may ravish her before the dotard's [her father's] face and then send his soul to hell" (123). Ardelisa's servant Joseph offers a messenger a drink and then "as he lifted the bottle to his head stabbed him to the heart with his knife. 'Go dog,' said he, 'go bear thy message to the Prince of Hell'" (126). This strong, unself-conscious writing in a rather formulaic romantic tale creates a sense of palpable threat. Knox speaks of executions by elephant trampling and dismemberment in exceptionally matter-of-fact ways, and Defoe has Crusoe tally up deaths as though he were doing inventory in Defoe's anchovy warehouse (171; see Backscheider, *Daniel Defoe* 470). That Aubin was a very early woman novelist and fills her text with violence—Christians who happily set fire to inhabited buildings, for instance—may shock students but still gives them insight into the kind of world these writers inhabited.

It has been said that almost all English majors harbor the wish to become creative writers, and one of the most attractive things about courses on the early eighteenth-century novel is the opportunity they provide to discuss the wheels and gears of fiction. For example, I ask what fictional strategies that we take for granted are awkwardly practiced in these texts. Simultaneity and transitions among characters and plot lines are among the most obvious. Both Knox and Aubin simply write such things as "Let us now make a Visit to the rest of our Country-men, and see how they do" (Knox 146) or "Let us now make enquiry after the good priest" (Aubin 134). These writers recognize constraints on a single person's perspective, and their method, although it seems awkward to us, is vernacular and realistic. That fiction writers today tend to ignore these technical problems, whether using a first-person or omniscient narrator, and jump from one character to another opens discussion of readers' horizons of expectations and demands then and now.

The greatest contrast between these writers' practices and today's is lack of suspense. Each of these three writers deliberately tells the reader what to expect, especially when it will be bad. "But blessed be the Name of my most gracious God, who hath so bountifully sustained me ever since in the Land of my Captivity, and preserved me alive to see my Father's word fulfilled!" Knox exclaims (125), and therefore in chapter 2 we know he will return safely to England. Before we suspect the massacre to come, Aubin tells us that Ardelisa and her father will never meet again. Shortly before the Turk captures the travelers, Aubin writes, "Full of joy and hopes, they cheerfully walked towards Domez-Dure, but nothing is to be depended on in this world" (130). Such cues are distinctive elements in Defoe's style and grow more prominent in his criminal fictions. Readers in the eighteenth century were being asked to read for different things and in different ways. How things come about, not how things are resolved, is the focus. The didactic strain present in the English novel from its earliest inception becomes obvious as readers are asked to learn about human nature, about how to act, and even about what the world—eternal and temporal—is like. The Aubin text introduces into the English novel a heritage different from the travel book, specifically that of Continental tales and romances. Its femino-centric story and some of its plot conventions, such as the use of coincidence, doubled characters, and interpolated life stories, are major elements in later eighteenth-century novels and, as William B. Warner and I have demonstrated, deserve serious attention (see esp. Warner 36–44; Backscheider, "Gendered Space").

All of us want students to share our belief that the history and development of the early English novel can be exciting, amusing, intellectually engaging, and, of course, revelatory. Beginning with this configuration of novels, in class or through students' independent research, I keep in the students' minds the importance of travel narratives and their evolving uses. Rather than *Humphrey Clinker*, I teach *Roderick Random*, and I may substitute Frances Brooke's *History of Emily Montague* for Oliver Goldsmith's *Vicar of Wakefield*. Fictions that encourage emigration and England's commercial aspirations can be set beside texts in which travel allows women or lower-class characters to test and revise assumptions about their "nature." In fact, travel fictions written in the century are one of the major sites for the nature-custom debate that we are still carrying on under terms such as nature versus nurture and sex versus gender. Why people travel and a culture writes travel narratives tell us a great deal, and the popularity of Mount Everest narratives, such as Jon Krakauer's *Into Thin Air*, makes that point easy for students to grasp.

NOTES

[1] I would put *A Journal of the Plague Year*, *The Political History of the Devil*, and *An Essay on the History and Reality of Apparitions* in this category.

[2] This text is in print and most conveniently available from Ayer (1977). Since I use only a small part that falls under fair-use guidelines, I scan and e-post with PIN access from the edition with an introduction by H. A. I. Goonetileke. Page numbers refer to this edition.

[3] *Calling* means a summons, perhaps divine, to a vocation, usually the ministry, or to a duty.

Thank God It's Friday: The Construction of Masculinity in *Robinson Crusoe*

George E. Haggerty

Robinson Crusoe is a useful text for teaching undergraduates about the construction of masculine identity in the eighteenth century. In fact, if students are not immediately ready to admit that gender is constructed, *Robinson Crusoe* makes a convincing case that gender emerges from complex material conditions, conditions that this novel both explores and codifies. Written as the various strands of early modern culture were coalescing, *Robinson Crusoe* can function as a primer in gender construction in the modern age. *Crusoe* is basic to the myth of modern Western culture and is part of the dominant fiction that helps form the ideological structure of which it is one of the prime examples. Ian Watt in *Rise of the Novel* long ago articulated the ways in which *Crusoe* anticipated the spirit of individualism. Even more interesting, however, are the ways in which *Crusoe* explores the always already compromised figure of masculinity itself.

Defoe's project involves the encounter with other cultures and with individuals who can be said to represent the other in *Crusoe*. Most crucially, of course, Crusoe's encounter with the "savage" Friday shapes the work and gives it cultural meaning. I try to impress on my students how Friday is central to the idea of masculinity. Friday is not a passive onlooker on the white masculinity that Crusoe establishes; he is essential to that masculinity and gives it not only a particular form but also a precise meaning.

Trial by Xury

Robinson Crusoe begins with a tale of dispossession. The hero is "the third Son of the Family, and not bred to any Trade" (4); and when he tells his father of his desire to go to sea, he is cursed. Then, when his first voyage goes badly, his captain blames him for disobeying his father. The poor hero has been overpowered by shame and reduced to a state of abjection: "uncertain what Measures to take, and what Course of Life to lead," he experiences an "irresistible Reluctance . . . to going Home" and instead he "lookt out for a Voyage." He then laments:

> That evil Influence which carried me first away from my Father's House, that hurried me into that wild and indigested Notion of raising my Fortune; and that imprest those Conceits so forcibly upon me, as to make me deaf to all good Advice, and to the Entreaties and even Command of my Father; I say the same Influence, whatever it was, presented the most unfortunate of all Enterprises to my View; and I went on board a Vessel

bound to the Coast of *Africa*; or, as our Sailors vulgarly call it, a Voyage
to *Guinea*.   (13)

The "evil Influence" that Crusoe speaks of here, the "wild and Indigested
notion of raising [his] fortune"—what are these but the desire to strike out on
his own and to realize himself in some way other than as the "middle Station"
(5) that his father so painstakingly explained to him? The desire for an adventure that takes Crusoe away from home begins to define him as a man and to
determine the form his masculinity will take. By the end of this paragraph of
lament, he is using the "vulgar" language of sailors and imagining himself on a
voyage. Crusoe in this way defines his need to be someone different from his
father, someone greater perhaps in Crusoe's mind. And in attempting this he
begins to define masculinity for the modern age: free from the encumbrances
of family and home and independent of the limits that society would impose.
This is a precarious course, but Crusoe feels an inner compulsion that he cannot resist.

On only his second voyage, Crusoe's ship is captured by a "*Turkish* rover,"
and he is made a slave by the captain (15). Crusoe passes very quickly over his
period of slavery (which lasted over two years) and concentrates instead on his
elaborate plan to escape. In a sense, he is unwilling to describe himself in a position of subjection and prefers to create a narrative of ingenuity and deception
that shows him to be a man worthy of participation in the Atlantic slave economy of the early eighteenth century. For this purpose, he depends increasingly
on the aid of a young "Maresco" called Xury (16).

Xury ends up as Crusoe's companion when Crusoe finally escapes, and he
seems prepared to instruct Crusoe in the demands of the masculine role Crusoe has chosen:

> [A]s soon as it was quite dark, we heard such dreadful Noises of the
> Barking, Roaring, and Howling of Wild Creatures, of we know not what
> Kinds, that the poor Boy was ready to die with Fear, and beg'd me not to
> go on shoar till Day; well *Xury* said I, then I won't, but it may be we may
> see Men by Day, who will be as bad to us as those Lyons; *then we give
> them the shoot Gun*, says *Xury* laughing, *make them run wey*; such *En-
> glish Xury* spoke by conversing among us Slaves, however I was glad to
> see the Boy so cheerful, and I gave him a Dram . . . to chear him up:
> After all, *Xury's* Advice was good.   (19–20)

Crusoe uses Xury here to determine how to proceed and, by depending on
the boy's being frightened, to hide his own fear. The bond between them extends to Crusoe's masculinity. For Xury knows when and how to use the gun
and believes that Crusoe will be able to use it when he needs to. This simple,
trusting support makes it possible for Crusoe to assume the masculine role to
which he aspires. Xury functions as an extension of Crusoe's masculine power.

Like a woman, or, rather, like the role that a woman usually plays in a masculinist culture, Xury admires that power and gives it its rationale. Because Xury is not a woman but a boy who begins to represent the wildness of Africa, he offers Crusoe cultural as well as personal affirmation.

Crusoe's and Xury's adventures along the African coast culminate in their rescue by a Portuguese trading ship. Once on the boat, Crusoe realizes that he is in the position to deal:

> As to my Boat it was a very good one, and that he saw, and told me he would buy it of me for the Ship's use, and ask'd me what I would have for it? I told him he had been so generous to me in every thing, that I could not offer to make any Price of the Boat, but left it entirely to him, upon which he told me he would give me a Note of his Hand to pay me 80 Pieces of Eight for it at *Brasil*, and when it came there, if any one offer'd to give me more he would make it up; he offer'd me also 60 Pieces of Eight more for my Boy *Xury*, which I was loath to take, not that I was not willing to let the Captain have him, but I was very loath to sell the poor Boy's Liberty, who had assisted me so faithfully in procuring my own. (26)

Crusoe thus learns that Xury functions as a possession in the world of circum-Atlantic trade, which makes sense when we realize that the novel takes place in the midst of a burgeoning slave trade and that Crusoe himself, more than once, is involved in such business. Recent discussions focus on this event to suggest how deeply implicated Crusoe is in the business of slavery from early on in the novel. See, for instance, the wonderful chapter on this novel in Srinivas Aravamudan's *Tropicopolitans*. But I would like to address the gender implications of this transaction. As a man, Crusoe needs Xury both to support him and to give him a reason to succeed, as the passage where Crusoe uses Xury to hide his own fear demonstrates. In the context of a slave economy, moreover, a boy like Xury could be an important possession, an entrée, as it were, into the world of cultural difference into which Crusoe has been plunged. In a sense, he needs Xury as a companion to support him in his desires. Instead Crusoe decides to treat him as a different kind of possession, a marketable one. The buying and selling of human cargo is a feature of colonialism, an always-present alternative to the bond I have described, and it is one that defines masculinity in the colonial context. The Portuguese captain understands this, and in a sense he is testing Crusoe here. That Crusoe is able to part with Xury as easily as he is, with only the slightest prodding from the captain, demonstrates that he is a man who imagines a particular place for himself in the economy of slavery. From the perspective of cultural mastery, Crusoe passes this trial of his masculinity with ease. From another perspective, a perspective he does not yet fully understand, he has failed. And it is that failure that structures the remainder of the novel.

The money that Crusoe makes by selling Xury enables him to set up a plantation in Brazil, and he is as successful there as anyone could hope. As a landowner, he has status and position, and his gender identity seems fully established. The sign of this achievement comes when his fellow planters are willing to trust him to trade on the African coast for slaves that he will bring back and share with them. These planters depend on slaves more intimately than they seem willing to admit. Crusoe's position as a trader in slaves makes him a fully recognized member of this planting community. As a slave trader, that is, he thinks he will become a man. His reflections are similar to those he experienced when he first left his father's house: "I . . . could no more resist the Offer than I could restrain my first rambling Designs" (31). Once again desire leads him on, but this time rather than the comparatively simple desire for adventure, he is prompted by a desire for gain.

Poor Robin Crusoe

On this voyage, Crusoe is shipwrecked and cast ashore on an unknown island. When he realizes what has happened to him, he busily sets up a home on the island and gathers animals about him: goats, a dog, a couple of cats, and a parrot at first constitute his little family. He is trained enough in ways of masculinity to understand that he must be in control of his surroundings, even if the context offers an ironic commentary on his role. Soon Crusoe sees himself as the "King and Lord of all this Country indefeasibly": "I descended a little on the Side of that delicious Vale, surveying it with a secret Kind of Pleasure . . . to think that this was all my own" (73). And at home he is a king as well:

> Then to see how like a King I din'd too all alone, attended by my Servants; *Poll*, as if he had been my Favorite, was the only Person permitted to talk to me. My Dog, who was now grown very old and crazy, and had found no Species to multiply his Kind upon, sat always at my Right Hand, and two Cats, one on one side the Table and one on the other, expecting now and then a Bit from my Hand, as a Mark of special Favour. . . .
> . . . With this Attendance, and in this plentiful Manner I liv'd.   (108)

His mastery of the island and his ability to survive in adverse circumstances give Crusoe the right to call himself king. But there is something ludicrous about this family gathering: it is a parody of the family Crusoe left behind. And while he may try to convince himself that he is a king, he never fully succeeds. His need to be king in this context is itself a kind of grotesque comment on his need to assert masculine ascendancy.

This ascendancy is at the same time a kind of abjection, as Crusoe finds repeatedly in dealing with life on the island. If left to itself, his domestic world threatens to explode in ways that he never expects:

> In this Season I was much surpriz'd with the Increase of my Family; I had been concern'd for the Loss of one of my Cats, who run away from me, or as I thought had been dead, and I heard no more Tale or Tidings of her,

till to my Astonishment she came Home about the End of *August*, with three *Kittens*; this was the more strange to me, because tho' I had kill'd a wild Cat, as I call'd it, with my Gun; yet I thought it was a quite differing Kind from our *European* Cats; yet the young Cats were the same Kind of House breed like the old one; and both my Cats being Females, I thought it very strange: But from these three Cats, I afterwards came to be so pester'd with Cats, that I was forc'd to kill them like Vermine, or wild Beasts, and to drive them from my House as much as possible.   (75)

This is a typical description of life on the island: it is rich and startlingly precise in its detail while showing Crusoe exercising his masculinity. His attempt to create a family is undermined by the profligacy of the (seemingly female) cats, and he has no recourse but to destroy them. As soon as the cats seem to exceed his ability to control them, they are treated "like Vermine, or wild Beasts." Crusoe is learning that the limits of the domestic are difficult to define and that the family arrangement is in constant danger of violence and collapse.

Poll is quick to remind Crusoe how abject his relation to the island really is. After being out on an expedition in a boat, Crusoe has to struggle back to a camp he has created at the center of the island. Here he collapses in exhaustion and hears a voice repeating:

> *Robin, Robin, Robin Crusoe*, poor *Robin Crusoe*, where are you *Robin Crusoe*? Where are you? Where have you been? . . .
> . . . [A]t last I began to wake more perfectly, and was at first dreadfully frighted, and started up in the utmost Consternation: But no sooner were my Eyes open, than I saw my *Poll* sitting on the Top of the Hedge; and immediately knew that it was he that spoke to me.   (104)

All the contingency of masculine power is revealed here. No sooner does Crusoe let down his guard than he finds himself abject and lost. The mournful cry of the parrot is after all the language that he taught the bird and might as well be coming out of the depths of his own consciousness. Crusoe's masculinity is a form of abjection because there is something missing in this fantasy of solitary control. He constantly reassures himself that he has control over his surroundings, but even he knows that his surroundings have control over him.

The cost of asserting masculinity is high. Crusoe achieves all he needs to survive on the island, but at the same time he feels lost, alone, and miserably lonely. His little family lets him down, and the division between the domestic and the wild becomes blurred to the point that he becomes deeply anxious. At first, he is only vaguely aware of what is worrying him. But when he finds first the footprint ("It happen'd one Day about Noon going towards my Boat, I was exceedingly surpriz'd with the Print of a Man's naked Foot on the Shore"

[112]) and then the evidence of ritualistic cannibal activity, the terms in which his fantasy of domestic harmony will be violated are more than clear.

> When I was come down the Hill, to the Shore, as I said above, being the S. W. Point of the Island, I was perfectly confounded and amaz'd; nor is it possible to express the Horror of my Mind, at seeing the Shore spread with Skulls, Hands, Feet, and other Bones of humane Bodies; and particularly I observ'd a Place where there had been a Fire made, and a Circle dug in the Earth, like a Cockpit, where it is suppos'd the Savage Wretches had sat down to their inhumane Feastings upon the Bodies of their Fellow-Creatures. . . .
>
> . . . I turn'd away my Face from the horrid Spectacle; my Stomach grew sick, and I was just on the Point of Fainting, when Nature discharg'd the Disorder from my Stomach, and having vomited with an uncommon Violence, I was a little reliev'd.   (119–20)

Crusoe's fantasy of masculine mastery is here so severely undermined that it makes him physically sick. The cannibals terrify him because they both violate his domestic happiness and challenge not only his tentatively established tenets of belief in God and in himself but also the very definition of human society that allows him to claim masculine privilege at all. Their threat to devour him renders him sick with anxiety, as if they represented a kind of cultural castration, undermining his masculinity and making a mockery of his claims to power. As human beings, they are the comfort he is looking for, but as "Savage Wretches" who are "inhumane" in their desires, they merely add to his abjection. This predicament seems utterly desperate and insoluble to Crusoe until his subconscious offers him a solution.

Crusoe's Dream

The solution occurs to Crusoe in a dream. The dream deals directly with this division between the domestic and the savage, and it does so in a way that is more than consoling to the increasingly desperate hero:

> I dream'd, that as I was going out in the Morning as usual from my Castle, I saw upon the Shore, two *Canoes*, and eleven Savages coming to Land, and that they brought with them another Savage, who they were going to kill, in Order to eat him; when on a sudden, the Savage that they were going to kill, jumpt away, and ran for his Life; and I thought in my Sleep, that he came runing into my little thick Grove, before my Fortification, to hide himself; and that I seeing him alone, and not perceiving that the other sought him that Way, show'd my self to him, and smiling upon him, encourag'd him; that he kneel'd down to me, seeming to pray

me to assist him; upon which I shew'd my Ladder, made him go up, and carry'd him into my Cave, and he became my Servant.   (144)

It is almost as if Crusoe plucks this savage like a fetish out of the fearful body of cannibals as a kind of talisman to ward off their evil intentions. This dream, which offers a useful prediction of what is to follow, insists on Crusoe's willingness to save one cannibal as a way of saving himself. Interestingly, in the dream he articulates a simple sequence of events: "I . . . show'd my self to him, and smiling upon him, encourag'd him, that he kneel'd down to me." Crusoe seems to understand that his own physical presence will act on the victim in this way. He but needs to show himself and smile, and the poor savage is on his knees.

The erotics of this encounter—presented to us as a dream-fantasy—are often overlooked. The situation in the dream is the deep, indeed ultimate, anxiety of castration, which cannibalism represents; this anxiety is displaced by a bond between Crusoe and a savage. Crusoe eroticizes the savage in the way that another fetishist might eroticize a lock of hair. In the fetish scenario the object is isolated for its protective power, its ability to protect masculinity from the threat of castration. In a native culture the fetish had spiritual and talismanic powers, and the erotic fetish is similarly invested. It can be used to ward off the evil that is threatened from outside the boundaries of culture. In other words, the savage offers himself as a protection from the threat of castration that the cannibals literally represent. He remasculinizes Crusoe by falling on his knees before him.

When this dreamscape is replaced by reality and Crusoe saves a savage who is about to be sacrificed, the scenario is nearly the same:

> I beckon'd him again to come to me, and gave him all the Signs of Encouragement that I could think of, and he came nearer and nearer, kneeling down every Ten or Twelve steps in token of acknowledgement for my saving his Life: I smil'd at him, and look'd pleasantly, and beckon'd him to come still nearer; at length he came close to me, and then he kneel'd down again, kiss'd the Ground, and laid his Head upon the Ground, and taking me by the Foot, set my Foot upon his Head; this it seems was in token of swearing to be my Slave for ever; I took him up, and made much of him, and encourag'd him all I could.   (147)

Crusoe's smiling and beckoning could be taken as seduction, but Crusoe's seduction, as he imagined in his dream, is to ward off the cannibals at large. If Crusoe can persuade one cannibal to agree to his wishes, he will survive. The savage's gestures of submission are even more vivid and fantastic than those of the savage in the dream, and Crusoe is quick to construe those gestures as giving him power and authority. If his seduction is successful, in other words, he will end up in a commanding position—on top, as it were. He will then have a savage who functions as an extension of himself. Ultimately isolating an individual from the group will prove to be an effective mode of colonization, one that worked for English colonizers in a number of different situations; but in this passage it works to reaffirm Crusoe's masculinity and to reassure him that the threat of castration at the hands of the cannibals is no longer real. He has armed himself with the perfect defense: a savage detached from his marauding brethren can serve as Crusoe's charm.

It is important that Crusoe's charm is a cannibal and that he represents the other of whom Crusoe has been so terrified. As Roxann Wheeler has said, "Friday is *Robinson Crusoe*'s 'solution' to the narrow boundary between legitimate Caribs . . . and cannibals" ("'My Savage'" 847). Friday is also the character Crusoe's "solution" to the terror of castration he experiences on the island. Crusoe invests this savage with a talismanic power because without him he cannot construct a masculinity that will function in this new world. The erotic component of this need becomes a part of masculinity itself: Crusoe's self is defined by and through his desire for the other. As Hans Turley has argued, the eroticization of male relations gives this process an intimate rationale (see *Rum* 144–48).

The next several incidents in the novel seem intended to demonstrate that Crusoe's masculinity is fully intact. Let one example suffice. After Crusoe has named Friday—and Crusoe's assumption of the power to do the naming is another sign of masculine privilege—he begins to teach him how to use the gun. Rather, Crusoe demonstrates the power that he maintains by having the gun:

> I loaded my Gun again, and by and by I saw a great Fowl like a Hawk sit upon a Tree within Shot; so to let *Friday* understand a little what I would do, I call'd him to me again, pointed at the Fowl which was indeed a Parrot, tho' I thought it had been a Hawk, I say pointing to the Parrot, and to my Gun, and to the Ground under the Parrot, to let him see I would make it fall, I made him understand that I would shoot and kill that Bird; according I fir'd and bad him look, and immediately he saw the Parrot fall, he stood like one frighted again, notwithstanding all I had said to him; and I found he was the more amaz'd because he did not see me put any Thing into the Gun; but thought that there must be some wonderful Fund of Death and Destruction in that Thing. . . .   (153)

Crusoe's gun is of course an extension of his masculinity, and this demonstration to Friday is also a way of threatening him. The ruthless destruction of a beautiful and potentially domestic bird, a parrot, is telling. To kill a hawk, a bird of prey, would not necessarily be anything worth remarking, but by making the bird a parrot Defoe suggests that Crusoe's violence is arbitrary. Friday's response to the execution of the bird is all that Crusoe could ask for, after all. For if Friday imagines that there is a "wonderful Fund of Death and Destruction in that Thing," then Crusoe can be certain that his servant will continue to respect him. This scene calls to mind earlier ones with Xury, and it is this connection that gives Crusoe the great satisfaction that it does. These simple demonstrations of masculine power are touching in their playful aggression. But they also represent the beginning of Crusoe's fulfillment as a figure of masculine power on the island.

The Generalissimo

Crusoe and Friday, master and servant, defend the island when it is invaded and in doing so manage to save Friday's father and a Spaniard from the fate that Crusoe most feared. Crusoe with his gun takes the lead, and he quickly establishes himself as the most powerful force on the island. He sees his situation in terms that are familiar, but now they begin to have some meaning beyond the parodic:

> My island was now peopled, and I thought my self very rich in Subjects; and it was a merry Reflection which I frequently made, How like a King I look'd. First of all, the whole Country was my own meer Property; so that I had an undoubted Right of Dominion. *2ndly*, My People were perfectly subjected: I was absolute Lord and Lawgiver; they all owed their Lives to me, and were ready to lay down their Lives, *if there had been Occasion of it*, for me. (174)

Crusoe expresses his power in this astonishing way because this is what the experience of the island has taught him. As "absolute Lord and Lawgiver," he can command the lives of his subjects. This is the achievement that Friday's submission has enabled.

When, a little later, Crusoe helps a captain who has been the victim of a mutiny to reclaim his ship, he shifts the metaphor from king to military commander. "At the Noise of the Fire," he says, "I immediately advanc'd with my whole Army, which was now 8 men, *viz*. my self *Generalissimo, Friday* my Lieutenant-General, the Captain and his two Men, and three Prisoners of War, who we had trusted with Arms" (192). Crusoe has achieved all he had hoped. The young boy who resisted the authority of his father is now generalissimo of this troop. With Friday as his lieutenant general, he can do anything. The bond that becomes the basis of Crusoe's power in the text is based on fealty and devotion, which many of Defoe's details make clear. That it is also an erotic bond, as Turley has argued, is a measure of its power. And it is also a measure of the power of the kind of colonial enterprise that Crusoe represents. Seducing the native, engaging him in aiding the colonist and in fighting his enemies, is an astonishing feat, but it is exactly what Crusoe achieves in this text.

Friday, then, is necessary to the full realization of Crusoe's masculine power. Without him, in fact, Crusoe is impotent, the potential victim of castration in a world of wilderness and destruction. Friday gives him the power to become the man he has always wanted to be: a master, a king, the generalissimo. Even more to the point, Friday gives Crusoe both the desire and the means to survive.

The implications of this configuration are as profound culturally as they are personally. If students can see that Robinson Crusoe and Friday offer a blueprint for gender and cultural relations for the centuries to follow, they will have come closer to understanding why this work continues to fascinate us. They will also understand how masculinity functions not only in this novel but also in the culture of which they are a part.

Robinson Crusoe and Early-Eighteenth-Century Racial Ideology

Roxann Wheeler

This essay sketches the texture of early-eighteenth-century racial ideology and indicates Defoe's particular interaction with it in *Robinson Crusoe*. An attentive reader of European travel narratives as well as an advocate for commercial expansion and slavery, especially in his articles for the *Review*, Defoe is indebted to both old and new modes of characterizing the appearance, behavior, and character of Englishmen and non-Europeans. Because Defoe's male characters are socially aspiring, piratical, or simply subject to misfortune, they travel most of the known globe, particularly the areas most commercially alluring to Britons, including the west coast of Africa, the East Indies, South America, and England's colonies in North America and the West Indies. In *Robinson Crusoe*, *Captain Singleton*, and *Colonel Jacques*, the myriad colonial and commercial encounters dramatize the way that racial ideology shaped the depiction of both non-Europeans and Britons, a phenomenon not as easily detectable in novels whose setting is England. This said, *Robinson Crusoe* neither perfectly reflects dominant English cultural ideology, which was aristocratic, nor does it simply reinforce dominant economic interests of the early eighteenth century, which were mercantile. Instead, *Robinson Crusoe* demonstrates the continuing hold that Christianity had in defining Europeans and a more recent interest that natural historians had in describing the physical body and thereby assigning a new value to it.[1]

Christianity was one of the oldest and most significant lenses through which Britons viewed other people and themselves. Most Britons would have explained the variety in human appearance and behavior as divinely ordained, based on the biblical account of creation. The ethnocentric assumption that all people were born with white skin or the more startling claim that Africans, among others, had white souls stemmed from the conviction of a shared descent from Adam and Eve, whom Britons often envisioned in their own image.[2] In this Christian worldview, diversities among humankind were superficial. While a belief in common parentage sometimes promoted toleration of differences, more often Christianity sanctioned a stratified view of the world's people, a sentiment reflected in and reinforced by English social order: hierarchical distinctions of rank were considered both natural and desirable.

A contemporary encomium reveals not only the key role of Christianity in dividing the globe but also typical assumptions about the general felicity of Europe. *The Compleat Geographer* (1723) notes that Europe's mild climate is complemented by "the Beauty, Strength, Courage, Ingenuity and Wisdom of its Inhabitants; the Excellency of their Governments, . . . and which Surpasses all, the Sanctity of their Religion." In this view, Christianity functions similarly to racial ideology: it flourished on its own and also worked in conjunction with other ways of articulating difference. Christianity was not merely a religious concept, it was also a political and cultural concept. A dense transfer point, Christianity provided a repertoire of positive qualities available for diversion into British national character and, much later, into a conception of whiteness. Protestantism was a significant subset of Christianity and a vital coordinate of British identity; it synthesized nascent individualism, English patriotism, and veneration of the Parliament-limited monarchy in the post–Civil War period. Britons' peculiarly liberal government, for instance, was believed to be part of the Protestant inheritance. Analyzing the ideological connection among Protestantism, freedom, and prosperity, Linda Colley's *Britons* argues that it was "on this strong substratum of Protestant bias from below that the British state after 1707 was unapologetically founded" (43). Arguably, Crusoe's religious conversion partakes in this overdetermined cluster of secular and Protestant meanings. Britons believed that changes in complexion and manners from biblical times, called degeneration, occurred naturally to people as they dispersed over the earth after the Flood or even if they migrated in contemporary times to the tropics. Variations in temperature, terrain, lifestyle, and even diet, compounded by long amounts of time in the places where the original biblical populations settled, made people look, act, and live distinctly. Indeed, it was well within eighteenth-century expectations that Europeans' complexions would darken if exposed to the sun in the torrid zone for any length of time. Crusoe, for instance, marvels that his complexion was "not so Moletta like" (109) as he expected after being on the island for decades.

Despite the Christian worldview accepting certain variation in appearance and behavior among people as natural, one of the most common overdetermined references to distant and non-Christian people was the term *savage*. Savagery was a religious, cultural, and political ideology that came into widespread use during the sixteenth century, according to the *Oxford English Dictionary*. Replacing and supplementing Roman notions of barbarians (which were focused on shared language and geographic proximity to Rome), savagery helped justify European empire in the New World and delineate stark human differences.[3] In general, the diverse tribes lumped under the generic term *Americans* or *cannibals* constituted the most significant population of savages, and the Caribbean islanders that Crusoe encounters were consistently distinguished for their political resistance to European domination: "Few groups were deemed more savage than island Caribs" (Boucher 10). Savagery embraced several attributes, including paganism, cannibalism, and nakedness; dark complexion was not ideologically necessary to the depiction of savagery, though it did bolster the perception of foreignness. Savagery focused on differences between European and Carib cultural behavior, and two of its main ideological effects involved erasing European territorial or commercial transgressions or helping justify them.

The negative representation of Indians often centered on their failure to be Christians. The Caribbean islanders are the ideological focus of savagery in *Robinson Crusoe* rather than the Moors, who were an older source of conflict, or the West Africans, who were a newer engine of England's economy. Most of Crusoe's musings about difference feature religion. Crusoe considers the terrible distinction between those to whom God reveals the light and those from whom God hides the light. Using Christian semiotics of light and dark, Crusoe accounts for this difference in terms of a rough geographic injustice, which permits some nations to be Christian and "forces" others to be sinners and punishes them in their absence from God (120). For example, Crusoe's delight in Friday prompts him to question his previous belief in a religious justification for European superiority: Crusoe observes that God had taken

> from so great a Part of the World of His Creatures, the best Uses to which their Faculties and the Powers of their Souls are adapted; yet that he has bestow'd upon them the same Powers, the same Reason, the same Affections, the same Sentiments of Kindness and Obligation, the same Passions and Resentments of Wrongs; the same Sense of Gratitude, Sincerity, Fidelity, and all the Capacities of doing Good and receiving Good, that he has given to us; . . . this made me very melancholly sometimes, . . . why it has pleas'd God to hide the like saving Knowledge from so many Millions of Souls.   (151)

Crusoe's religious speculations make unequal access to God's will seem divinely ordained at the same time that he highlights the extensive commonalities between cannibals and Europeans.

The historian Hayden White elucidates Crusoe's assumption about sin and savagery in his analysis of the wild man, which was an older construction of human difference in Europe:

> Christianity had provided the basis of belief in the possibility of a humanity gone wild by suggesting that men might degenerate into an animal state in *this* world through sin. Even though it held out the prospect of redemption to any such degenerate humanity, through the operation of divine grace upon a species-specific "soul," supposedly present even in the most depraved of human beings, Christianity nonetheless did little to encourage the idea that a true humanity was realizable outside the confines either of the Church or of a "civilization" generally defined as Christian.   (186)

Crusoe offers a purely religious explanation for the Caribs' plight rather than the secular rationale common to early natural historians who cited climate and other geographic causes.

The other outstanding characteristic of the savage was cannibalism, a putative practice linked to military victory that for many Europeans was considered tantamount to a religious belief. Through mid-century, Caribbean islanders conjured up "the most extreme form of savagery. Truculent by nature and eating human flesh by inclination, they stood opposed to all the tenets of Christian and civilized behaviour" (Hulme and Whitehead 4). The historian Frank Lestringant contends that Defoe's influential characterization of monstrous cannibals in *Robinson Crusoe* represented the mainstream English attitude (141). Not surprisingly, then, cannibalism is the motivating fear most characteristic of Crusoe's (fictional) subjectivity and of his extended reflections on the appropriate course of action toward native islanders.

A final key component of savagery was nakedness or, more precisely, clothing that did not completely cover torsos and legs.[4] Nakedness signified "a negation of civilization" on several counts, and clothing assumed a new value in the repeated confrontations between fully garbed Europeans and lightly clothed inhabitants of other regions of the world (Sayre, *Sauvages* 152–53). Some Africans, Malaysians, Pacific Islanders, and Americans substituted ointments and other external preparations for textile protection, especially in warm regions of the world. Part of the British Christianizing process, albeit weakly pursued in North America and the Caribbean, involved clothing. The degree to which native assimilation to religious instruction was gauged successful was perceptible in the clothing that native converts adopted—or failed to adopt (Sayre, *Sauvages* 146). Native adoption of European clothing was a reassuring sign to Britons of proper gender and political subordination as well as of healthy economic exchange.

As many critics note, Friday is not a perfect savage, and this insight is crucial to understanding his ambiguous place in the novel. Despite Crusoe's preoccupation with the implications of a Christian worldview for the disposition of entire populations around the globe, Crusoe's interaction with Friday often takes place in an altogether different register. Crusoe's attention to Friday's spiritual welfare and physical appearance may be explained in part by the tradition of Europeans representing Indians positively, which was fostered predominantly by French writers and is now called the noble-savage tradition (Boucher 10, 117).[5] In this view, traceable to classical conceits about a golden age, Indians were considered gentle and intelligent; they lived simply without the corruption of luxury or other aspects of civilization. Their natural nobility derived from the combined absence of artifice and distinctions of rank.

One of the most memorable scenes in *Robinson Crusoe* is not related directly either to Christian ideology or to civility. The sustained description of Friday's physical body is best understood as part of a newer constellation of racial ideology that we now associate with the field of natural history, but it also bears traces of the ideology of noble savagery. Crusoe precisely describes Friday for the reader:

> He was a comely handsome Fellow, perfectly well made; with straight strong Limbs, not too large; tall and well shap'd, . . . twenty six Years of Age. He had a very good Countenance, not a fierce and surly Aspect; but seem'd to have something very manly in his Face, and yet he had all the

Sweetness and Softness of an *European* in his Countenance too, especially when he smil'd. His Hair was long and black, not curl'd like Wool;
his Forehead very high, and large, and a great Vivacity and sparkling
Sharpness in his Eyes. The Colour of his Skin was not quite black, but
very tawny; and yet not of an ugly yellow nauseous tawny, as the *Brasil-
ians*, and *Virginians*, and other Natives of *America* are; but of a bright
kind of a dun olive Colour, that had in it something very agreeable; tho'
not very easy to describe. His Face was round, and plump; his Nose
small, not flat like the Negroes, a very good Mouth, thin Lips, and his
fine Teeth well set, and white as Ivory.   (148–49)

To eighteenth-century Britons, Crusoe's detailed observation of Friday carries positive connotations, including his seeing European features in Friday's
visage. Crusoe's description distinguishes Friday from a stereotypical Negro
after the fashion of racial taxonomies and differentiates him from a stereotypical cannibal in terms of attitude and skin color. The historian Philip Boucher
contends that this idealized portrait of Friday is a physically flattering picture
by European standards. According to Carib custom, a young man like Friday
would have likely had ear and lip plugs, a flattened forehead and nose, as well
as facial scarification and red paint (126–27). The hybrid physical description
embraces Friday's multiple narrative roles: he is alternately Crusoe's laboring
slave, willing servant, affectionate companion, as well as fellow Christian. Friday is visibly packaged to elicit contemporary sympathy and to minimize the
extent of his cultural and physical variation from Europeans.

Other than the noble-savage literary tradition, a primary factor explaining
Friday's makeover is that when most Britons explained skin color or human variety in general, they did not yet conceive them as deep or rigid constructs.[6]
Nevertheless, it is the visible difference between Europeans and savages that
triggers Crusoe's anger and results in the massacre of the cannibals. Skin color
was an unpredictable indicator of identity throughout the eighteenth century,
and European attempts to represent the indigenous people of the Caribbean
and Americas highlight the imprecise way that most Britons perceived complexion.[7] Savages and other Indians appear as white, copper, tawny, and black in
written texts and in illustrations throughout the century. Some Europeans believed that Indians who seemed dark complected were actually white because
they were only artificially colored by ointments, dirt, or the like.[8] Even for most
Britons, who thought that climate influenced physical appearance and who thus
held that exposure to the sun and other natural forces made skin darker, Indians
were often perceived to be similar in coloring to the Portuguese, Spaniards, or
Italians. Their precise color was never as important to Europeans as their scanty
clothing, simple living conditions, oral culture, or paganism.

Because of their perceived physical resemblance to Europeans, Indians
often appeared in natural history classifications with Europeans, which is evident in François Bernier's "A New Division of the Earth, according to the Dif-

ferent Species or Races of Men Who Inhabit It" (1684). One of the first modern taxonomies based solely on physical appearance, Bernier's classification included American Indians and Europeans in a group that also embraced the people of North Africa, Thailand, and the northern inhabitants of East India. Bernier observes that the Americans are "olive-coloured, and have their faces modelled in a different way from ours. Still I do not find the difference sufficiently great to make of them a peculiar species different from ours" (362). In a similarly expansive fashion, Defoe's contemporary Richard Bradley imagined the world divided into two kinds of white men (with or without beards), two kinds of black men (with curly or straight hair), and the intermediate category of mulattoes. Indians, Bradley speculates, occupied the category of white men without beards and so differed the least from Europeans. Typical of his contemporaries, Bradley was unwilling to associate physical variations with mental differences, even though he uses white men with straight hair as the standard by which to measure others: "as to their [non-Europeans'] Knowledge, I suppose there would not be any great Difference, if it was possible they could all be born of the same Parents, and have the same Education, they would vary no more in Understanding than Children of the same House" (169).

In examining eighteenth-century ideology in *Robinson Crusoe*, it appears that race as we understand it today did not fully anchor European difference at this time and cannot be the basis for analyzing Crusoe's relationship to Friday. *Robinson Crusoe* corresponds to a particular phase of the colonial process when slavery and other exploitative practices were not justified by coherent racial ideology. In this early stage of colonialism, the representation of racial differences was not systematized but in flux. Indeed, the novel suggests that only some differences were cobbled together to justify European domination of Caribbean and African people: a coherent ideology had not yet emerged to match the de facto situation.

Nevertheless, *Robinson Crusoe* may be read as using available racial ideology to vindicate the British colonial spirit in Crusoe's initial, negative assumptions about Africans and Caribbean islanders and in his conviction that Europeans are technological and cultural superiors to all other people. Focusing on Crusoe's mercenary approach to the slave trade, especially his selling Xury, or on Crusoe's recalling his murder of Carib islanders who have not harmed him emphasizes the ways that Crusoe values Europeans more than any other group. In addition, the novel revises colonial relations considerably by featuring a more palatable version of power differences than existed in practice; for instance, the depiction of Friday, Crusoe, and Xury envisions slavery as an individual and even temporary phenomenon and not as the systemic oppression necessary to a successful empire based on large-scale sugar production in the West Indies.

Despite the compelling textual evidence mentioned above, the novel is not best read as a simple vindication of the colonial enterprise. *Robinson Crusoe* also suggests the fissures in racial ideology, especially through incidents such as

Friday's recounting the way that his community incorporated stranded Europeans: the peaceful coexistence characteristic of Friday's model is the opposite of Crusoe's immediate transformation of all newcomers into subordinates. Moreover, several additional aspects of the novel question a monolithic conception of empire or race at this time: Crusoe's revision of his negative assumptions about Africans and the hesitation Crusoe shows in his treatment of Caribs, not to mention the disconcerting questions that Friday asks about Christian doctrine or the lack of coherent logic in many of Crusoe's musings.

Studying early-eighteenth-century racial ideology and *Robinson Crusoe* permits a glimpse at changes in modes of racialization carried out between the seventeenth and nineteenth centuries. *Robinson Crusoe* invites analysis of the significance that Europeans attributed to religious belief, clothing, technology, and even the division of living space to define themselves and others. Older European modes of racial ideology were gradually subsumed in and partially replaced by attention to the body's surface. Speculations about the meaning of skin color or the correlation between bodily structure and intellectual capability took on a new urgency in scientific realms, particularly natural history and comparative anatomy. Crusoe's conviction of the multitude of Caribbean and European similarities proves to be a historically temporary vision that erodes over the next 150 years as scientific classification promotes an epistemology based on detailing physical difference and as science assumes a new cultural prominence.

NOTES

[1] Portions of the argument presented here have been adapted from chapter 1 of Roxann Wheeler, *The Complexion of Race: Categories of Difference in Eighteenth-Century British Culture*, © the University of Pennsylvania Press, 2000. Reprinted by permission of the University of Pennsylvania Press. On taxonomies, see Foucault, *Order*.

[2] Thomas Clarkson speculated that Adam and Eve's skin color was dark olive (120). John Mitchell suggested that all people were originally black (146). Others, such as Goldsmith (1: 376), Blumenbach (264), and the *Encyclopedia Britannica* ("Complexion" 5: 287) offered that Africans, like other people, were born with white or reddish skin. William Blake's "Little Black Boy" in *Songs of Innocence* (1789) most memorably attributes white souls to Africans.

[3] On the Roman concept of foreigners, see Hannaford 76–80. Savagery is a traditional discourse of difference traceable to Herodotus. See Hulme for excellent historical and analytical work on savagery in the Caribbean.

[4] For one of the richest treatments of the European perspective on the cultural habits of Indians, see Kupperman.

[5] Boucher is particularly helpful in showing lines of influence from French authors to English writers. In the last quarter of the seventeenth and in the early eighteenth century, there were several popular books that made somewhat more positive views of Caribs available (108–10). See Fairchild; also consult Novak, *Defoe and the Nature of Man*, for a rich sense of contemporary ideas about *Robinson Crusoe*, the state of nature, and natural man.

⁶Stories frequently told in myriad eighteenth-century documents testify to a super-ficial notion of human variation. Among the most popular anecdotes was the susceptibil-ity of noses, head shape, and skin color to environmental changes and to human manip-ulation. Many Europeans believed that black Africans and Native Americans had wide nostrils because as children they were carried on their mothers' backs; the constant rub-bing of the infant's nose against the mother's back flattened the nose's "natural" shape.

⁷See Vaughan for an analysis of an eighteenth-century shift in representations of In-dians, particularly as it applies to Euro-American texts. He gives extensive documenta-tion about Europeans viewing Indians as naturally white and thus artificially colored by paints and other ointments. While I find much to agree with in his argument about In-dians, Vaughan has simplified British views of Africans.

⁸As excerpts from travel narratives in *Wild Majesty* make clear, sixteenth- and seven-teenth-century travelers commonly noted the Indians' applied color (53, 68). This belief was also on occasion extended to Africans, particularly Hottentots (see Buffon 400). On the artificial color of Indians, see Buffon 3: 415.

Teaching the *Crusoe* Trilogy

Robert Markley

Many teachers of *Robinson Crusoe* never have read its sequels, *The Farther Adventures of Robinson Crusoe* (1719) and *The Serious Reflections* (1720), and, for their part, most critics have downplayed the significance of these works, treating *The Farther Adventures* as a slapdash sequel and the *Reflections* as a collection of miscellaneous moral essays that try to cash in on the popularity of Defoe's first novel.[1] While other contributors to this volume offer valuable approaches to teaching *Crusoe*, I want to suggest that *Farther Adventures* and parts of *The Serious Reflections* have a place in the classroom and that teachers and students need to consider seriously Defoe's insistence that both works are essential to understanding his hero's "indefatigable application and undaunted resolution under the greatest and most discouraging circumstances" (*Reflections* xii). In his preface to *The Farther Adventures*, the novelist claims that this sequel

> is (contrary to the usage of second parts) every way as entertaining as the first, contains as strange and surprising incidents, and as great variety of them; nor is the application less serious or suitable; and doubtless will, to the sober as well as ingenious reader, be every way as profitable and diverting. (vii)

His contemporary readers apparently agreed: published four months after *Robinson Crusoe*, *The Farther Adventures* went through seven editions by 1747 (only two fewer than the original) and was republished regularly with its predecessor well into the nineteenth century. Most students are astounded to learn that in this novel Crusoe, now over sixty, embarks on a series of adventures that take him first back to the island; then on to a career as a merchant in Southeast Asia and China; and finally on a trek from Beijing, across Siberia, to Europe. Their surprise is one indication of how deeply ingrained our assumptions have become about Crusoe and the significance of his adventures. Both the second and third installments of the trilogy offer radical revisions and expansions of the Crusoe myth. Although time is at a premium in most eighteenth-century novel and survey courses, both undergraduate and graduate students may benefit from rethinking the default view that Defoe's first novel is a primer for an emergent modernity or a parable of colonial aggrandizement.[2]

In the context of the trilogy as a whole, the assumptions and values that critics have associated with Crusoe's twenty-eight years on the island—puritanical self-scrutiny, economic self-reliance, religious proselytizing, and the exploitation of the natural world and non-European peoples—constitute only one-half of a dialectic. Once Crusoe leaves his colony midway through *The Farther Adventures*, Defoe develops the narrative strategies and emphasizes the ideological concerns that shape the rest of his novelistic career, notably his vision of an infinitely profitable trade to Asia, an obsession that marked his journalism from the 1690s on. The fiction of economic self-sufficiency so crucial to *Robinson Crusoe* is abandoned in the sequels for a discourse of international trade; as a merchant in the East, Crusoe pursues his fortune while trying to protect a religious and national identity that can insulate him from cosmopolitanism and contamination. Consequently, the submissive figure of the cannibal as convert, prostrating himself before European technology and religion, is replaced by the hero's, and the novelist's, obsession with far more dangerous others, the Chinese. Over the course of his adventures, Crusoe's moralistic self-recriminations become increasingly formulaic and gradually give way to fervid assertions of European superiority to Asian cultures in a world in which "Infidels possess such Vast Regions, and Religion in its Purity shines in a small Quarter of the Globe" (Defoe, *Vindication* 4). While a full-scale analysis of *The Farther Adventures* and *Serious Reflections* is beyond the scope of this essay, I outline three areas for classroom discussion and student essays suggested by these works: Defoe's tendency in *Serious Reflections* to elaborate, rewrite, and refashion Crusoe's "original" narrative of his twenty-eight years on the island; the novelist's abandonment of the island and its accreted values and assumptions in *The Farther Adventures*; and Crusoe's obsession in both works with the marginalization of Christianity in the Far East. Taken together, these approaches may lead students and their teachers to reconsider both the nature of *Crusoe* and the subsequent course of Defoe's career as a novelist.

Crusoe's seemingly scattershot reflections in the last installment of the trilogy, I have found, can be turned to advantage in the classroom. Looking back to his years on the island, Crusoe recounts at length several episodes that testify to the psychological trauma of his isolation. In *Serious Reflections* Defoe extends and revises the portrait he offers in *Robinson Crusoe* to dramatize the periodic "return of . . . vapours" (253) that haunt the hero's imagination. As a means to think through the implications of the novelist's rewriting of his hero's plight, consider the following passage. I quote it at length to suggest something of the meticulous care with which the novelist retouched his original rendering of Crusoe:

> [O]ne night, after my having seen some odd appearances in the air, of no great significance, that coming home, and being in bed, but not asleep, I felt a pain in one of my feet, after which it came to a kind of numbness in my foot, which a little surprised me, and after that a kind of tingling in my blood, as if it had been some distemper running up my leg.
>
> On a sudden I felt, as it were, something alive lie upon me, as if it had been a dog lying upon my bed, from my knee downwards, about half way up my leg, and immediately afterwards I felt it heavier, and felt it plainly roll itself upon me upwards upon my thigh, for I lay on one side, I say, as if it had been a creature lying upon me with all his weight, and turning his body upon me.

It was so lively and sensible to me, and I remember it so perfectly well, though it is now many years ago, that my blood chills and flutters about my heart at the very writing of it. I immediately flung myself out of bed and flew to my musket, which stood always ready at my hand, and naked as I was, laid about me upon the bed in the dark, and everywhere else that I could think of where anybody might stand or lie, but could find nothing. "Lord deliver me from an evil spirit," said I, "what can this be?" And being tired with groping about, and having broke two or three of my earthen pots with making blows here and there to no purpose, I went to light my candle, for my lamp which I used to burn in the night either had not been lighted, or was gone out.

When I lighted a candle, I could easily see there was no living creature in the place with me but the poor parrot, who was waked and frighted, and cried out, "Hold your tongue," and "What's the matter with you?" Which words he learned of me, from my frequent saying so to him, when he used to make his ordinary wild noise and screaming that I did not like.

The more I was satisfied that there was nothing in the room, at least to be seen, the more another concern came upon me. "Lord!" says I aloud, "this is the devil!" "Hold your tongue," says Poll. I was so mad at the bird, though the creature knew nothing of the matter, that if he had hung near me, I believe I should have killed him. I put my clothes on, and sat me down, for I could not find in my heart to go to bed again, and as I sat down, "I am terribly frighted," says I. "What's the matter with you?" says Poll. "You toad," said I, "I'd knock your brains out if you were here." "Hold your tongue," he says again, and then fell to chattering, "Robin Crusoe," and "Poor Robin Crusoe," as he used to do.

Had I been in any reach of a good temper, it had been enough to have composed me, but I was quite gone; I was fully possessed with a belief that it was the devil; and I prayed most heartily to God to be delivered from the power of an evil spirit.   (253–54)

Although Crusoe convinces himself that this numbness is a "disease," its recurrence over a period of months leads him to go "about with a melancholy, heavy heart, fully satisfied that the devil had been in my room, and lay upon my bed" (255). If *Crusoe* is a novel that turns the Protestant ethic outward in the hero's fashioning a civilized lifestyle on a remote tropical island, his conviction that he is plagued by the devil turns his self-scrutiny inward: moral evil appears both as an external threat and as an effect of his melancholy. Crusoe is explicit in his belief that the objective existence of the devil is confirmed by the "propensity to evil rather than good [that] is a testimony of the original depravity of human nature" (256). Yet this conclusion seems less a moral tag imposed on his adventures than a believable consequence of his isolation: Crusoe's recollection dramatizes, with compelling specificity, the physiological as well as psychological effects of his religious convictions. For many students, such descriptions lend convincing narrative form to what otherwise might be poorly understood abstractions such as "puritanical morality" or "psychologized interiority."

My interpretation of this passage and others like it has developed over the years in response to classroom discussions of how such scenes affect our perception of Crusoe's character. In its density of detail, its careful description of the "palsy" in the hero's leg (*Farther Adventures* 256), and Poll's humorous and uncanny comments, this scene supplements Crusoe's narrative of his years on the island. In his preface to *Serious Reflections*, Defoe asserts that "there is not a circumstance in the imaginary story [that is, *Robinson Crusoe*] but has its just allusion to a real story, and chimes part for part and step for step with" the narrator's life history (xi). Defoe's emphasis on the correlation between fictional strategies (the story of Crusoe's shipwreck) and "real" life provides one way for students to approach the question of why Defoe returns two years later to focus on the workings of his hero's imagination. Crusoe's insistence that he is naked in bed when he imagines another body next to him suggests to many readers that the footprint in the sand has triggered repressed and forbidden sexual desires. When the laughter in class dies down, discussion tends to focus on the problem of why this scene has been "left out" of the original novel, and, in different ways, many students argue that in *Crusoe* Defoe adopted a form of self-censorship. Once his first novel was successful, they maintain, he could go back and emphasize those aspects that make his hero seem more vulnerable and (to use a word that comes up frequently in class) "neurotic." This approach can be used to hone students' abilities as critical readers: I have received some excellent papers that have returned to *Crusoe* to focus on those passages that gloss over episodes that find the hero "pensive and sad" (173), and even a few that suggest where Defoe hypothetically might have inserted this scene had he revised and expanded his first novel instead of writing sequels.

If passages in *Serious Reflections* lead students to revisit their initial impressions about Crusoe, their responses to his *Farther Adventures* range from slack-jawed amazement to profound skepticism about Defoe's claims for his sequel. The first half of the novel, set on Crusoe's island colony, is didactic, even theologically coercive, and does not always go over well in the classroom. Battles with natives are interspersed with long colloquies about the necessity for religious toleration and the virtues of Christian marriage, and Crusoe devotes much of his time and energy to converting indigenous women and marrying them off to their European lovers. When Defoe abruptly abandons the projects of colonization and conversion midway through the novel, however, classroom conversation picks up. Having placed the colony in the hands of his nameless partner, Crusoe declares, "I have now done with my island, and all manner of discourse about it; and whoever reads the rest of my memorandums would do well to turn his thoughts entirely from it" (374). His vehemence is startling to most students: as an experiment in or a model of colonialism, Crusoe pronounces his island a failure. Neither ideals of religious toleration nor the discourses of virtuous self-control can prevent the nameless island from succumbing to the characteristic problems of early-eighteenth-century colonies—diminishing resources, political conflicts, and external threats:

> [T]he last letters I had from any of them was by my partner's means; who afterwards sent another sloop to the place, and who sent me word, tho' I had not the letter till five years after it was written, that they went on but poorly, were male-content with their long stay there; that [the governor Crusoe had appointed] was dead; that five of the Spaniards were come away, and that tho' they had not been much molested by the savages, yet they had had some skirmishes with them; and that they begg'd of him to write me, to think of the promise I had made to fetch them away, that they might see their own country again before they dy'd.
>
> (*Farther Adventures* 374–75)

By the time Crusoe receives this letter, he has succumbed to the lure of trade; it is as though Defoe has recognized that the languages of administrative self-policing are incompatible with his visions of profits to be made in the Far East. For many students, Crusoe's abrupt departure suggests that the realism of *Robinson Crusoe* has been predicated from the start on the fantasy that one man is an island—psychologically and economically. This passage in particular can foster discussions about Defoe's purpose in having his hero abandon the fledgling colony. Asking students why Crusoe leaves the island gives them the opportunity to think about issues of narrative strategy and about eighteenth-century conceptions of character and commerce.

When Crusoe leaves the island, he leaves behind as well the "reflections" of a man well aware of his own "follies" (374). Although Friday is killed in a battle at sea and Crusoe is forced off his nephew's ship after remonstrating with the crew for massacring villagers on Madagascar, he realizes a fortune from his years as a merchant. In the process, Crusoe's moralistic self-doubts and upbraidings give way to denunciations of the "pagan" civilizations he encounters and ultimately, in Siberia, to external acts of violence (*Farther Adventures* 422). In an important sense, the idolatry of the Americas poses no threat to Defoe's vision of Protestant civilization or to the narratives that anchor his hero's identity in volume 1. In *The Farther Adventures* and *Serious Reflections*, however, the Chinese emerge as the embodiment of a fundamental contradiction that Defoe cannot resolve—a virtuous and prosperous "heathen" civilization that threatens to undermine the mutually reinforcing discourses of unending profit, religious zeal, and national identity (*Farther Adventures* 422).

The *Crusoe* trilogy appears at a significant time in British efforts to open new markets in the Far East and amid ongoing debates about the value of the East India trade. Although a critic of the India trade, Defoe consistently, even obsessively, advocated British expansion into the South Seas; trading posts on the west coast of South America, he maintained, would establish a profitable trade with both New Spain and the nations of the Far East (Markley, "So Inexhaustible"). In his final novel, *A New Voyage round the World* (1724), Defoe voices his long-standing critique of the East India trade: "we carry nothing or very little but money [to the Orient], the innumerable nations of the Indies, China, &c., despising our manufactures and filling us with their own." He characterizes these imports as either "trifling and unnecessary"—"china ware, coffee, tea, japan works, pictures, fans, screens, &c."—or as "returns that are injurious to [Britain's] manufactures," such as "printed calicoes, chintz, wrought silks, stuffs of herbs and barks, block tin, cotton, arrack, copper, indigo." A few merchants in the East India Company might profit, but England as a whole was threatened by its trade imbalance with the Far East. "The innumerable nations of the Indies, China, &c." become, for Defoe, *both* an imaginative space of infinite profits and a nightmarish realm where personal and national identity are threatened (155). To counter the prospect of "China's world economic preeminence in production and export," *The Farther Adventures* develops compensatory narratives that deny or repress the limitations of European power in the Far East (Frank 111; Pomeranz).

As Jonathan Spence notes, Defoe's obsessive vilification of China is without precedent in the vast European literature on the Middle Kingdom of China published between 1500 and 1800 (67–69). Defoe rejects eyewitness accounts, which almost uniformly agreed that "of all the Kingdoms of the Earth *China* is the most celebrated for Politeness and Civility, for grandeur and magnificence, for Arts and Inventions" (Le Comte, *Memoirs* A3r; [translator's pref.]).[3] The prospect of an empire resistant to his critiques of tyranny, sin, and idolatry forces Defoe to counter the challenges that China poses to his vision of an infinitely profitable trade. In both *The Farther Adventures* and *Serious Reflections*, Crusoe castigates the Chinese at greater length than he does any other people or culture. In his survey of non-Christian cultures, he dismisses the Mogul empire in two sentences and the entire Islamic world in a paragraph but devotes twenty-three hefty paragraphs to castigating the Chinese for their pride, immorality, technological backwardness, tyrannical government, and hideous art. His long digression on China, he tells the reader, is the only time in his travels that he singles out a nation for explicit comment: "this is the only excursion of this kind which I have made in all the account I have given of my travels," he maintains, "so I shall make no more descriptions of countrys and people; 'tis none of my business, or any part of my design" (*Adventures* 423).

When students are asked why descriptions of other countries are not part of Defoe's "design," many respond that the novelist wants his readers to focus on the hero's tribulations. Fair enough. As most teachers recognize, students will often write about the ways in which Crusoe either maintains a steadfast character throughout his years on the island or adapts to and transforms his island wilderness. Crusoe's attacks on China, however, cannot be shoehorned easily into traditional conceptions of his character. Although few students know much about China in the eighteenth century, there are a number of accessible histories, such as the works of Spence, Andre Gunder Frank, and Kenneth

Pomeranz, that offer them opportunities to think about why China threatens to undo the principles of theology, economics, and identity that underlie *Crusoe*. Cannibals, like Friday, can be converted; Catholics, like the French priest on Crusoe's island, can become allies against idolatry. But the Chinese disinterest in European culture and trade poses a greater threat than the dangers on the island because the Middle Kingdom judges Western barbarians by its standards of civilization and conceptions of reality.

Defoe is shrewd enough to know that he cannot re-create the density of detail that characterizes firsthand accounts of China so generic diatribes substitute for the descriptive strategies of literary-cartographic realism. Describing a land he has never seen only in relation to European standards of civilization, power, and technology, Defoe offers compensatory fictions for the wealth and greatness of the Chinese empire. His tirades, however, cannot disguise the fact that Chinese goods remain objects of desire, such as the £3,500 worth of raw silk, cloth, and tea that Crusoe brings back to sell in Europe.[4] All the eyewitness accounts that Defoe conceivably could have read testify to the wealth, business acumen, and ingenuity of the Chinese. Louis Le Comte's description is a typical characterization of commerce in the Middle Kingdom:

> There is no Nation under the Sun, that is more fit for Commerce and Traffick, and understand them better: One can hardly believe how far their Tricks and Craftiness proceeds when they are to insinuate into Mens affections, manage a fair Opportunity, or improve the Overtures that are offered: The desire of getting torments them continually, and makes them discover a thousand ways of gaining. . . . Every thing serves their turn, every thing is precious to the *Chinese*, because there is nothing but they know how to improve. . . . The infinite Trade and Commerce that is carried on every where, is the Soul of the People, and the *primum mobile* of all their Actions.   (237)

With some rhetorical changes, this passage could be lifted from Defoe's *Complete English Tradesman*, as a former graduate student pointed out to me. Chinese merchants embody the very strategies that Defoe's heroes and heroines adopt over the course of their careers. Like Moll and Roxana, these profit seekers thrive on their ability to outmaneuver European men. Most threateningly, for Defoe, China's "infinite Trade" marks the sinicization of capitalism, a preemptive appropriation of the strategies of bourgeois self-definition, including the psychological "torments" of Crusoean obsession. In contrast to the fictions of economic self-sufficiency, labor, and the love and devotion of a virtuous servant, China presents Crusoe with confusing networks of "infinite Trade and Commerce," double-dealing, and dependency. The prosperity and acumen of the Chinese in this regard undermine the links between sin and scarcity, virtue and abundance that are crucial to a Protestant vision of self-identity and national greatness. Consequently, Defoe must gloss over how an empire "imperfect and impotent" in "navigation, commerce, and husbandry" (*Farther Adventures* 428) can produce the riches that to a significant extent dominate European markets for luxury goods and for reexport to the Americas. His invective can be acted on only after he has left the Qing Empire and can assert the superiority of Christian culture against a far weaker antagonist.

My scholarly interest in Defoe's views of China was initially aroused by oral presentations given by undergraduates some years ago. Students with access to a reasonably good undergraduate library can locate a wealth of material to allow them to explore the eighteenth century in global as well as national terms. Assigning relatively straightforward research projects can offer students the opportunity to contextualize Defoe's fascination with trade and travel, and many of them choose to investigate the economic realities that underlie his fictions of infinite profits.

Several years ago, one student came to me asking why the novelist creates a fictional Russian caravan to get Crusoe back from Beijing to Europe. The nine caravans that traversed Siberia between 1696 and 1719, she found, were the monopoly of the czar and offered nothing like the fantastic profits that Crusoe reaps in *The Farther Adventures* (Mancall 201). Yet Defoe evidently was fascinated by the narrative possibilities that such an epic trek offered. Students, then, might ponder the similarities and differences between Crusoe's travels across Asia and Singleton's trek with his shipwrecked band of pirates across Africa or, for the intrepid, the journey of fifty sailors across South America at the end of *A New Voyage*. In the latter novels, the sailors accumulate vast amounts of gold in regions that are free from competition: the natives in Africa are relatively few and the Amazon basin is a bucolic and unpopulated countryside of verdant hills, abundant game, and rivers of gold. While all three novels play to English fantasies of advantageous trade by finding "savages" eager to exchange gold for beads and utensils, *The Farther Adventures* is theologically as well as economically Eurocentric. Crusoe's verbal attacks on the Chinese are externalized in Siberia when the hero, now seventy-one, burns a pagan idol and then escapes with his caravan, never acknowledging to his Russian fellow travelers his role in what becomes a major incident on the fringes of the czar's empire. His actions ultimately pose no threat to the safety of the caravan or the hero's profits because, once outside the borders of China, Christian merchants can use deception as a strategy of survival, profitability, and self-definition; they can adopt, in effect, the characteristics and strategies of their Chinese counterparts.

If *The Farther Adventures* disorients students who may expect another tale of "man's" triumph over "nature," it also forces in them and their teachers a reorientation of the values and assumptions that traditionally have defined *Robinson Crusoe* and the realist "rise" of the novel. In one sense, *Serious Reflections* might represent the moralizing passages left out of the second half of *The Farther Adventures*, belated efforts to bridge the gaps and resolve the inconsistencies in the Eurocentric ideologies of selfhood, economic individualism, and colonialist appropriation. If Defoe's moral and aesthetic imperatives remain the same in the first two volumes, as the novelist claims, *The Farther Adventures* experiments with a broad range of narrative possibilities, many of which Defoe subsequently exploits: the protean self whose integrity can be guaranteed only by protestations of faith, the balance sheet that shows only profits and not the costs or consequences of moneymaking, the business enterprise that can be left at a moment's notice without affecting profits, and a nationalism that picks its rhetorical fights carefully. For students, the value of the second and third installments of the trilogy lies in the opportunities it offers them to rethink their Eurocentric conceptions of early modern literature. In contrast to Defoe's fable of conquering the island wilderness, *The Farther Adventures* and *Serious Reflections* offer a more complex and frightening view of the world, and both novels, in my experience, have provoked pointed questions about Crusoe's fantasies of empowerment in the Caribbean. If *Robinson Crusoe* seems to offer a "thoroughly known text and context," its sequels reveal that the novelist felt compelled to rewrite one and radically expand the other (Liu 757). By teaching these texts, we may get a better sense of how Defoe conceived of the achievement—and limitations—of his best-known novel.

NOTES

[1]Recent critics who have dealt with the second and third installments of the *Crusoe* trilogy include Neill; Hopes; and Jooma. Neither *Farther Adventures* nor *Serious Reflections* has been edited in a century.

[2]Hans Turley reads the trilogy as Defoe's effort to describe a piratical, homosocial self as an alternative to the domestic ideology of a feminized, psychologized identity ("Protestant Evangelism"). According to Turley, Defoe yokes capitalist expansion and Protestant evangelism to privilege Crusoe the Christian apologist over Crusoe the emergent, bourgeois, and psychological self. The argument of the following two paragraphs is developed at greater length in Markley, "'I Have Now Done,'" which includes a bibliography of seventeenth- and eighteenth-century works on European responses to China.

[3]Defoe indicates that he read Le Comte's work (*Reflections* 125). On the voluminous literature available in Europe on the Far East, see Lach and van Kley.

[4]Throughout the first half of the eighteenth century, Britain imported far more from the East than it exported, and as late as 1754 eighty percent of its shipments to Asia were in bullion.

Robinson Crusoe as Literary Art

Timothy C. Blackburn

It may seem like stating the obvious to say I would like to discuss teaching the canonical *Robinson Crusoe* as a work of art. For students who have struggled with Defoe's resolutely functional prose, the book's lack of chapters, and Crusoe's nonaesthetic approach, however, my statement might sound not obvious but odd. Although students are likely to be sensitive to postcolonial perspectives and to be absorbed by the issues the book excites, they do not think of *Robinson Crusoe* as well crafted in the same way that *Pride and Prejudice* or *The Sun Also Rises* is, and they find it downright primitive compared with *A Portrait of the Artist as a Young Man* or *To the Lighthouse*. They follow in a long tradition, since at least Jean-Jacques Rousseau, of judging the preisland and postisland sections "irrelevant" (*Émile* 147). If they read criticism, they are likely to discover reinforcing views about Defoe's "artless veracity" (Watt, "Defoe" 215) and "journeyman" style (Richetti 13), the novel's "narrative inefficiency" (Zimmerman 20), and the "inert" nature of the opening and closing sections (Boardman 42); they will find little about the subject of Defoe's art. In other words, students, like many scholars, tend to think of *Robinson Crusoe* as a classic or even a myth but not as a work of literature with careful, conscious structure requiring close reading to best appreciate.

I am not suggesting a formalist approach merely for its own sake. Over a period of twenty-five years I have taught *Robinson Crusoe* more often than any other work, first to college and more recently to high school students. I have found that approaching it as a work of art, that is, as a highly conscious, well-crafted literary achievement, can be an engaging experience for students that deepens their readings. Regardless of their arguments about the book's meanings, students respect *Robinson Crusoe* much more when they sense its complexity and beauty and see Defoe as more than an opportunistic hack.

I first began teaching *Robinson Crusoe* in college composition classes. It was the sole work of fiction on the syllabus, and the students were only rarely English majors. I chose it because I liked it and because it explored the basic underpinnings of Western culture. I also chose it because I thought it would be easy, for I theorized that the relatively unsophisticated student readers might match the kind of audience Defoe had in mind. Although I was quickly divested of the idea that it would be easy for students or teacher, I learned that, compared with the upper-division English majors I was to teach later, the relatively unlettered students responded as richly and often with more liveliness, both because of the book's inherent quality and because they sensed it was different from the literature they had previously studied. As more than one student put it, *Robinson Crusoe* doesn't feel literary.

The first paragraph of the novel presents a perfect starting point for deciding just how literary—or artful—the novel is. What could be more straightforward than "I was born in the Year 1632" (4)? On hearing "let's analyze this opening," students are naturally eager to mention the overt forecasting in the second paragraph, but I suggest they first focus on the long opening sentence. To the questions, Why would Defoe make Crusoe's father from Germany? and Why would he have their last name change?, students quite reasonably bring up realism or verisimilitude. Aside from guesses about politics and geography that offer opportunities to discuss some of the historical background, including the death of Gustavus Adolphus in 1632 and the Hanoverian accession, the catchall of realism tends to finish the discussion. What else could there be, they ask, in such a simple start?

With the discussion stuck at this point, I ask students to examine their assumptions about the quality of *Robinson Crusoe*. Would it change their approach to the opening if they assumed *Robinson Crusoe* is a careful, conscious work of art by a great artist instead of the simple, less-accomplished work they have assumed from the narrator's plain speaking? Although assuming quality can lead to distortions, so can assuming incompetence; the assumption of quality causes odd or accidental effects to gain aesthetic stature, whereas the assumption of incompetence causes the art that hides art to stay hidden. Such problems face readers trying to deal with errors in the narrative: who to blame, the author or his uneducated narrator? "What more natural," asks James Sutherland, than "for a Crusoe or a Singleton to make mistakes when he has a pen in his hand? Their very mistakes and awkwardness are a kind of guarantee of their authenticity: Defoe can't lose" (*Critical Study* 127). Since more often than not Defoe *has* lost on this count, it is instructive to try the experiment of assuming high artistic quality.

Once the opening has been seriously considered in these terms, students might point out that the emphasis on Crusoe's father as an immigrant suggests a world where people constantly move and change. In this world of change, something as stable as identity itself—one's very name—can, "by the usual Corruption of Words in England" (4), change in a very short time. Furthermore, Defoe shows that Crusoe's father himself left home as a young man and was for a brief time at sea, spending the rest of his life far from home, on an island. The student contributing this observation has the sense of a real revelation, a sense shared by the class. Students will disagree about what to do with this observation—is it an irony undercutting or augmenting Crusoe's father's authority?—but they begin to see possibilities beyond what the narration obviously invites. They can go on to see that the death of Crusoe's elder brother deepens the world of the novel from one of change to one with war and violence in the most civilized places. At the same time they see in Crusoe how stubbornly resistant to such insight human beings can be. Taking Defoe's details seriously makes the whole conflict between Crusoe and his father more tragic and enriches the narrative beyond the pieties punctuating it.

By considering everything in the preisland section as purposeful beyond the needs of realism or exposition—Why this particular detail of exposition? What are the implications?—students discover patterns that affect other parts of the novel. For instance, they note the Edenic overtones of the offer Crusoe's father makes him—obey this one command and you can otherwise do what you wish—which heightens Crusoe's later interpretation of his disobedience as his "Original Sin" (141) and of his father as a quasi deity. Yet at the same time students catch Crusoe's subtle ambivalence toward his father. By making an imperfect analogy to the father in the prodigal son parable (12), Crusoe undercuts his father's stubborn intransigence, for the scriptural father sent the son off with the blessing of his inheritance. Thus alerted to Crusoe's ambivalence, students note that Crusoe again undercuts his father at the very end of the book, when he provides the kind of sea training for his nephew he presumably wishes his father had given him (219).

Always asking questions that assume Defoe was doing more than telling an adventure story or suggesting trade routes to exploit, students animatedly ponder the ways the pirate Moors, Xury, and the West Africans further enlarge the novel's world in terms of geography and religion and race and slavery. It is conventional to say Defoe threw in the pirates for sensationalism, but, by resisting that and instead looking at the way the pirates are described and what they value and do, students begin to see how carefully and thoroughly Defoe has prepared Crusoe, not to mention his audience, for the island task of re-creating civilization: Crusoe begins in civilization, which he neither understands nor values; experiences what might be called its opposite with the pirates, who subvert the rules of civilization for their benefit; and then witnesses its absence (in Defoe's and Crusoe's terms) along the West African coast.

Once students have built a case for Defoe's careful composition of the preisland sections of *Robinson Crusoe*, they are better able to explain why these sections (and, later, the postisland sections) bothered them. Mainly, the myth precedes the book. They know the island is coming and they want to get to it.

Although it can be shown that in some senses *Robinson Crusoe*'s "movement is dramatic" (Hunter, *Reluctant Pilgrim* 18), Defoe's narrative techniques do not seem anything like the kinds of suspenseful buildups with which students are familiar from popular culture. Crusoe's matter-of-fact recitation of events and details is so undramatic that it flattens tone and equalizes incidents, forcing students to respond in a new way. For instance, Crusoe's behavior after the footprint episode has an implied aesthetic: he assumes any of his noises or actions, however minimal, has the potential for consequential, even mortal, events. He survives by paying attention to everything, just as he previously sought spiritual survival by examining trivial details for evidence of God's providence, even resorting to bibliomancy. By choosing for his story *"an Hundred Thousand to one"* (47) occurrence, Defoe is revaluing the normal significance given things, which includes the way a story is told. A conventional consequential pattern would create an entirely different kind of world from the one Defoe exhibits in *Robinson Crusoe*. Students are challenged in the way Crusoe is when he considers the rice and barley miracles; both need to resist easy interpretations and keep an eye on details, even adventitious ones.

Student papers that use close-reading techniques often lead to insightful analyses. Students have charted imagery of being swallowed up (by both ocean and cannibal); worked through Crusoe's inveterate metaphors of civilization, such as calling the tree in which he sleeps the first night "my Apartment" (36); compared and contrasted the four different accounts of his landing; traced the repeated groupings of eleven people; or examined a single passage, especially if seemingly unimportant. But even well-known passages have shown untapped potential for scrutiny. For example, papers have argued that the description of the shipwreck includes Dutch and French expressions because this is Crusoe's real break with Europe; that the powerful accumulation of first-person plurals in the clauses immediately preceding Crusoe's going overboard accentuates the powerful loneliness of the relentless singular *"I's"* that follow; and that Crusoe's poignant comment that he never again saw anyone from the ship, "or any Sign of them, except three of their Hats, one Cap, and two Shoes that were not Fellows" (35), is as vivid as an imagistic poem and has effective sound patterns and rhythms that, once established in readers' ears, echo in many ways throughout the text.

Some students have admitted to being liberated by realizing that Defoe's prose does not often get the close-reading scrutiny given to poetry or to modernist prose. Reading Defoe closely makes them feel more like a discoverer than like a performer following others' scripts. I confess to encouraging that view at the expense of some critical discussions of *Robinson Crusoe*. For instance, we discuss Crusoe's apostrophe to gold coins as a useless "Drug" and his immediate "Second Thoughts" to take the money anyway (43), trying to decide if Defoe's portrayal is too crude to be considered irony. After they have read critical opinions from both sides of this debate, I suggest their own method of assuming literary quality might help them decide. Eventually someone notices that Crusoe says his swim back to the island is imperiled by the water's roughness and "the Weight of the Things I had about me," a subtle complication of the irony missed by commentators. The more confident students become about their own assumptions, the less they question the author's intentions, thus opening themselves to the kinds of arguments students often resist, such as those about fascinating structural dimensions of *Robinson Crusoe*: Crusoe's "rebirth" nine months after landing on the island (Hunter, *Reluctant Pilgrim* 149); the possible parallel of Crusoe's imprisonment on the island with England's imprisonment (in Defoe's opinion) from the Restoration to the Glorious Revolution (Seidel, "Exile" 365–66); and the implied symbolic and providential fathering of Friday by Crusoe, who is twenty-six when he lands on the island and spiritually rescued by the twenty-six-year old Friday twenty-six years later (Blackburn 367–68).

Friday always invigorates discussions. Because he has become such an important focus of the book and a mythic character in his own right, it is helpful for students to be as precise as possible in their responses, paying attention to the details Defoe gives and considering the formalist implications. Most students are bothered by Crusoe's brutality in giving Friday his name, but some recall that the very first paragraph of the novel showed a name change happening less dramatically but just as involuntarily to Crusoe's family. While the first account of name change does not absolve Crusoe, it complicates the picture. Name changes are thus depicted as an act similar to Friday's wielding of the sword—he "at one blow cut off his Head as cleaverly, no Executioner in *Germany* could have done it sooner or better" (148); students therefore need to account for how Defoe uses Friday to direct satire and irony at civilization before making sweeping condemnations about Crusoe's or Defoe's brutality. Friday is forced to learn Crusoe's language, but, in a careful parallel not often noticed, the Spaniards held by Friday's tribe are forced to learn the tribe's language. Whatever case students make about *Robinson Crusoe*'s portrayal of Friday, it is strengthened by being precise and by considering Defoe's larger thematic and artistic intentions.

Paper topics that specifically challenge students to investigate *Robinson Crusoe*'s complex structure and texture work particularly well. When asked to take some very small detail from the postisland section and to compare and contrast it with something from the island section or, alternatively, the preisland section, students raise, for themselves and their readers, questions about artistic design, control, and intention. Some of the results are predictable, though still interesting, such as the many Xury and Friday parallels or the parallels between the wolves and the cannibals, the Spaniards, and the animals Crusoe fears along the African coast. The most interesting and challenging parallels involve more specific topics, such as a repeated image or an interpretation of Crusoe's misjudgments in his first and last great dangers, the storm at sea and the wolves. Students write most successfully when they have a genuine sense of discovery.

Dr. Johnson may have wished *Robinson Crusoe* longer, but its ending has disappointed many readers. Students who have sought the aesthetic dimensions of the novel, working from the premise that the ending represents a carefully considered set of artistic choices, probe the import of choices that readers have long found frustratingly inefficient, such as Crusoe's coming to England not once but twice, the detailing of wealth, and the truncating of personal information about, for example, Crusoe's marriage. They find that the episode with the wolves proclaims the dangers of Europe and Crusoe's need to avoid smugness and shows that the world established in the first part of the novel remains the same, complex and dangerous. They assess from various critical perspectives the implicit (and generally sad) biographies of the persons mentioned in the final episodes and the odd workings of chance or providence in details like Crusoe's inadvertent conversion of Brazilians to Catholicism, but they are always struck by the understated relentlessness of Defoe's portrayal of mortality, randomness, and, in ever mobile Robinson Crusoe, restlessness. As students often say, you can see the ending as great if you're willing to see it as subtle.

Is *Robinson Crusoe* a great work of literary art, with carefully planned effects and subtle complexity in virtually every part and detail? Obviously, that's a difficult question, but teachers approaching it as if it were will find their students have some intriguing answers.

Messages in Bottles: A Comparative Formal Approach to Castaway Narratives

John Barberet

> Defoe is possibly the only author by proxy (*auteur d'antici-pation*), in so far as he supplied his successors with images.
> —Pierre Macherey, *A Theory of Literary Production*

As fans of *Gilligan's Island* are well aware, a deserted, isolated island in the ocean can often become a busy port of call: visitors arrive and depart; intriguing flotsam washes up on the shore, only to be swept away by high tides and storms; and there is always the strange sensation that someone may already be living there. The same can be said, not just for Crusoe's island, with its supporting cast of cannibals and conspirators, but for the novel itself, a veritable intertextual intersection where all roads come from and lead to other island narratives. Woven from, among other texts, Montaigne's essay "On Cannibals," Denis Vairasse d'Allais's *The History of the Sevarites or Sevarambi* (1675), Shakespeare's *The Tempest*, and the Alexander Selkirk narratives, *The Life and Adventures of Robinson Crusoe* seems to reveal its textual fabric all the more fully once it begins to unravel, beginning with Defoe's own sequels and from there into a series of strands, of versions and variants, such that an entire genre—the Robinsonade—has been coined in an attempt to capture them.

The Robinsonade—let us prefer the term *castaway narrative*, to allow for precursors—belongs to or is in close proximity to several other genres, among them the travel narrative, the adventure tale, and the imaginary voyage. It is, however, perhaps best defined in contradistinction to the genre of the utopian narrative despite—and maybe because of—some unusual similarities between the two (in fact, the syllabus in the appendix at the end of this essay was designed as a bookend for a seminar on utopias). First, both genres derive their names and to a large extent their formal features from one original book and its title. Also, both genres yield less-idyllic counternarratives in the twentieth century: the anti-Robinsonades of William Golding and J. M. Coetzee on the one hand and the dystopias of Yevgeny Zamyatin and Aldous Huxley on the other. In addition, utopias and castaway narratives involve islands, that is, controlled and delimited settings where the projects being undertaken by the contemporary historical community (colonialism, industrialism, urbanization, etc.) can be more easily grasped and mapped by readers. Hence both genres emphasize the role of sight (vision, visibility) and of showing (descriptions of the island, descriptions of the utopian community): the first thing a castaway does is find the highest point from which to view his or her predicament; in utopia, the guide offers the visitor a complete tour of the city.

Yet this socialization of space yields two distinct results, for whereas castaway narratives seek to reproduce the same—Crusoe rebuilds the plantation he had left—utopias seek to produce the different or the alternative. Although both genres are highly ideological (see Nerlich; Marin), it is clear that classic Robinsonades seek to reproduce the society from which the castaway hails. The castaway recapitulates the dawning of civilization and repeats the rise of Homo sapiens—fire, agriculture, corrals, metalworking, bread making—all is rediscovered, as if to reaffirm and retrace the wisdom of our ancestors. To be sure, certain improvements are made (in Defoe, for instance, the freedom of religion is exercised), but pathological social formations do occur: just about everyone owes his or her life to Prospero in Shakespeare's *The Tempest*, to Crusoe in Defoe, and to Captain Nemo in Jules Verne's *The Mysterious Island*. Castaway communities (there is usually, eventually, a community that forms) are patriarchal, often racist, and hierarchized according to functions. In a sense, castaway narratives end with what utopian narratives begin with: the social problems of human beings.

Let us begin, then, with the end of Defoe's novel; and for the sake of accuracy, we can begin precisely where the most widely taught edition of the novel ends. On the last printed page of the Norton second edition of Defoe's *Robinson Crusoe* (436), following the Selected Bibliography, the reader finds the following appended note: "For a suggestive fictive rendering of the Crusoe story, see J. M. Coetzee, *Foe* (London: Penguin Books, 1987)." This supplement, literally the last words of the book, presents a host of problems that students can consider. First, why is Coetzee's "rendering" the only one mentioned? (Is Norton in financial cahoots with Penguin, and is this note a marketing ploy—a possibility Defoe himself would surely have appreciated?) What about Verne's *The Mysterious Island*, where the narrator explicitly compares his characters' situation with that of Crusoe? What about Michel Tournier's *Friday*, arguably more faithful to Woodes Rogers's Selkirk narrative than Defoe's novel itself, since for Tournier the fall off the precipice while pursuing a goat is a crucial event, whereas Defoe simply omits it? What about J. G. Ballard's *Concrete Island*, where the castaway's automobile plunges through a barrier into an interstate no-man's-land, leaving the disabled driver to fend for himself? What about an anti-Robinsonade such as Golding's *Pincher Martin*, which portrays the survivor-castaway motif as an entirely imaginary scenario played out in a dying man's mind? Remarkable new Robinsonades appear regularly, most recently from Umberto Eco (*The Island of the Day Before*) and Yann Martel (*Life of Pi*). Why single out Coetzee?

Second, what is a "suggestive fictive rendering"? Does this imply, as indeed it seems to, that Defoe's novel is an accurate, nonfictional account of Crusoe's the story—that, in other words, it is the original whose uniqueness is proved by the subsequent emergence of indebted imitators? Do other writers from other times, cultures, and continents wander Crusoe's island like pale shades, pointing suggestively but disturbing nothing? To be sure, English departments have transplanted Crusoe's island firmly back to English soil, a recuperative process continued in the Norton second edition, which still lacks an essay with a comparative, internationalist approach. The very presence of the various scholarly prefaces, documents, essays, and appendixes in the Norton edition and others, including excerpts from the *Farther Adventures* and other paratexts, leads to the third problem: what exactly is "the Crusoe story"? And if there is such a story, can Defoe's novel also be considered a "suggestive fictive rendering" of this story?

We can begin by answering this last question in the affirmative, although this may seem counterintuitive. As a general rule, once we start comparing texts devoted to a particular literary topos, the problem of origins rears its head. With *Robinson Crusoe* the problem is doubled, as it were, because the novel is about (in the sense of rotates or hovers around) the problem of origins—and specifically, as Pierre Macherey has argued in his discussion of *Mysterious Island*, of false origins, for example, the description of the origin ex nihilo of *homo economicus* is countered and denied by the availability of the ship's vital cargo.

This point can be taken much further: despite the playful earnestness of Defoe's prefaces, it is clear not only that Crusoe's tale is a fictional one but also, more important, that any account of a castaway's complete exile and redemptive survival is always already fictional and allegorical. In the real world, the abandoned *enfant sauvage* brought up by wolves cannot be rehabilitated, and adults would fare no better. To be human is to interact with other human beings, and absolute solitude—especially these days—is an impossibility, and therefore a myth, an escape, an ideology, and an illusion. (To whom would you narrate your solitude? And would that not be the end of it?) Entire philosophies crumble under the weight of absolute solitude; readers of Tournier's *Friday* will recall the slow collapse of the narrator's normative definitions of consciousness and perception, as well as the existentialist and poststructuralist concepts the narrator uses to explain this collapse.

Those who would invoke the presence of a deity in such a situation might be surprised that gods do appear on the various islands, though often in the guise of tricksters (think of Prospero) and perhaps of the author himself. In Verne's *The Mysterious Island*, the narrator boasts of the ingenuity of human beings as the castaways, armed only with one watch, one match, and one grain of corn, recreate by themselves the stages of technological evolution. Overlooked by the narrator is that the reclusive Captain Nemo has been secretly providing them with the necessary tools and chemicals, disguised as coming from bounteous nature (they even begin calling Captain Nemo God and imagining his countenance). That everything happens as the paradox of origins, in case we missed it in *Robinson Crusoe*, is perpetuated in Verne by exploring it, compelling us to reevaluate and resituate our reading of Crusoe as a castaway; Crusoe had tools, supplies, even guns and ammunition, largely because he was on a slave-finding trip for his plantation. He is already *homo economicus* even before landing on the island; more precisely, as Michael Nerlich argues, the adventurer Crusoe represents belongs to an age that was already over by the time the novel was written, and he exists to placate the lower classes with the illusion that wealth through adventure is a real historical alternative. The recent popularity of the *Survivor* reality-television series, where the last castaway gets the money, proves that such an "ideology of adventure" still resonantes in our culture.

In just such ways, "renderings" of Crusoe's "story" unfold, erode, or reconfigure what we can call the original version, revealing as much about themselves as about the contradictions they explore. Pursuing the theme of the hidden island trickster at the origin of the plot, for instance, we can recall how Prospero's magic holds the key to the castaways' situation; how the mysterious proprietor of H. G. Wells's *The Island of Dr. Moreau* is behind the strange events that occur on the island (see also the remarkable *The Invention of Morel*, by Adolfo Bioy Casares); and we can apply these "renderings" back to Defoe's novel in order, for example, to better appreciate the concealment strategies Crusoe uses to make himself appear more numerous to the cannibals and, at the end, to the mutineed crew. To look at Defoe's novel in this manner—finding themes, transpositions, stock images, and plot devices echoed and remodulated in "suggestive . . . rendering[s]" from many different literatures—is to understand how a novel not only can belong to its descendants but also can constitute a separate genre—in this example, the Robinsonade.

When one reads comparatively and across borders both geographic and textual, it quickly becomes difficult to isolate and distinguish one castaway narrative from another without some form of classification besides date of publication and country of origin. However, one can distinguish through comparative analysis certain features such narratives have in common and thereby arrive at a fuller understanding of "the Crusoe story." Students should be encouraged not to deduce such recurring motifs arbitrarily but to peruse two, three, or more castaway narratives before identifying them. Student readers quickly grasp the simplicity of the main elements and the complexity and fragility of their comparative arrangements. For illustrative purposes let us briefly discuss four such recurring motifs: scapegoating, storms, island topographies, and the body. I conclude with two absolutely essential motifs, that of the other and that of the diary or journal.

It is a basic structuralist tenet that elements in a series (chess pieces, the colors of the spectrum or of a traffic light) have meaning with respect only to one another and not to a transcendental signified. A comparative approach to castaway narratives quickly turns up a series of permutations over time and space involving specific events, situations, and topographies that can be arranged into a flexible framework or narrative template. Each element or "image" (as Macherey terms it [141]) is not necessarily stable but may be composed of contradictions. For instance, there is always a reason why the protagonist (or the group of protagonists, when one considers Robinsonades about collective castaways) is cast away from society. Perhaps the best example of this is the biblical tale of Jonah, where the protagonist is on a mission of avoidance and where the scapegoating scenario implicit in the term *castaway* becomes explicit through the drawing of lots and Jonah's being cast overboard. Similarly,

Tournier's Robinson begins his journey by submitting himself to a prescient reading of tarot cards, and indeed he too has been singled out. The balloon-riding collective in Verne are refugees from the United States Civil War, a chosen and not surprisingly representative few. Other protagonists display various imperfections that seem to explain their exclusion: besides Sebastian and Antonio in *The Tempest*, we should note that Ballard's Maitland wrecks his car while returning from an adulterous tryst and Stephen King's medical student in "Survivor Type" is smuggling drugs. Another recurring motif is the event that actually performs the casting away of the castaway, and it takes the form of a big storm—a force of nature and not of culture—thus contradicting the first motif, scapegoating, according to which it is society that performs the casting away. This contradiction is collapsed in *The Tempest*, where the storm is a curse, a spell, a magician's trick, as well as a political strategy and a form of revenge. As for Crusoe, his restlessness signals a certain willful anomie characteristic of modernist antiheroes. In a larger sense, of course, the storm is usually an alibi for the rejection of the protagonist (and what he or she represents) by society.

The topographies of the islands onto which the castaway is tossed also merit comparative analysis, since each castaway finds an island he or she seems to deserve. Most such islands contain caves of various shapes and sizes, certain flora and fauna (goats are predominant), and other features that serve to create what can be termed a moral landscape. Tournier's Speranza, for example, contains an erotic glen; a stinking *souille*, or mud pit; and a cave in the shape of a womb. Defoe's Crusoe is well aware of this moral aspect of the island's landscape; he leaves his first boat intact, "as a *Memorandum* to teach me to be wiser next Time" (99). The protagonist's attempts to impose culture onto this representation of nature reveals in the end another contradiction, since the island's topography is a textual and cultural construct itself, with its own history: islands in twentieth-century Robinsonades progressively shrink like Honoré de Balzac's wild asses' skin, to such a degree that Gary Larson's comic castaways barely have room to lie down. Students are encouraged to draw maps of the various islands; to collect popular representations of island topography (from cartoons, advertisements, art, etc.); and to locate and describe isolated, separated spaces that function as islands (e.g., the traffic island) on campus, in the suburbs, and in the malls.

Another topography that merits comparative analysis is the body of the castaway, a feature of the Robinsonade I had ignored until a class composed largely of nursing students brought it up. They suggested performing a health assessment of each castaway based on textual evidence. We began with the body of Caliban then moved on to Crusoe and other characters, all of whom display a variety of phobias and especially manias. The initial results, posted on the class Web site, were as follows:

> The health (mental and physical) of subject Caliban was assessed by sixteen student nurses, nutritionists, psychologists, and psychiatrists

(coincidentally, all students in the same literature course). The following diagnoses are based (admittedly somewhat loosely) on Carol Jarvis, the American Psychiatric Association's *Diagnostic and Statistical Manual of Mental Disorders*, and other standard texts in these fields.

Acute confusion
Diversional activity deficit
Dysfunctional grieving
Chronic pain
Self-esteem disturbance
Absent father syndrome
Altered family processes
Altered nutrition
Developmental problems
Altered role performance
Powerlessness
Impaired skin integrity
Self-care deficit (hygiene)
Diarrhea
Anxiety/generalized anxiety disorder
Vitamin B deficiency (long term)
Flatulence
Dowager's hump (curvature of the spine)
Panic disorder
Rheumatoid arthritis
Acute stress disorder

Subsequent health assessments of castaway characters yielded further information, including the difficulties faced by a disabled protagonist (Ballard's Maitland, whose broken leg prevents him from moving around the island). More provocatively, the ample presence of textual data supporting such assessments suggests that the castaway genre may be closely linked to that of the illness narrative. If one pushes this idea even further, it is often hard to evade the notion that the Robinsonade portrays, at a basic level, an experiment conducted on a chosen subject placed in the wild by a detached scientist—a notion that is confirmed in more than one of the narratives under discussion, particularly in the story "Survivor Type," a tale King admits was inspired by a conversation with a doctor concerning the will to survive in extreme circumstances.

To be sure, these recurring motifs or "images"—scapegoating, storms, island topographies, and bodies—provide content and context for the castaway narrative while allowing for the kind of variation befitting a touchstone genre like the Robinsonade, which often seems to be a sort of writing exercise for authors. Perhaps the best example of this dialectic between theme and variation involves the representation of the island's other, whether Caliban (or Ariel or even Miranda—all native islanders) or the various Fridays (of Defoe, Tournier, Coetzee) and his thematic descendants, the most recent of which takes the form of a volleyball with dried blood on it in the film *Cast Away* starring Tom Hanks. As this last example proves, there is no reason the other has to be an actual human being; Golding's Christopher Martin builds "a man to stand here for me" out of rocks and a piece of tinfoil and refers to him as "the Dwarf" (*Pincher Martin* 61, 107). Significantly, before the arrival of Friday in Defoe's novel, the role of the other had several premonitory incarnations: in addition to "my Boy Xury," sold to the Portuguese captain for "60 Pieces of Eight" (26), there are the confrontations with the parrot and the dying goat. Both of these confrontations reward close attention, since the encounter with the other turns out to be an encounter with the self-estranged. It is not a coincidence that Crusoe's mirror stage—his famous description of his own appearance resulting from his habit of "frequently [standing] still to look at my self" (108)—takes place between these encounters with the parrot and the goat. In the first case, Crusoe, while sleeping in his "County House" (103) is awakened "by a Voice calling me by my Name several times, *Robin, Robin, Robin Crusoe,* poor *Robin Crusoe,* where are you *Robin Crusoe*? Where are you? Where have you been?" (104).

He is reassured when he discovers that this voice belongs to his "Poll," yet he immediately admits that "just in such bemoaning Language I had used to talk to him" (104), leaving the reader to conclude that Crusoe spent at least some of his time on the island talking to himself ("you") as if he were another, thereby creating a gap, as it were, out of which an eventual other will emerge. In the second case, Crusoe, having just described himself as clad almost entirely in goatskin, encounters a goat dying "of meer old Age" at the mouth of a cave (129). His self-estrangement takes the form here of his metaphoric transformation into a goat. Both of these encounters have their echoes in other castaway narratives: Caliban's famous pronouncement, "You taught me language; and my profit on't / Is, I know how to curse" (1.2. 365–66) bears an odd resemblance to the parrot's "Language." A similar mimetic estrangement can be found in Martin's relationship with the figure he built from stones and reflective tinfoil:

> . . . he was clinging to the Dwarf and the stone head was rocking gently, rocking gently, and the sun was swinging to and fro, up and down in the silver face.
> "Get me off this rock!"
> The Dwarf nodded its silver head, gently, kindly.
>
> (Golding, *Pincher Martin* 162)

As for the castaway's identification with goats, when Tournier's Friday finally succeeds in wrestling and killing the patriarchal goat, Andoar, he proclaims, "The great goat is dead, but I shall make him fly and sing fly and sing" (190). He then transforms the goat's skin into a kite, fashions his skull and entrails into an aeolian harp, and is moved to observe, "Andoar was myself. I myself was that solitary and stubborn old male, with his patriarch's beard and his fleece sweating lubricity" (209).

One does not have to be an animal-rights activist to discern the intense and complicated relationships between castaways and animals on the island. Defoe's Crusoe calls all of his tame animals "part of my Family": this includes goats, parrots, his dog, his cats (though at first he is "oblig'd to shoot several" and later to drown their litters), and even various "Sea-Fowls" that he ties to stakes after cutting their wings (131).

Tournier's Crusoe, after a poor start—"It [the goat] was the first living creature he had encountered on the island, and he had killed it" (19)—gradually develops a more nurturing relationship with the other animals and even with "vegetables" (115), though he continues to be wary of the vultures. Those who read French might wish to see how Michel Gall pursues this theme of animal friendship in his novel *La vie sexuelle de Robinson Crusoë*.

Generally, the way a castaway treats animals prefigures the way the other will be treated. It is somewhat disturbing to note that when the other arrives and takes human form, the encounter almost invariably takes the form of Hegel's master-slave dialectic: at first the master conquers the slave, but gradually the slave comes to exert power over the master, who is in an important sense dependent on the slave for mastery. It is even more disturbing to discover that students often take for granted the necessity of an indigenous slave for the castaway, as if enslavement is an unproblematic and unmediated form of natural human interaction. This can be tested by asking students, If someone saves your life, should you become that person's slave? Students' reaction suggests that the imagery of colonial domination is a powerful obfuscation; the antidote, as Roberto Fernández Retamar has shown in his famous essay on Caliban, originally published in 1971, involves applying the dialectical reversal. The best example of such a reversal is Tournier's depiction of Friday, who becomes a powerful agent for transformation and initiates Crusoe into a higher form of existence; but there are plenty of others. In the filmic domain alone, Luis Buñuel's *Adventures of Robinson Crusoe* or Lina Wertmuller's *Swept Away by an Unusual Destiny in the Blue Sea of August*, where the master-slave dialectic is a matter not of race but of class and gender. To be sure, not all Friday figures perform such a dialectical reversal: Coetzee depicts a Friday whose tongue has been cut out, perhaps by Crusoe himself (but how can we know?), and who becomes a symbol for repressed stories ("the true story will not be heard til by art we have found a means of giving voice to Friday" [118]). Ballard's Friday figure, Proctor, is "plainly a mental defective of some kind" (86), because, according to his runaway caretaker, Jane, of injuries received while employed as a trapeze artist. The Crusoe figure, Maitland, concludes that Proctor bears an "unconcealed strain of violence, a long-borne hostility to the intelligent world on which he would happily revenge himself" (95)—a description strikingly reminiscent of Prospero's description of Caliban and of course to

Crusoe's reaction to the cannibals. Maitland thus justifies (at least to himself) humiliating and dominating Proctor.

Finally, one last other is present, if not actually on the island: the reader. There is perhaps no better time to keep a diary than when one is alone and isolated, and the act of diary keeping involves both isolation and withdrawal, the same casting away of the self that motivates the Crusoe story. The journal or diary usually serves both as a narrative device and as an event performed by the castaway to maintain sanity: even castaway narratives devoid of actual journal keeping, such as the movie *Cast Away*, released in 2000, nevertheless include scenarios of writing, in this case on the walls of the cave the main character inhabits. A classic example of one variety of the diary as a castaway narrative form, the message in a bottle, is provided by Edgar Allan Poe's "Descent into the Maelstrom"; but the castaway's journal also partakes in the isolation, the uncertainty and the absurdity of writing to no one, a form of address that invokes reflexivity in the face of absence. (Students who keep journals can understand and explain this phenomenon; a good example is the habit of beginning each entry with "Dear Diary," as if the journal itself is the addressee.) Such a mode of narrative production recapitulates the origin of writing itself: the plot moves chronologically, like days marked with a knife on a tree, and usually contains inventories and lists of cargo, among the oldest texts known to archaeologists.

Maurice Blanchot argues that the "intimate diary" ("le journal intime") is the purest form of writing: it portrays the loss of the subject into an absent object and the entry of the self into writing as an autonomous and self-engendering act. Blanchot's notion of writing without an addressee coincides with the definition of literature as an autonomous zone of articulation. This important feature—writing in the face of radical absence—is certainly common to or implicit in castaway narratives (see the remarkable lyrics to "Message in a Bottle" by The Police), even when third-person narration is predominant. Verne's castaway journalist keeps a record, but all is lost—including the journal—when the island blows up. Tournier's Robinson keeps two journals, the first written with a vulture's quill using ink from a sea porcupine, the second reflecting his transformation through the use of blue woad ink and an albatross's feather, both a gift from Friday. Ballard's Maitland does not keep a diary, but through trickery he gets the brutal, mentally deficient island native to write messages on concrete—"HELP CRASH POLICE"—which are immediately erased by the illiterate man, who thinks he is scrawling vulgarities (150–53). Coetzee's Crusoe kept no written account, but significantly Susan Barton's letters to "Foe" are returned unopened. Leave it to King to take this self-consuming narrative mode to its extreme: his protagonist, a greedy and immoral medical student cast away on a tiny island, armed only with a scalpel and plenty of painkillers, describes in his journal the process whereby out of sheer hunger he gradually eats most of his bodily appendages, except the few fingers needed for the act of writing and those he is in the process of consuming ("ladyfingers" [426]) when the diary breaks off. The body of the text follows the amputation of the body, as performed by the scalpel/pen. One certainly has to agree with Blanchot here that the diary chronicles the loss of the self in the act of writing.

At the origin of this particular theme, of course, are Crusoe's reasons for keeping a journal:

> I drew up the State of my Affairs in Writing, not so much to leave them to any that were to come after me, for I was like to have but few Heirs, as to deliver my Thoughts from daily poring upon them, and afflicting my Mind.   (49)

Crusoe the journal keeper is not out to know himself but instead is using writing as self-help therapy, as a way to purge himself of obsessive ideas through textual externalization. Here we find all the features of the "message in a bottle" motif plus an intriguing reversal of the castaway's situation: for writing is what the castaway casts away.

The futile-diary mode of narrative transmission is certainly one of the most important aspects of the castaway narrative and yields a wide variety of permutations—even in Defoe's novel, where we find a pseudodiary re-created and then abandoned by the narrator. Once again, we are close to a better understanding of how "renderings" relate to an original text: not so much as misreadings or anxieties of influence as a playful exploration of the contradictions, gaps, concealed perspectives, and reversible binarisms already present in the original. And we can perhaps start speaking of "the Crusoe story" as many books but one text and as one dominant narrative form, the existential solitude of the writing self.

APPENDIX

Course Syllabus for Castaway Narratives (excerpt)

Required texts

> William Shakespeare, *The Tempest*
> Daniel Defoe, *Robinson Crusoe*
> Jules Verne, *The Mysterious Island*
> William Golding, *Pincher Martin*
> Michel Tournier, *Friday*
> J. M. Coetzee, *Foe*
> J. G. Ballard, *Concrete Island*

Texts to be distributed

> Michel de Montaigne, "On Cannibals"
> Isidore Ducasse (comte de Lautréamont), *Maldoror* (excerpt)

William Dampier, Edward Cooke, Woodes Rogers, Richard Steele, Accounts of Alexander Selkirk (see Defoe, *Robinson Crusoe*, Norton ed.)
Stephen King, "Survivor Type" and "Notes"
Stacey Richter, "An Island of Boyfriends." *My Date with Satan*

Castaway movies (choose one)

Swiss Family Robinson. Dir. Edward Ludwig. 1940.
Las aventuras de Robinson Crusoe [Adventures of Robinson Crusoe]. Dir. Luis Buñuel. In Spanish. With English subtitles. 1954.
Forbidden Planet. Leslie Nielsen (the castaway), Walter Pidgeon (Prospero), Anne Francis (Miranda), and Robby the Robot (Caliban). 1956.
Swiss Family Robinson. Dir. Ken Annakin. 1960.
Robinson Crusoe on Mars. Dir. Byron Haskin. With Adam West. 1964.
Lost in Space. Dir. Stephen Hopkins. Based on 1960s TV series. 1998.

Paper Topics

1. *Comparative island topography.* (a) Write a comparative and/or historical study of the various dwellings the castaway inhabits in at least three of the novels we have read. It might help to use Robinson Crusoe's dwelling(s) as a "beginning," then treat the other dwellings as variations on a theme.

(b) "More and more, the island was becoming an exact model of his head" (Ballard 69). What is the relation between the castaway and the island in at least three of the novels we have read? Does the island shape the castaway, or is the island an extension of the castaway's character?

2. *The body of the castaway.* Lately (in Coetzee and Ballard, not to mention King) the castaway's health has been declining. Ballard's Maitland is our first disabled castaway. How does this change the nature of his situation in comparison with previous castaways? What importance does the castaway's health play in his island experience?

3. *From Friday to Proctor.* Lately (in Coetzee and Ballard) Friday is getting more disturbing and intractable. Is Ballard's Proctor the return of Caliban? What do Proctor and Coetzee's Friday have in common?

4. *Ballard's "concrete island."* How does the "island" differ from the previous novels we've read? How is it similar? What aspects of an "ocean" island does Ballard attribute to this one, and how?

A Semester on Crusoe's Island

Matthew Wickman

Inspired by an article in the MLA's *Profession 1998* (see Mazella), frustrated by my own experience in introduction to literature courses (once as a student, now as a teacher), and intrigued by the possibilities that seemed intrinsic to Brigham Young University's year-long approach to such introductions, I decided to renounce my class's involvement with distended literary anthologies in favor of a more intensive engagement with *The Life and Adventures of Robinson Crusoe*. The problem to which *Crusoe* seemed to pose a solution can be described as one of diffusion. Students were expected over the course of two semesters to digest the distinguishing features of and subdivisions in the major literary genres (e.g., under the rubric poetry, the difference between a lyric, an ode, an elegy, etc.), learn key rhetorical terms (from *allegory* to *zeugma*), absorb a dozen or so critical approaches to literature (from formalism through feminism and new historicism), and use this knowledge in producing lucid and cogent analytic essays.

In turning toward *Crusoe*, I aimed to employ this tendency toward diffusion in the students' favor. Believing like most of my colleagues that introductory literary courses should resemble workshops rather than warehouses and emphasize processes of analytical labor over inventories of information, I decided to try not to fill students with terminology but to engage them intensively with a text that they already seemed to know without having read. For, while we can acknowledge the impact of the Shakespeare and, more recently, Jane Austen industries on our modern cultural landscape, *Crusoe* arguably pervades it more than any other canonical work of literature. Reincarnations of Defoe's novel range from Bugs Bunny cartoons and *Gilligan's Island* reruns to the 2000 movie *Cast Away* and the television series *Survivor*. (References to *Crusoe* also pervade not only literary history but also economic and sociological analyses of Karl Marx and Max Weber and even the category in my high school yearbook entitled "person with whom you would most like to be stranded on a desert island.") Consumed primarily as image rather than text, *Crusoe* has acquired an iconic status that transcends its origins in eighteenth-century British culture. Thus an extended engagement with Defoe's novel in an introductory literary course would seem to afford students a unique opportunity to heighten their awareness of myriad cultural and mass-mediated forms.

With this hypothesis as my impetus, I considered a number of approaches for teaching *Crusoe*. I thought of creating a multimedia course in which we would read *Crusoe* alongside a later work such as Elizabeth Bishop's poem "Crusoe in England," J. M. Coetzee's novel *Foe*, or Derek Walcott's play *Pantomime* and consider avatars of *Crusoe* in other generic forms, from television to film to hypertext. Or, addressing this subject from a theoretical angle, I thought of building a course around a critical history of the media, using *Cru-*

soe as the primary text amidst an array of secondary sources by authors ranging from Herbert Marcuse and Marshall McLuhan to Walter Ong and Fredric Jameson. In the end I organized courses that are more congruent with my department's standard curriculum for introductory literary courses, which places the emphasis on exposing students to a variety of critical approaches and cultivating the ability to interpret literature from a multiplicity of perspectives.

One problem with this curricular aim is that it tends to produce polarities of theory and practice. Students are first exposed to psychoanalysis, poststructuralism, and other theories and then asked to write critical essays and research papers using this knowledge. In addition to the oversimplification, sloganeering, and short-term memory that such a diffuse approach inspires, it encourages students to engage literature as a pathological organism: texts exhibit symptoms that a particular critical approach dissects and diagnoses. Or else this approach promotes an engagement with literature that seems redolent of scriptural exegesis, in which texts are treated as sacred repositories of meaning that theory somehow helps us tease out. Hence, and despite its better intentions, the crash-course approach to literary theory blunts critical thought by transforming theories into tools that elude evaluation except, perhaps, when read against one another.

I have been trying to hurdle this challenge by supplementing or replacing the standard-issue literary anthology with *Robinson Crusoe* and by striving to cultivate in my students an intimate knowledge of one (culturally pervasive) text. I have opted to approach criticism by modifying the so-called critical approach. Although the feminist, psychoanalytic, Marxist, and other readings in critical editions are often exemplary, they tend to foster the pathological sensibility in which the primary text becomes a repository of symptoms that critical approaches diagnose. My introductory course is attentive to a fairly broad range of theories but focuses less on particular camps of critical thought than on processes of intellectual discussion whose end lies primarily in the sheer experience of grappling with critical texts. In other words, I have been trying to divert the analytical focus from a search for symptoms to the process of engagement.

To this end, I select theoretical essays that may be read not only in relation to *Crusoe* but also against one another. For instance, I have assigned Walter Benjamin's "The Storyteller" alongside Michel Foucault's "What Is an Author?" and Jean-François Lyotard's "Answering the Question: What Is Postmodernism?" alongside Jürgen Habermas's "Modernity: An Unfinished Project." Since *Crusoe* engages questions of colonialism, I have assigned Gayatri Spivak's "Can the Subaltern Speak?" with Homi Bhabha's "Of Mimicry and Man." In the final two weeks of the term, I turn our attention to essays that represent a convergence of *Crusoe* scholarship and literary theory, such as Lydia Liu's article "Robinson Crusoe's Earthenware Pot," which addresses *Crusoe*'s implication in commodity fetishism.[1] The essays with which I conclude the term underscore the relation between not only *Crusoe* and literary theory but also contemporary theory and the traditions (in Freud, Benjamin, Foucault, and others) from which it draws.

The course proceeds in two-week blocks. After reading through *Crusoe* in the first two weeks, the students and I discuss one theoretical essay during the initial meeting of the week and spend the second meeting discussing that essay in relation to Defoe's novel. The following week we analyze that first essay's companion piece and then read both pieces in relation to *Crusoe*. In these units I aim to create an environment of conversation, bred from a familiarity with the material and from discussion devoted to the interpretive process. Replacing an anthology with *Crusoe* as the primary text to which we return several times throughout the term gives students sufficient time not only to formulate rudimentary interpretations of a particular novel but also to revise these interpretations, enunciate alternative arguments, and become more familiar with their own tendencies as critics. Anonymous student evaluations from these courses attest to the benefits derived from this approach:

> I enjoyed studying one text the entire term. I found more things in it each time I had to write about it.

> *Crusoe* was an interesting read. I'd first encountered it when I was twelve, and it made very little sense. Now, with more skill in analysis and writing, it made more sense and intrigues me.

> I appreciated the fact that the class was not based on an anthology. It was helpful to have in-depth discussions on one book.

This conversational approach becomes crucial in the way we discuss the secondary essays. We talk about fundamental premises in these essays that the students are unlikely to have gleaned from the reading itself and then focus on particular passages that seem important or enigmatic. With Benjamin's "The Storyteller," for instance, I first sketch a historical and conceptual outline of Hegelian and Marxian dialectics, and then we review key passages from the essay: the etiolation of authoritative experience in the modern world, the relation between epic and memory, the premodern affiliation of storytelling and craftsmanship, the correlation between capitalism and the rise of the novel, and so on. We cap our discussion by summarizing one or two main ideas from the essay, such as the tendency of narrative form to register socioeconomic transformations, or the capacity of and necessity for criticism to apprehend these transformations in a politically active manner.

Most fruitfully, however, we read Benjamin's essay in relation to *Robinson Crusoe*. For example, we turn to the episode shortly after Friday's rescue, in which Crusoe and Friday return to the scene of the sacrificial feast and Friday animatedly narrates for Crusoe the doom he would have faced had Crusoe not saved him:

The Place was cover'd with humane Bones, the Ground dy'd with their Blood, great Pieces of Flesh left here and there, half eaten, mangl'd and scorch'd; and in short, all the Tokens of the triumphant Feast they had been making there, after a Victory over their Enemies. I saw three Skulls, five Hands, and the Bones of three or four Legs and Feet, and abundance of other Parts of the Bodies; and *Friday*, by his Signs, made me understand that they brought over four Prisoners to feast upon; that three of them were eaten up, and that he, pointing to himself, was the fourth: That there had been a great Battle between them, and their next King, whose subjects it seems he had been one of; and that they had taken a great Number of Prisoners, all which were carry'd to several Places by those that had taken them in the Fight, in order to feast upon them, as was done here by these Wretches upon those they brought hither.   (150)

We review this passage together and postulate the arguments, positions, or cultural assumptions that Crusoe may have been conveying. Here, we take up a modified heuristic of the critical approach, less as a search for symptoms than as an indicator of differences. Then we discuss the episode from four distinct angles corresponding, roughly, to a reading of Benjamin with *Crusoe* (that is, of the writers' expressed or tacit arguments as running parallel to each other's) to a reading with Benjamin against *Crusoe* to a reading with *Crusoe* against Benjamin and to a reading against both *Crusoe* and Benjamin. That is, we discuss first how Friday's narrative seems to exemplify Benjaminian storytelling; second, how Friday's narrative and Crusoe's interpretation of it seem to provide evidence of social fragmentation commensurate with a space that Benjamin affiliates with the novel; third, how the episode, with Benjamin, evokes a premodern sense of community, a community based on race or religion rather than (as Benjamin suggests) class; and fourth, how the episode reflects and distorts hierarchical relations of class (contrary to Crusoe's professions of magnanimity), but in such a way that it attests to a long and complex history of abuses that challenges the nostalgic view of community as once whole and subsequently degenerated. Often I break students into four groups and ask them to present their findings to the class.

This exercise gets students to think about texts and relations between texts in terms of rhetorical positions, ideological constructions, and imaginative possibilities. Most students claim that it is an illuminating and even empowering experience that goes beyond an understanding of individual works. One student wrote in a course evaluation:

I've really enjoyed the class and what I have learned about critical thinking. I'm planning to go into psychology, but at the same time see many of my views and beliefs in opposition to much of what is popular and accepted in psychological circles today. I really want to develop my critical skills and become better versed in the philosophies and methodologies that will help me to intelligently approach these issues and propose acceptable alternatives.

Other evaluations have been similar: "This class really stretched me intellectually. The reading and discussing of the critical essays was really a rigorous mental exercise." There are always students, however, who are less enthusiastic: "I enjoyed [reading *Crusoe*] more than an anthology, but had a hard time comprehending many of the [theoretical] ideas." "I did not appreciate the value [of] the majority of the supplementary readings. I would have preferred readings that had stronger ties to *Robinson Crusoe* or [that might have been more] useful without [requiring] a strong background in critical theory." Even these more skeptical students, though, seem to take something positive from firsthand exposure to the theory: "The essays were difficult at times. . . . [But] I liked the way the class was organized."

Since I conceive of this course as a workshop with practical aims, I try not to play Vergil in guiding lower-division students into the infernal crucible of theory or the elysian fields of eighteenth-century studies. Instead, I try to enhance students' engagement with their writing. In keeping with the theme of conversation, I place a philosophical as well as pragmatic emphasis on the process of revision. If students are required to write three essays, I usually ask them to write the first as a five-to-seven-page interpretive essay on *Crusoe*. For the next assignment students are permitted, even encouraged, to revise that paper, but only on the condition that they incorporate either library research or at least one of the secondary readings into the body of their argument. Then, for the third paper, I give them the option of revising their papers once again but ask them to expand it to eight to twelve pages and to provide evidence of further research. The students who choose to remain with their original topic are able to refine their ideas over the course of the semester, while building their papers into projects of greater complexity and sophistication. Their work and scores tend to improve, which increases their confidence in themselves as writers and in the legitimacy of their ideas. My hope is that this experience will help students construct more complex arguments, write stronger papers in their upper-division courses, and begin to establish a degree of mastery over the process of revision as it applies to critical reflection about ideological positions as well as interpretive arguments and compositional mechanics.

Not surprisingly, student work in these courses tends to show more dramatic improvement than work in courses in which each assignment is discrete and each grade terminal. The students seem to understand that despite the difficulty of the assigned material this pedagogical approach boosts their final grades, and thus they are far more willing to sail intellectually into uncharted waters. Their course evaluations bear this out: "The emphasis on the revision process improved my writing immensely. The class didn't allow me to produce the same carbon-copy papers that are easy to punch out but forced me to increase the depth of my writing." "I enjoyed studying one text the entire term. I found more things in it each time I had to write about it."

Students who do not profess to enjoy the course still tend to favor the emphasis on revision, chafing instead at the emphasis on theory or on a single work of fiction, like *Crusoe*. From my standpoint as a teacher mostly of upper-division and graduate courses, however, I gladly shoulder the burden of such criticism because the cumulatively crafted essays from these *Crusoe* courses are often more sophisticated than those of upper-division students. I have watched students shape and develop brilliant arguments on suppressed images and representations of femininity in *Crusoe*, on postcolonial ramifications of Crusoe's rapport with his parrot, on Weberian analyses of the overlay in *Crusoe* of religion and economics, and on many other subjects. Such student-generated projects are, I believe, the result of extended exposure to and engagement with a primary text, the opportunity to develop and revise a topic of research, and a climate of rigorous intellectual inquiry whose tone is set when the instructor takes a conversational approach to a series of dense theoretical essays that raise the bar of discussion.

Perhaps as a function of my own perversely iconoclastic pleasure, I consider these experimental lower-division courses a success if my students manage to arrive at a measure of self-reflexivity regarding their inculcation in critical thought. Recently during a discussion of Foucault's "What Is an Author?" a student cross-examined me whether—if it is true, as Foucault argues, that discourse is the medium of a power that operates productively rather than repressively—we might include my particular insistence on coherent thesis statements under a discursive rubric. Might we not, this student continued, classify critical thought and its elaboration in introductory literary courses as mere conventions? This protest might be demystified by most instructors of English under more familiar headings: Do I have to write an essay, or can I do something different? Why are you assigning this material instead of short stories? Doesn't the B-minus I got on the last paper prove that grading is subjective?

In this introductory course, however, such protests seem to take on greater poignancy; students often express them with unusual sophistication, given the climate of discussion. After all, Crusoe's hegemonic dominance over Friday and Friday's catechism in Western (religious) thought have been the subjects of protracted examination. And yet despite, or perhaps because of, this subversive climate, I regard these moments of potential uneasiness—moments when the parameters of thought instilled by our discipline become more perceptible, however self-interested a particular student is in bringing them to light—as signs of the success of the course. Such instances point beyond the utilitarian mastery of any conglomerate of texts or theories and toward the kind of dialectical engagement with issues that students seem increasingly to require not only for success in the English major but also, and more important, for success in evaluating and negotiating the heavily mediated cultural labyrinths of a global society.

NOTE

[1]Other suggested texts that I have either used or considered include essays that directly address *Crusoe*, such as those by Novak ("Friday"); Svilpis; Wheeler ("Complexion"); and Clowes, as well as essays that make only casual reference to *Crusoe*, such as those by Said; Armstrong and Tennenhouse; Michaels; Baskerville; de Certeau; and Sharpe.

The Robinsonade: An Intercultural History of an Idea

Carl Fisher

> Robinson Crusoé dans son isle, seul, dépourvu de
> l'assistance de ses semblables et des instruments de tous
> les arts, pourvoyant cependant à sa subsistance, à sa
> conservation, et se procurant même une sorte de
> bien-être, voilà un objet intéressant pour tout âge.
> —Jean-Jacques Rousseau, *Émile*

> Robinson Crusoe on his island, alone, deprived of the
> assistance of his fellow man and of all artificial aids, yet
> providing for his own subsistence, for his own safety, and
> even achieving a sort of well-being—there is a matter of
> interest for any age.

If imitation is the greatest form of flattery, then *Robinson Crusoe* is much flattered indeed. Literary works rarely have made such an immediate impact and yet remained so popular for so long. A "private Man's Adventures in the World," as the supposed editor described the novel in the preface (Defoe, *Robinson Crusoe* 3), became a source of inspiration and imagination not just for the reading public but for every subsequent generation of writers. The first imitation was published within months of the original novel, and, while the novel needed no advocate, Jean-Jacques Rousseau's comments in *Émile* on the exemplary education that the novel provides spawned an even greater number of adaptations. Hundreds, perhaps thousands, of literary texts find their originary idea in Defoe's novel. Many of these works are ephemeral, mere footnotes to the prevailing taste of their time, market-driven imitations meant to exploit commercial possibility, and commentators often critique the nonliterary aspects of many Robinsonades. However, Robinsonades should be considered not for their aesthetics but for their international cultural impact. Some variations were extremely popular, went into multiple printings, and were themselves translated into many languages. (Campe's *Robinson der Jüngere* for a time was more popular than the original, was translated into English to great success and multiple editions, and spawned its own imitations.) Almost every culture has its own Crusoe story, a Robinsonade that reshapes the character and often revises the plot drastically, sometimes containing just a kernel of the original story and character.

In the broadest definition, a Robinsonade repeats the themes of *Robinson Crusoe*; usually it incorporates or adapts specific physical aspects of Crusoe's experience and is an obvious rewriting of the Crusoe story. Other times, it shares ideas or narrative style. Critics debate the parameters of the Robinsonade, from the narrowest variations found in translations to the broadest incorporation of popular themes. Margit Hoffman says that a Robinsonade requires only "a repetition of a similar situation, a castaway on an uninhabited island, with completely different people involved" (142). In describing a library collection of Robinsonades that runs to 130 titles, Hoffman distinguishes between authentic Robinsonades on the one hand and "pseudo-Robinsonades" (this category is from Ullrich's 1898 bibliography) on the other. The first category includes editions, translations, abridgments, as well as a reader written in one-syllable words (only the names Xury and Friday are two syllables) and published in 1868 that dramatically changes the style and sometimes the facts of Defoe's narrative. The pseudo-Robinsonades avoid the island solitude but incorporate Crusoe themes and make direct references to Robinson, often in the titles. Among many interesting pseudo-Robinsonade examples, Hoffman cites *Jungfer Robinsone oder die verschmitze Junge-Magd* ("Young Miss Robinson or the Cunning Young Maid" [1723]), a novel about the trials and tribulations of a young girl, a runaway, whose story includes criminal activity, domestic service, masquerading as a man, seduction, and prostitution, the plot sounding more like *Moll Flanders* than *Robinson Crusoe*. Another is *Zwey gehlerte Robinson* ("Two Learned Robinsons" [1748]), which claims that the original Robinson fathered many children, none of them well educated, then follows the difficulties of two monks who wish to escape religious orders and become Protestants (148). To be connected to *Robinson Crusoe*, even tangentially, renders a kind of authenticity. The resonance of the title and the concept can be seen in other pseudo-Robinsonades. For example, Frederick Marryat's *Masterman Ready; or, The Wreck of the Pacific* was quickly translated into German (*Sigismund Rüstig*) with the addendum *Ein neuer Robinson* (see Hoffman 147).

Writers knew that Defoe had struck gold and tried to mine the same vein. Sometimes a publisher rather than a writer would rename a work to take advantage of the Crusoe popularity: *Der niederländische Robinson* (1724) was a renaming of the Dutch novel *Vermakelijke Avonturier* (1695). *Der spanische Robinson* (1726) was merely a new edition of Alain René Le Sage's *Gil Blas*, while *Le Robinson americain* (1851) was a translation of James Fenimore Cooper's *Crater* (Rogers, *Defoe* 23). Commercial interest outweighed ethical concerns, or truth in packaging. *Crusoe* captured imaginations around the world, and there are few places without a specific national Robinson, as denoted in book titles: the French Robinson, the Dutch Robinson, the German Robinson, the American Robinson; there is "The Austrian Robinson, The Upper Austrian Robinson, Robinson in the Pacific, Ivan, Robinson of the North, The Hungarian Robinson" (Hurlimann 105); "Every region of Germany—Saxony, Silesia, Thuringia, Swabia—had its own *Robinson*. In 1723 appeared a *Geistlicher* [Clergyman] *Robinson*; in 1732 a *Medizinischer* [Doctor] *Robinson*" (Robertson 209). Some of these are chapbook titles, but still they testify to the popularity of the concept.

Within the conventions taken from the original—food, dress, menagerie, living environment—there are myriad permutations. Robinsonades alter the physical elements of the story, such as the shipwreck, living conditions, exotic setting, taming of nature, available resources, number of castaways, and length of isolation; they alter the castaways' reason for travel, adventures before and after their shipwreck, experiences in isolation, creation of community, and ultimate reabsorption into the world; they incorporate discernible thematic aspects of the novel, such as the psychological and emotional stress of survival and solitude, philosophical meditation, and religious beliefs. Writers tried to make their imitation distinct, either to fit a niche audience or to distance their version from the original, sometimes for ideological purposes. Just to give one example here, Johannes Bachstrom's *Land der inquiraner* (1736) has a group of prisoners escaping inquisitional persecution take over a ship, hoping to sail to freedom in western Africa. The refugees are shipwrecked, scattered on a number of islands, and eventually reunited on a central island. This story shows the lineaments of the *Crusoe* story, but the increased numbers and the splintering of experience give a perspective different from that of the isolated individual. Interestingly, the survivors, when reunited, decide that they are still too close to the horrors of civilization, symbolized by the Spanish Inquisition. Thus, when they build a ship, they sail for Africa and hope to create an ideal community.

The development of the Robinsonade, not surprisingly, can be traced through literary and social history. Each period and national context chooses its own modes of imitation, adapting the novel's center to its own needs. While issues of genre and nationality are often prominent, equally interesting are moments when they are not. There is rarely a pure version of the story, since each Robinsonade can be read not just in the context of time and place of production but also in juxtaposition to Defoe's text and subsequent imitations. The preface to a French version in 1800 claims that the difference between the British and the Continental Robinsonade is that the British prefer the image of the isolated individual, whereas Continental versions have emphasized "man as a social being and the central interest in the family" (Charles Montlinot, qtd. in Peterson 47). This is a Rousseauvian reading of the novel and is not necessarily any more correct for the French Robinsonade than it is for the British. There are just as many common patterns among national versions of the story as exceptions. Given the intercultural, interlingual quality of the tale, the many permutations, the multiple editions, and the many translations, the argument that there are distinct national Robinsonades does not hold up.

The remarkable versatility of the Robinsonade across cultures does not, however, preclude a coherent structure for understanding developments of the form. To provide such a structure, I look at some of the national traditions of the Robinsonade, particularly British, French, and German variations. Many of the comparative examples might appeal primarily to specialized readers; still, knowing more about how *Robinson Crusoe* is mimicked can help students understand the endurance and influence of the novel, especially in a world-comparative context. Even a list of titles, a recitation of dates, or a comparison among Robinsonades in national literatures can provide a grounding in the genre's ubiquitous quality. Several other essays in this volume deal with teaching *Robinson Crusoe* as a Robinsonade (i.e., Barberet on castaway narratives, Stevens on the female Robinsonade, Lundin on the children's Robinsonade, Mayer on filmic Robinsonades), and I do not want to tread the same ground. However, I hope that the information here will offer readers and teachers of the novel a sense of the pervasive influence of the novel and suggest a number of classroom uses. The Robinsonade can be taught in straightforward background courses and those structured to suggest correspondences between texts and cultures and across representational periods. *Robinson Crusoe* is fitting in a national-literature course or as the starting point for an all-Robinsonade class; the multimedia forms of the Robinsonade can tell students much about the changing history of the idea. Students brought up on the Internet will be particularly appreciative of the virtual world that *Robinson Crusoe* creates, not just in the text but in the broad dissemination of the novel around the world.

British Imitations: No Man Is an Island

In Great Britain, not surprisingly, there are numerous imitations and variations of *Robinson Crusoe*. The first direct imitation, published within months of the original in 1719, was meant to capitalize on the success of the original: *The Adventures, and Surprizing Deliverances, of James Dubourdieu, and His Wife: Who Were Taken by Pyrates, and Carried to the Uninhabited-Part of the Isle of Paradise. Containing a Description of That Country, Its Laws, Religion, and Customs: Of Their Being at Last Released; and How They Came to Paris, Where They Are Still Living.* This was published in tandem with *The Adventures of Alexander Vendchurch, Whose Ship's Crew Rebelled against Him, and Set Him on Shore on an Island in the South-Sea, Where He Liv'd Five Years,*

Five Months, and Seven Days; and Was at Last Providentially Releas'd by a Ja-maica Ship. In these two works we can see not only the attempt to stay close to the original *Robinson Crusoe*—the plot elements in the descriptive titles—but also immediate differences from it. *Vendchurch* is notable because the cast-away is put on an island instead of shipwrecked and has a relatively brief stay, whereas *Dubordieu* allows the castaway a mate and describes an idealized and unknown society that hearkens back to *Utopia* and looks forward to *Gulliver's Travels*. In fact, *Gulliver's Travels*, despite generic differences, an expansion of venues, and a focus on travel instead of being shipwrecked, owes a great deal to *Robinson Crusoe* and perhaps even started as a parody of the adventure-shipwreck concept (see Braverman's essay in this volume). Defoe himself used the formula of adventure and shipwreck and survival in *The Consolidator* (1705) and returned to it not only with his two sequels to *Crusoe* but also in works as varied as *Captain Singleton* (1720) and *A New Voyage round the World* (1724).

Two of the better known eighteenth-century British Robinsonades, often still read for their literary merit, follow the pattern of hewing to the original but diverging in obvious ways. The main character of Peter Longueville's *The Hermit; or, The Unparalle[le]d Sufferings and Surprising Adventures of Mr. Philip Quarll, an Englishman. Who as Lately Discovered by Mr. Dorrington a Bristol Merchant, upon an Uninhabited Island in the South-Sea; Where He Has Lived above Fifty Years, without Any Human Assistance, Still Continues to Reside, and Will Not Come Away* (1727) refuses opportunities to leave the island and idealizes the solitary life that Crusoe never fully embraced. Quarll tries to re-create the state of nature before the Fall and glories in an Adamic, Edenic existence that deifies nature and avoids ambition. While there are Robinsonian conflicts with cannibals and a shipmate who becomes Quarll's Fri-day—as well as a pet ape named Beaufidele instead of a parrot—Longueville's narrative comes closer to More's *Utopia* than Defoe's *Crusoe*, especially in its sustained critique of European society, which is described as unhealthy and unbalanced. Robert Paltock's *The Life and Adventures of Peter Wilkins* (1751) combines elements of *Robinson Crusoe* and *Gulliver's Travels*. Shipwreck forces Wilkins to live like Crusoe for a time, near Antarctica, but then he finds hidden caves that lead him to the land of the Glumms and the Gawrys and is visited by flying Indians. The fantasy elements shift the narrative flow and sug-gest a hybridity to the early novel that would be discouraged in later texts.

The Robinsonade remained a consistent model throughout the century. In the British tradition alone there are hundreds of texts that center on a desert-island narrative. Here is a chronological selection of titles to suggest the range:

John Barnard, *Ashton's Memorial. An History of the Strange Adventures, and Signal Deliverances, of Mr. Philip Ashton, Who after He Had Made His Escape from the Pirates, Liv'd Alone on a Desolate Island for about Sixteen Months. With a Short Account of Mr. Nicholas Merritt,*

Who Was Taken at the Same Time. To Which Is Added a Sermon on Dan. 3.17 (1725)

Authentic Relation of the Many Hardships and Sufferings of a Dutch Sailor, Who Was Put on Shore on the Uninhabited Isle of Ascension, by Order of the Commodore of a Squadron of Dutch Ships (1726)

John Kirkby, *The Capacity and Extent of the Human Understanding: Exemplified in the Extraordinary Case of Authomates; A Young Nobleman, Who Was Accidently Left in His Infancy, upon a Desolate Island, and Continued Nineteen Years in That Solitary State, Separate from All Human Society* (1744)

Ralph Morris, *A Narrative of the Life and Astonishing Adventures of John Daniel, a Smith at Roylston in Hertfortshire, for a Course of Seventy Years* (1750)

The Travels and Adventures of William Bingfield, Esq.: Containing, as Surprising a Fluctuation of Circumstances, Both by Sea and Land, as Ever Befell One Man (1753)

The Life and Surprizing Adventures of Friga Reveep, of Morlaix, in France; Who Was Sixteen Years in an Uninhabited Part of Africa, and How He Met with a Young Virgin Who Was Banish'd . . . together with Their Surprizing Deliverance to Their Own Country Again (1755)

The Life and Surprizing Adventures of Crusoe Richard Davis (1756)

John Elliott, *The Travels of Hildebrand Bowman* (1778)

Thomas Spence, *A Supplement to the History of Robinson Crusoe, Being the History of Crusonia, or Robinson Crusoe's Island, down to the Present Time* (1782)

The Admirable Travels of Messieurs Thomas Jenkins and David Lowellin through the Unknown Tracts of Africa (1783)

Thomas Day, *The History of Little Jack* (1788)

Charles Dibdin, *Hannah Hewit; or, The Female Crusoe* (1796)

The Rival Crusoes; or, The Shipwreck (1826)

William Henry Anderson, *The Catholic Crusoe; Adventures of Owen Evans, Set Ashore on a Desolate Island 1739* (1862)

Mortimer Gilbert, *Six Hundred Robinson Crusoes* (1877)

This list is far from complete. As with the French and German examples that follow, there are hundreds of possible titles. All the works chosen here make overt references to *Robinson Crusoe*, usually in the title, and in their often strange yet self-evident adaptation provide an interesting map for the power of the original concept and the continuing influence of the novel.

French Robinsonades: From Shipwrecked Self-Reliance to Sentimental Longing

Early French Robinsonades followed predictable patterns; the imaginary voyage and the adventure story were predominant. When a French edition of imaginary voyages was published in forty-one volumes (1785–89), *Robinson Crusoe* occupied the first three volumes, "[qu'il] tient par-tout le premier rang parmi ce genre de roman" (Garnier qtd. in Gove 36; "as it holds everywhere the first rank in this type of novel" [my trans.]), and most of the other narratives are discussed by the editor in relation to *Robinson Crusoe*, including islands inhabited only by lovers, by Greek shepherds, and by troglodytes (see Gove 40). After Rousseau, although the adventure story does not disappear, the French literary models begin to focus on sentiment rather than on rationalized survival. Guillaume Grivel's *L'ile inconnue* ("The Unknown Island" [1783]) is notable because the author openly acknowledges the resemblance to *Robinson Crusoe*; he claims to have used Alexander Selkirk's history too, but he expands on Defoe's design and purposefully gives his castaway a female rather than a male companion (see Peterson 29), which according to one contemporary reviewer lends Grivel's novel "sweet sensibility" (qtd. in Peterson 30). Bernardin de Saint-Pierre's *Paul et Virginie* (1788) creates a sentimental island paradise where young lovers learn virtue. In *Histoire de Sudmer; ou Robinson Crusoé rétabli dans son intégrité* (1802), the anonymous author, deciding that all narrative interest is gone once Crusoe leaves the island, rewrites the story to tell of a castaway who never returns, "in order to stress Crusoe's courage, industry, and especially his trust in the Lord" (Peterson 47).

Other noteworthy French Robinsonades:

> Guillard de Beaurieu, *L'élève de la nature* (1763)
> Louis Laurent Joseph Gain de Montagnac, *Les mémoires de chevalier de Kilpar* (1768)
> François Guillaume Ducray-Duminil, *Lolotte et Fanfan, ou les aventures de deux enfans abandonnés dans une isle déserte* (1788)
> Lemaire, *Le petit Robinson, ou les aventures de Robinson Crusoé, arrangées pour l'amusement de la jeunesse* (1810)
> Madame Mallès de Beaulieu, *Le Robinson des douze ans, histoire interessante d'un jeune mousse français abandonné dans une ile déserte* (1818)
> Ernest Fouinet, *Le Robinson des gláces* (1835)
> Eugènie Foa, *Le petit Robinson de Paris, ou le triomphe de l'industrie* (1840)
> E. de La Bedolliere, *Le dernier Robinson* (1860)

The German Robinsonade: Education and Citizenship

The German response to *Robinson Crusoe* was swift and prolific. While many aspects of the story obviously stand out in the German context—Crusoe's education, morality, and middle-class background undoubtedly added to the novel's appeal—it should not be forgotten that Crusoe's father was "a Foreigner of Bremen" (5) and that Crusoe's real family name is Kreutznauer. To say that the German audience embraced the Robinsonade concept is to put it mildly; Crusoe became a German figure and his model one of the building blocks in the development of the bildungsroman.

Many German examples fit closely to the British models with interesting variations. For example, a 1727 German Robinsonade, rendered into English as *Gustav Landcron, a Swedish Nobleman's Remarkable Life and Travels during Which He, as a Real Robinson, Together with a Baptized Turkish Woman, during Twelve Years Miraculously Survived in an Uninhabited Island, and Besides, with Astonishing Perseverance, Suffered and Overcame the Most Terrible Fates until He Finally Quite Unexpectedly Could Reach a Real Happiness*, has the Robinson figure, near death, breast-fed for nine months by his female Turkish companion (see Hoffman 147). Three German Robinsonades remain well known today. Johann Gottfried Schnabel's *Insel Felsenburg* ("Felsenburg Island," four volumes of which were published between 1731 and 1743), which actually coined the term *Robinsonade*, was more popular than any other German novel for nearly forty years. The novel indulges in tongue-in-cheek humor about the many Robinsonades already in existence and comments on how readers are often enthralled by false stories claiming to be true. Set during the Thirty Years' War, the main character shares with Crusoe the sea travel and castaway status he experienced, but not alone; he travels with others who are trying to escape the social and political turmoil of Europe. They set up an ideal community as a counterpoint to the violent society left behind, and they have no desire to leave their island.

Joachim Heinrich Campe's *Robinson der Jüngere* (1779–80) proved almost as popular as the original *Crusoe* and was translated into many languages and adapted in many ways (including an Eskimo version serialized in Greenland, a modern Greek version from before Greece's liberation from Turkey [see Hoffman 146–47], and a Yiddish version that emphasizes the dialogical qualities of the Crusoe story as a sign of Enlightenment values [see Garrett 220–21]). Campe's work is structured as a pedagogical exercise, as a dialogue between father and children, and on a teacher-pupils model, in which the father describes incidents in Robinson's life, allowing the children to ask questions and draw conclusions. It incorporates Rousseauvian ideas about human development, but it disagrees with Rousseau's sense of Crusoe's innate resourcefulness; Campe's "younger Robinson" is shipwrecked without tools. He must build his civilization entirely with his hands and natural resources, and his struggle is meant to highlight the benefits of society. Campe also critiques Crusoe's seeming acceptance of slavery and argues for a common good as opposed to the insistence of individual will. Campe's Robinson, as opposed to Defoe's, returns to his father and civilization as a happy, productive citizen.

While the original *Robinson Crusoe* was written for an adult audience and often adapted for juvenile literature, Campe's work was intended for children but adapted for adults. A similar process of multiple audiences goes on with Johann David Wyss's *Der schweizerische Robinson, Oder der Schiffbrüchige Schweize-Prediger und Seine Familie* ("The Swiss Robinsons; or, The Shipwrecked Swiss Pastor and His Family" [1812]). The subtitle to an English version shows the balance between castaway adventure and pedagogy: *Adventures of a Father and Mother and Four Sons in a Desert Island: Being a Practical Illustration of the First Principles of Mechanics, Natural Philosophy, Natural History, and All Those Branches of Science Which Most Immediately Apply to the Business of Life.* The book that most Anglo-American audiences know as *Swiss Family Robinson* has been immensely successful, and the emphasis on education and natural history situates it as a Robinsonade seen through the lens of Rousseau's *Émile* but with Campe's sense of family authority. Still, critics reading the novel through the context of its history and not of contemporary popular culture interpret it as far from the innocent version adapted for modern audiences. Hoffman analyzes the novel as a response to children's fears of isolation; although the family has many adventures, its members never face the isolation and loneliness of an individual castaway, and so strength is found in the family community. Martin Green claims the story is a reaction to the French Revolution, that Wyss was a reactionary, "appalled by the bloodshed of the Paris terror," whose adaptation of the Crusoe story "reinforced patriarchy and justified by implication the patriarchal state" (*Seven Types* 51).

Other German Robinsonades of interest:

Der Teutsche Robinson oder Bernhard Creutz (1722)
Americanische Robinson (1724)
Heinrich Texel, *Der Holländische Robinson* (1751)
Robinson vom Berge Libonon (1755)
Emma, der weibliche Robinson (1837)
Die Familie Waldmann. Eine Robinsonade (1842)

The Crusoe Legacy; or, The Robinsonade in the Twenty-First Century

The primary development of the Robinsonade occurs in Britain, France, and Germany, but it has truly been a global phenomenon. It could not be easily categorized then, nor can it be entirely quantified now. Since many of the better-known twentieth-century examples are discussed in other essays in this book, I have focused on some of the lesser-known and earlier examples, to suggest the variability, popularity, and endurance of the form. The novel and its retellings capture the values of every age. It is both timeless and rooted in its time; each generation and each historical, social, and political context allow for a rewriting with the essential elements intact. In the modern age, the archetype becomes an antimodel, the colonial creates the other, and feminist or postcolonial *Crusoes* vie for recognition (see essays in this volume by Backscheider, Stevens, Barberet, and Zimmerman) against *Crusoes* that continue to proliferate in popular culture (children's books, film). There have been theatrical adaptations, from serious stagings to melodrama, pantomime, and puppet shows. Variations of Crusoe can be found in many popular incarnations, from science fiction novels to television miniseries to contemporary advertisements to pornographic films. Some adaptations stretch the original in ways that bear but a dim resemblance to Defoe's tale. As Michael Seidel writes, "Crusoe's adventures form the basis of everything from a jokebook to a cookbook; he even appears in animal narratives as a dog" (*Island Myths* 8). Even news reporting uses *Crusoe* as a reference point; often when a boat is lost at sea and recovered, *Robinson Crusoe* is invoked.

The Robinsonade remains a vital form, evident not only in past adaptations, which clearly strike chords for authors and audiences alike and retain both aesthetic and commercial value, but also in the explosion and popularity of contemporary *Crusoes*, several of which are discussed at length in other essays in this book, including Muriel Spark's *Robinson*, Michel Tournier's *Vendredi*, and J. M. Coetzee's *Foe*, as well as the many contemporary film adaptations and imitations. Few works can be said to have spawned their own genre or subgenre, but *Robinson Crusoe* fits that category. If many of these works, important in the period and culture of their production, are but pale imitations of Defoe's *Crusoe*, it is less an indictment of the form than a testament to the endurance of the original.

Robinsonade Bibliographies

An essay such as this one is deeply indebted to bibliographers, and in the case of *Robinson Crusoe* there have been many dedicated to documenting the traces. The first German bibliography of the form, Johann Haken's *Bibliothek der Robinsone* (1805–08), deals with twenty-six German novels, as well as two British, two Italian, two French, and one Dutch. Less than a century later, Hermann Ullrich's monumental *Robinson und Robinsonaden* (1898), which though incomplete could still list over seven hundred Robinsonade titles (including almost two hundred British editions, over two hundred translations and revisions, and almost three hundred imitations in multiple languages). It was designated part 1, but Ullrich never completed a second part. Geoffroy Atkinson's two-volume *The Extraordinary Voyage in French Literature* includes examples before 1720, and Philip Babcock Gove's *The Imaginary Voyage in Prose Fiction*, which focuses exclusively on 1700–1800, also highlights prominent Robinsonades (122–78). Many other bibliographies are interesting but often focus narrowly on national literatures, library collections, or specialized comparisons, such as the one compiled by Fritz Brüggemann in *Utopie und Robinsonade*, and most are not current. The complete bibliography of the Robinsonade has yet to be (and may never be) compiled.

Reading the Hermit's Manuscript:
The Female American and Female Robinsonades

Laura M. Stevens

Unca Eliza Winkfield, the narrator of *The Female American* (1767), begins the story of her life by observing:

> The lives of women being commonly domestick, the occurrences of them are generally pretty nearly of the same kind; whilst those of men, frequently more vagrant, subject them often to experience greater vicissitudes, many times wonderful and strange. Though a woman, it has been my lot to have experienced much of the latter. (35 [2001])

Winkfield's story is indeed an unusual one for a woman in the eighteenth-century Atlantic world: it involves biracial ancestry, education in classical and Native American languages, and survival on a remote island filled with strange animals and ancient tombs. To call it exceptional would be an exaggeration, however, for this story is an example of a genre Jeannine Blackwell has termed the "female Robinsonade," or retelling of the Crusoe narrative with a female heroine. Blackwell notes, "Between 1720 and 1800 over sixteen female castaways appeared in German fiction, followed by at least three French, three Dutch, three British, and one American variation of the genre" (5). Teaching *Robinson Crusoe* almost always benefits from some engagement with the novel's vast intertextual involvement. Having adapted much material from non-fictional travel narratives, spiritual autobiographies, and other types of texts, Defoe's narrative has exerted an even greater influence on countless literary and cinematic descendants. Presenting *Robinson Crusoe* to students alongside a female Robinsonade such as *The Female American* is an especially fruitful approach to intertextual study. It can open productive conversations in the undergraduate classroom about the early novel; the repetition and reworking of cultural myths; and eighteenth-century British notions of gender, religion, empire, and race.

The Female American, which is of unknown authorship, tells the story of Unca Eliza Winkfield, the daughter of an American Indian princess and an Englishman who meet in circumstances echoing the story of John Smith and Pocahontas. Orphaned by her mother when she is a baby, Winkfield spends her first seven years in Virginia with her father. She then travels to England to live with her father's brother, an Anglican clergyman. While sailing back to Virginia after her father's death, Winkfield is abandoned on a remote island because she refuses to marry the ship captain's son. The eighteen-year-old Winkfield encounters more favorable circumstances than Crusoe, such as finding an intact dwelling established by a prior castaway. Living for several months on the island, she Christianizes the natives from a neighboring island and then is discovered by a search party dispatched by her uncle and his son. She eventually marries this cousin, and, after he makes a brief trip to England for supplies, the two settle down to a life of seclusion and missionary work on the island.

I have taught *The Female American* alongside Defoe's *Robinson Crusoe* in an upper-level undergraduate course titled Transatlantic English Literature before 1800 and in a graduate course with a similar scope. Teaching this novel or other female Robinsonades was not a practical possibility until recently, because few have been in print since the nineteenth century. *The Female American* had been out of print since 1814, but Broadview Press's new paperback edition offers a convenient option for classroom use. The text's editorial introduction by Michelle Burnham frames the novel effectively for an undergraduate reader, and a series of brief supplementary readings helps students understand the novel in its historical and generic context.

Most of my students have found *The Female American* to be among the most engaging texts in the course syllabus, and they have been interested in approaching the text from several angles. Since students have already read documents relating to exploration and colonialism when they encounter this novel, they are eager to discuss how this fictional account was modeled on nonfictional travel narratives and missionary writings. The students have been fascinated with Winkfield's biracial identity and hybrid acculturation—truly unusual qualities in the protagonists of eighteenth-century English novels—and they have puzzled over behavior they view as inconsistent with her diverse background, such as her ownership of American Indian slaves. The text's idealistic but condescending depiction of indigenous Americans has interested them, as has the novel's complex moral stance on colonialism. Winkfield tells us that before her father first settled in Virginia her uncle warned him, "We have no right to invade the country of another, and I fear invaders will always meet a curse" (37 [2001]). Winkfield's paternal grandfather is Edward Maria Winkfield, a real historical figure and one of the founders of the Jamestown colony (Winkfield 24 [2001]). With the exception of Winkfield's father, the colonists do indeed come to a disastrous end, in an attack modeled on the Jamestown massacre of 1622. Yet Winkfield herself is the positive result of that violent colonial encounter. The child of an interracial marriage who exhibits stereotypical virtues of both parents' cultures, she launches her own campaign of Christian imperialism on the island's inhabitants. Accompanying the novel's initial condemnation of conquest, then, is a Christian fantasy that benevolent imperialism, emblematized by interracial marriage, is a path to global salvation (McCarthy 164–65).

Because this novel addresses colonialism and transatlantic culture in such direct yet complex ways, it has come to occupy a pivotal position in the course. Winkfield herself is a transatlantic figure. Her hybridity and multidirectional movement exemplify the interactions and reciprocal influences I try to convey to the students throughout the semester. This text also has helped me make transitions between separate units in the course, linking more traditional literary genres with less canonical writings and connecting chronologically distant texts. Although *The Female American* is set in the seventeenth century and imitates an early-eighteenth-century novel, the publication of this book in the decade of tensions preceding the American Revolution adds another layer to the text's treatment of colonialism.

When considered alongside the biracial identity of Winkfield, the timing of the novel's appearance suggests several approaches to interpreting its broader cultural significance. The publication of this narrative coincided with the increased appearance of both real Indians and images of them in Britain. During 1767, the year of *The Female American*'s first printing, the Mohican and Presbyterian minister Samson Occom was in the midst of a widely publicized preaching tour of Britain, raising money for the Indian charity school of New England that would become Dartmouth College (Love 130–51; Richardson). His sermons and public appearances presented Britons with a living example of an Indian who had been converted and largely assimilated into their culture. The large sums of money he raised indicated the renewed hope many felt that in the wake of the Seven Years' War more Indians might become both Protestants and British loyalists. Whether or not the novel deliberately took advantage of the publicity surrounding Occom's preaching tour, *The Female American*'s focus on missionary work and British acculturation presented the fictional embodiment of similar hopes. The novel also claimed American Indian authorship—at least in the conventions of novelistic assertions of authenticity—five years before Occom wrote what was the first English publication by an Indian.

Besides coinciding with Occom's journey to Britain, *The Female American* appeared at a time when images of Indians were being used as propaganda both for and against Britain's rebellious American colonists. These competing images were related to the broader phenomenon Philip Deloria has termed "playing Indian," in which Anglo-American culture defines itself by appropriating behaviors and appearances of Indians as noble savages. Deloria has noted, "Between 1765 and 1783, the colonies appeared as an Indian in no fewer than sixty-five political prints" in British newspapers (28). The Indian princess was an especially evocative figuration of America in Britain because she often was marked as an exotic sexual object and she thus depicted "the colonies as available and vulnerable to the desires of men" (29). In contrast, "Colonial papers . . . whitened Indian figures . . . and clothed bodies that had been naked when they first appeared in London publications." These "more chaste" images of female Indians became icons of threatened political virtue and plucky resistance to tyranny (30). Half English, bold, virtuous, and immersed in her father's culture, Winkfield would seem to be aligned with colonial presentations of Indian princesses, although other aspects of the novel suggest overlap with a British perspective. Comparing the character of Winkfield with depictions of Indians in contemporary newspapers can enrich seminar discussions of this text, prompting students to consider the political contexts of literature and to discuss the ways in which Anglo-American culture has constructed itself by appropriating American Indian voices.

The narrator's gender has tended to interest my students at least as much as her Indian and English identity and has provoked speculation about the author's sex. In this way the novel's anonymity yields pedagogical benefits because it prevents students from leaping into biographically determined readings of the text or making easy generalizations about gender. Asking students to consider the implications of imagining a male or female author, instead of simply debating the authorship, can lead to productive discussions of gender in the eighteenth-century novel. Janet Todd has observed that in the mid-eighteenth century, "Prose and poetry were considered firmly gendered, and sensitive readers could immediately tell the sex of the author. A woman writer was expected not simply to express her sex but also to call attention to her femininity, her delicacy and sensitivity" (126). Although such an approach could be problematic for less-advanced students, those with sophisticated interpretative skills and some understanding of eighteenth-century British notions of gender and genre might enjoy debating whether *The Female American* would have been received by its first readers as "feminine writing" (Todd 126).

The use of female pseudonyms and narrators by male authors of course was a standard practice in eighteenth-century novels, including Defoe's *Moll Flanders* and *Roxana*. Several scholars have explored the significance of what has been termed, with varying implications, "narrative transvestism" by Madeleine Kahn, "female impersonation" by Eve Sedgwick (64–65), "narrative cross-dressing" by James Carson, or "pseudo-feminocentrism" by Nancy K. Miller (49). A male author might write through a female voice for many reasons, for example, to enhance homosocial ties and facilitate homoerotic exchange (Sedgwick; Miller), provide a path to crossgender sympathetic identification (Carson 97), or simply offer a marketable commodity for a predominantly female readership. Kahn's analysis of narrative transvestism as "an integral part of the emerging novel's . . . investigation of how an individual creates an identity" (6–7) would have particular relevance to *The Female American* in a genre-based course, and any of these critical texts would be useful for a class on women and literature in the eighteenth century.

Whether or not *The Female American* was wrtten by a woman, it provides an important but unusual example of eighteenth-century fiction that is focused on women's lives. Through comparison it highlights how *Robinson Crusoe* makes use of early modern notions of masculinity, a topic that is often overshadowed by other topics in discussions of Defoe's novel. My students have spent much of their time examining the ways in which the castaway story changes with a female or a male protagonist, and they have applied these comparisons to a discussion about the difference between biological sex and socially shaped gender. Their interest in the roles that sex and gender play in the unfolding of castaway narratives makes sense to me because part of the pleasure of reading a castaway story is seeing how a human being might act when removed from his or her society and, when isolated, might re-create aspects of that distant world. As we read Crusoe-like stories we wonder, what conventions would and could we abandon if stranded on an island? How would we survive, and what would we look like after the survival? Reading a female castaway story along-side Defoe's text focuses these questions on the topic of gender.

The protagonists in Defoe's and Winkfield's novels often behave in pre-dictably gendered ways. Crusoe is more physically active than Winkfield and more inclined to alter his environment. Although Winkfield changes the cul-ture of her neighbors and orders the pagan idols destroyed, she leaves her nat-ural surroundings relatively unchanged. She also seems more capable of pa-tience and calm. While both describe unusual natural phenomena, Winkfield sits down for hours to observe a strange animal (101–04 [2001]). Although we know Crusoe keeps a diary, it is hard to imagine him sitting still at all for de-tailed observations, since we read about the exhausting regimen of farming, building, digging, and patrolling that promotes his physical survival and iden-tity as a civilized person. Crusoe, who uses a discourse of ownership more often than Winkfield does, says at one point, "How like a King I look'd" (174 [2001]). He keeps goats in captivity, while she lures them to her door to be milked. He fences in farms, while she gathers wild roots. Most striking, Wink-field avoids violence, while Crusoe does not. He fantasizes about murdering cannibals and later does kill a few, while she complains even about the un-pleasantness of killing goats for meat.

But however unpleasant the task is, Winkfield does slaughter the goats when she must. These and other events show us that, although *The Female American* presents a castaway story that is more suitable for a woman, the imperative of survival allows the novel to present unladylike behavior in a favorable light. For all their adherence to gender norms, these two stories reverse some of the traditional behaviors we assign to men and women. Crusoe, for example, is more domestically focused than Winkfield. He is more a farmer, while she is more a hunter-gatherer. Crusoe is much more cautious about exploring than she is, and he is far more dedicated to the "nesting" activity, however frenetic, of establishing a home. In certain ways she is also more courageous, displaying more presence of mind and less panic when events such as earthquakes occur.

Besides challenging common assumptions about gender, the female cast-away story opens up narrative avenues for women. Blackwell has noted that fe-male Robinsonades "creat[e] a new type of female consciousness and a revised plot framework for women characters living in the 'objective' world outside" (8). Because they feature women outside their proper domestic setting, these novels overlap with several contemporaneous genres: the female picaresque, American Indian captivity narratives, shipwreck and Barbary captivity narra-tives, stories of female pirates, and Gothic novels. Important differences exist among these genres, however, especially in the narrative and imaginative possi-bilities they offer female readers. Female picaresque and pirate narratives align adventure with immoral behavior, and captivity and shipwreck narratives link the adventures that their more virtuous heroines experience with physical violation, torture, forced marriage, or death.

Blackwell has distinguished the female Robinsonade from the *pícara*, noting that protagonists of Robinsonades tend to be middle class, law abiding, educated, and virtuous (9). Female castaways stretch norms of acceptable femininity, mainly because they have not chosen their circumstances, but do not break those norms. In this way they are distinct from more transgressive figures such as female pirates, who also were depicted by Defoe (Greene). While they do not choose their adventures and share with female Robinsonades a virtuous character, the heroines of American Indian and Barbary captivity narratives are more likely to appear as icons of violation rather than isolation. Robin Miskolcze has shown that "women came to figure prominently in" fictional Barbary captivity narratives even though "there were never any female British or American women held in captivity by any of the Barbary states" because they enhanced a drama of white, Christian, and Anglo virtue under attack from barbaric others (42, 50). Similarly, many late-eighteenth-century American Indian captivity narratives in English "degraded and effaced [the female captive's] body," with lurid scenes of torture, creating a racist and sensationalist drama by showing virtuous white women in the hands of dark brutes ("Communion" Sayre 51). Female Crusoes suffer loneliness and fear death, yet they are not in the hands of the enemy, although savages sometimes appear on the horizon or lurk on nearby islands. Winkfield is marooned because she resisted a forced marriage, but the threat of marriage ends when her time on the island begins. Female Crusoes are captives of circumstance, removed from the violating touch and objectifying gaze of others. In this way they present a fantasy of self-determination and heroism within limits, quite different from the possibilities presented by captivity narratives.

Of all these genres, only the Gothic matches the Robinsonade in expanding the imaginative horizons of female readers while meeting eighteenth-century European moral codes and adhering to "a new bourgeois ideology of femininity" (Spencer 15). Unlike the picaresque or the captivity narrative, the Gothic "took the heroine out of the constricting world of the realistic novel into an imaginary world of adventure, and widened the fantasy of female power offered by romance by exploring other kinds of power than that of heroine over adoring lover" (Spencer 192–93). Both the Gothic and Robinsonade genres generate notions of female power through the construction of dramatic physical spaces—castles and crypts on the one hand, islands and oceans on the other—that also imprison their protagonists. The pagan ruins on Winkfield's island, which include subterranean passages and tombs, resemble the interiors of Gothic novels, and the episodes involving these settings arguably count as Gothic interludes. Jane Spencer has argued that eighteenth-century women novelists responded to contemporary treatments in three ways: by protesting societal expectations of women, by absorbing those expectations in a didactic narrative, or by presenting "a fantasy that transformed the feminine position"

(107). Like many Gothic novels, female Robinsonades fit in this last category, since they use life-threatening circumstances and exotic locales to break away from conventionally acceptable portrayals of women without directly confronting them.

While eighteenth-century novels are well known to have enriched women's imaginative worlds by "making women central to their own stories" (Brophy 40), most of those stories remain rooted in the domestic sphere that was in the process of being marked as a woman's world. Women's stories usually are generated from emotional intrigue and the exertions of resistance to immorality, whereas men range the earth and experience adventures. If, as Martin Green has argued, "*Robinson Crusoe* is one of the most important genres of that huge literary form, the adventure tale," which has provided "the liturgy—the series of cultic texts—of masculinism" (Robinson 1–2), then it is perhaps fitting that some of the few novels describing women's adventures would derive from the Crusoe story.

Although most of the adventure stories generated from Defoe's novel have indeed been stories of boys and men, the castaway plot also has provided one of the only avenues for realistic stories of female adventure. I think it is no accident that some of the most fondly remembered novels young women have read over the past few decades draw on the Crusoe story. Some modern variations of the female Robinsonade include two Newbery Award–winning novels: Jean Craighead George's *Julie of the Wolves*, the story of a thirteen-year-old Eskimo girl who runs away from home and is adopted by a pack of wolves, and Scott O'Dell's *Island of the Blue Dolphins*, which tells of an American Indian girl, Karana, who lives on her own for eighteen years after she is accidentally left behind during an evacuation of an island. Several of O'Dell's novels show girls transforming into self-sufficient women through shipwreck, solitude, or survival in the wilderness. These include *Sarah Bishop*, the story of a girl who takes refuge in the wilderness during the American Revolution, and *The Serpent Never Sleeps*, in which an English girl lives through a shipwreck off Bermuda to play a pivotal role in the Jamestown Colony's encounters with Pocahontas and Powhatan. In Harry Mazer's *The Island Keeper*, Cleo Murphy comes to terms with the death of a sister by escaping to an island but then finds herself trapped there for the winter. Robert C. O'Brien's *Z for Zachariah* is set in a green valley, an island of life in a postapocalyptic landscape of death, where Ann Burden lives on her own for more than a year. Like Crusoe she keeps a diary, retreats to a cave, and is terrified but thrilled to find the footprint of a man who eventually will threaten her life.

Whether or not they take place on physical islands, these stories all carve out solitary spaces in which characters reach maturity through trials that involve self-reliance, innovation, and strength rather than passive adaptation to social norms and familial demands. It is fitting for the future of this subgenre, then, that Winkfield is stranded on her island because she will not agree to a marriage she does not want. It is perhaps indicative of the intense social pressures adolescent women must confront that there is an entire subgenre of coming-of-age stories that take place in isolation. The castaway narrative provides a vehicle for a female bildungsroman, or novel of development, that involves more self-realization than societal containment. However female Robinsonades end, the story of a young woman's maturation through the conquering of adversity supersedes a traditional plot of courtship, moral education, and marriage.

It is interesting that few film versions of the Crusoe story empower women in the way that much young adult fiction has. Although a few films from the mid-twentieth century such as *Wolves of the Sea* show girls or women surviving in the midst of physical adversity, there are few if any female equivalents to contemporary films such as the very popular *Cast Away*, which shows Tom Hanks fending for himself Crusoe-style. Commercial films seem to have taken the idea of a woman on a desert island as an opportunity for the depiction of standard heterosexual romance and scantily clad bodies in an exotic setting rather than for the exploration of female survival. Women are mainly sexual objects and not adventurers in films such as *The Blue Lagoon*, *Six Days Seven Nights*, and *Swept Away*, not to mention pornographic films such as *The Erotic Adventures of Robinson Crusoe*. The only filmic alternatives to the woman as sexual object in a Robinsonade seem to be the daughters or mothers in films such as *Lost in Space*, which derive from the *Swiss Family Robinson* narrative, or—in television—the competitors in the Hobbesian societies of the *Survivor* reality shows. If the castaway plot is any indication of broader trends, mainstream film and television lag far behind novels in the range of women-centered adventures they present.

Even in novels, however, the female castaway story is rarely a straightforward vehicle for protofeminist fantasy. Some early female Robinsonades, such as Marguerite Daubenton's *Zelia in the Desert*, use the desert-island setting for the narration of otherwise conventional, though improbable, events. When Zelia and her friend Nina are cast ashore in a storm while they are en route to Batavia with Zelia's family and fiancé, the two women do not engage in more physical exertion or display more resourcefulness than they would have without the shipwreck. An aged Frenchman, also a castaway, takes them in until Nina, pregnant by a man whose family forbade their marriage, dies shortly after childbirth; the Frenchman dies a few months later. Zelia raises the child, Ninette, in solitude until eight years later she is reunited with her fiancé, who had been marooned several miles away. After two years of courtship, the lovers marry, bear two children, and live in domestic bliss until the adolescent Ninette runs away to find civilization in the more populated regions she discovers in what is Sumatra. Ninette is rewarded for her adventurousness when she is taken in by a Dutch family whose son falls in love with her and whose acquaintance with Ninette's father makes possible a happy reunion. With the exception of Ninette's wandering, the novel does not really depart from the plotlines or characters of eighteenth-century sentimental novels. Aside from providing Nina and her illegitimate daughter with physical exile instead of societal ostracism, the castaway plot does little more than supply an unusual setting in which upper-middle-class young women act as they would have at home. The suspense of the novel lies not in whether Zelia and Ninette will survive but in who will marry whom.

Retellings of the Crusoe story with female protagonists can complicate the traditional dichotomies between male and female stories, but not as much as we might at first think. Had I taught *The Female American* in a more traditional course on the eighteenth-century novel, I suspect the class would have spent more time addressing the ways in which Winkfield's narrative both continues and departs from the domestic story lines usually assigned to women. Of English novels of the mid-eighteenth century, Todd has argued that "above all readers appeared to want to read of the young heroine, of virtue in distress made potent, of the chaste passive female woman humbling patriarchy" (145). The female Robinsonade offers a variation on this formula without really breaking from it. For all its extraordinariness, *The Female American* generates its island adventure from the standard sentimental plot of a young woman forced into an undesirable marriage and ends with a marriage between Winkfield and her cousin, an Anglican clergyman. He takes the unusual step of following her to the island, but the reasons for this decision seem to be more religious than romantic. Although their parish is Indian rather than English, the couple settles down to the quiet life of a rural clergyman and his dedicated wife, similar to the marital lives anticipated at the end of Jane Austen's novels. Even if examined apart from its colonial framework, *The Female American* provides a useful link in the history of the novel, especially with its variation on what Carolyn Heilbrun has called the marriage plot (48).

Reading *Robinson Crusoe* in contrast to *The Female American* thus can lead to sophisticated discussions about the transatlantic context of the eighteenth-century novel and about the narrative use of gender. A more ambitious approach, one that I have attempted in a graduate class, is to read *The Female American* as a text that both exhibits and explores intertextual engagement as a means of making room for literate women and their stories. Jacqueline Pearson has noted, "Between 1752, when Charlotte Lennox published *The Female Quixote*, and 1824, when Sarah Green wrote *Scotch Novel Reading*, a number of novels, tales, poems and educational works centre on full-scale critical analyses of female reading practices" (8). *The Female American* makes an unusual contribution to this late-eighteenth-century preoccupation with the reading woman as "not only historical reality but also sign, with a bewildering range of significations" (1). It combines an argument for the importance of literacy to female survival with an Anglican critique of Defoe's Puritan perspective. The unknown author of *The Female American* obviously is writing after having read Defoe, but he or she also is writing about the acts of reading and rewriting Defoe.

When Robinson Crusoe finds himself marooned on an uninhabited island, he is able to survive by scavenging the wreckage of the ship on which he was a passenger. When Winkfield is stranded on her island, she preserves herself by stumbling across the dwelling, supplies, and manuscript of a hermit who had lived on the same island for forty years and who apparently has retreated to die. The "wonderfully extraordinary" life of this hermit, as recounted in the manuscript, closely resembles that of Robinson Crusoe. Having spent his first thirty years "in more than useless follies," the hermit became stranded on the island, experienced a religious conversion, and spent the remaining forty years of his life in a state of pious solitude (72). The fresh water and food in the hermit's dwelling stave off imminent death, but it is the manuscript that saves Winkfield's life for the longer term. Containing descriptions of the island's geography, flora, fauna, and neighboring indigenous inhabitants, it provides all the information that a resourceful, English-reading castaway might need to survive.

And Winkfield is a resourceful castaway. As we watch her roll a locked chest of clothing off a cliff to break it open, leave lamps to mark her path in a labyrinthine tunnel, and convert the visiting natives by climbing into and speaking from within the idol they worship, we suspect that she never would have made the mistakes Crusoe did, such as carving a canoe that is too heavy to be carried to the water. In this example, however, we learn that in addition to being pragmatic and smart, Winkfield must have had experience in carving canoes. With her dual ancestry and upbringing she has enjoyed a life of challenging physical activity. Her ability to "shoot a bird on the wing," a skill taught to few eighteenth-century Anglo-American women, epitomizes this atypical background (49 [2001]).

Although her inventiveness is evinced in action, the font of her resourcefulness is her multilingual literacy. Fluent in "several of the Indian dialects," she also has been taught Latin and Greek (83 [2001]). Winkfield has read widely and wisely under the tutelage of her uncle, and this education guides her through exile. Calling attention to Winkfield's literacy could produce a discussion about the various ways in which Winkfield approaches the task of surviving on the island as a skilled reader. When she stumbles on the hermit's dwelling, for example, she is able to anticipate who the residence's absent occupant might be, because she "had read of hermits, who frequently retire from public life to enjoy their devotions in private" (57 [2001]). Besides studying the manuscript, Winkfield learns from several other texts. She has an almanac, with which she anticipates the annual arrival of the neighboring Indians (69 [2001]). By reading inscriptions in the Egyptian-like tombs of the island she comes to understand the religion of the tombs' deceased inhabitants and thus becomes a more effective missionary. She always has with her a New Testament in the original Greek, which she interprets with a sophisticated hermeneutics instilled in her by her uncle. In contrast to Crusoe, who sometimes selects biblical verses in a random fashion and then applies them literally to his experience, Winkfield remembers her uncle's firm Anglican warning: "Beware . . . of the practice of some enthusiasts of our times, who make the word of God literally an oracle" (59 [2001]). She also opens her Bible and finds a relevant verse by accident, but she reads the entire chapter, ponders, and prays before accepting the verse's applicability. These acts of careful reading allow her to flourish in and transform the land on which she has been marooned.

Whereas Crusoe first gathers tools and objects from his wrecked ship, Winkfield spends most of her time gathering and weighing written information to deal with exile. That Winkfield substitutes textual acquisition for material scavenging distinguishes her from Defoe. The replacement of the ship with the text as the means of survival also is suggestive of a complex imitative relation between *The Female American* and *Robinson Crusoe*.

Besides studying the several instances in which Winkfield survives by reading, upper-level students might be directed to the ways in which this female protagonist reads. For having taken her uncle's advice not to read texts as oracles, Winkfield adopts much of the advice dispensed in the Crusoe-like hermit's manuscript but does not follow all of it, especially the suggestion that she hide when the neighboring Indians visit the island. It is true that, as April London notes, "[m]asculine writing . . . gives way to female orality" when Winkfield Christianizes the local natives by "preaching through the mouth of an idol" (99 [2001]). I would argue, however, that she is emboldened to disregard the hermit's advice because of her wide and sophisticated reading. By departing from the hermit's advice when she sees fit and by weighing his text against other sources of information, she is able to improve on the model of the hermit's life, transforming a remote island into a flourishing mission. Likewise, the novel itself borrows from many more precedents than Defoe's story, ranging from travel accounts and missionary writings to domestic fiction. In so doing it exposes inadequacies in Crusoe's actions, such as his failure to convert more than one of the neighboring Caribs. Winkfield's evangelical labors may be an insidious form of imperialism, but her benevolent intentions and nonviolent actions highlight Crusoe's acquisitive and domineering behavior.

Encouraging students in an advanced class to focus on Winkfield's literacy opens up a range of possible interpretations of this female Robinsonade. Just as the character Winkfield subtly criticizes Crusoe's actions, the author of *The Female American* revises Defoe's project. For if *Robinson Crusoe* is the minute recounting of extraordinary experience distilled through one text, the Bible, *The Female American* is a meditation on the importance of reading carefully and widely, of balancing imitation with evaluation and initiative, in order to survive. Published during an era of worry that women could corrupt themselves by reading, this narrative shows a woman saving herself and the souls of her pagan neighbors through her ability to read and think.

Ultimately, *The Female American* is a story about both a heroine and an author who are reading and rewriting a hermit's manuscript. Selective textual appropriation takes place in a way that makes room for a female protagonist and narrator. Gender also becomes a fulcrum of intertextual critique. While Crusoe either does not know or will not acknowledge the degree to which his story draws on preceding texts, Winkfield is consciously intertextual to the point of competitiveness, suggesting that Crusoe's narrative is a male imitation of her authentic story (105 [2001]). In this way *The Female American* uncannily antic-ipates J. M. Coetzee's *Foe*, the story of a woman who has washed up on Cru-soe's island, survived to be rescued along with Friday by a passing ship, and then found herself written out of her own adventure story by the man the booksellers have hired to publish her tale. Coetzee's postcolonial novel calls our attention to the silences imposed by patriarchal and imperialist structures. These silences are spoken in eloquent detail by the text's narrator, Susan Bar-ton, and they are symbolized painfully by the tongue that has been cut from Friday's mouth. Although *The Female American* forwards no equally graphic image of patriarchal silencing, it delivers and perhaps seeks to profit from a similar accusation, that the male castaway and his author have stolen stories from their female or colonized counterparts.

Studying the difference that gender makes in a castaway story is one ap-proach to *The Female American*. In the advanced classroom, another approach is to explore how gender provides an opening for one text to appropriate from and rewrite—dare I say cannibalize?—another. The female castaway not only is a fascinating subject in her own right but also provides an opportunity to consider the ways in which intertextual reading takes place in the eighteenth century, as writers work amidst a literary network of unprecedented complex-ity. If *The Female American* is on one level an allegory of reading and writing, on another level it might be understood as a fantasy of writing taking place in blessed but lonely solitude, away from the borrowings and influences of others.

NOTE

I would like to thank the students in my spring 2001 class Transatlantic English Lit-erature before 1800 at the University of Tulsa for contributing several ideas to the writ-ing of this article. Thanks also to the students in my fall 2001 class Restoration and Eighteenth-Century English Literature for suggesting titles of modern female Robin-sonades and to Kate Adams, Thomas Buoye, Michelle Burnham, and Lars Engle for reading drafts of this article.

Contexts for *Crusoe*: Colonial Adventure and Social Disintegration

Everett Zimmerman

Robinson Crusoe is easily adapted to courses that engage central concerns of current literary study: for example, studies of colonialism, material culture's shaping effects, and the instrumental nature of much Enlightenment thought. In its New World context, colonialism is associated with the voyages of Columbus and the subsequent European settlements in the Caribbean and South and North America (Hulme 2–5). These ventures resettle subjects of a European country in order to manage the resources of the colony, including its indigenous peoples, in ways that profit the settlers and the colonizing country. Justification for seizing the land includes its putative vacancy, inefficient exploitation, and the cultural and moral backwardness of its inhabitants, who require improvement or, in cases of resistance, punishment. Eventually the New World plantations were a major impetus to the African slave trade, the demand for cheap and hard labor (on sugar plantations, for example) being far in excess of what was supplied by the indigenous inhabitants.

 Robinson Crusoe exemplifies these colonial practices. Crusoe establishes a plantation in Brazil on which he uses slave labor, and he is marooned on an island while on a voyage to acquire slaves at a rate lower than that charged by the authorized dealers in this profitable and carefully regulated trade. He assumes possession of a seemingly uninhabited island and defends it fiercely against the subsequent incursions of native cannibals. On his departure, he plans to maintain his ownership, leaving behind Spaniards and English sailors to continue the cultivation he had begun. In Defoe's continuation, *The Farther Adventures of Robinson Crusoe*, Crusoe returns to the island, orders its developing society, and ensures the continued subjugation of the native population. The implications of the discovery of a New World required a rethinking of European natural philosophy and theology (then the nearest approximations to some of what we now include in the human sciences). These newfound lands and their cultures and material circumstances were absent from the received versions of history and geography. Thus their relation to biblical salvation history—the Judeo-Christian versions of the development of the human relationship to God—was also ambiguous. Did this ambiguity signal a lack in these peoples or in the received versions of salvation history? Thus not just the status of indigenous New World inhabitants but also the thought and culture of the Old World became problems. Relatively early in the New World colonial enterprise, there were sustained attempts to understand the culture of the indigenous peoples in relation to a critique of the legitimacy and morality of colonialist practice. For example, Bartolomé de las Casas and Jean de Léry wrote of the culture of New World peoples and of the deficiencies and evils of

Spanish and French colonial administration in the sixteenth century. Accounts like theirs raise some of the prominent themes of subsequent colonial fiction.

What is at stake in critical accounts of colonialism is the nature and value of both cultures, and also their interaction. Each culture is tested and changed by the other. The eventual result of such interaction is at the root of the complexities of postcolonialism: the return or attempted return of former colonies to an independent political status makes recovery of a precolonial cultural status appear desirable yet almost impossible. Sometimes, years of colonial interaction and education created a cultural complex whose even partial unraveling can be achieved only through delicate negotiation.

An acknowledgment of the effects of interaction between colonized and colonizer needs to be extended also to the relationship between the observer and the observed in colonial narratives. However sympathetic to an alien culture, the observer-narrator sees details of the culture from outside their context. Such seeming objectivity has long been a matter of concern in anthropological theory (Fabian). On the one hand, it seems important to avoid the failure of understanding that results from an observer's merely repeating how an alien culture sees itself. On the other hand, an external analysis is determined by the observer's subjectivity: the object of attention is subsumed under the categories of the observer's markedly different culture, and how the object is described reflects the observer's cultural assumptions. Implicit in the notion of an intelligible encounter with an alien culture is the need for interactivity with that culture and the recognition that achieving an entirely external understanding of that culture is possible.

But the conception of a common human nature that makes possible an understanding of the other also makes possible the colonist and observer's implication in, even absorption in, the observed culture. It is the tensions related to this possibility that colonial fiction often explores. At one extreme we find what has been imagined as "going native"—a nearly full absorption into an alien culture. At the other extreme we find rigid, repetitive rehearsals and insistent enforcements of the behavioral codes of the observer and disciplinary practices that function as a defense against erosion of the observer's cultural values. Thus, the observer and colonizer's violence against indigenous peoples can sometimes be interpreted as a refusal to acknowledge an unwelcome affinity between two cultures, not an act of economic aggression alone.

Many fictional works that deal with the complexities in the relationship of colonist to colonized and observer to observed share thematic patterns with *Robinson Crusoe* (1719). Aphra Behn's *Oroonoko* (1688) rationalizes the slavery that provides labor for the plantations. Behn exempts her hero from slavery (in contrast to other blacks) by describing him in terms that assimilate him to European standards of appearance and culture. His deviations from Europeans are inessential except in cases where European culture is seen as defective. Joseph Conrad's *Heart of Darkness* (1899) represents the rapacity of European colonization of the Congo and also the deleterious effects of the Congo on

Europeans: the reality of European pretences of moral superiority is exposed in the example of Kurtz, whose program for civilization ends in his own descent into savagery. William Golding's *Lord of the Flies* (1954) traces the degeneration of a group of schoolboys on an island beyond the reach of the enforcers of their civilization's moral and cultural codes. Their savagery cannot be attributed to some external force but appears to be something released from them.

Robinson Crusoe's place in the history of colonialism is more apparent to us than to its original audience, although the proponents of empire were often aware of the inhumane goals and methods of their enterprise, even if the long-term consequences remained unknown. The cumulative force of the physical and cultural destruction that resulted from European imperialism can be seen clearly with hindsight, although individual instances of particularly destructive colonialism were recognized then as well as now. I compare Behn, Conrad, and Golding to accommodate the insights into colonialism both of Defoe's time and of other times. Although Defoe's book is appropriately contextualized in its contemporaneous texts, its significance needs also to be assessed in a longer historical continuum. Comparisons enable students to see interpretive possibilities that may not be fully realized in Defoe's book. Interpretive cruxes may then be seen as evidence of long-standing problems in colonialism and commercial society instead of being dismissed as remnants of the otiosity of an earlier writer or society.

At least since Ian Watt's influential analysis in *The Rise of the Novel*, *Robinson Crusoe* has been regarded as a representation of the changes occurring in the European economic and social landscape as a result of the advent of individualism. Crusoe rejects family and an established social position to make his own way in the world, eventually returning to England with a fortune garnered from sources outside the society he left, an illustration of the dynamic forces of emergent capitalism. As Peter Hulme has shown, such an analysis has been used in subsequent considerations of Defoe's book in the context of colonial adventures (175–222). After many years Crusoe returns to England as claimant to an island on which he has been shipwrecked. He is accompanied by his Amerindian servant, Friday, whose status as rescued or captured depends on perspective and thus whose seeming loyalty is produced by natural gratitude or inculcated subordination.

Analyses of *Robinson Crusoe* in the context of the history of colonialism tend to subordinate Crusoe's explicit religious concerns to the consequences of individualism and the development of imperialism. These analyses regard Crusoe's frequent reflections on his position in a divine order as manifestations of the presumed uneasiness of Europeans at their depredations of non-European peoples and goods. They assume that the economic and military work designed to satisfy European desires is being accomplished while conscience is in fact expediting this work by demonstrating European moral superiority to those dispossessed by force.

But the book Defoe wrote puts difficulties in the way of a narrowly colonialist interpretation. The religious structuring of the narrative resists the reconciliation of the particulars of Crusoe's moral system to the demands of individual-ism and colonialism (Damrosch 187–212). The retrospective narration assimi-lates much of Crusoe's story to important conventions of spiritual autobiogra-phy, makes a conversion experience central to the narrative, and attributes the preservation of Crusoe's life to providential intervention (Hunter, *Reluctant Pilgrim*; Starr, *Autobiography*). Crusoe's rationalizations—his according pri-macy as occasion demands to material advancement, self-preservation, or moral restraint and outrage—are those of a character in exigent conditions who must work out a balance among competing ideologies and practical actions in unusual, even unique, circumstances. In his retrospective narration, Crusoe's struggles with his past reveal the process by which judgment and interpretation are forged out of personal choices and not fully consistent ideologies.

Crusoe's analysis of his "original sin" reveals a complex interaction among differing ideological strands in his thought. Crusoe brings his regret at having rejected his father's advice to remain in the middle station of life into religious, economic, and colonial contexts:

> [F]or not to look back upon my primitive Condition, and the excellent Advice of my Father, the Opposition to which, was, *as I may call it*, my ORIGINAL SIN; my subsequent Mistakes of the same Kind had been the Means of my coming into this miserable Condition; for had that Providence, which so happily had seated me at the *Brasils*, as a Planter, bless'd me with confin'd Desires I might have been by this Time; *I mean, in the Time of my being in this Island*, one of the most considerable Planters in the *Brasils*.   (141)

Crusoe's use of the term *original sin* continues his practice of placing seem-ingly secular adventures in a religious context, relating decisions about survival and accumulation to an assumed providential structure for his life. Crusoe rue-fully estimates that if he had stayed in Brazil he would by now have been worth "an hundred thousand *Moydors*" (141). But this kind of analysis does not expose its moral foundations, resembling as it does a cost-benefit assessment. Crusoe then explicitly introduces the slave-trading voyage that led to his being a cast-away on his island. For the modern reader, this account of getting and spending provides an opening for moral judgment: "what Business had I to leave a settled Fortune to turn *Supra-Cargo* to *Guinea*, to fetch Negroes" (141). Crusoe does not, however, recognize the buying and selling of people as a trigger for moral judgment: "Patience and Time would have so encreas'd our Stock at Home, that we could have bought them at our own Door" (141). He construes his sin only as that of having abandoned a stable and profitable situation.

In the classroom, teachers and students are tempted to introduce their own varieties of providence into this passage. Even if we don't believe in provi-dence, we would like Crusoe to be punished for his involvement in the histori-cally demonstrable evils of slavery. Recourse to Defoe may here be plausible: Defoe would not have been unique in his time if he had acknowledged the evils of slavery. John Locke's writings were well known to provide support for an antislavery perspective: despite the ambiguities created by Locke's justification for enslaving the proponents of an unjust war, his work also made a powerful case for the inalienable ownership of self. Thus Defoe may be expecting the reader to see Crusoe's moral blindness. Even if that is true (and I am not sure that it is), there is no suggestion before or after the passage that Crusoe is willing to subordinate his need for cheap and hard labor to the rights of black Africans to their own persons. Crusoe's commitment when he is a plantation owner and afterward (in the time of narration) to the economic progress portended by the colonial plantation system appears to override any concern about the evils of slavery, even if they are recognizable from some other perspective.

A character's choices can be violations of our norms yet also be rationally motivated and defended according to their historical context, however multiple the ideologies that produced its norms, a context where our assured hindsight would require foresight. Reading a past text with historical consideration of a character's perspective is beneficial to us because it potentially yields a past that is complex and not merely a ratification of the present. Many more historical issues than those raised in this present discussion have been explored by interpreters of *Robinson Crusoe* (e.g., Mayer, *History* 181–97; Novak, *Realism* 23–46). Yet specific interpretive problems in a text are not necessarily resolved by historiographical reflection: for example, is slavery being excused in *Robinson Crusoe* only by the exigencies of the plantation system, or is Crusoe unthinkingly assuming slavery is acceptable? Students and teachers are not likely to be content with an exclusively theoretical insight into the complexities of historical interpretation.

Some practical teaching problems can be mitigated by the analysis of cognate texts. The advantage of a comparative approach to teaching *Robinson Crusoe* is that texts addressing similar issues but in different ways can be linked to particular times and circumstances rather than left as hypothetical formulations. While this approach leads to a regression in which each text commenting on *Robinson Crusoe* may raise equally difficult interpretive problems, the comparisons build a network of responses to related issues and thus suggest the complexity of the past and the limitations of any one response to *Crusoe* or related issues in it. Even our own interpretations and responses may not be final and definitive. By studying texts before and after *Robinson Crusoe*, we are creating an interpretive situation for ourselves that is analogous to the temporal complexities in Defoe's book, where the temporalities of character and retrospective narrator interact with each other. Interpretation must be focused and refocused to accommodate the ever-changing standpoints of then and now—Crusoe's pasts and ours.

I wish now to sketch briefly several possibilities for comparison to those texts mentioned earlier as contexts for our understanding of *Robinson Crusoe* in relation to the colonial enterprise. Even these few of the many potentially relevant texts may be difficult to include while meeting the other demands of a single course. (The explicit Robinsonades, retellings of the Crusoe story such as Michel Tournier's *Vendredi* and, most notably in our time, J. M. Coetzee's *Foe*, are not considered here because they raise somewhat different problems.) However, the following comparative analyses suggest important relations that might be pursued in much more detail in classroom discussion.

Behn's *Oroonoko* is set in an English colony that produces sugar using slave labor. Behn combines a discussion of the colonial venture of Surinam with the justification of a political order based on royalism. Although an evaluative structure based on class is reinforced by having the upper classes behaving distinctly better than their social inferiors, all of the English no matter what their class status are involved in the same enterprise—making profits from sugar-cane through the employment of slave labor (Frohock 451–52). *Oroonoko* directly confronts the racial issues implicit in *Robinson Crusoe*. The slavery needed for plantation labor is rationalized by distinguishing Oroonoko, the "royal slave," and his aristocratic partner, Imoinda, from other slaves who do not have equal birth, bearing, and courage. Oroonoko, later "Caesar" (36–37), sympathizes with the English king Charles I: "he had heard of our Civil Wars in *England*, and the deplorable Death of our great Monarch; and wou'd discourse of it with all the Sense, and Abhorrence of the Injustice imaginable" (13). He is represented as culturally superior to the native West Indians but is associated with their fierce warrior code, which causes fear in the colonists. The exemption of the intractable indigenous peoples from slavery provides a seeming rationale for the enslavement of those Africans whose nature is presumed to be adaptable to slavery. In contrast to the status of other Africans, the royal status of the titular character should, in the narrator's view, exempt him from slavery. As Roxanne Wheeler has shown ("Savage"), *Robinson Crusoe* too includes complexities of racial distinction—Moors, West Africans, and native Caribbeans—which have an important bearing on the treatment for Xury, Friday, and the African blacks who are made into plantation workers. *Robinson Crusoe*, however, does not modify these distinctions through adherence to a mystified respect for hereditary aristocracy. Middle-class Crusoe has no hesitation in calling himself king, although he may see some humor in so doing.

Robinson Crusoe is a pivotal narrative between *Oroonoko*, which foregrounds political ordering, and later texts that also include a powerful emphasis on the personal disintegration occurring outside functioning social boundaries. Behn's view in *Oroonoko* is that if stability is to be maintained in a colonial slaveholding society dedicated to the pursuit of profits, a hierarchy from aristocrat to slave must be grounded in a natural order; otherwise the forces for insubordination will have to be contained by violence alone. The references to the murder of Charles I and to the wrongfulness of the grisly execution of Oroonoko or Caesar call attention to the instabilities of English society as well as of colonial government. In contrast, Defoe's story of an island of despair visited by cannibals appears in many respects far removed from these explicit political warnings. Yet Crusoe at least cursorily ponders the basis of the society he is building—the legitimacy of its order and the sources of his authority. He is also obsessed with order on a personal level, as reflected in the tidiness of his storeroom and his mind. Crusoe has brought the values of his former world with him, and he attempts to instantiate them on this desolate island.

The cannibals conflict with the commercial values that shape Crusoe's moral and social perspective (Boucher 125–27; Lestringant 137–43; Cottom 157–60). They, like the warrior West Indians of *Oroonoko*, are an impediment to colonialism. For Crusoe, they also represent the obliteration of European moral boundaries because he will become one of them if his resistance is insufficient. Crusoe's interactions with the cannibals thus provide perhaps the broadest synthesis of the themes of the book, since the cannibals appear to threaten both his possessions and his morality, his external and internal geography. For Crusoe, the cannibals are both repulsive and fascinating: "I was satisfy'd I might sit and observe all their bloody Doings, and take my full aim at their Heads" (123). In an attempt to restrain his self-consuming rage, he canvasses the arguments against punishing those who have not attacked him, arguments that include legal, moral, religious, and prudential grounds (124–26). His restraint is temporary, and he eventually recounts the killing of seventeen in one party (171). Despite Crusoe's frequent moral reflections and restraint, we can see an affinity to Kurtz in Conrad's *Heart of Darkness*: "Exterminate all the brutes" (51).

Conrad's *Heart of Darkness* represents vividly the horrors perpetrated by colonialism in King Leopold's Congo. Just as vividly it represents colonialism's destructive effects on its perpetrators. Conrad regards the colonial world with its hypocrisies of those in office and deep alienation from customary values as sufficient to destroy the morale of even the well intentioned. But he derives the core destructiveness of colonialism from its inner complicity with savagery—not with indigenous savagery alone but with the far greater savagery released by colonial demoralization. Europe and the Congo are both required to make a Kurtz. The geography of the heart of darkness is that of the Congo and of humankind. The Congo represents the pull of desire away from duty, principle, and, finally, work. Work is for Conrad's character Marlowe the limited truth underlying the grander terms; as a shared enterprise, work is capable of subordinating cannibalism. Yet even Marlowe on one occasion "confounded the beating of the drum" with his heartbeat (64). Marlowe's situation is analogous to Crusoe's. Crusoe is barely able to rationalize, let alone justify, his murderous rages against his island visitors in the contexts provided by law and Scripture. His strategies of accumulation and accounting, however, provide an effective counterbalance to the metaphoric cannibal drums that call him.

Kurtz represents one dismal possibility of what Crusoe might become, whereas the "harlequin" Marlowe encounters (53) represents Crusoe's actual position. Going up the river, Marlowe's group comes across an astonishingly neat woodpile prepared for them in the wilderness. In an empty hut is one tattered book, *An Enquiry into Some Points of Seamanship*, which seems irrelevant on this narrow, uncharted river. Yet Marlowe's perusal of the book makes him "forget the jungle and the pilgrims in a delicious sensation of having come upon something real" (39). At Kurtz's settlement they meet the benefactor who prepared their wood. He is dressed in rags "beautifully" patched in many colors, making him resemble a harlequin (53). Although he has become Kurtz's acolyte, the harlequin also tries to restrain Kurtz. His description of traveling to the heart of darkness is monitory: "I went a little farther," he said, "then still a little farther—till I had gone so far that I don't know how I'll ever get back" (54). Like Crusoe, he is an adventurer desperately clinging to the bearings of civilization through work, neatness, and a book embodying real activities. The harlequin has saved himself from fully succumbing to Kurtz—but not perhaps from a disabling encounter with the knowledge that darkness lurks in the received abstractions enabling conventional life. In addition to his Bibles, Crusoe too appropriates "Compasses, some Mathematical Instruments, Dials, Perspectives, Charts, and Books of Navigation" (48). Yet Crusoe, like the harlequin and Marlowe, may not "get back": before Crusoe's adventures end, his "farther" adventures are adumbrated. However fervently he repents, Crusoe's life appears not to lead back to his father's house.

Golding's *Lord of the Flies* does not refer explicitly to the colonial situation. It does, however, explore the fate of human values in a situation analogous to the colonial one. It shows the psychic mechanism behind Crusoe's loathing and fear of his beast, the cannibals. We see a group of schoolboys rapidly regress from behaving with conventional respectability to acting like savages when they are released from the coercions of the adult world. They are stranded on an island as a result of the massive war waged by their seemingly civilized society, an irony that undercuts any easy generalizations about the values they abandon. As in *Heart of Darkness*, values appear to be ungrounded conventions without authority. Yet the gradual disappearance of those values leads to an increasingly violent and ritualized—as opposed to rationalized—society, with cannibalism as its potential climactic event.

Ralph, the leader who endorses and generally embodies democratic procedures and humane practices, has lost his position of authority because the boys prefer Jack's authoritarianism and the exciting rituals Jack devises, which are organized around obtaining savory meat. Ralph learns that in preparation for his impending capture, "Roger sharpened a stick at both ends" (175), a menacing statement in itself and also because it is associated with the ritual of killing pigs for food, an event that now prognosticates what is planned for Ralph.

Although the boys overcome the taboo against killing only gradually and with difficulty, they are eventually able to kill pigs without compunction. They are thus on the path to abandoning the conventions they brought to the island and are aware of the terrifying possibility that nothing is forbidden; they also have acquired the invigorating knowledge that they themselves may produce terror:

> The sow fell and the hunters hurled themselves at her. The dreadful eruption from an unknown world made her frantic; she squealed and

bucked and the air was full of sweat and noise and blood and terror. Roger ran round the heap, prodding with his spear whenever pigflesh appeared. Jack was on top of the sow, stabbing downward with his knife. Roger found a lodgment for his point and began to push until he was leaning with his full weight. The spear moved forward inch by inch and the terrified squealing became a high-pitched scream. Then Jack found the throat and the hot blood spouted over his hands. The sow collapsed under them and they were heavy and fulfilled upon her.   (125)

This description evokes a catalog of transgressions—against life, mothers, and sexual regulation. And when the devastation produced by Roger's stick is noticed, linguistic prohibitions and sodomy are added to the catalog of transgressions: "Right up her ass" is the phrase "received uproariously," followed by "Did you hear?" and a round of repetitions (126).

After the killing, the already-established bloodless reenactment begins. But as twilight falls and the boys become fearful, Jack adds a new element to the ritual: "Sharpen a stick at both ends" (126). The sow's head is placed on the stick, an offering to placate the beast that haunts their waking and sleeping imaginations, while they take the rest of the sow's carcass back for their feast. The boys' violence and the terrors of the beast are in reciprocal relation: the beast, as the now-murdered Simon tries to explain, is inside as well as outside (81–82). Jack had earlier outlined the concept of the reciprocal relation between terror produced and terror experienced: "If you're hunting sometimes you catch yourself feeling as if you're not hunting, but—being hunted, as if something's behind you all the time in the jungle" (47).

These books emphasize the need for a benign and effective political order. Yet each also represents the basis of such a political order as potentially arbitrary and irrelevant. Practical action and convention are the most persistently persuasive guarantors of social values, but they provide only a fragile barrier against the stresses generated outside the structures of long-established societies. Savagery and cannibalism appear as markers of the usually unheeded instabilities at the heart of a seemingly modern society ordered by commercial values.

Robinson Crusoe remains a central if enigmatic text in relation to colonialism. Studying it in the context of these cognate texts connects aspects of Defoe's book that are easily separated: discussion tends to isolate Crusoe's colonial depredations from his personal disturbances and rationalizations. The classroom contextualizing of *Robinson Crusoe* with *Oroonoko*, *Heart of Darkness*, and *Lord of the Flies* supports a sustained and specific interrogation of the connection between colonial ventures and their psychic and social costs.

Teaching Contemporary Responses to *Robinson Crusoe*: Coetzee, Walcott, and Others in a World Literature Survey

Charles W. Pollard

On the fourth anniversary of his shipwreck, Robinson Crusoe reevaluates his predicament and concludes that the island has become his home and the civilized "world" has become "a thing remote," exclaiming *"Between me and thee is a great Gulph fix'd"* (94). Alluding to the parable of the rich man and Lazarus, Crusoe views his old life as hell and his new life as heaven. Students in my world literature survey often consider *Robinson Crusoe*, the first book on their syllabus, in similar terms: while the book is perhaps not quite hell, it surely is "a thing remote," and they cannot imagine crossing the "great Gulph" between their own experience and Defoe's. One way to bridge this gulf is to teach *Robinson Crusoe* in relation to two of the richer contemporary Robinsonades, J. M. Coetzee's *Foe* and Derek Walcott's Crusoe poems. By examining how Coetzee and Walcott recast Defoe's enlightenment and his colonial and Puritan assumptions about life, students appreciate more readily not only the specific contours of that great gulf but also the surprising continuities between their contemporary postmodern and postcolonial culture and Defoe's world.

As a white South African novelist and literary critic, Coetzee understands experientially and intellectually the complex continuities and gaps between his world and the world of Defoe, and he explores them skillfully in *Foe*, his award-winning fifth novel. I begin the first of three class days on *Foe* by asking students to identify how Coetzee changes Defoe's story. They quickly respond with narrative details, noting, for instance, that Coetzee's Cruso (his spelling) has no chest of carpenter's tools that can be used to transform the island into a paradise, only a knife that he uses to survive; no goats that can be domesticated, only wild apes that must be killed; no miraculous barley that can be made into bread, only bitter lettuce, fish, and bird's eggs that must be eaten to live. These details strike them as a more realistic depiction of a deserted island, and we discuss the gulf between Defoe's providential realism and Coetzee's naturalist realism. We then consider how Coetzee's changes in the narrative call into question Defoe's optimistic view of human rationality and utility. Coetzee's Cruso keeps no journal to tell his story or to record his use of time—he has neither the tools nor the desire to write—instead, he spends his days clearing rocks from fields to make stone terraces, even though he has no seeds to plant in those fields. This image suggests the distance between Defoe's Enlightenment view of human work as productive and an absurdist's view of it as futile. Like a Kafkaesque character, Coetzee's Cruso says, "We have nothing to plant—that is our misfortune. . . . Clearing ground and piling stones is little enough, but it is better than sitting in idleness" (33). Coetzee's Cruso is no longer the optimistic hero of the emerging, eighteenth-century middle class but an ontological castaway of the twentieth century who stoically works in a world in which meaning seems ever-receding.

Indeed, as students are quick to point out, Cruso is not even the central figure of *Foe*. Coetzee shifts the narration to a woman, Susan Barton, who spends most of the novel absorbed by the task of trying to get the author, Daniel Foe, to tell her story of the island. Students readily grasp how Susan's character calls into question not only the almost complete absence of women in *Robinson Crusoe* but also, and more important, the cultural and material difficulties of a woman trying to write in the eighteenth century. Susan tells a wonderful oral story, but she is afraid that she has "no art" to write it down and that the "book-sellers will hire a man to . . . put in a dash of color" (40). While she resists losing control of her story, she acknowledges that she does not have the material conditions necessary to write—money, leisure, and education. With a nod toward Virginia Woolf, Susan complains to Foe that "to tell the truth in all its substance you must have quiet, and a comfortable chair away from all distraction, and a window to stare through; . . . and at your fingertips the words with which to capture the vision before it fades. I have none of these, while you have all" (51–52).

Coetzee historicizes this struggle over authorship in the context of the rise of the novel by self-consciously imitating different narrative techniques in each of the four sections of his novel: an oral account similar in style to Defoe's, an epistolary style in the manner of Samuel Richardson, a first-person narration like many nineteenth-century novels, and a concluding section in which Coetzee himself becomes a character and narrates two alternative conclusions. In fact, Coetzee intensifies both the self-conscious artifice and the gender struggle of the novel by having Susan and Foe disagree explicitly about the plot of the story. Foe wants a five-part plot that focuses on Susan's search for an imaginary daughter, whereas Susan wants a three-part plot that focuses on her experiences on the island. She even begins to fear that Foe will exclude her from the story altogether, concluding that it would be "better without the woman," a not so subtle critique of Defoe's actual novel (72). Eventually, Coetzee resolves the conflict between Susan and Foe through a sexual encounter that both reenacts the traditional myth of the Muse and reverses conventional gender expectations. Susan takes the dominant position in their lovemaking because she sees herself as the Muse who does "whatever lies in her power to father her offspring" (140). Similarly, she speaks of Foe as her "mistress" or "wife" whom she loves "for welcoming me and embracing me and receiving my story" (152). In other words, the female Muse impregnates the male author with the story—a trope that underscores the power of metaphor to change the cultural construction of gender. Coetzee's use of this familiar feminist strategy reveals the cultural and material transformations that have taken place since *Robinson Crusoe* and that have enabled women to become writers.

Students typically have strong opinions about whether Coetzee successfully conveys Susan's story and whether his metaphoric recasting of gender is a satisfying response to the history of patriarchy. They are more puzzled and intrigued by his representation of Friday. They recognize that Coetzee distinguishes his Friday from Defoe's character by describing him as distinctly African: "he was black: a Negro with a head of fuzzy wool, . . . the flat face, the small dull eyes, the broad nose, the thick lips" (5–6). However, students are less certain about how to interpret a Friday who has lost his tongue and who has likely been castrated, stripped of the power to represent or reproduce his identity through stories or children. It is presumed that this violence occurred at the hands of slave traders, but there is no way to know for sure because Friday cannot communicate. Susan tries to learn the story of Friday's mutilation through a variety of arts—teaching him new words, drawing pictures for him, playing music with him, and dancing next to him—but she is frustrated at every turn. She concludes that his story is "properly not a story but a puzzle or a hole in the narrative" (121). This poststructuralist language is intentional as Coetzee suggests that Friday's story is an aporia, evident not only in the triumphant "history of fact" described in Defoe's preface (*Robinson Crusoe* 3) but also in Coetzee's self-consciously reflexive and ethnically sensitive novel. The story of slavery is the aporia, in other words, of Western culture from the Enlightenment to the postmodern present. While poststructuralism is often criticized for undermining ethical or ideological commitments, Coetzee accepts responsibility for the historical and cultural oppression of ethnic others by expressing a poststructuralist doubt about the capacity of his language to tell that story without furthering the oppression.

Although Coetzee hesitates to represent Friday's story, he recognizes its power and offers some hope of Friday's being able to convey it. At the end of section three of the novel, Susan and Foe watch as Friday puts on Foe's robes and wigs and begins to write. He is only able to write the letter *o* over and over again, another trope for the absence at the heart of his story, but as Foe says to Susan, "it is a beginning. . . . Tomorrow you must teach him *a*" (152). Similarly, in the first of two conclusions to the novel, Coetzee becomes a character in the novel and bends down to Friday's mouth and hears a sound like "the roar of waves in a seashell; . . . From his mouth, without breath, issue the sounds of the island" (154). In the second alternative conclusion, the Coetzee character discovers the other characters of the novel submerged in the shipwreck of history. When he pries open Friday's mouth this time,

> from inside him comes a slow stream, without breath, without interruption. It flows up through his body and out upon me; it passes through the cabin, through the wreck; washing the cliffs and shores of the island, it runs northward and southward to the ends of the earth. (157)

In both these passages, Coetzee represents Friday's story as deeply significant in shaping contemporary culture—Coetzee hears the sounds of the island and feels the pressure of the stream that flows to the ends of the earth—but Coetzee remains ethically restrained from representing that story because his cultural forebearers, people like Defoe, exercised power over the Fridays of this world by retelling their stories. Contrasting Coetzee's restraint here with his willingness to represent Susan's story typically generates a lively discussion about the ethics of representation. Is it a viable ethical distinction for Coetzee to speak for Susan but not for Friday? Should and how does Coetzee's position as a white South African in an apartheid state affect his ethical obligations as a novelist? What are the ethical parameters of representing others' experience in both art and life?

Representing Friday's story as an aporia underscores the paradoxical presence of absence in contemporary fiction and theory. Indeed, the animating absence in *Foe* is the absence of God. Whereas Defoe's Crusoe makes sense of the world primarily through his Puritan understanding of God's providence, Coetzee explores what it means to live life without a metanarrative. Susan says that if God does write, "he employs a secret writing, which is not given to us, who are a part of that writing, to read" (143). Defoe relies heavily on biblical stories to authorize his story of Crusoe, whereas Coetzee relies ironically on Defoe's story to represent his characters' lives as contingent. In *Robinson Crusoe*, God controls the stories of Crusoe's and Friday's lives to bring them to salvation. In *Foe*, Susan gains the contemporary equivalent of salvation, individual freedom, by controlling the representation of her story: "I am a free woman who asserts her freedom by telling her story according to her own desire" (131). The difference between Defoe's faith and Coetzee's doubt is clearly a defining feature of the "great Gulph," but the common concerns that emerge from these different starting points—the importance of storytelling, the quest for meaning, the defining of self in relation to others—also suggest a strong cultural continuity about the central questions addressed in fiction. Coetzee clearly interrogates the aesthetic, philosophical, and religious ideas that underlie Defoe's novel, but he also respects the novel's role in initiating the genre through which he can explore these issues with such felicity.

Walcott also understands this cultural dynamic of simultaneously resisting and honoring Daniel Defoe. Walcott is the Nobel Prize–winning poet and dramatist from the brown middle-class of Saint Lucia in the Caribbean, an island located not far from Crusoe's mythical deserted island in the gulf of the "mighty River *Oroonooko*" (*Poems* 155). Although Walcott's education and early experiences were thoroughly colonial, he considers them a privilege, since, as he puts it, "like any colonial child I was taught English literature as my natural inheritance" ("Muse" 62). Part of that inheritance is Defoe's *Robinson Crusoe*, a novel about which Walcott has written an essay, "The Figure of Crusoe"; several poems written in the mid-1960s, "The Castaway," "Crusoe's Island," and "Crusoe's Journal"; and a play, *Pantomime*. Each of these works could be used to illustrate Walcott's reworking of different aspects of the Crusoe myth, but I typically devote at least one class to "Crusoe's Journal," a particularly rich poem that has become the most readily available of Walcott's

"Crusoe" texts in recent anthologies of world literature. This poem offers another telling example of the gulf between Defoe's religious and cultural assumptions and the burden and privilege of creating art from the legacy of those assumptions in the Caribbean.

I begin by asking students to examine the prosody of the poem. Walcott writes "Crusoe's Journal" in alternating lines of regular iambic pentameter and iambic trimeter. Such a conventional form may seem unremarkable except that the poem is set in one of Walcott's favorite liminal spaces, a beach. Slowly, the reader begins to feel the undulating regularity of Walcott's poetic lines, which conveys the cadence of waves rolling on a shore. "Like those plain iron tools" that Defoe's Crusoe salvages "from shipwreck" to make the island his kingdom, Walcott redeploys conventional prosodic devices of an "Old World" tradition to convey the unique rhythm of his "New World" island landscape and culture ("Crusoe's Journal" 2957). Walcott embraces Crusoe's pragmatic utilitarianism both because it is the best method for a contemporary Caribbean artist to use to create and because it is the historical method that the slaves used to survive the oppression of colonialism. As he argues in his essay "The Muse of History," "the slave converted himself, he changed weapons, spiritual weapons, and as he adapted his master's religion, he also adapted his language, and it is here that . . . our poetic tradition begins. Now began the new naming of things" (48).

Walcott's "new naming" includes a renaming of Crusoe, a controversial choice when so many other Caribbean writers were choosing to write from the perspective of figures who were marginalized in the canonical texts, figures such as Caliban or Bertha Rochester. Walcott explains the choice by suggesting that Crusoe aptly reflects the "elation" and "despair" of the contemporary Caribbean writer: the "elation" of being one of the first to be able to "name" a magnificent natural world and new culture emerging from the shipwreck of colonialism and the "despair" of being isolated culturally and ontologically by the legacy of colonialism ("Interview" 63). Walcott thus suggests a "catalogue" of new names that Crusoe becomes in this poem: "My Crusoe, then, is Adam, Christopher Columbus, God, a missionary, a beachcomber, and his interpreter, Daniel Defoe" ("Figure" 35). Early in the first verse paragraph of "Crusoe's Journal," the speaker claims Defoe's *Robinson Crusoe* as "our first book," both the first book set in the New World and the first novel in the English language. Walcott recognizes that this appropriation of Defoe is not innocent. He describes "our first book" as also "our profane Genesis" ("Crusoe's Journal" 2957). *Robinson Crusoe* is "profane" because it perpetuates racial and colonial myths, but it is also a "Genesis" because, like Adam, writers in the Caribbean have the privilege to name things for the first time, to speak "that prose / which, blessing some sea-rock, startles itself / with poetry's surprise" (2957).

Walcott transforms his Crusoe into another discoverer of the New World, Christopher Columbus, and plays with the religious etymology of the name

Christofer to develop an elaborate and richly textured metaphor of baptism—
the Christian ritual of naming:

> like Christofer he bears
> in speech mnemonic as a missionary's
> the Word to savages
> Its shape an earthen, water-bearing vessel's
> whose sprinkling alters us
> into good Fridays who recite His praise,
> parroting our master's
> style and voice, we make his language ours,
> converted cannibals
> we learn with him to eat the flesh of Christ. (2957)

Punning on the name *Christofer* (which literally, and for Walcott ironically,
means "bearer of Christ"), Walcott suggests that this Crusoe/Columbus figure
is a missionary of European culture; he christens others as "savages" and im-
poses on them his rituals of language and religion. It is a violent baptism—in
Walcott's imagination the shape of the baptismal font resembles the ships of
the Middle Passage—but it is baptism that has forever altered (punning with
altar) the savages into "good Fridays." The irony of this new name embodies
Walcott's understanding of slaves' strategic response to such a cultural baptism.
Slaves in Walcott's poem accept their role as suffering servants, which gives
them more of a claim to be true representatives of Christ. They thus transvalue
the significance of conversion to claim the power of the master's language and
religion—they "wrested God from [their] captor" ("Muse" 47).

Claiming power through strategic acquiescence also explains how Walcott
sees the relationship between Crusoe and Friday. When Walcott introduces
Friday, it is the first time in the poem that he suggests the possibility of an opposition between characters rather than a conflating of them. He employs his
pronouns carefully to distinguish between Crusoe/Columbus ("he") and the
"good Fridays" ("us" and "we") ("Crusoe's Journal" 2957). This distinction is a
small but telling way for Walcott to recognize the hierarchical relationship between master and slave and to identify himself with the slaves. However, he
does not leave the relationship in opposition. The slaves expose the master's
prejudices by ironically participating in another of his religious rituals, communion, "converted cannibals, we . . . eat the flesh of Christ". Yet at the same
time, by participating in the ritual together, Friday and Crusoe form a new
identity as they re-create communion in the New World, "*we learn with him* to
eat the flesh of Christ" (emphasis added). In other words, Walcott accepts the
coerced baptism of colonialism but also looks to shape the new communion of
independence. He recognizes the colonial stereotypes perpetuated by Defoe's
Crusoe but also claims the right to rewrite that figure to create a new independent cultural tradition for the region.

In the final verse paragraph, Walcott's Crusoe becomes more like Samuel Beckett's tramps, "posing as naturalists, / drunks, castaways, beachcombers," ontological scavengers piecing together an art and culture from the driftwood of various cultures (2958). In Defoe's novel, God providentially meets Crusoe's spiritual and practical needs on the island, and Crusoe creates in order to exercise dominion over the land. In Walcott's poem, Crusoe is existentially isolated with no assurance of God's existence, so he creates art to bridge that loneliness and connect to others. Indeed, the great gulf between Defoe's religious and Walcott's aesthetic sensibility is underscored in Walcott's conclusion. Walcott's Crusoe grounds his faith in art by "hoarding such heresies as / God's loneliness moves in His smallest creatures" (2958). Ironically, Walcott suggests that if human beings are created in the image of God and if his own desire to create emerges out of a desire not to be alone, then God must have created human beings in order not to be alone, which amounts to a heresy about God's self-sufficiency. Defoe's God shipwrecks Crusoe on the island to bring him to salvation; Walcott's Crusoe is existentially shipwrecked, and his salvation comes through an art in which he can imagine a God who shares his loneliness. By having the multiple figures of Defoe, Adam, Columbus, a missionary, castaways, beachcombers, and God merge in the figure of Crusoe, Walcott transmutes their accepted cultural contexts and thus reconceives their function in his tradition. Through this reordering, he wants to create a tradition in which he can affirm both his love for the English language and its literature and his love for the Caribbean landscape and its people. Walcott's Crusoe stands as a figure of the ambivalence of a colonial Western tradition, since he is a figure of both artistic ingenuity and violent exploitation, creates tools to survive and then uses them to rule, and saves Friday but then enslaves him. Walcott sees the ambivalence of Crusoe's legacy as an unavoidable part of a Caribbean literary tradition. He responds by reorienting that legacy in new contexts that reflect his pragmatic perspective on how best to master that legacy to create an independent future:

> So from this house
> that faces nothing but the sea, his journals
> assume a household use;
> we learn to shape from them, where nothing was
> the language of a race.   (2958)

I typically teach Coetzee and Walcott at the end of my world literature survey course, and their texts serve not only to illustrate the gulf between *Robinson Crusoe* and the students' contemporary culture but also to review and develop larger themes of the entire course. Coetzee's choice of a woman narrator complicates the feminist issues that have been raised in our discussions of Goethe's *Faust*, Mary Shelley's *Frankenstein*, Henrik Ibsen's *A Doll's House*, and Virginia Woolf's stories and essays. Moreover, students delight to see the connection between the absurd worldview of Crusoe in Coetzee and Walcott and their earlier reading of Fyodor Dostoevsky's *Notes from the Underground*, Franz Kafka's *The Metamorphosis*, and Beckett's *Endgame*. Coetzee and Walcott also question the belief in a just God in the light of the evil of slavery, a question of theodicy that the students have already encountered in slightly different forms in Voltaire's *Candide*, Elie Wiesel's *Night*, and Shusaku Endo's *Silence*. Walcott also offers his perspective of the postcolonial condition as part of the African diaspora, which contrasts engagingly with the students' reading of Chinua Achebe's *Things Fall Apart* and Coetzee's *Foe*. Finally, Walcott skillfully reworks themes and forms of the Western poetic tradition in ways that enable me to appraise and distinguish the salient points of other poets that the students have read such as William Wordsworth, Henrich Heine, Charles Baudelaire, and T. S. Eliot.

Coetzee and Walcott have written two of the more engaging contemporary Robinsonades, but they are not alone in the contemporary renewal of this subgenre. Muriel Spark's *Robinson*, Michel Tournier's *Friday*, or even Robert Zemeckis's film *Cast Away* all could be effectively used in the classroom to help students better understand the significance of *Robinson Crusoe*. The depth and quality of these contemporary works testify to the continuing influence of Defoe's novel. At their best, these contemporary Robinsonades help students achieve the maturity that Crusoe himself achieves when he recognizes the gulf between his contemporary island world and his previous life: "I gain'd a different knowledge from what I had before. I entertain'd different Notions of Things. . . . I look'd now upon the World . . . as a Place I had liv'd in, but was come out of it" (93–94). Similarly, teaching these contemporary works helps students see how Crusoe's world is still a place that they have both lived in and come out of, a place that remains useful because it helps them understand themselves by understanding their past.

Robinson Crusoe in Hollywood

Robert Mayer

The most striking films based on works of fiction are often those that clearly depart from the text. The best motion picture based on a novel by Ernest Hemingway is Howard Hawks's *To Have and Have Not* (1945), and, although there is something very Hemingwayesque about the behavior and style of the character Harry Morgan (Humphrey Bogart) in that film, the picture that Hawks made owes almost nothing to the book. Neil Sinyard has suggested that *Sunset Boulevard* (1950) may well be a more interesting cinematic reworking of *Great Expectations* than David Lean's 1946 film adaptation of the novel, which in many ways follows Charles Dickens very closely (124, 119). And Brian McFarlane, in a recent study of the move from novel to film, argues that "there are many kinds of relations which may exist between film and literature, and fidelity is only one—and rarely the most exciting" (11). The starting point for this essay, then, is the view that the best films based on novels are often not faithful renderings of texts but imaginative reworkings of them. The history of the adaptation of *Robinson Crusoe* to film demonstrates the tendency to transform rather than simply adapt the novel. This essay briefly surveys the films based on *Robinson Crusoe* that have been made in North America and in England and then focuses on Robert Zemeckis's *Cast Away* (2000). As many of the *Crusoe* films reveal, the book presents considerable cinematic opportunities to a filmmaker—voyages, storms, disasters, physical and psychological torments, encounters with exotic others—but it also poses undeniable problems, particularly what to make of the Crusoe-Friday relationship in the late twentieth and the early twenty-first centuries. Exploiting the cinematic potential of the novel and addressing the thorny problem of Friday and Crusoe have made for some interesting, even powerful films. However, the motion pictures based on Defoe's novel have often gone seriously against the book's grain; this aspect of many films based on *Robinson Crusoe* creates exciting possibilities for using film to teach Defoe's most famous narrative.

The history of the adaptation of *Robinson Crusoe* is almost as old as the history of film itself. There are cinematic renderings of the novel as early as 1903, and the earliest film version of Crusoe available in the Library of Congress dates from 1917. From the beginning, filmmakers adapting Defoe's text have assumed a familiarity with the novel based on the plotline alone that allowed them to loosely portray the story, leaving the audience to fill in any gaps. Thus the 1917 cinematic *Robinson Crusoe* tells the story in a few scenes in which an actor representing Crusoe is seen in silhouette against a changing series of backdrops, representing, for example, a ship at sea and the shore of an island. Like many other early films, this one seemingly aims to please by rendering the familiar in moving images, however crude those images may have been even in 1917.

Since then, Defoe's novel has served as the basis for short and feature-length live action films, cartoons, and animated features. It has been filmed in Russia, France, England, the United States, and Mexico, among other countries, and the character has been interpreted by Douglas Fairbanks, Jackie Coogan, Laurel and Hardy, Porky Pig, and Bugs Bunny as well as by less unlikely performers such as Dan O'Herlihy, Peter O'Toole, Aidan Quinn, Pierce Brosnan, and Tom Hanks. *Robinson Crusoe* has served as the basis for a fourteen-part serial about a Polynesian detective fighting saboteurs on a Pacific island (*Robinson Crusoe of Clipper Island* [1936]) and for *Robinson Crusoe on Mars* (1964) by the minor-cult director Byron Haskins. Renderings somewhat closer to the novel include *Crusoe* (1988) by Caleb Deschanel and one film by an indisputable cinematic master, the Spanish filmmaker Luis Buñuel. Defoe's novel has been adapted more than any other eighteenth-century work of fiction, with the possible exception of *Gulliver's Travels* (A. Chalmers 71). The reason may be that *Robinson Crusoe* is more than a novel; it is, in Ian Watt's words, a "myth of modern individualism" (*Myths* 141–92). The novel has inspired many adaptations mainly because its story is familiar and crucial. However, its fame and importance have also made it a narrative ripe for transformation in myriad ways, some comic and some serious, some intellectually or aesthetically compelling, and some thoroughly debased.

Three of the most important Crusoe films (which I discuss in detail in "Three Cinematic Robinsonades")—Buñuel's *Adventures of Robinson Crusoe* (1952), Jack Gold's *Man Friday* (1975), and Deschanel's *Crusoe*—reveal the problematic character of the novel for filmmakers in the last fifty years. Of these films, only Buñuel's could be regarded as a faithful rendering of Defoe's novel, and even his movie blatantly works against values and beliefs frequently associated with the book, such as its Puritan religiosity and its celebration of the "middle State" as "the best State in the World" (5). All three films, furthermore, are troubled by the Crusoe-Friday pairing. Whereas earlier films, including the Fairbanks vehicle, *Mr. Robinson Crusoe* (1932), frequently highlighted Friday and Crusoe by being egregiously racist, the motion pictures by Buñuel, Gold, and Deschanel embody critiques of the pairing and refigure the relationship between the Occidental master and the non-Western other (Mayer, "Robinsonades"). The three films focus our attention on race or ethnicity. Friday is of African descent in Gold's and Deschanel's films and is an Indian in Buñuel's picture, made in Mexico. Thus in all three movies Friday is a representative of a prime racial or ethnic other in the society in which the film was made. Also, the three films call into question Crusoe's view of Friday as his natural subject; indeed, they rework the Crusoe narrative by representing his relations with Friday as an index of Crusoe's need for (or, in Gold's *Man Friday*, his inability to achieve) spiritual and moral growth.

Zemeckis's film, *Cast Away*, which is based on a screenplay by William Broyles, Jr. (who also wrote the Hanks hit *Apollo 13* and had a hand in writing the recent *Planet of the Apes*), also transforms the Crusoe story. A simultaneously thoughtful and compelling reflection on the Crusoe myth and a Hollywood romance, the film plays it safe by focusing on a love story but takes great risks by daring to be something akin to a silent movie through more than half of its playing time. *Cast Away* treats the Crusoe figure as a representative of economic man by telling the story of Chuck Noland (Hanks), a systems-operational engineer working for Federal Express, whom the audience first sees in Moscow as he tries to instill the values of the 1990s multinational corporation into Russian FedEx employees. Noland tells the Russians "we live or we die by the clock" and declares "we must never allow ourselves the sin of losing track of time." He is seen on Red Square, oblivious to the setting because he is concerned with finishing "the sort" in time to return to Memphis with the packages that are his sacred responsibility. Time, then, is crucial in this film as it has been in many of Zemeckis's pictures, including *Back to the Future* and *Contact*. In *Cast Away*, time is at first equated with money. However, Noland's plane goes down in a storm in the South Pacific, and he drifts in a raft to a deserted island, where he discovers his watch and his beeper have stopped working. He must therefore learn and adjust to a new sense of time, one dependent on the sun and moon, the seasons, and tides. Implicit in these developments is a muted critique of contemporary American life, dominated by a faith in entrepreneurial capitalism and peopled by workaholics. Before the crash, Noland exemplifies such capitalist values. For example, he is called away from a Christmas dinner, where he is ensconced in the large, jovial family of his girlfriend, Kelly Frears (Helen Hunt); the look on Kelly's face when she realizes he must leave bespeaks resignation mingled with a hint of reproach. His constant comings and goings clearly threaten their relationship; late in the film, when Noland returns to Memphis after four years on the island to find Kelly married and with a child, he tells her, "I never should have gotten on that plane." Zemeckis's film thus evokes Crusoe's father's "[c]ounsel against" (4) his son's becoming a man "of aspiring, superior Fortunes . . . who went abroad upon Adventures" (5) and the father's injunction to his son to remain at home and embrace the safety and well-being of "the middle Station of Life" (5).

Zemeckis and others engaged in making this film have declared their belief that *Cast Away* is about Noland's "spiritual journey." Hanks, for example, argues that Noland's ordeal on the island is "the best thing that ever happened to this guy" (*Making*), presumably because it taught him that he "never should have gotten on that plane," that human relations are more important than watching the clock and counting packages. Noland's journey, however, is not a religious one; when the body of one of the plane's crew members washes ashore, Noland buries him but says no prayers and in fact rejects (with a shrug) the idea of prayer as pointless. In short, if the film is preoccupied with the hero's "spiritual journey," it treats that phenomenon by focusing on and, like Defoe's narrative, being deeply fascinated by the particulars of the castaway's ordeal.

From the moment the plane crashes until after Noland is rescued, Hanks is the only actor in the film. Furthermore, although it features a rich soundtrack, the movie dispenses with music while Noland is on the island, underlining his isolation and the challenges he faces through the sound of waves, wind in the trees, thunder, and Noland's own voice. Noland speaks mainly to himself and Wilson, the Friday of this film (about which more shortly). For well over an hour the film consists primarily of the camera's observation of Noland's experience: his body, covered with sweat, wounds, and dirt; his hair, growing longer and more tangled; his shedding of fifty or more pounds (shooting on the film was suspended for more than a year while Hanks slimmed down); his discovery of how to make fire and primitive tools; his struggle to find food and potable water; his extraction of an aching tooth; and his building of a raft and eventual escape. David Denby in the *New Yorker* declares that the focus of the film is in fact Hanks's body, and in a way he is right. Hanks, however, simply becomes the most prominent element in the mise-en-scène in a film that suggests the harrowing nature of a castaway's ordeal.

Noland's psychic torment—the film's rendering of this Crusoe's experience on what the novel's hero calls his "*Island of Despair*" (52)—is mainly registered through his relationship with Wilson, the volleyball that takes on human qualities when the mark of Noland's bleeding hand imprints something like a human face on it. This reimagining of Friday works in at least two distinct ways. First, because Noland imparts a personality to the ball and talks to, quarrels with, and seems harried by it, Friday here becomes a projection of the film's Crusoe. Wilson clearly emanates from Noland's profound loneliness and his need for human company. It is only after the four-year gap in the film's treatment of Noland's life on the island, when we see that Noland is emotionally and psychologically shaky, that the relationship between Wilson and Noland becomes important. This single-sided Crusoe-Friday relationship, seen from the viewpoint of the deeply disturbed hero, is nonetheless credible because of Hanks's acting and the many shots of the volleyball in the midst of Noland's colloquies with it.

A second effect of the film's representation of Friday as a product of Crusoe's torment is its erasing of him from the narrative. Whereas earlier films critiqued the Crusoe-Friday relationship, *Cast Away* addresses the relationship by sweeping it aside, and in the process removes the non-Western other who has always been a crucial part of the Crusoe myth. This act of erasure might be seen as the filmmakers' solution to the problem of Friday because it critiques Crusoe's racist aspect by depriving Crusoe of the savage whom he dominates in other versions of the story. However, it might also be seen as a more insidious act, a dispensing with the troublesome savage in favor of a rendering of the myth that shows that the world beyond the metropolitan center has been emptied of any impediments to its occupation. Perhaps even worse, Wilson may be seen not as an erasure but as a transformation of the exotic other in the Crusoe myth—given a savage aspect by the wild hair at the top of the ball, resulting apparently from the volleyball's having been cut or torn—into a true object, something that can be thrown away, tied down, or otherwise subjected to

Noland's will. Interestingly, however, no matter how much of an object Wilson may seem to be, Noland clearly loves and needs the other with whom he shares his island.

Whether Wilson strikes one as a solution to or as a serious deepening of the problem of Friday, there is no question that Wilson is a striking revision of Defoe's narrative. Films like Zemeckis's (and the other Crusoe films discussed here) thus demonstrate that making a motion picture based on a novel often involves something more like transformation or metamorphosis than adaptation (Bluestone). Such malleability makes these films particularly valuable to scholars and teachers who may want to use cinema to heighten their own and their students' understanding of the novel. Most of these films are so much at odds with the novel that they cannot be used as a substitute for it. Buñuel's film is in some ways a faithful rendering of the book, but Gillian Parker has rightly observed that "Defoe used the experience of the island shipwreck to tell one story, Buñuel to tell another" (16). Thus students can use the films to see the book itself more clearly and to understand how it has been understood and transformed in our time, but they cannot use them as a shortcut to experiencing Defoe's novel.

Instead, the films, as pedagogical tools, work best as a series of sharp contrasts with the text. Several of the cinematic adaptations, for example, treat the sexual component of Crusoe's torment, thus putting the motion pictures at odds with the novel, which leaves sex out and therefore, according to James Joyce, embodies the "sexual apathy" of the Anglo-Saxons (323). Both Buñuel's *Robinson Crusoe* and Gold's *Man Friday*, furthermore, depict only Crusoe's experience on the island, thereby eliminating his connections to the larger world and his family, although Buñuel does introduce Crusoe's father in a nightmare that marks his most striking addition to the narrative. *Cast Away*, the film that most heavily revises the Crusoe story by setting it in contemporary America and introducing a love story, offers an ending very different from the one in the novel. Zemeckis's ending, which emphasizes Noland's loneliness and isolation even after his return from the island, is a fascinating refusal to make a typical Hollywood picture and is, therefore, a serious reflection on Defoe's text. Noland does not win Kelly back (unlike Cary Grant in the 1940 comedy *My Favorite Wife*, who is reunited with Irene Dunne seven years after she was shipwrecked), and at the end of the film he is "at sea" again, although this time the oceanic expanse in which we see him is not the Pacific but the Texas Panhandle. Noland may be headed to a new romance (with a beautiful sculptor whose FedEx package he has kept intact while on the island as a talisman meant to ensure his return and which he returns to her home near the end of the film), but he may also be headed on to "farther adventures." In the last scene he is at a crossroads, and his fate is uncertain; the film thus dispenses with a traditional happy ending and at the same time rethinks the nature of Crusoe's persistent "wandring Inclination" (4), apparently attributing it to deep loneliness that overtakes him on the island.

Revisions, then, are the norm and not the exception in the filmography of *Robinson Crusoe*. The Crusoe films, taken together, offer a series of illuminating crosslights on the book. Classes might use several different filmic versions of Defoe's novel in combination, either as a way of concluding and extending their consideration of the novel or as part of a discussion of the process of moving from fiction to film. Several films viewed together, each one perhaps presented to a class by individual students or groups of students, can yield insights on Defoe's and the filmmakers' treatment of Crusoe's ordeal, his attempted "Master[y] of every mechanick Art" (51), his sexuality, his piety or lack thereof, his sense of time, his wanderlust and love of things, his links to his family and the outside world, and his relationship with Friday—all key elements in the complicated and rich Crusoe myth. Cinematic adaptations of the novel focus our attention on how the Crusoe myth is constructed in Defoe's text and how it functioned in his world and can also illuminate the ways in which the story has been read and transformed in our own day. Film thus potentially helps students of *Robinson Crusoe* achieve a richer view of the novel than they might otherwise attain if they only see it in terms of its early modern contexts.

Teaching *Robinson Crusoe* in the Introduction to Literature Course

Christina Sassi-Lehner

Why teach *Robinson Crusoe* in an introduction to literature course for nontraditional, multicultural, urban college students? How can it be taught in a way to make this early-eighteenth-century novel immediately relevant and engaging to adult students who do not as a whole have much of a literary background and who rarely—if ever—read novels outside the classroom? I had to address these questions when I decided to include the book as the one novel that we would read in the required seminar entitled Modes of Analysis, designed to introduce undergraduates to critical readings of poems, short stories, one play, and one novel.

I always begin the first day of class by having students write responses to a questionnaire about their educational background, their prior experiences with reading and writing about literature, their strengths and weaknesses as writers, and their favorite author or book. Over the years I have learned that they prefer to read self-help and self-improvement guides, followed by romance novels and thrillers of the Danielle Steele and Stephen King variety. It was their preference for popular self-help books that led me to choose *Robinson Crusoe* as the one novel that we read. I have found it useful to focus on the novel as a mythic archetype of self-invention, and I suggest to them that this is one of the reasons Crusoe's story is so compelling. In this sense we may read Crusoe as the ultimate self-made man who forges for himself an identity and a life that are in direct opposition to the steady, stolid, middle-class existence that his father had intended for him. Whether because of inner compulsion or providential design (both possibilities are entertained by the main character), Crusoe embarks on a life of great variety and extraordinary adventure that tests his most deeply held beliefs, his ingenuity, his survival skills, and his will to dominate his surroundings and succeed economically. From this angle, I try to show students how *Robinson Crusoe* in particular, and imaginative literature in general, takes hold of us, gives us pleasure, and seems to fulfill a fundamental need for moral and spiritual guidance and enrichment. I also remark that if we are to read only one novel in this course, why not choose one of the earliest in the English language by one of the founders of the novel, a work that has become mythologized over time and that has passed into popular culture across the globe. (Indeed, although none of my students had read the novel, all of them knew of it—many thought that it was a children's book—and were familiar with Crusoe's story.) What is it about this book and the telling of Crusoe's story that has taken such a powerful hold on our imaginations from the first moment of its appearance in print in 1719 to the present?

My classes were composed of returning students anywhere from age twenty to sixty-five and from many different ethnic backgrounds. Almost all of them had families to support and consequently worked full-time. They also had in common maturity and seriousness of purpose as they prepared themselves for careers in the social services. Our seminar met once a week for four hours over the course of fifteen weeks. I encouraged students to begin reading *Robinson Crusoe* early in the semester since we would be covering the book during weeks 9 through 11, at which time they would have to read roughly one hundred pages each week. Most were daunted by the prospect of this reading load and took my advice. Some students began reading the novel on their own, got as far as the first two or three pages, and by the next class announced that they did not like it because they found it difficult to read. In particular, they wanted to know why so many words were capitalized and asked why I had chosen a book written in "old English."

I taught this course for four semesters, and each class initially reacted negatively to the book: students found the diction frustrating and the long paragraph-length sentences hard to follow. Many became defensive. I reassured them that once they became accustomed to certain orthographic features of early-eighteenth-century writing, they would read with greater ease and soon get caught up with the story. The first time I said this I was only hoping that reading would get easier for them, but in successive classes I always found my statement to be true.

The students' questions gave me the opportunity to talk about the development of the English language and the beginning of the English novel. I explained to them that the book was not written in Old English, a Germanic language that one could not read and understand without study and application. I brought in a book of autograph manuscripts for them to see how Old English, Middle English, and early modern English texts looked. The students were fascinated by the significant changes in the language's forms; I now always introduce students to such manuscripts, which never fail to spur a lively discussion about the rationale for spellings of words today that retain their earliest forms but not their original pronunciation. My ESL students found this particularly interesting because it explained why they find the spelling of such words as *light* and *night* strange and difficult. We also discussed influences changing the language and creating new words today: advances in technology, medicine, and communications and the use of the popular slang terms. I noted the importance of the dictionary in establishing and stabilizing words and the rules of usage and explained that because Defoe lived before Samuel Johnson published the first authoritative dictionary in the English language, his spelling, like that of other authors of his time, was erratic. All of this, of course, is a departure from *Robinson Crusoe* itself, but it is a wonderful, exciting, and useful excursus for students new to English-language studies or to Western culture. That *Crusoe* readily lends itself to a discussion of how language evolves is one of the reasons this novel works well in an introductory genre course for the students that I teach.

As an introduction to the novel, I discuss Defoe's life, emphasizing his modern education, multifarious professional involvements, bankruptcies, and prolific—and disputed—literary output. I provide some historical background and discuss the cultural contexts for the emergence of the novel as the dominant literary genre. We begin with a close reading of the preface and the claims made by the purported editor of Crusoe's autobiography. Many of my students are deeply religious, know their Bible well, and immediately read the book as spiritual autobiography or religious allegory: Crusoe's wrestling with his conscience, his interpretations of the events that befall him—such as his resistance to his father's wishes and his reaction to his first storm at sea—become symbolic of the human condition and the journeys that each of us makes through life. My students relate to such symbolism naturally, instinctively, and so enthusiastically that I am always amazed at Defoe's extraordinary ability to reach readers and move them on such a visceral level. Without any prompting on my part, students observe the providential significance of the repetition of dates and identify the biblical allusions in the novel. I ask students to think about what makes Crusoe's story believable and gripping. Inevitably they point out the painstaking attention to detail in the accounts of how Crusoe salvaged essential items from both his own and a later shipwreck; planned and constructed his well-concealed fortresslike home; made hideous but functional earthenware; and even, over a period of months, built two different canoes. Crusoe's indomitable spirit and sheer will to succeed at any task wins over readers despite his arrogance and condescension to characters such as Xury and Friday.

In our discussions I emphasize the importance of close readings and note that a novel as rich and complex as *Robinson Crusoe* invites different critical approaches and interpretations that can be both valid and contrasting because they relate to themes that arise from the words of the novel. At the beginning of the course I find that a number of students have difficulty accepting the notion that different interpretations of a poem or short story can coexist without necessarily contradicting one another. There are always a few students who ask impatiently how it is that a text can have more than one meaning. They want to know who comes up with these interpretations, and they argue that if a text can mean anything, then it is just a free-for-all; if anyone can say that a text means anything, then no one can say what it really means. I point out that the words on the page lend themselves to these different readings and so different interpretations may be valid. For this reason I conduct close readings of texts with students in class to help them discover that a fruitful ambiguity may increase a text's richness and resonance for readers. In this way my students become less distrustful of literary criticism and of interpretations that they had not previously considered or even thought possible. Nonetheless, I always have a few students who resist ambiguity and who are genuinely angered by the idea that we are reading different interpretations into a work that should rightly have one and only one meaning. By the time that we finish *Crusoe*, however, most students have become more adept at literary analysis and more comfortable with the idea that texts can have different readings, even though readers may make wrongheaded or misguided interpretations that are unfounded by the text.

To get students to a point of heightened critical awareness, I first have them focus on four different elements of the novel: formal realism, psychological realism, economic values, and allegorical signification as spiritual biography. This focus helps the students discover on their own that these elements and themes are very much present throughout the book. Only then do I have students read short critical essays that address *Robinson Crusoe* from each of these different perspectives, which they now acknowledge to be legitimate. In class I divide them into groups of four and ask that each group work together to identify passages in the text that substantiate or call into question one of these critical interpretations. This exercise works extremely well because it makes students confront the text and take ownership of their interpretative process. They have intense animated discussions among themselves, and at the end of the small-group discussions each group presents its findings to the class as a whole. In the process they learn how one can construct meaning from a text, and they begin to understand and appreciate the complexity and richness of Defoe's novel and, by extension, of great novels in general. For students who have had no prior experience analyzing literature, this becomes an eye-opening, powerful, and deeply rewarding experience. Of course all novels may be taught in this way, but something elemental about Crusoe's will to survive and dominate the self-created desert-island world speaks to these students, who by dint of hard work and sheer willpower are also involved in the task of reinventing themselves and transforming their lives.

For a final in-class assignment on *Robinson Crusoe*, I give students an exercise that asks them to imagine what choices they would make if shipwrecked and left to fend for themselves on a desert island. I give them ten minutes to come up with a list of ten items that they would need to fulfill all the different aspects of their lives while on the island. The list must take into account their own particular religious or spiritual, dietary, clothing, entertainment, and safety needs. At the end of ten minutes, students are divided into groups and asked to explain, justify, and rationalize their choices and then get feedback from the members of their group. I then tell them that they have been rescued and have managed to take everything with them except for the list. Now they have to imagine who finds the list: an explorer, a missionary, another islander from nearby, or a person like them who has been stranded there. On the basis of the list of items alone, they are to analyze what kind of person this character would imagine them to have been. This exercise in critical thinking makes students aware of how one's values affect one's critical judgments about others. It also brings home the point that our interpretation of Crusoe depends to an extent on our own values. Students enjoy this assignment and take it quite seriously, although they find the list making to be the most challenging part. I find that this is an effective way of concluding our critical journey into the novel. Crusoe's "true" adventures provide Defoe's readers with paradigms for choosing, valuing, judging, and appreciating what we are given in life. In a very direct way, this in-class assignment encourages students to think about the process of critical analysis and to make the connection that critical thinking is as relevant to our everyday lives as it is to our understanding of imaginative literature. *Robinson Crusoe* is a perfect text with which to make these connections.

"Great Labour and Difficulty": *Robinson Crusoe* as Introduction to Literary Analysis

Anne Chandler

Among the requirements for English majors at Southern Illinois University, Carbondale, is a methods course titled Introduction to Literary Analysis. Intended to map out generic conventions, literary terms, and critical schools, the course also stresses intensive familiarization with a very few texts of the instructor's choosing. Thus, although labeled "writing-intensive," the course becomes in practice one in critical reading and one that must explore the epistemic implications of its title. A seminar-style approach to this exploration is made possible by a strict maximum of twenty students in a class. Nonetheless, the constituency is mixed: the notion of literary analysis strikes some students as hopelessly easy and self-evident and others as hopelessly difficult and cryptic. Mediating these extremes is a worthwhile challenge, since even the most confident students can use a more tangible conversance with analysis as an activity and with textuality as a phenomenon. *Robinson Crusoe* aids this cause on several planes. It draws students ineluctably to the problem of pinning down what makes a text seem difficult or easy; its prolixity, reflexiveness, and disorderliness make for a steep readerly climb riddled with fingerholds for analysis; and of course the novel thematizes difficulty, ease, and work of all kinds—including the work of analyzing texts.

In exploiting the analogy between Crusoe's work and our own, I consider my task to be twofold: to promote the process of getting one's hands dirty, so to speak, in the work of reading *Robinson Crusoe* closely and to encourage a running commentary on that process and all it entails. In my course, students read *Robinson Crusoe* after studying Renaissance and Romantic texts that are far more economical and lyrical. Having heard the case for doing microscopically close readings of these texts and for considering them as works of art, students now confront a sprawling narrative that just seems like work—initially because of eighteenth-century orthography and idiom and later because of all the problematics of excess and lack in the novel that have impelled decades of Defoe criticism. Yet one can resituate the very concept of difficulty, first by encouraging a certain insouciance about Defoe's verbal tics and plot blips (if you lose track of which voyage he's on, you're not alone) and then by nudging students' questions toward issues of interpretation. These larger difficulties—most broadly, the difficulty of prioritizing information—so thoroughly imbue the fabric of *Robinson Crusoe* that students quickly perceive oddities such as Crusoe's fluctuations of prodigality and paternalism, his inventorying mania, and his variant accounts of first landing on the island. My message is this: tempting though it is to explain away these problems as functions of plot or of individual psychology, it is more constructive to keep alive a troubling sense of their irresolution, as inherent to the novel's texture, preoccupations, and cultural functioning. Two discoveries attend this higher critical plane: that an element of instability helps us construct original, defensible theses and that these fresh arguments require us to be certain about what the text actually contains.

An apt point of entry is found in the novel's mixed rhetoric of effort, especially in the first hundred pages. As prominent as is the refrain of "great Pain and Difficulty" (39), "great Labour and Difficulty" (40), "a great deal of Time and Labour" (44), "very laborious and tedious Work" (49), and so on, the text also exults in "ease": not only the "easy Circumstances" of the imagined middle class ("sliding gently thro' the World" [5]) or the creature comforts that result from Crusoe's labors but also the sense of leisure or luxury that infuses the representation of hard work. Crusoe bemoans "the Folly of beginning a Work before we count the Cost" (93), yet his calculations of man hours and emotional stress are so numerous, formulaically redundant, and internally contradictory as to overwhelm their ostensible purpose. To be sure, modern Defoe scholarship enables us to reconcile Crusoe's work obsession with a psychological need for mastery, the compulsions of *homo economicus*, or the tendentiousness of Puritan discourse. But if we view it first as a pleasure of the text, a narrative drive that steamrolls the facts in its way, or a fulcrum of competing rhetorical "needs," the class can defer these summations while we sift related discursive curiosities, such as the heavy mediations and reworkings of the so-called journal, Crusoe's highlighting of specialized terms and personal coinages, and his fluent appeals to ineffability and blocked expression. The parallels among these rhetorical modes are well worth pursuing, but the larger pedagogical point here is that to get such a ripple effect started, one first has to do a lot of page scanning and note taking. In short, the literary analysis of *Robinson Crusoe* requires the thoughtful, and assiduous, gathering of data. The information is not arrayed conveniently before us, as in a sonnet; yet there are rewards in carving out for ourselves chunks of the novel that can be scrutinized, whether locally or in aggregate, as we would a sonnet.

In teaching *Robinson Crusoe*, then, I employ what might be termed a concentrated formalism, in order to facilitate broader narratological and cultural insights. Our immersion in the text—or, rather, our search for discursive patterns in the apparent wilderness of details—allows us to distance ourselves from Crusoe: we hover above the island, trying to reflect on what makes one set of details seem to go somewhere and another seem like a dead end. I ask students to consider how we might conceive of the labor-language matrix that the novel flaunts as extending from Crusoe to us and from text to interpretation. More directly, however, I walk them through exercises designed to show what it feels like to do the work of data gathering and analysis and where that work can lead. In sum, I have found that I can turn the difficulties of *Robinson Crusoe* to advantage in an undergraduate methods course by mining certain lodes of teachable textuality with a specifically incremental series of writing assignments.

Laying the Groundwork: Course Placement and Assignment Structure

I design my syllabus so that *Robinson Crusoe* falls over four weeks in the middle of a fifteen-week semester. Students are asked to buy Michael Shinagel's second Norton Critical Edition (1994) and to read the novel in four fifty-page installments. They write two to three very brief essays on the novel and on selected criticism from the Norton in preparation for a four- to six-page paper that must incorporate at least one additional source. Befitting the concerns behind Introduction to Literary Analysis, the midterm placement of *Crusoe* helps reinforce prior reviews of basic literary-critical history and paradigms while also addressing the need for some modicum of continuity, or of consensus, about the types of exploration involved in writing critical essays. The foundation for my approach to *Robinson Crusoe*, then, is partly laid in texts studied earlier in the course—*King Lear*, *Frankenstein*, and a collation of lyric poetry—for which formalist methodologies, and the waves of reaction to them, are fairly easy to outline. Such schematizing is somewhat trickier with *Robinson Crusoe*, but the slower working-through of this process helps to convey the message that even the most boldly antiformalist criticism relies in some ways on principles of close reading.

The bridging function of my approach to the novel is anchored in brief writings known variously as "one-page papers," "two-paragraph assignments," or "your two observations." These assignments are distinguished from more diffuse journal entries or reaction papers and are meant to showcase specific findings in primary texts or specific points of contention with assigned criticism. Students are asked to view these exercises as presentations they might make at a business meeting, and indeed—as in a seminar—the exercises form the basis for discussion on the days they are due. The option of integrating such findings into a longer essay is always available; alternatively, when students begin a longer paper (such as the one I assign for *Robinson Crusoe*), the one-page assignment is used for partial drafts, on which pairs of students advise each other in class. The overarching advantage of the one-page papers or their equivalents is that close reading and content analysis are instituted as a kind of civic responsibility that reflects well on oneself, like mowing the lawn. The observation is made public and in the process is given a critical valence of its own. Moreover, it becomes clear that developing a context for the observation, defining its boundaries for oneself but in consultation with others, is a key aspect of original thought.

Getting to Work: Dividing Tasks and Developing Expertise

For *Robinson Crusoe*, I reinforce these premises by interspersing one-page assignments with in-class activities designed to rearticulate the assignments' function. The initial assignment derives from the first fifty pages of the novel (up to Crusoe's balance sheet of good and evil) and asks students to identify the smallest possible nugget of expressive or logistical strangeness they can find. In class discussion, we experiment with broadening these items into categories (definitional, topical, and so on) and, sometimes, with distilling them further or exploring their importance in a particular passage. In this way, students gain an area of textual expertise that they can develop if they wish. Then, on the second day of discussion, I isolate several passages from the first hundred pages—the "O Drug!" homily (43), Crusoe's illness (64–65), and the bird-hanging episode (85) are a few sample foci—for a fifteen-minute written explication. I provide page numbers and brief labels for these passages on the blackboard. The idea is for students to refer freely to the passages while writing, and the stated task is to make a case for the indispensability, both rhetorically and thematically, of the passage they choose. The arguments are necessarily experimental, but the ensuing discussion challenges a prevailing sense that important commentary must be axiomatic or that one must espouse a fully formed critical argument before doing the textual legwork. Instead, the exercise leads students through the sort of hypothesis negotiation that constitutes critical novel reading. (How might the bird-hanging episode, for example, be regarded with respect to all episodes involving birds—or to all those involving retribution?) It also blunts the pervasive anxiety that if someone else is discussing the same topic, one's own line of thought cannot be original. Finally, the exercise injects the act of discovering dramatic ironies, narrative inconsistencies, and conflicts of interest—the things that tempt us to throw up our hands at *Robinson Crusoe*—with an ongoing incentive to collect more data.

A sample line of inquiry involves the novel's concern with animals and animalism. Crusoe's early encounters with wild beasts may strike one on first reading as simply situational and less ideationally resonant than, say, his treatment of Xury. But if even one student questions the frequently used terms *wild* and *tame* or compares Xury's competence as a hunter with Crusoe's hotheadedness, the class can apply those observations to Crusoe's later boasts about managing the animals on the island. Crusoe's theories of attachment and domestication in these anecdotes transfer all too readily to his relationships with Xury and Friday. Thus an element that at first seems flatly concrete turns out to be implicated in almost any thematic context we can imagine. If we expand our purview a bit, we can see how the literal and novelistic treatment of animals impinges on race, ethnicity, and colonialism; on the economics of desire, including what Crusoe calls "confin'd Desires" (141); on the phenomenologies of religious mania and xenophobic violence; on the manipulation of material objects; and on the characterization of the natural world. Later, when students read Carol Houlihan Flynn's discussion of cannibalism (which deals with questions of animality and embodiment), they are well equipped to engage her argument not only topically but with an experienced sense of how Flynn places a microscopic attentiveness to both material and idiomatic detail within a far-reaching sociological framework. As challenging as the essay is, students can see what the argument is doing because they have done it themselves.

It is this kind of confidence, and a sense of what backs it up, that I try to encourage in the students' readings of criticism. When the class has read about
three-quarters of the novel, I assign Ian Watt's "Robinson Crusoe as a Myth"
for a sort of whole-group rehearsal in apprehending and testing the premises
of a critical argument. As professional scholars, Flynn and Watt clearly know
more than most about the histories involved. But when it comes to the novel itself, we're on an equal footing, or can be, as long as we answer their interpretive efforts with a good-faith effort of our own. If we grant that what these ex-
perts say is interesting, what might they have *missed* (or, downplayed) that we
ourselves noticed in the novel?

To further a healthy sense of entitlement to this question, I have devised a
note-taking exercise in which the class makes its own study guide in lieu of the
name-brand digests to be found in bookstores and online. Each four-to-five-
person group is assigned about fifty pages to gloss under two rubrics: "pivotal
events" and "key issues, images, or modes of expression." A composite of the
best results (ten pages or so) is photocopied for everyone as a reference tool.
Along the way, some interesting things happen. Most groups elect to divide the
work further so that each student reviews some ten to twenty pages. There is
discussion about how best to reference events and how to explain in shorthand
the permeable boundaries between such events and the thematic and formal
issues they raise. To shape and delimit their notetaking, some students choose
to retain the original two rubrics, essentially going over the same ground twice;
others replace them with an encyclopedic table of contents for the assigned
section; still others collaboratively determine more specific themes, such as
"labor, punishment, deliverance" and a "progression from isolation to compan-
ionship." The chance to sharpen a category heading or even to reimagine what
potentially counts as a category is not, of course, seized by all students; but for
those who do take it up, the process brings a lasting sense of readerly power.

This exercise also brings forth in most students a willingness to clarify things
for one another—stemming possibly from a sense of enlightened self-interest—
and encourages a good deal of actual writing: students explode the table-of-con-
tents format into full sentences and reproduced quotes, and they carefully signpost the distinctions between similar episodes. Defoe's loquacity becomes
contagious, moving them from reportage to an evaluative, sometimes sardonic
engagement: students note significant repetitions and omissions, place scare
quotes around Crusoe's favorite terms, and refer summative statements to textual evidence. Thus one student's heading, "Strong longing of Crusoe for com-
panionship," was supplemented with the plangent citation, "my Hands would
clinch together, and my Fingers press the Palms of my Hands" (136). A desirable side effect of the exercise, then, is that students find themselves lingering
over, if not actually copying out, the words—considering, as they do so, what
makes one reproduction more telling or more valuable than another.

A final pair of assignments leads to the major paper; here, the goal is to divide and conquer the difficult process of synthesizing data. Students are given

instructions to find in the library a single journal article or book chapter on *Robinson Crusoe*, using the search capabilities of the online *MLA Bibliography*. They then collaboratively (in pairs) negotiate their topics and arguments in a thesis-building exercise designed to help them build on their prior practice in close reading and content analysis. With drafted introductions in hand, students elicit each other's responses to the following template:

1. Generally, I am interested in the way _____ relates to _____ in *Robinson Crusoe*.
2. The "smallest," most concrete manifestation of my topic would be (the image of the) _____.
3. In a sense, that image or picture could serve as a governing metaphor for a bigger phenomenon in the novel because _____.
4. The episode or situation that shows this (relation, phenomenon) most straightforwardly is _____.
5. An episode or situation that shows the issue to be "more complex than meets the eye" is _____.
6. What I'm discussing is interesting
    a. because it complicates our view of Crusoe as a person by showing us _____;
    b. because it leads us to scrutinize Crusoe's statement about _____;
    c. because it illuminates the following pattern or method in Defoe's construction of the novel: _____.

   The rationale here is to promote relational thesis statements that integrate broad evaluations with specific evidence and, beyond this, to parlay the celebration of detail in *Robinson Crusoe* into implications that are constructive, perhaps social, and certainly interpretive. In the past several students have used the language of the template to help structure their introductory paragraphs—a welcome price to pay for the practice they get in setting up a layered argument and in formalizing their own ideas about how to read this novel. Crafting an essay by characterizing the relations among examples is something that does not come naturally to most students; it takes practice and reading. And no other novel I can think of forces this issue so bluntly or models such virtuosic amplifications on material details as *Robinson Crusoe* does.

   These in-class exercises operate on the basic principles of textual explication, generative freewriting, and categorical searching. Their shared, workaday quality helps greatly in negotiating the students' overwhelming sense that the novel is full of too much detail, on the one hand, and their impulse to impose broad moral and psychological truisms, on the other. In concentrating the search for and the sense of the novel's form, the exercises help students to stop worrying about getting past the text's profusion and perseveration and to begin instead to engage intellectually with these tendencies as the hallmarks of its cultural work.

From *Beowulf* to Virginia Woolf:
Is There Room for *Robinson Crusoe* in an
English Literature Survey Course?

Carl Fisher

> Culture is simply the ensemble of stories we tell
> ourselves about ourselves.
>
> —Clifford Geertz

The British literature survey course is a standard of the English major.[1] The trajectory is similar, almost identical, in hundreds of Brit-lit surveys (part 1), from the venerable Bede through *Beowulf*, *Gawain*, Chaucer, Langland, Malory, Sidney, Spenser, Shakespeare, Donne, Jonson, Herrick, Herbert, Marvell, Milton, Dryden, Pope, and Johnson. It is a marvelous journey; over a thousand years are packed into a scant fifteen weeks. Yet as anyone who has taught the course knows, there is never enough time in a British literature survey course to do full justice to the length and breadth of the literature. This point is made clear by the ever-growing length of the first volume of the standard anthologies, *The Oxford Anthology* (2,376 pages), *The Norton Anthology* (2,974 pages), and the even more voluminous *Longman Anthology of British Literature* (3,028 pages). All the anthologies offer far more material than can be covered even cursorily.[2]

How do you skip the mystery plays or More or Marlowe or Swift? If you choose a work slightly off the beaten track, the *Taliesin* or one by Mary Herbert or Dekker and Middleton, what do you cut from the canon? To a degree, some of these choices are dictated by the institution, which may have a relatively set syllabus. Also, one always hopes that outside the required surveys students will take the right combination of period courses, genre courses, and special-topics courses to fill in larger gaps in literary history. However, in the current splintered curriculum, which has fewer required courses, we cannot assume any kind of common knowledge or even that students, who are increasingly resistant to longer reading assignments, have had a novel course. When an instructor merely follows the dictates of the traditional anthology and institutional custom in teaching the Brit-lit survey, students can gain a false sense of canonicity and cultural continuity that will not find a balance in other courses. Using a novel in the survey, specifically *Robinson Crusoe*, can complicate a discussion of British literature and culture in extremely productive ways.

The survey, after all, should not just be about authors and is rarely any longer a matter of art. The authorial trajectory I suggest above is just as much about the stories that a culture creates, how it tells them, and what they mean. Throughout these thousand years, ideas develop and paradigms shift; power transfers, beliefs transform, and British society grows in ebbs and flows that are mirrored in and to a degree developed through representation. It is through recognizing the evolution and transitions of the literature, and the dialogue between literary text and the contexts of literary production, that the British literary survey can come alive as a vibrant documentation of a culture. Ideally, such a survey would utilize cultural studies and incorporate contemporary theories of anthropology, psychology, social history, and political science while not neglecting significant backgrounds from the periods, such as reigning philosophical ideas or developing scientific theories. In this model, the concept of art or literature needs to be interrogated, especially for implicit value judgments, and the privileging of certain forms divorced from the "large network constituted by many other life practices" (During 1) creates a false analysis. Critical theories that try to get beyond the text to better understand it include Mikhail Bakhtin's sense of the carnivalesque and the dialogical potential in literature, Pierre Bordieu's concept of "fields" in which products of the imagination take material form in power relations, Frankfurt-school theories about ideology and material culture, and Stephen Greenblatt's analyses of colonial and imperial representations. Topics standard for a cultural studies approach to the survey might include the structures of nationalism and national identity, concepts of sexuality and gender, the commercialization of literary production, changing audiences, and the rise of popular fiction, or the tension between elite and popular culture, as well as examples of visual culture.

It could be argued that this cultural material has little to do with a standard British literature survey. However, *The Longman Anthology* proceeds in the direction of cultural studies, incorporating more women's writing, interrogating convenient periodicity, and arguing for a literary geography that questions the traditional concept of British literature. It intends to include "the full sweep of literary history" in order to highlight "works' original cultural contexts and their lasting aesthetic power" (xxxv) and incorporates Celtic and Gaelic and influential translations from the French, among other less-heard voices. *The Longman Anthology* emphasizes the shifting winds of culture, the development of new forms, the rise of popular culture, and changes in literacy as important for understanding the course material. A seventh edition of the *Norton Anthology* remains more traditional but still incorporates a culturally oriented approach; the newest edition includes more women writers and new sections with titles such as "The Wider World" (889–906), "The Science of Self and World" (1528–95), "Debating Women: Arguments in Verse" (2584–605), and "Slavery and Freedom" (2806–821; Abrams and Greenblatt).

This cultural orientation adds bulk to an already-weighty literary history. It could be argued that because of the growing weight of cultural contexts the sheer mass of material would be reason enough to exclude a novel from the survey. However, a novel like *Robinson Crusoe* can tie together many of the traditional elements of teaching literary history with some of the more prominent aspects of cultural study. Far from standing out as an anomaly, the novel can be integrated in a survey course to show the continuity and shifts in aesthetic, thematic, and social development. *Crusoe* works in the survey to demonstrate the growth of narrative and the unfolding of forms, not in isolation or as the product of an active imagination and individual genius, but as a response to previous literature and as an example of changing audiences. The novel exemplifies trends in literary production and, in the broader parameters of literary history, can be easily seen as part of a changing genre, from epic, romance, and lyric. Each genre tells its own story in specific ways and has its own ideological underpinning. Students in a survey course should see the movement toward realistic fiction as a major shift. Perhaps more important for any student in the traditional survey structure is the valuable exercise of close reading and textual analysis of such a nuanced novel as *Crusoe*. In my experience teaching the novel in a survey, students are grateful for syntax and diction that seem closer to their language, and they are easily engaged in the kinds of textual analysis that they felt too difficult in earlier works (as complex and sometimes archaic as *Robinson Crusoe* can seem from a modern perspective, after a two-week immersion in Milton it appears remarkably straightforward).

Despite my love of heroic couplets and a real inclination for reading and teaching satiric verse, I am not sure that John Dryden's *Absalom and Achitophel* or Alexander Pope's *Rape of the Lock* tells us more about literary history than *Robinson Crusoe* does, and I think that to fully understand British literature of the period you need both, and not in separate instructional contexts but in juxtaposition, to discuss genre, audience, and the historical forces that shape textual production and to project what will come. The novel can certainly be studied in the social and political context of the satire that characterized the previous fifty years, whether the Restoration comedies of William Wycherley and William Congreve or the mock epic of Samuel Butler's *Hudibras* and Dryden's *MacFlecknoe* and Pope's scathing *Dunciad*. If "the proper study of mankind is man," as Pope claims in *An Essay on Man*, then *Robinson Crusoe* is an apt object and subject of study in the survey. The novel is about the force of civilization carried inside each individual—in the British tradition, the "blessed plot" of England—and it demonstrates how culture shapes the individual's sense of identity. Crusoe's middle-class work ethic and ideals of self-sufficiency, his providential beliefs, and his sense of self and other are conceptual frameworks of self-definition and can be seen tied to other ideological social mechanisms such as law, religion, family, economics, and education. Here it is easy to fall back on the useful background of J. Paul Hunter's *Before Novels*, where the precursors to the early novel are discussed: the adventure story, spiritual autobiography and diary writing, and confessional narrative. Since an essay in this volume deals directly with the influence of John Bunyan's *Pilgrim's Progress*, I need not dwell on this connection, but I always set up the juxtaposition for students. And, as more than one commentator would note, even in impoverished and less-literate eighteenth- and nineteenth-century households, there were likely to be three books: the Bible, *Pilgrim's Progress*, and *Robinson Crusoe*.

However, is the popularity of *Crusoe* a selling point for including it in the survey? Moreover, although I have discussed the novel in some eighteenth-century contexts, where does it fit in the larger survey? I would argue that when you get beyond the formal structures and generic shifts, *Robinson Crusoe* truly holds its place in British literary history. As narrative, it can be discussed in the context of storytelling traditions. Comparing the novel with *Beowulf* or *Utopia* allows students to develop their critical sense of narrative structure and purpose. Other useful methods include analysis of mythic structures; pointing out ahistorical and archetypal elements of the story versus specific period-bound historical features; and looking at the symbolic images, such as the ship and shipwreck, the tools, the clothing, the umbrella, the footprint, the island itself—all of which can be seen in relation to similar elements in other texts. Questions can be formulated that allow students to look at themes across time periods; sharpen their sense of what each text can mean; and develop and demonstrate their understanding of the evolution of themes, the changing structures of belief, and shifts in social power. For example, how does Caedmon's vision compare with Crusoe's sense of Providence? How does Beowulf compare with Crusoe as hero? How does Grendel's cannibalism compare with that of the natives on Crusoe's island? How does Gawain's quest compare with Crusoe's rebellion? In what way can Caliban and Friday both be seen as social others? Can Donne's claim that "no man is an island" help shed light on Crusoe's island discontent? While some of these questions are admittedly a bit precious for a well-trained professional, they serve as wonderful tools for allowing students to make synthetic connections and demonstrate their analytical ability with specific texts and across time periods. Once students start to recognize how these processes work, it almost makes *Crusoe* seem overdetermined.

The literature survey developed as a way to understand literary form, tradition, and history with a great-books rationale; while cultural studies may dissent from many aspects of this tradition, it incorporates important elements albeit with a different emphasis. If nothing else, both models share the idea that understanding the past is critical to understanding the present. Instead of radically revamping the curriculum, I suggest incorporating *Crusoe* into the standard syllabus, which will not untrack or degrade the tradition but enhance an understanding of the length and breadth of the British tradition. This essay tries to create an argument for why *Robinson Crusoe* belongs in a British literature survey course. It would be disingenuous of me to fail to admit that I can come up with almost as many reasons not to include the novel, some of which I mention above. Perhaps the best reason for including it is the least theoretical and critical: it works. I have taught the British literature survey both without a novel and with other novels, such as *The Castle of Otranto* and *Pride and Prejudice*. Despite the length and complexity of *Robinson Crusoe*, students pay it great attention, usually read it avidly, and see in it one of the first truly modern voices. They often comment in their class evaluations that it is one of their favorite works of the semester. Incorporating the novel allows a perspective, as I hope is indicated by the arguments above, that gives even greater depth to the already broad survey.

NOTES

¹I am assuming a standard fifteen-week semester in which the first part of the survey focuses on British literature through the eighteenth century. Some departments start the second semester with the eighteenth century—making *Robinson Crusoe* an appropriate early choice, while in the quarter system *Robinson Crusoe* would come early in what is probably a 1660–1832 time frame.

²The editorial choices and apparatus of these standard anthologies are far too broad a topic to be covered here. Interesting, however, is how Defoe, who casts such a shadow on the rise of journalism and the development of the novel and who was no mean poet himself, is usually given short shrift. The *Norton* has a snippet of *Roxana*, while the *Oxford* has three pages of *The True and Genuine Account of the Life and Actions of the Late Jonathan Wild* and one page of *Moll Flanders*. The *Longman Anthology* increases the coverage of Defoe dramatically. While the only selection from *Robinson Crusoe* is the ledger sheet of good and evil accounting, *Longman* also includes selections from *The Apparition of Mrs. Veal*; *A Journal of the Plague Year*; *Jonathan Wild*; and three excerpts from *A Review of the State of the British Nation*, included with periodical excerpts to highlight the rage for news, manners and customs, and economic discussions. There are also selections from Richard Steele, Joseph Addison, Eliza Haywood, Anne Finch, and others that construct a cultural context perfect for studying the period and the novel.

Teaching *Robinson Crusoe* in a Survey of the Novel Course

Maximillian E. Novak

If, as some believe, the novel began in 1740 with the publication of Samuel Richardson's *Pamela*, then *Robinson Crusoe* has no place in a survey course of the novel, except perhaps as a primitive example of the form. Approaching the novel by narrowly demarcating the genre, however, lost considerable support with a revival of interest in the romance, in women novelists such as Aphra Behn and Eliza Haywood, and in the comparative approach of Mikhail Bakhtin. This critical revival also represents something like a return to what was once the norm for teaching the novel. Surveys of the novel developed in American higher education around the turn of the twentieth century. Whereas the emphasis in courses devoted to the study of national literatures was on periods, in novel courses the emphasis was essentially on considering the novel as a work of art, sometimes but not always in a historical framework. The impulse for such courses came from comparative literature courses. At the beginning, the comparative approach tended to treat an emphasis on national literatures with some latitude. As championed by Irving Babbitt and Joel Spingarn, such "type courses" were considered to have broad social and ethical goals (see Ehrenpreis). Today, versions of such courses continue to be taught in American universities and in universities throughout the world, and the publication of Daniel Defoe's *Robinson Crusoe* in 1719 is often used in such classes as a kind of introduction to the study of the novel or, at least, as a way of illustrating a significant moment in the history of fiction.

Since I have taught a novel survey course for over forty years, I use my own experience to describe some of the critical changes that have occurred over the past decades and the ways they have influenced and may continue to influence the teaching of the novel in general and *Robinson Crusoe* in particular. In addition to undergraduate courses of varying sizes, I have taught undergraduate and graduate seminars treating theories about the novel. In such courses the novels may serve as examples for certain theoretical approaches, but in some sense, they were still surveys.

I start with the survey of the novel that I took as an undergraduate—the kind of survey that had been taught throughout the United States for some fifty years. Admittedly, such a course is unlikely to be taught today, but it may be useful for what it tells us about the development of the modern survey course. When I was an undergraduate, around 1950, the curriculum of the University of California, Los Angeles, had both period courses and type courses. Under the semester system, in addition to courses divided up according to periods, there were year-long courses in poetry, drama, prose, and the novel. The first semester of the novel course was essentially a history of fiction until 1832. The lectures began with Greek romances, wound their way through Rabelais and Cervantes, and eventually reached England with Robert Greene, Thomas Deloney, and Thomas Nashe. At this point the lectures slowed somewhat, but they still managed to get through Jane Austen, Sir Walter Scott, and early Charles Dickens. *Robinson Crusoe* and Defoe's other novels were presented as part of the development of realism. Of course, this did not mean that anyone had to read a novel by Defoe. Each week, students were allowed to select one book from eight to ten fictional texts, fifteen for the entire semester. The lectures covered everything that was happening in Britain and on the Continent. Students listened to lectures on works they were unlikely to read in their lifetime; the titles and dates might appear on the final examination.

It is unlikely that today any teacher would want to duplicate such a course, which offered little time for close reading or theorizing about the nature of fiction. It was unabashed literary history. Yet some aspects of such an approach could return. For example, Margaret Doody's *The True Story of the Novel* (1996) uses the Greek romances and their various archetypes as the origin of all subsequent works of fiction. As an undergraduate, I found the lectures informative and useful. I did not expect my professors to teach me how to read a text; I thought I could do that on my own. But I knew some students who were bewildered by the mass of dates, titles, and authors. To them the course seemed more like abstract history than a study of literary works.

Classes of this kind did indeed resemble, or tried to resemble, what was conceived to be history. For many scholars of this generation, history had the attraction of truth and science, and they scorned the notion of literary criticism as trivial and subjective. If such an attitude seems naive today, it is because their use of history was frequently as subjective as the belletristic critics they scorned. We might ask whether some version of the history of the novel is possible in a survey course. In trying to defend the historical approach to scholarship and, by implication, to teaching, Robert Hume argues against searching for a "history of the novel" as an acceptable quest. Although he accepts various forms of "story telling" (biography, for example) as valid, he says:

> [t]he history of the novel . . . [is] another matter altogether. One cannot sufficiently demonstrate connections between novels or the influence of one novel on another, and the historian is free to select so radically from an enormous range of largely unconnected material that almost any story can be concocted and justified. (402)

Nevertheless, despite Hume's doubts, there are all kinds of stories that we can tell our students about the way novelists were influenced by the techniques of earlier novelists, and if we want to ignore the authors, we can easily demonstrate intertextuality as a principle in the history of fiction. In writing *Robinson Crusoe*, Defoe drew on a variety of texts as disparate as the Old Testament book of Jonah and William Dampier's *A New Voyage round the World*.

I had the advantage of returning to the scene of the crime, that is, to what most people today consider the outrageousness of the old literary history as a pedagogical method. When I returned to the University of California, Los Angeles, as an assistant professor in 1962 and had the opportunity to teach the first part of the fiction survey, it was being taught in exactly the same way by the same teacher I had as an undergraduate. I looked over the notes I had taken. I had forgotten how much material had been given to us in these lectures, but by 1962 the course seemed like a dinosaur. Four years earlier, I had taken a position at the University of Michigan and started teaching a course on the novel and short stories. The emphasis of Michigan's English department was on close reading of selected passages and discussions about the unity of the text. It was pure New Criticism, which was looking less and less satisfactory as a method. Ian Watt's *Rise of the Novel* (1957) had already given respectability to judging fiction by taking into account contemporary literacy, epistemology, economics, and social life. Watt was attracted to New Criticism and to an evolutionary theory of the novel throughout his life, but his approach to the novel form through types of realism remains a valid method even today. Most important for my essay, Watt showed how central *Robinson Crusoe* was for any consideration of the novel in a survey course. For in *Crusoe* can be found a new sense of individualism and of the social world, a concept of economic man, a world that needed to be reminded of how things worked (making pottery and bread), and a style based on ordinary speech. We may be skeptical of origins, but for many teachers, Watt showed one way to begin the survey of the novel.

The theoretical approaches that followed *The Rise of the Novel* are important to any consideration of teaching *Robinson Crusoe* in a course devoted to the novel, since such courses may likely be the basis for later courses in the novel. If courses in the twentieth-century novel have to teach how to read stream of consciousness and mythic structures, a survey course in the novel is likely to use *Robinson Crusoe* when the teacher is trying to get the students to understand the complexities of first-person narrative—the ways in which it both involves the reader and limits the reader's knowledge. Perhaps Hume is right in suggesting that a survey of the novel is a doubtful kind of story we are telling. Nevertheless we can construct thematic and formal connections that provide intellectual excitement and an integral foundation for the study of literature. Whatever historical connections we may want to make, we should be sure that students learn how to read fiction. From that standpoint *Robinson Crusoe* is an appropriate text with which to begin.

When I started to teach the first part of the novel survey, I shortened the reading list somewhat and turned the lectures to discussions of the individual texts and their backgrounds. As long as I was teaching under the semester system, I could take advantage of beginning with early models for the novel, such as the Greek romance. However, I found that I could extract enough about the romance from *Don Quixote* and that I could also use it as an example of why realism in the novel was always an illusion, by looking at such episodes as Sancho

Panza's account of bringing animals across a river along with Don Quixote's admonition to summarize. I then proceeded to *Robinson Crusoe* as a work introducing a new kind of realism—a realism that embodied social, economic, and political contexts.

Watt was right enough about Defoe's serious use of what he called formal or circumstantial realism, but what might be called the Defoe effect is a blend of the real and something more numinous. This is what Maria Graham meant when she wrote in 1821, "The language is so homely, that one is not aware of the poetical cast of the thoughts; and both together form such a reality, that the parable and the romance alike remain fixed in the mind like truth" (158). The account in *Crusoe* of all the things and activities needed for the making of bread is about the realities of economic life, but it also functions as a larger allegory for human progress from hunting and gathering to pastoral living and farming. Crusoe's speech on the uselessness of gold on the island, so much admired by Samuel Coleridge, echoes larger themes of the human economy in the state of nature.

I often found it helpful to begin my discussion with a brief survey of Defoe's career, emphasizing his work as a spy and his ability to assume different identities and voices. Lucien Goldmann argues that early novelists were almost all figures who were somehow displaced in their society. This was quintessentially true of Defoe. I also stressed his authorship of various literary forms—newspaper articles, memoirs, satires—along with political, economic, and social tracts, all of which had a role in the writing of *Robinson Crusoe* and which were important for the development of the realist novel.

In looking forward to discussions of Richardson's and Henry Fielding's novels, one can show, following Watt, how, despite Watt's attempt to limit Defoe's gift to the novel to circumstantial realism, Defoe focused on the inner psychological state of Crusoe as Crusoe reacted to the natural world and how Defoe, like all of the best novelists who followed him, turned adventure and plot into occasions for moral commentary on the human condition. I always avoided two approaches that are common enough in surveys of the novel: a simplified idea of the evolution of the form and the creation of a major distinction between its early and later incarnations. The first is a too easy adaptation of Darwin to the history of the novel. Alan D. McKillop in his *Masters of English Fiction* was right in his plea for the greatness of Richardson's *Clarissa* (96–97). Just because the fashion for epistolary novels may have faded and just because the idea of feminine virtue has never been the same since Mae West does not mean that the greatness of *Clarissa* is any less apparent. The second concept represents a false historicism. J. Hillis Miller once argued, with only slight exaggeration, that *Don Quixote* contained in some form or other everything that the novel would become. Though Watt tried to explain why La Fayette's *Princess of Cleves* was not a novel, his arguments have grown weaker with the years. The volume of novels written during the last half of the seventeenth century (mostly written in French and translated into English) was hardly negligible. This is not to deny the innovative techniques of Richardson and Fielding. They added greatly to prose fiction from the standpoint of psychology and aesthetics. Both laid claim to creating a new species of fiction. Defoe too stressed the originality of *Robinson Crusoe*.

Even while conceding the originality of Richardson and Fielding, we do not have to believe their claims that what they wrote was different in kind from what had come before. With *Crusoe*, we have a sense of concentration in a situation involving nothing very new from day to day. Of course there are the cannibals and Friday, but great events during the twenty-eight years include such banal matters as manufacturing pots, arranging the shelves of the hut, and domesticating the goats. Compared with these activities, Pamela's adventures with Mr. B are genuinely exciting. Richardson and Defoe are both writers of realist fiction, but Richardson focuses more on the psychology of human relations. Defoe, as Watt suggests, creates individualists—characters who are much more concerned with themselves than with those with whom they interact. The distinction between Richardson and Defoe hardly seems to demand that we classify them as working in different genres.

Before I discuss specific generic approaches to *Robinson Crusoe* below, I want to make a few generalizations. If we are going to impose generic distinctions on the flow of fiction, we should do so with some of the sophistication offered by Michael McKeon in his *Origins of the English Novel*. McKeon attempts to take into account attitudes toward epistemology along with a profound awareness of social and political change in arriving at his conclusions. Teachers who provide a simple statement such as "the novel began in 1740" present students with what amounts to a convenient lie or with an idea so complicated that it would take more time to explain than is available in a survey course. When my institution went over to the quarter system, which limits courses to ten weeks, I had to abandon any notion that I was presenting a history of fiction. The time frame shrank to what we now call the long eighteenth century, from 1660 to 1832. After I found that I could only teach about five or six books in the ten weeks, I concentrated on each text as an individual experience for the reader and retained a general chronological order. Though I flirted with the notion of reversing chronology—of beginning with, say, Mary Shelley's *Frankenstein*, which has many of the same themes as *Robinson Crusoe*—I could never rid myself of the conviction that students would find such an organization confusing. When I introduced J. M. Coetzee's *Foe* into the class (of approximately fifty students), no matter how often I explained why I was using such a text, I always had complaints from some students to the effect that a twentieth-century text did not belong in such a course. No one ever complained that the books were taught in the approximate order in which they were written. However, the advantages of moving from an eighteenth-century text with a colonialist mind-set to a modern anticolonial text provide glimpses into history and culture that create a beneficial learning experience, despite the risk of bewildering a few students.

Although I kept to a chronological order, I usually selected texts that enabled me to organize the course around themes that might be carried forward. If I wanted to stress adventure and colonial themes, I began with Behn's *Oroonoko*, proceeded to *Robinson Crusoe*, and included Coetzee's *Foe*. I could then either focus on English society and teach William Godwin's *Caleb Williams* and Austen's *Mansfield Park* or focus on the novel of experience and growth and include Fielding's *Tom Jones*. When I was feeling excessively optimistic about my students' abilities, I would attempt teaching Laurence Sterne's *Tristram Shandy*. Austen's *Northanger Abbey* also works well with these themes. On occasion I would try to establish a connection between *Robinson Crusoe* and the Gothic. Both exploit the sublime and share storms and shipwrecks, isolation and caves, anxiety and the constant threat of some unknown terror. And just as the Gothic exploits the possibilities of the supernatural, so does Defoe in the episode involving the discovery of the dying goat in the mysterious grotto. Although Defoe never ventured to compose lengthy descriptions like those that fill the novels of Ann Radcliffe, his two descriptions of the ocean in storm are wonderful in their feeling of motion and terror; connections abound.

Other patterns emerge from *Robinson Crusoe*, such as the discovery of the self, a theme that deals with identity and education. Such themes work particularly well with first-person narrative, with works like Richardson's *Pamela*, Tobias Smollett's *Roderick Random*, Godwin's *Caleb Williams*, and even Dickens's *David Copperfield*. Gérard Genette has pointed out the complexities of making simple divisions about what he prefers to call "voice" (213–61), and while it might make some sense to deal with novels that are "*Written by Himself*," as *Robinson Crusoe* was advertised, Fielding's *Tom Jones* and Austen's *Emma* or even *Pride and Prejudice* work well in treating the type of novel in which the main character undergoes a form of education through a series of experiences.

Occasionally, I have organized the novels along formal lines of discussion, treating such problems as the nature of realism, point of view, the handling of time, repetition, plot, the creation of character, and genre in an attempt to stress the varieties of techniques in the writing of fiction. Beginning with Robinson Crusoe as the isolated narrator, I would gradually move to the complexities of Austen's indirect discourse, suggesting that each author found a way to familiarize us with his or her characters. Although Bakhtin's notion of heteroglossia and the dialogic nature of the novel would seem to make *Robinson Crusoe* into a fairly narrow work, I point out how many voices we actually hear: Crusoe's father, the captain of the ship that is wrecked on the way to London, Xury, the Portuguese captain, Friday, the Spanish captain, the mutineers, the English captain who rescues Crusoe, and even the parrot. And I would suggest that the insertion of Crusoe's journal provides both a new kind of narrative form and a somewhat different type of narrator from the aged, moralizing teller of the tale. It also gives the reader a sense of immediacy in retelling Crusoe's encounter with the problems of daily life. The full text includes Crusoe's lengthy ruminations, such as his internal struggle with whether attacking the cannibals is just, that are contemporary with his life on the island and other meditations that reflect the older and perhaps wiser Crusoe who contemplates the meaning of his adventures from the comforts of England. There are moments of sensibility, in which he is overwhelmed by his emotions, and moments of self-mockery. Moreover, the realist narrative is interrupted by mysterious dreams, ominous warnings, and strange events.

The question of genre, both literary and nonliterary, is important in considering *Robinson Crusoe*, but, in contrast to a number of other critics, I have never regarded it as central. As we state in our introduction, anyone reading the title page of *Crusoe*, which promises adventures and designates Crusoe as a "Mariner," would expect to read a volume about travel and adventures. It seems to me that the mere fact that travel narratives were often suspected of lies and exaggerations does not mean that the reader was constantly concerned about the "indeterminate" (Bakhtin's term, qtd. in McKeon, *Origins* 4) nature of the fiction. Rather, Coleridge's "suspension of disbelief" must have kicked in from the very start. But I also believe that George Starr's arguments about the structural importance of spiritual autobiography is entirely correct (see *Spiritual Autobiography*). And J. Paul Hunter has made us aware of a number of other early fictional kinds besides spiritual autobiography—the guide tradition, the wonders tradition, the meditation tradition—pointing to a body of didactic and religious literature that has considerable importance for Defoe's work. Nevertheless, there are often long passages, such as the rescue from the island, in which there will be no specific biblical references or allusions at all. It was not at all uncommon for genuine, firsthand accounts of adventures at sea to turn into spiritual autobiographies or for the seamen who wrote such accounts to quote scriptures at some length. The reader, then, may subsume such manifestations in *Robinson Crusoe* as one more aspect of the real. Of course, the work may also be read (and has been by me and others) as an economic treatise and a treatise on the nature of government. I have used all these approaches at one time or another in my survey course.

Finally, I want to comment on the accessibility of *Robinson Crusoe* to students in the novel survey. Although I have never been sure why, students seem to have a difficult time with *Clarissa* (less so with *Pamela*), and my last attempts at teaching *Tristram Shandy* or *The Heart of Midlothian* met with genuine resistance. Students seem to be willing to follow the association of ideas in modern texts but to resent their presence in an eighteenth-century novel. And Sir Walter Scott's rendering of the accents of his nation put off a large number of students. However, Defoe's prose is still open to them—and, as the popularity of the movie *Cast Away* made apparent, *Robinson Crusoe* is still an exciting story.

Robinson Crusoe and Children's Literature

Anne Lundin

Somewhere off the coast of Narnia, beyond Middle Earth, through the Hundred-Acre Woods, and near the land where the wild things are lies an island. It is a green oasis in a wine-dark sea, a tropical paradise of wild headlands and blue lagoons, a treasure hoard of pirates' gold, a land of milk and honey. It lies beyond the borders of the map and it is found through the geography of "what if." It is the home of Robinson Crusoe.

Crusoe found this island over two and a half centuries ago. It was a speculative world based on the bare bones of a story. In the spring of 1703, a young Alexander Selkirk ran away to sea and, while having a quarrel with his captain, asked to be marooned on a desert island off the west coast of South America. He stayed on the island for four years and four months; then he was rescued and returned to London, dressed in goat skins. Selkirk was the talk of the town. Daniel Defoe, an aging journalist, took Selkirk's story and turned it into his own island fantasy, *The Life and Strange Surprising Adventures of Robinson Crusoe, of York, Mariner Written by Himself.* Defoe transformed Selkirk's story into a universal fantasy, a story that holds its spell over the centuries. Instead of the island of Juan Fernandez, where Selkirk stayed and which could easily be found, Defoe placed his hero on a remote, distant isle beyond our knowing. The four years of exile became twenty-eight as the author dwelled on the revelations of a solitary existence, on the meeting of character and place.

This surprise encounter begins after an abandoned youth. The story unfolds as a picaresque tale of adventure: Crusoe's defiant decision to go to sea, despite parental warning; his profitable voyages as a private trader; his capture by Moorish pirates and escape on an open boat with a companion, Xury; Crusoe and Xury's rescue by a Portuguese ship and four years in Brazil. The components of this tale are told before Crusoe clambers ashore on the "Island of Despair," as he calls his refuge (52). These adventures fit the pattern of travel literature current in the eighteenth century, a time of geographic curiosity. Where Defoe breaks new ground is his concentration on the island and his hero's solitary adaptation to that environment.

And adapt he does, with great English ingenuity. Crusoe retrieves items from the shipwreck and builds a cave spacious enough to accommodate them. He dwells on toolmaking "with as much thought as a statesman would have bestowed upon a grand point of politics, or a judge upon the life and death of a man" (61). He explores inland and finds valleys of wild grapes, melons, and sugarcane. He makes pots, baskets, furniture, a canoe. He erects a post on his arrival and keeps track of each moment by making notches on it, a cross on which his beginning is marked as a constant given. He tames a goat and befriends a parrot, who cries, "Poor Robin Crusoe! Where are you? Where have you been? How come you here?" (104).

These questions become ominous as Crusoe comes on a lone footprint in the sand, the promise of company. He eventually rescues a savage from the cannibals, naming him Friday, "Which was the Day I sav'd his Life" (149). Friday becomes civilized and learns to put on trousers, to pray, and to carry a gun. Castaway and companion are finally rescued as mutineers take their place on the island, well versed in defense and husbandry by Crusoe the teacher. Crusoe returns home to England, with more roving ahead and an audience around the world awaiting each word.

Robinson Crusoe was published in April 1719, with five new editions to come that year. Within ten years a host of imitations made it possible for nearly any nationality to identify with the far-flung Crusoe. Swedish, German, American, Saxon, Magyar, and even Chinese Robinsons were offered by enterprising publishers. In almost three hundred years, the editions of the book itself exceed one thousand, and a multitude of pseudo-Robinsons, with or without the island, populate literature with Crusoe progeny. With boy Crusoes, girl Crusoes, Arctic Crusoes, prairie Crusoes, and even a dog Crusoe, castaway stories have become a world phenomenon termed by the French Robinsonades: stories based on the ancient conflict of human beings in nature, in the particular setting of a real or imagined island. It stirs deep questions about human existence and our place in the natural world as survivors and creators.

The fascination of this book is indefatigable. Jean-Jacques Rousseau called it "the one book that teaches all that books can teach" ("Rousseau" 52). Its lessons keep surfacing in myriad volumes: trial-by-wilderness books for young and old; literature of postnuclear survival; space exploration and the building of new worlds; the perennial fantasy of islands and wish fulfillment. Television indulges our daydreams with the popular series *Survivor* and with commercials that speculate that aspirin is the preferred analgesic on a desert island. In England, the BBC program *Bookmark* recently featured a show called "Crusoe's Children," with a modern lexicon of images from the slave trade to Club Méd. Harvard University, under the direction of Children's Literature New England, held a summer seminar in 1987 titled Robinson Crusoe and His Heirs, which is also the title of a course taught at Tufts University. Defoe's classic seems to be a basic imaginative kit, capable of infinite do-it-yourself variations.

The Crusoe myth is most potent in children's literature. Although *Robinson Crusoe* was not written specifically for a young audience, children have been its principal readers through the years. Moreover, it reaches across all classes: it has been published both as a popular chapbook and in deluxe editions. Children, on the whole, ignore Crusoe's soul-searching to view the tale as folklore. *Crusoe* satisfies the child's hunger for freedom and discovery, the dreams of young humanity. Recognizing this magic, Sir Walter Scott wrote, "There is hardly an elf so devoid of imagination as not to have supposed for himself a solitary island in which he could act Robinson Crusoe, were it but the corners of the nursery" (qtd. in Tucker 165). Thomas Bewick, the magnificent wood engraver of the eighteenth century, remembered running as a boy across hills, stark naked, in imitation of the savages in *Robinson Crusoe* (Bewick 16). Many a child longs to be cast on some palm-strewn shore in the uttermost parts of the earth.

The allure of vicariously experiencing Crusoe's existence in the wild spawned many imitations. Each of the following classic novels enlarged and energized the myth by giving the castaway new motives or circumstances. The worlds of such novels created the contemporary Robinsonade by kindling the imagination and by depicting Crusoes all over the globe. The most famous re-creation of *Robinson Crusoe* was *Swiss Family Robinson* (1814), by Johann Wyss, the father of four sons who were eager for island literature. In creating this home-spun tale, Wyss included every member of his family. The solitary castaway thus sprouted into a family of six: a clergyman, his wife, and their four sons—all on an island that could only exist in the imagination. While Crusoe owed his comforts to his own exertions, the Swiss family found all their needs met in their new Eden. Every flora and fauna desired were found growing right at their feet. Through this paradise strode Father Robinson, a natural scout-master, a living textbook of universal knowledge, who even paused in the midst of the shipwreck to explain the principle of the lever, "as well as I could in a hurry" (1954 ed., 17).

Masterman Ready was written by Captain Frederick Marryat as a corrective to *Swiss Family Robinson*, a book dearly beloved by his children who begged for a sequel. Marryat was critical of Wyss's seamanship and determined to write a great English naval romance based on authentic detail. "Fiction, when written for young people, should at all events be *based* on truth" (xii), Marryat declared. His intention was to land his castaways, the Seagrave family, on a South Pacific island, where they would be aided by the wise old salt, Master-man Ready. He taught them how to build a shelter, find water, fish, catch turtles, blaze a trail, and survive. Mr. Seagrave was the religious and cultural guardian, and the whole island became, in a sense, a school.

R. M. Ballantyne's *The Coral Island* (1858) was a departure from didactic tales about island life. The children in this book are alone. A trio of young friends—Ralph Rover, Jack Martin, Peterkin Gay—enjoy their island paradise, discovering the pleasures of coconuts, breadfruit, and oysters. They are also, however, fearful of the threat of sharks, warring cannibals, and pirates. The graphic realism and focus on children influenced Robert Louis Stevenson's *Treasure Island*, J. M. Barrie's *Peter Pan*, and William Golding's *Lord of the Flies*. In *Coral Island*, the island-adventure story was finally emancipated from the moral tale; and new mysteries were to unfold.

Jules Verne in *The Mysterious Island* shaped the island tale in accordance with the strange new frontiers of science fiction. His massive three-part novel told the story of five Americans who escaped to a Pacific island at the time of the Civil War, stranded with only one match, one grain of wheat, one metal dog collar, and two watches. Verne deliberately stripped his characters to the barest essentials. Unlike the imaginary heroes of Defoe and Wyss, who fortuitously found supplies in stranded vessels or washed ashore, "here not any instrument whatever, not a utensil. From nothing they must supply themselves with every-thing," wrote Verne (1965 ed., 37). The creation of something from nothing would later become instrumental in Verne's fiction and in Robinsonades.

Stevenson in *Treasure Island*, an acknowledged masterpiece among adven-ture stories, re-created the stock-in-trade island imagery into an entirely origi-nal tale. The novel, narrated by the young hero, Jim Hawkins, traces the lust of both pirates and the gentry for gold. These factions battle for possession of Treasure Island, described as a melancholy place with a stagnant smell. The castaway, Ben Gunn, appears as a "terrible apparition," tattered and demented (79). Indeed, even with the prospect of treasure remaining, Hawkins declares at the end, "Oxen and wain-ropes would not bring me back again to that ac-cursed island" (187).

The lost paradise is mythologized in Barrie's *Peter Pan; or, The Boy Who Wouldn't Grow Up*, first performed in 1904 and published in 1911 as *Peter and Wendy*. The subject of this island fantasy is the loss of innocence that growing up demands, a theme similar to that in *Treasure Island*. Peter Pan, a mother-less, half-magical boy, teaches the Darling children to fly through the skies to Never Never Land, a fantastic land of Indians, mermaids, wolves, crocodiles, and pirates. Barrie drew on island imagery from Ballantyne's *The Coral Island*, about which he wrote, "To be born is to be wrecked upon a desert island" (qtd. in Tucker 165).

Robinson Crusoe and his most famous descendants, *Swiss Family Robinson*, *Masterman Ready*, *The Coral Island*, *The Mysterious Island*, *Treasure Island*, and *Peter Pan*, opened up new mythic possibilities for the adventure story. Defoe took the ancient tale of a voyage, which goes back at least as far as the *Odyssey*, and transformed it into a powerful psychological novel, a spiritual autobiography. Wyss lightened the intensity by creating a compliant nature and a colony of castaways. Ballantyne portrayed children on their own on a coral is-land of diamond caves and blue lagoons. Verne created a technological commu-nity on an island of mystery. Stevenson deepened the moral and spiritual inter-pretations of adventure as the book moves from the romanticized island to its bloody reality. Barrie fantasized childhood as a lost paradise, a costly freedom.

The themes of good and evil, innocence and experience, life and death, sur-vival and creation are played out in the Robinsonades of the twentieth century. The Crusoe myth seems particularly suited to the modern temper and its view of the human condition as isolated and conflicted. Golding's *Lord of the Flies*, an adult novel adopted by youthful readers, portrayed the inevitable moral cor-ruption that overcomes the rage for order. While several Robinsonades written for adults have addressed these themes, particularly Michel Tournier's *Friday* and Muriel Spark's *Robinson*, children's literature has traditionally been the landscape for island exploration and the homeland of the castaway.

The island is a geography of limits. This patch of land is bordered by the sea, large enough to explore and conquer, small enough to seem like home. It is here in this self-contained world that the castaway can experience pleasure and risk pain in an allegory of growing up. Island literature is replete with the children who came and played: *Baby Island*, by Carol Brink, in which two girls find themselves island-bound with a boatload of babies; *The Tale of Little Pig Robinson*, by Beatrix Potter, where the shore is covered with oysters and sweets grow on trees; *Swallows and Amazons*, by Arthur Ransome, where the children play the roles of mariner, explorer, pirate, or castaway on Wild Cat Island; *The Sailor Dog*, by Margaret Wise Brown, whose hero learns to build a beach shack and then gains the confidence to repair his boat to return home; *The Islanders*, by Roland Pertwee, where two boys are given free run of a salmon river, an island, and five hundred acres of Devon countryside; *Where the Wild Things Are*, by Maurice Sendak, where Max tames monsters and plays king before returning to his mother and a warm meal; *Hey, Al*, by Arthur Yorinks, where a New York janitor and his dog enjoy an exotic island paradise, which they finally relinquish for home, since "Paradise lost is sometimes Heaven found" (Yorinks 32).[1]

This paradise is a limited world of infinite possibilities, fortunate and unfortunate. The island is as realistic as it is romantic. A bittersweet sense underlies *Abel's Island*, by William Steig, the *New Yorker* cartoonist and Newbery medalist. Steig makes his Robinson a rodent named Abel who gets swept away in a torrential stream to an island, where he makes a log home and, in his painful solitude, becomes an artist, turning isolation into spiritual realization. The island as crucible is also portrayed in Harry Mazer's *The Island Keeper*, where teenage Cleo flees in despair to an island retreat in Vermont. Her stay is prolonged through the winter, until she feels healed and ready to return. As Cleo leaves, she invokes "the strength of the island close around herself" (165). Karana in Scott O'Dell's *Island of the Blue Dolphins* is a solitary child, abandoned on an island for eighteen years. Based on historical fact, this novel traces her growing wisdom and compassion toward the natural world. In his Newbery Award acceptance speech, O'Dell writes that Karana learns: "first we must be an island secure unto ourselves. Then, that we must 'transgress our limits' in reverence for all life" (316).

In these island tales the limits transgressed are cultural and gender ones. Karana must break the taboos of her tribe that restrict women from hunting. She also befriends her enemies: the wild dog that killed her brother, the Aleut girl whose people betrayed her people. In Tournier's *Friday and Robinson*, a juvenile version of his adult novel, the castaway learns to live on a desert island by watching his servant, Friday, and accepting his values as well as domestic customs—a total reversal of attitude. Friday becomes the tutor and Crusoe the convert to the natural life. Matt in Elizabeth George Speare's *The Sign of the Beaver* begins a similar conversion when he reads *Robinson Crusoe* to a Native American boy, who reacts to the master-servant relationship and views the story from a different perspective. In Jane Yolen's *Children of the Wolf*, the orphan boy Mohandas protects two young girls raised by wolves. These feral children are a taunt and mystery to all but Mohandas, who sees in them "my other self, different, full of unspoken words, and alone" (12).

This taming of nature and struggle to survive while stranded is the meaning of the island tales. The subduing of nature is an act of control and surrender that creates new values and vision. It leads the boy in Antoine de Saint-Exupéry's *The Little Prince* to learn through a fox that "if you tame me, then we shall need each other" (80). It carries Miyax in Jean Craighead George's *Julie of the Wolves* to cross the tundra in a wolf pack and sing to the spirit of Amaroq. It calls Buddy in Virginia Hamilton's *The Planet of Junior Brown* to support others in his shelter, living by the credo, "We are together because we have to learn to live for each other" (210).

The Robinson Crusoe myth looks beyond earthly limits to the possibilities of space, to the taming of new worlds, to the survival and creation of the human race on the fragile earth that is our island home. The source is there in that familiar figure stalking the shore, with the long beard and pointed hat, his body covered with animal skin, his gun and parasol by his side, and the parrot perched on his shoulders, calling us by name.

NOTE

[1]Titles listed appear in the appendix below.

APPENDIX: A SELECTIVE BIBLIOGRAPHY

The following list contains a number of current books for children that develop themes related to *Robinson Crusoe*: survival and creation on a desert island. The island may be an interior or a physical place; the castaway experience may be accidental or intentional. Some of the books are more firmly in the Robinsonade tradition, while others reflect the theme more than the story pattern. Trade editions and paperbacks are listed.

Picture Books

Brown, Margaret Wise. *The Sailor Dog*. Illus. Garth Williams. Golden, 1981. 32 pp.
The restless sailor-dog, Scruppers, has plentiful adventures on land and sea.

Goffstein, M. B. *Natural History*. Farrar, 1979. 32 pp.
This picture book is a tribute to shared survival of the human race with the natural world.

Lionni, Leo. *Frederick*. Pantheon, 1966. 32 pp.
This fable depicts in a family of mice the inner life necessary for survival.

Potter, Beatrix. *The Tale of Little Pig Robinson*. 1930. New ed. 1987. 112 pp.
The island is the culmination of Pig Robinson's adventures and is where he still may be found.

Sendak, Maurice. *Where the Wild Things Are*. Harper, 1963. 48 pp.
Max travels to an island of monsters where he is made king.

Spier, Peter. *Noah's Ark*. Doubleday, 1977. 44 pp.
The ark is an island of survival, and Spier draws on the creative possibilities of
the myth.

Steig, William. *Brave Irene*. Farrar, 1986. 32 pp.
Irene is indeed brave as she battles a blizzard to deliver a gown to the duchess
in this realistic tale of fortitude.

Yorinks, Arthur. *Hey, Al*. Illus. Richard Egielski. Farrar, 1986. 32 pp.
Al, a janitor, and his faithful dog, Eddie, are whisked away to a tropical paradise, which they abandon for home and a new perspective.

Books for Middle Grades

Brink, Carol. *Baby Island*. Macmillan, 1973. 154 pp.
Two girls are shipwrecked with four babies on a tropical island.

George, Jean Craighead. *My Side of the Mountain*. Dutton, 1967. 178 pp.
Sam Gribley escapes to the Catskills and learns to live off the land.

Jarrell, Randall. *The Animal Family*. Illus. Maurice Sendak. Pantheon, 1985.
200 pp.
A peaceable kingdom is created when a solitary man on an island is joined by a
mermaid, a bear cub, a lynx, and a boy.

Konigsburg, Elaine. *From the Mixed-Up Files of Mrs. Basil E. Frankweiler*.
Macmillan, 1967. 168 pp.
Two children run away to the Metropolitan Museum of Art where they solve
an intellectual mystery.

Moeri, Louise. *Save Queen of Sheba*. Dutton, 1981. 116 pp.
Two pioneer children search for their parents after a massacre.

O'Dell, Scott. *Island of the Blue Dolphins*. Houghton, 1960. 184 pp.
Karana lives alone on an island where she learns reverence for all life.

Paterson, Katherine. *The Bridge to Terabithia*. Crowell, 1977. 144 pp.
Jess and Leslie discover an imaginary kingdom in the woods where they reign
as royalty and retreat for solace in tragedy.

Saint-Exupéry, Antoine de. *The Little Prince*. Harcourt, 1943. 96 pp.
This philosophical fantasy traces the search of an alien boy on earth for the meaning of life.

Sperry, Armstrong. *Call It Courage*. Macmillan, 1968. 96 pp.
A Polynesian boy endures many harrowing adventures to prove himself worthy of the name "Stout Heart."

Steig, William. *Abel's Island*. Farrar, 1976. 128 pp.
Mouse Abel develops character on an island with many parallels to the story of *Robinson Crusoe*.

Tournier, Michel. *Friday and Robinson: Life on Speranza Island*. Knopf, 1972.
     118 pp.
Tournier adapted his adult novel *Friday* to this juvenile novel where Friday converts Crusoe.

Books for Upper Grades

George, Jean Craighead. *Julie of the Wolves*. Harper, 1982. 176 pp.
A thirteen-year-old girl learns how to become part of a wolf pack in order to survive on the Arctic tundra.

Hamilton, Virginia. *The Planet of Junior Brown*. Macmillan, 1971. 240 pp.
Buddy Clark survives while supporting others in his shelter.

Holman, Felice. *Slake's Limbo*. Macmillan, 1974. 117 pp.
Slake escapes to the subway where he builds a little home and some hope in the future.

Levin, Betty. *Put on My Crown*. Lodestar, 1985. 128 pp.
A boatload of pauper children are shipwrecked on a strange island where children die young.

Mark, Jan. *The Ennead*. Kestrel, 1978. 252 pp.
Isaac lives as an outsider on Erato, the lone surviving planet.

Mazer, Harry. *The Island Keeper*. Laurel-Leaf, 1981. 165 pp.
Cleo experiences emotional growth during an island survival in Vermont.

O'Brien, Robert. *Z for Zachariah*. Macmillan, 1975. 256 pp.
A girl struggles to survive a nuclear war in a safe valley, which becomes threatened by another survivor.

Orlev, Uri. *The Island on Bird Street*. Houghton, 1984. 176 pp.
Alex compares himself to Robinson Crusoe in this Holocaust survival story that has won many international awards.

Paulsen, Gary. *Hatchet*. Bradbury, 1987. 195 pp.
Physical survival and spiritual awakening are portrayed in this adventure of a boy alone for fifty-six days in the Canadian wilds.

Pertwee, Roland. *The Islanders*. Illus. Ernest Shepard. Oxford, 1967. 269 pp.
Two boys rely on their own resources in the English countryside.

Ransome, Arthur. *Swallows and Amazons*. Merrimack, 1981. 352 pp.
This is the first of twelve novels that chronicle the adventures of children on vacation in the lake country of England.

Sleator, William. *The Boy Who Reserved Himself*. Dutton, 1986. 161 pp.
Two youths struggle for freedom in the fourth dimension in this science fiction thriller and spoof.

Speare, Elizabeth George. *The Sign of the Beaver*. Houghton, 1984. 135 pp.
Matt is left alone in a cabin in the Maine woods of the 1700s and befriends a Native American who teaches him much about survival.

Taylor, Theodore. *The Cay*. Doubleday, 1969. 160 pp.
This controversial novel concerns a black adult and a white child marooned on a desert island, with racial harmony as its theme.

Townsend, John Rowe. *The Islanders*. Lippincott, 1981. 256 pp.
Strangers are banished to a barren island where they meet an extraordinary survivor who has much knowledge to impart.

Townsend, John Rowe. *Noah's Castle*. Lippincott, 1976. 256 pp.
This is a disturbing science fiction novel where a father is determined to turn his home into a contemporary Noah's Ark.

Yolen, Jane. *Children of the Wolf*. Viking, 1984. 144 pp.
Based on history, this fictional story centers on a relationship between the orphan boy Mohandas and two girls raised by wolves.

Accounting for the Self: Teaching
Robinson Crusoe at a Business School

Cheryl L. Nixon

Equating Crusoe with economic individualism may be a reading well known to literary critics, but it is an interpretation alien to the typical undergraduate student. Expecting *Robinson Crusoe* to be an adventure tale, my students read Crusoe's island experiences of building a home, producing food, and battling natives as acts of physical survival, not capitalist theory. My students are surprised that Crusoe spends over twenty-eight years planting seeds and raising goats; often, they want to skim through these nonadventurous tasks, and they show relief when the novel returns to action scenes (even if that action includes the slaughter of savages). When I teach the novel, then, I encourage my students not to discount Crusoe's economic life but to see how Crusoe—and they themselves—use economic accounting as a means of accounting for the self. I hope to convince them that Crusoe's "Account" of the economic self provides the adventure they seek (3).

My approach to *Robinson Crusoe* is furthered by a challenging teaching context: for four years, I taught the novel at a business school to freshman students enrolled in a required writing course. Although my students were often resistant to reading this "old" novel, they taught me much about making *Robinson Crusoe* relevant to today's undergraduate, and it is their response to the novel that I examine here. At the start of their undergraduate business careers, these students often see little connection between their business aspirations and their required liberal arts courses; rather than ignore this supposed schism, I have come to recognize that their business interests can provide a foundation for a complex understanding of *Robinson Crusoe* and a complex appreciation of literature's role in the construction of the idea of the self. Fascinated by the rise and fall of the dot-com industry, my students approach the stock market as a force to master and envision career paths with strategic zeal; if *Robinson Crusoe* is connected to these interests, the adventure inherent in Crusoe's business of the self becomes readily apparent. Indeed, Crusoe's life becomes a business start-up that requires the entrepreneurial thinking my students hope to experience in the workplace: creativity, problem solving, strategic planning, and power accumulation—even new product development! And, Crusoe's learning by doing parallels my students' business learning, specifically the hands-on workshops and real-world internships they see as crucial to their education. My students become more invested in this challenging novel once they realize that it imagines the impulse behind their education—to gain power over economic systems—as an extreme survival game.

Learning that business concerns provide the material for the first English novel, my students grapple with the idea of creating meaning out of work: is economic activity an essential part of the self and must it be accounted for in telling the story of the self? Ultimately, my students learn to read the novel for the questions it raises concerning the equation of economic development with self-development. The novel encourages them to think deeply about questions that they have not yet answered but certainly will confront: Am I the sum of my goods? Do the practices I use to gain wealth define who I am? What would I sacrifice for wealth? What constitutes "enough"? How does the desire for ownership connect to morality and spirituality? How much of the natural world will I domesticate to gain goods? Who will I enslave to gain goods? Global capitalism has only intensified these questions; my students need not go to an island to experience Crusoe's concerns, since the island's demands have come to them in the form of debates over trade law, child labor, minimum wages, and global warming. Paradoxically, the stripped-down economy of Crusoe's island reveals the moral and intellectual complexity of today's global economy. Emphasizing *Robinson Crusoe*'s economic themes not only raises these difficult questions but also allows my students to see how literature provides a space in which to think deeply about the implications of and contradictions in economic theory and practice.

My discussion-based classes are small; students are expected to practice their close-reading skills, contribute to the class's understanding of the novel, and build thematic readings for a final paper. However, my freshmen often have difficulty locating the concepts existing behind Crusoe's actions and tracing the novel's development of those concepts. In addition, they are often easily frustrated by the novel's paragraph and sentence structure. To respond to their difficulties, I have developed three assignments: a thematic paper, a comparative speech, and a series of creative-writing exercises.

First, each student's reading culminates in a thesis-driven essay that explores one of the economic themes we have developed in class discussion. As a preliminary draft for this paper, each student must write an open-ended, self-reflective piece that states his or her analytic paper's thesis, connects that central thesis to his or her own experiences, and explains what questions *Robinson Crusoe* has raised about his or her business assumptions or expectations. The final paper cannot include this self-reflection, but this draft work helps the student become invested in the analytic paper by mimicking Crusoe's activity of self-reflection. Because my students often have difficulty understanding how literature can use ideas and actions as plot structure and, simultaneously, question those ideas and actions, the essay must explore how Crusoe's economic activities function as both an external plot structure of adventure and an internal moral, emotional, or psychological structure of the self. The analytic paper thus encourages my students to create bridges between economic accounting and self-accounting.

Second, as we work our way through the novel, each student must prepare a brief in-class speech that places *Robinson Crusoe* in the context of seventeenth- and eighteenth-century philosophic thought. Students compare the novel with short excerpts from John Locke, Thomas Hobbes, and Jean-Jacques Rousseau; the speeches locate and analyze passages that share key concepts and phrases. By positioning the novel as engaged in political and economic philosophy, the speeches demonstrate literature's voice in such seemingly non-literary debates.

Third, I assign a series of short creative-writing assignments, balancing our thematic readings with an emphasis on Defoe's difficult writing style. Crusoe's lists, accounts, and ledgerlike entries often embody an economic approach to the world. The creative-writing assignments encourage my students to try on this economic writing style by looking for Crusoe-like descriptions in today's pop-culture magazines, making Crusoe-like lists of the objects in their dorm rooms, and keeping a Crusoe-like journal. I challenge my students to see how certain types of texts, in their very form, equate economic gain with the progress of the self; I ask my students if *Robinson Crusoe* is critiquing these forms of textual self-representation by using them.

Our preparation for the final, theme-based paper provides the class with a loose interpretative framework. Our discussions focus on Crusoe's success and failure as an entrepreneur of the self, investigating how his extreme circumstances force him—and the reader—to connect economic activity to moral, psychological, and social self-definition. Most obviously, we start our interpretation by reading the novel's first three pages together out loud; students readily understand that Crusoe's father's lecture on being content with "the middle Station of Life" (5) represents an outlook that Crusoe—and they—rebel against. The students empathize with Crusoe's "Notion of raising my Fortune" (13); I ask them to consider what conflicts that desire raises for Crusoe (why must Crusoe be caught in two terrible storms and shipwrecked? why must the enslaver be enslaved by Moors?). Examining the details of Crusoe's first business transaction—his voyage in which forty pounds of toys are turned into three hundred pounds of gold dust—the students wonder why those "aspiring Thoughts" of wealth presage "Ruin" (14). We open the text, then, by recognizing a basic question that *Robinson Crusoe* asks us: Should we place happiness in opposition to wealth, curtailing the impulse toward material accumulation in favor of other forms of self-definition (such as the family or spirituality)? Or, should we connect wealth and happiness, seeing the impulse toward self-improvement as necessarily tied to the quest for economic gain?

When business students examine Crusoe's life on the island, they inevitably see basic business concepts in the novel. We begin by discussing how Crusoe's island economy imagines a pure or stripped-down experience of supply and demand, production and consumption, and credit and debt. Students are excited to see Crusoe creating multiple meanings for business terms such as "Labor" (75), "Business" (77), "employment" (78), "invention" (87), "operations" (87), and "enterprise" (100). They are shocked to see abstract concepts such as "Evil" and "Good" analyzed "very impartially, like Debtor and Creditor" (49), and listed in an "Accompt" (50). Students observe that Crusoe immediately sees the island in economic terms, as in the famous passage, "I was King and Lord of all this Country indefeasibly, and had a Right of Possession" (73). Students learn that, after attempting to make the business of the island actually work, Crusoe must create a new economic model. Although Crusoe proudly proclaims, "I was Lord of the whole Manor; or if I pleas'd, I might call my self King, or Emperor over the whole Country which I had Possession of," he also must come to realize "[t]hat all the good Things of this World, are no farther good to us, than they are for our Use; and that whatever we may heap up indeed to give to others, we enjoy just as much as we can use, and no more" (94). Lively discussions often result from Crusoe's decision to rescue coins from his shipwreck (43) and the Spaniard's ship (140). Students ask, for example, why he takes the gold if he knows it is useless; they revisit these discussions when Crusoe's decision is rewarded because he takes the money when he leaves the island (200).

As we chart Crusoe's progress on the island, I ask students what business practices, both good and bad, they see Crusoe using to ensure success. Successful experimentation allows Crusoe to control supply and demand. His most pressing concern—the need to "secure a constant Supply" of food (86)—teaches him to predict, plan, and enact a cycle of regulated production and consumption. For example, Crusoe learns the correct season and location for planting rice and barley after losing seed to drought. As student papers have argued, he is able to conduct more plantings because he saved a portion of seeds; he has understood the need for experimentation and correctly accounted for failure as part of his business plan. Reflecting on his successful harvest, Crusoe exclaims, "by this Experiment I was made Master of my Business" (77). As his growing "Stock of Corn" demands bigger and bigger barns, Crusoe notes that his self-regulation and "resolve" is rewarded with "increase" (90).

Student papers have developed unique business-inflected readings of Crusoe's island activities. For example, they see Crusoe's attempt at making pots (87–89) or his construction of the umbrella (99) through the lens of innovative production and design. Although I typically place these scenes in the context of the Protestant work ethic, my students' business background encourages a more subtle reading of the scenes. They notice Crusoe's repeated attempts, in his making of clay pots, to match process with product: he tests each pot's clay composition, shape, and size and experiments with the methods of baking in the sun, burning in the fire, and glazing with sand (88). In Crusoe's exclamation, "No Joy at a Thing of so mean a Nature was ever equal to mine, when I found I had made an Earthen Pot that would bear the Fire" (89), students see excitement born out of the process of experimentation: imagining, testing, creating, and reduplicating imbues the product with meaning. Although they can recognize Crusoe's work as an internalization of discipline and his pots as a symbol of the civilization of nature, they tend to read the pot-making scene sympathetically. They see a creative drive overcoming obstacles and designing a product, revealing the science and art that underlies useful work. Student papers have positioned Crusoe's luxury-good creation of the clay pipe as a just reward for the labor of making the pot (105) and interpreted his citation of scripture as a reference to this labor, "[A]s we are all the Clay in the Hand of the Potter, no Vessel could say to him, Why hast thou form'd me thus" (152).

The class complicates our business reading of the novel by exploring the individual's role in systems of exchange, examining how Crusoe's stripped-down economic system becomes more complex when it must interact with other systems, cultures, and persons. Brief excerpts from Hobbes, Locke, and Rousseau give students a more sophisticated understanding of the layers of meaning underlying Crusoe's seemingly simplistic survivalist actions. Suddenly, Crusoe is attempting to create a civilized economy in a state of nature; his unique society of one rewrites the definition of power, property, and society. In part 1 of Hobbes's *Leviathan*, I often assign the first pages of chapters 10, "Of Power," and 11, "Of the Difference of Manners"; chapter 11 provides a striking description of man's "perpetuall and restlesse desire of Power after power" (161). In Locke's *Two Treatises of Government*, I often assign book 2, chapter 2, "Of the State of Nature"; I also find chapter 5, "Of Property," helpful, since it describes a solitary man creating *"Property"* out of nature by the Crusoe-like *"Labour"* of collecting acorns (288). Finally, I also often assign Rousseau's *Of the Social Contract*, specifically book 1, chapters 1, "The Subject of Book I"; 2, "The First Societies"; and 9, "Of Property."

In the speech assignment, I ask my students to perform a close reading that connects a scene from the novel to specific phrases, actions, and concepts presented in the assigned philosophical text. For example, student speeches have recognized Crusoe's situation in Rousseau's chapter on property, locating passages such as,

> To justify the right of the first occupant to any piece of land whatever, the following conditions must obtain: first that the land shall not be inhabited by anyone else; secondly, that the claimant occupies no more that he needs for subsistence; thirdly, that he takes possession, not by an idle ceremony, but by actually working and cultivating the soil.   (66)

Confronted with this definition, a student can now ask, Was Crusoe the first occupant of the island? Does Crusoe take more than he needs? And, does Crusoe see the activity of work as preceding his right of ownership?

In addition, we read excerpts from the philosophical texts addressing slavery and the state of war and juxtapose them with the scenes in which Crusoe engages in war with the savages; rescues and befriends Friday; and saves the Spaniard, Friday's father, and, later, the English captain. Although there are many ways of approaching Crusoe's relationship with the savages and Friday, the philosophical texts allow us to maintain and complicate our economic reading, helping my students see war and slavery as the consequences of power and property. Our earlier focus on Crusoe's island economy encourages the student to compare and contrast Crusoe's role in the business of land with his role in the business of people. I assign part 1, chapters 13, 14, and 15 in the *Leviathan*, in which the equality of men, laws of nature, and conditions of war are explained. Similarly, in *Two Treatises of Government*, I assign book 2, chapters 3, "Of the State of War," and 5, "Slavery." And, in *Of the Social Contract*, I assign book 1, chapters 3, "The Right of the Strongest," and 4, "Slavery." For example, Crusoe's reasoned reflection on the moral foundations of an attack on the cannibals—"what Right I had to engage in the Quarrel of that Blood" (124)—can easily be linked to any of the philosophical excerpts concerning war.

Crusoe's fear of the cannibals provides my students with an entrance into Crusoe's self-construction. They are often amazed that his business self is sacrificed to his emotional self; he admits, "I confess that these Anxieties put an End to all Inventions, and to all the Contrivances that I had laid for my future Accommodations and Conveniencies," and goes as far as to move "that Part of my Business which requir'd Fire; such as burning of Pots" to a part of the island where smoke would not be seen (128). Student speeches have connected Crusoe's confession to Hobbes's assertion that in the "condition" of war "there is no place for Industry; because the fruit thereof is uncertain." This passage ends with the famous statement that the state of war brings "continuall feare, and danger of violent death; And the life of man, solitary, poore, nasty, brutish, and short" (186). Students' close readings recognize that the economic balance created by one is a false business model; the true test of the self comes in the creation of an economic enterprise that, in turn, forms relationships with others in a social enterprise. For example, student speeches have questioned the ethics of Crusoe's decision to wait six months to rescue the Spaniards so that he can account for the grain needed to feed them (177–79). Students have also used these speeches to raise questions concerning Crusoe's need for both subjects and family and his lack of need for women.

Exploring Crusoe's relationship with Friday, students examine Crusoe's application of economic principles to personal relationships. For example, Crusoe explains, "I was greatly delighted with him, and made it my Business to teach him every Thing, that was proper to make him useful, handy, and helpful" (152). Student speeches have asked if Crusoe's relationship with Friday is one of business or family: is Friday a "Slave" (147), "Servant" (151), or "Child to a Father" (151)? They have focused on passages that construct Friday as an economic good, such as when Crusoe describes Friday as "swearing to be my Slave for ever" (147) and as learning "to say *Master*" (149). Student speeches have cited Locke's argument that "a Man, not having the Power of his Own Life *cannot*, by Compact, or his own Consent, *enslave himself* to any one, not put himself under the Absolute, Arbitrary Power of another, to take away his Life," and his explanation that "if once *Compact* enter between them, and make an agreement for a limited Power on the one side, and Obedience on the other, the State of War and *Slavery* ceases" (284–85). After saving Friday's life, Crusoe reports that Friday "lays his Head flat upon the Ground close to my Foot, and sets my other Foot upon his Head, . . . and . . . made all the Signs to me of Subjection, Servitude, and Submission imaginable" (147). As a result, students have wondered whether the two have entered into some sort of compact. This comparison of texts allows students to question Friday's actions, Crusoe's descriptions, and Locke's definitions and helps students understand the richness of the concepts underlying Crusoe's actions.

Finally, and most successfully, I use creative-writing assignments that encourage students to mimic Defoe's writing style. The creative-writing assignments address the difficulty students have with the novel's form, specifically Crusoe's excessive listing, inventorying, detailing, and charting. To show that accounting is an everyday eighteenth-century cultural practice, I display manuscript accounts that I have located in the Chancery Records held at the National Archives (formerly the Public Records Office). These lists provide a striking comparison with *Robinson Crusoe*'s form and content; for example, the account submitted for *Douglas v. Burnett* (1719) lists activities such as thatching a barn, making a gate, and building a wall (see fig. 1, lines 6, 8, 10, and 11). The last entry in this account quantifies one of Crusoe's activities, reading, "For three parts in four of 6:10:0 for ploughing and sowing of winter corn upon the farm in 1717--} 4.17.6." Intrigued by these glimpses of eighteenth-century life, students start to question how and why Defoe's fiction captures real ways of thinking about and organizing the world. Again, I encourage my students to see that the novel's formal qualities are born of an economic outlook on life that they share with Crusoe. Although Crusoe cannot check his bank account on the Internet or print graphs of a stock's changing value, he engages in a textual charting of progress that my business students recognize. Just as Crusoe catalogs every object and action on the island as a means of accounting for his life, the creative writing assignment encourages my students to make a similar equation between the form and content of accounting for themselves.

This creative-writing assignment has evolved to have several steps. In an essential preparatory step, students must note examples of Crusoe's accounting. Crusoe lists objects rescued from the shipwreck (41–43), actions in diary form (52–55), and steps in making objects (57); these early scenes often frustrate students. Crusoe's table of evil and good (49–50), chart of the seasons (78), and list of the savages killed (171) provide strikingly visual examples of accounting. After recognizing the elements of Defoe's form, I give students the first step in their creative-writing assignment: students must locate an example of Defoe's writing style in current popular culture. Looking in magazines, students must find a person who gives an account of him- or herself by describing his or her belongings, home, or daily routine. Students often bring in *People* (which lists famous people's routines), *Sports Illustrated* (which lists athletes' activities), and *Glamour* (which lists clothes in women's closets). I have had students bring in exercise-oriented articles, detailing steps for getting in

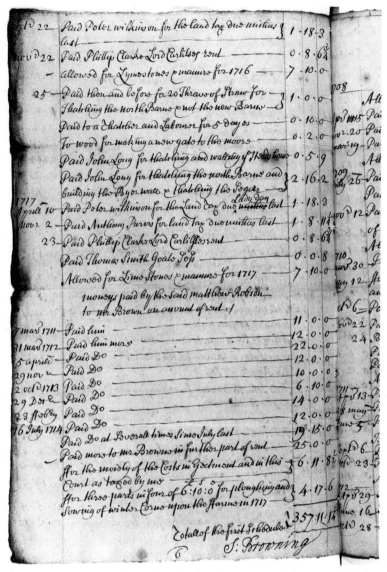

Fig. 1. An estate account submitted to the Chancery Court in 1719 as part of *Douglas v. Burnett* and recorded in the Court's Master's Reports. Source: National Archives (Public Records Office, Kew): c38/348.

shape, and home-decorating articles, featuring photographic inventories of objects. Students quickly recognize that Defoe's formal techniques are still alive and well.

After sharing these popular-culture examples of Defoe-like writing, students must then turn to their own lives. This step of the assignment requires each student to make a list of all the objects in his or her dorm room or of all the steps he or she takes in doing a simple task. Using these lists, the student then writes up a one-page "island" journal. In creating an account of the self, the student must choose objects and events that offer insight into who he or she is. This assignment works particularly well for freshmen who have just been "shipwrecked" on a new college campus and are self-consciously trying to create a new identity. This twenty-first-century journal must use eighteenth-century writing style; students must imitate Defoe's style on the level of the sentence and word, using similar punctuation, capitalization, and spelling. Students copy their journal entry on an overhead transparency. We share these creative-writing pieces by displaying them and reading them out loud in class. This assignment forces students to experience Defoe's writing style (if not live a Crusoe-like moment or two!), which helps them understand how Defoe's form illuminates Crusoe's obsessions, fears, hopes, and desires. The creative-writing assignment has been very successful because, in the process of taking account of themselves, the students come to see the connections between not only Defoe's form and content but also writing and self-construction.

When I first attempted a business reading of *Robinson Crusoe*, I feared the novel would be reduced to a simplified text. The exact opposite has happened. I have found that an economic emphasis enables my business students more readily to enter the text and to ask ever-widening questions of the novel and themselves. A variety of assignments—attempting thematic, comparative, and creative approaches—has helped me encourage this questioning. Obviously, I have a Crusoe-like goal for these assignments: I hope my students will experience reading and writing as a form of self-interpretation and self-creation. Crusoe's physical survival dictates many of his activities on the island, but, as my students come to realize, his survival as a human being depends on his writing down and meditating on his activities.

NOTES ON CONTRIBUTORS

Paula R. Backscheider is Philpott-Stevens Eminent Scholar in English at Auburn University and a past president of the American Society for Eighteenth-Century Studies. She is the author of the biography *Daniel Defoe: His Life* and four critical books, including *Daniel Defoe: Ambition and Innovation* and *Spectacular Politics*. She is the editor of *Selected Fiction and Drama by Eliza Haywood* and, with John Richetti, edited the anthology *Popular Fiction by Women, 1680–1730*. Her forthcoming book is *Eighteenth-Century Poets and Their Poetry*.

John Barberet is assistant professor of French at the University of Central Florida. He has published articles on Baudelaire and Balzac and served as host and cochair for the twenty-seventh meeting of the Society for Utopian Studies. He is working on a book-length study entitled "Scenarios of Diffusion from Balzac to Baudelaire," which discusses narrative strategies adopted in relation to shifts in the book trade in the nineteenth century.

Timothy C. Blackburn has taught at several colleges, the Marshall School in Minnesota, and Newark Academy in New Jersey. He is chair of the English department at Forsyth County Day School in North Carolina. He has published articles on *Captain Singleton*, *Robinson Crusoe*, and *My Ántonia*.

Richard Braverman teaches in the Department of English and Comparative Literature at Columbia University. He is the author of *Plots and Counterplots: Sexual Politics and the Body Politic in English Literature, 1660–1730* and numerous articles on Restoration and eighteenth-century literature and culture.

Anne Chandler is associate professor of English at Southern Illinois University, Carbondale. Her research focuses on the confluence of educational philosophy and sex-gender ideology in eighteenth-century Britain. She has published essays on Thomas Day, Mary Wollstonecraft, and William Godwin. These and other figures are discussed in a book in progress on Rousseau, gender, and late-eighteenth-century fiction.

Carl Fisher is professor of comparative literature at California State University, Long Beach. His publications include articles on Defoe, Sterne, Rousseau, Godwin, Hannah More, and the representation of pigs in the eighteenth century. He was coeditor, with Clorinda Donato, of the book review section of *Eighteenth-Century Studies* (2001–04).

George E. Haggerty is professor and chair of English at the University of California, Riverside. His books include *Gothic Fiction / Gothic Form*, *Unnatural Affections: Women and Fiction in the Later Eighteenth Century*, and *Men in Love: Masculinity and Sexuality in the Eighteenth Century*. He edited *Professions of Desire: Lesbian and Gay Studies in Literature* and *Gay Histories and Cultures: An Encyclopedia*.

Roxanne Kent-Drury is associate professor at Northern Kentucky University. Her recent publications focus on the literature of travel and exploration and include articles on colonial-exploration narratives and pirates and bandits. She also edited Catherine Cockburn Trotter's *Love at a Loss* for the *Broadview Anthology of Restoration and Early Eighteenth-Century Drama*.

Anne Lundin is associate professor of Library and Information Studies at the University of Wisconsin, Madison, where she teaches courses on children's literature. Her most recent publication is *Constructing the Canon of Children's Literature: Beyond Library Walls and Ivory Towers*. Her work is represented in a variety of journals, including *Children's Literature, Journal of Children's Literature, The Lion and the Unicorn, Children's Literature in Education*, and *Library Quarterly*.

Robert Maniquis teaches in the Department of English, University of California, Los Angeles. He is the author or editor of several volumes on eighteenth- and nineteenth-century literature, including *Lonely Empires: Personal and Public Visions of Thomas De Quincey, The English Opium-Eater, The Encyclopédie and the Age of Revolution, Les revolutions dans le monde ibérique*, and *British Radical Culture of the 1790s*.

Robert Markley is professor of English at the University of Illinois, Urbana. He is the author of fifty articles on seventeenth- and eighteenth-century literature, cultural studies, and the relations between literature and science. His books include *Two-Edg'd Weapons: Style and Ideology in the Comedies of Etherege, Wycherley, and Congreve*; *Fallen Languages: Crises of Representation in Newtonian England, 1660–1740*; and *The Far East and the English Imagination 1600–1730*. He is editor of *Eighteenth Century: Theory and Interpretation*.

Robert Mayer teaches British literature and film at Oklahoma State University. He is the author of *History and the Early English Novel: Matters of Fact from Bacon to Defoe* and editor of *Eighteenth-Century Fiction on Screen*.

Cheryl L. Nixon is assistant professor of English at the University of Massachusetts, Boston. She is completing a book entitled "Surrogate Family Plots in Eighteenth-Century Law and Literature: Guarding Estate, Blood, and Body," which explores the fictional and factual construction of surrogacy by juxtaposing the novel with manuscript Chancery Court records. She has edited *The Committee*, a Restoration comedy by Sir Robert Howard, and has published essays on Richardson, Austen, and eighteenth-century law.

Maximillian E. Novak has published numerous works on eighteenth-century literature. His books on Defoe are *Economics and the Fiction of Daniel Defoe*; *Defoe and the Nature of Man*; *Realism, Myth, and History in Defoe's Fiction*; and *Daniel Defoe, Master of Fictions: His Life and Ideas*.

Charles W. Pollard is president of John Brown University. He has published essays and reviews about British modernism and postcolonial literature in *Twentieth Century Literature, Interventions*, and *Christianity and Literature*. He is also the author of *New World Modernism: T. S. Eliot, Derek Walcott, and Kamau Brathwaite*.

Christina Sassi-Lehner is assistant professor of English at Bronx Community College, the City University of New York. Her critical and historical edition of Defoe's *The Storm* is forthcoming.

Gordon Sayre is associate professor of English at the University of Oregon. He is the author of *Les Sauvages Américains: Representations of Native Americans in French and English Colonial Literature* and *The Indian Chief as Tragic Hero* (forthcoming from the Univ. of North Carolina Press). He also edited *American Captivity Narratives: An Anthology*.

Manuel Schonhorn is professor emeritus of English and American literature at Southern Illinois University, Carbondale. He is the author of *Defoe's Politics* and the editor of *Daniel Defoe's General History of the Pyrates*. He has written on Pope, Fielding, Twain, Hemingway, and political theory. He serves as coeditor of the Stoke Newington Daniel Defoe Edition.

Geoffrey Sill is chair of the Department of English at Rutgers University. He has edited books on Walt Whitman and the plays of Fanny Burney and is the author of articles on Defoe and two books, *Defoe and the Idea of Fiction* and *The Cure of the Passions and the Origins of the English Novel*.

Laura M. Stevens is associate professor of English at the University of Tulsa, where she teaches English, American, and transatlantic literature of the seventeenth and eighteenth centuries. She is the author of *The Poor Indians: British Missionaries, Native Americans, and Colonial Sensibility*.

Roxann Wheeler is associate professor of English at Ohio State University, Columbus. She is at work on a second book on eighteenth-century literature about the West Indies and its connection to domestic English issues. Her first book, *The Complexion of Race: Categories of Difference in Eighteenth-Century British Culture*, examined the significance of both physical and cultural attributes to assumptions about racial similarity and difference in the eighteenth century.

Matthew Wickman is assistant professor at Brigham Young University. He was a Clark Library dissertation fellow at the University of California, Los Angeles, while completing his PhD on narratives of the Scottish Highlands. His published work appears in such journals as *PMLA* and *Eighteenth-Century Fiction*, and he is currently completing a book manuscript about Scottish Highland romance and the rupture of experience from knowledge in modernity.

Everett Zimmerman was professor of English at the University of California, Santa Barbara. He authored *Defoe and the Novel*, *Swift's Narrative Satires*, and *The Boundaries of Fiction: History and the Eighteenth-Century British Novel*.

SURVEY PARTICIPANTS

Paula R. Backscheider, *Auburn University*
John Barberet, *University of Central Florida*
Sandra Beckett, *Brock University*
Timothy C. Blackburn, *Newark Academy*
Gene Blanton, *Jacksonville State University*
J. P. C. Brown, *Middlesex University*
Frederick Bracher, *Pomona College*
Leo Braudy, *University of Southern California*
Margaret Bruzelius, *Harvard University*
Jill Campbell, *Yale University*
Anne Chandler, *Southern Illinois University, Carbondale*
DeAnn De Luna, *Johns Hopkins University*
Aparna Dharwadker, *University of Oklahoma*
Donald Eddy, *Cornell University*
Martin Green, *Tufts University*
Daniel Hoffman, *Swarthmore College*
Jeffrey Hopes, *Université du Maine, Le Mans*
Sarah Jordon, *Albion College*
Betty Joseph, *Rice University*
Roxanne Kent-Drury, *Northern Kentucky University*
Shelley King, *Queen's University, Canada*
William Kinsley, *University of Montreal*
Deborah Knuth, *Colgate University*
Mark Koch, *Saint Mary's College*
David J. Leigh, *Seattle University*
Anne Lundin, *University of Wisconsin, Madison*
Robert Maniquis, *University of California, Los Angeles*
Robert Markley, *University of Illinois, Urbana*
Robert Mayer, *Oklahoma State University*
John Middendorf, *Columbia University*
John Morillo, *North Carolina State University*
Cheryl L. Nixon, *University of Massachusetts, Boston*
Jo Alyson Parker, *Saint Joseph's University*
Charles W. Pollard, *Calvin College*
Christina Sassi-Lehner, *Bronx Community College, City University of New York*
Gordon Sayre, *University of Oregon*
Manuel Schonhorn, *Southern Illinois University, Carbondale*
Geoffrey Sill, *Rutgers University*
Rebecca Taylor, *Washington University*
Matthew Wickman, *Brigham Young University*
Lance Wilcox, *Elmhurst College*
Everett Zimmerman, *University of California, Santa Barbara*

WORKS CITED

Abrams, M. H., and Stephen Greenblatt. *The Norton Anthology of English Literature*. 7th ed. Vol. 1. New York: Norton, 2000.

Adams, Percy. *Travelers and Travel Liars: 1660–1800*. Berkeley: U of California P, 1962.

———. *Travel Literature and the Evolution of the Novel*. Lexington: UP of Kentucky, 1983.

Adventures of Robinson Crusoe [*Aventuras de Robinson Crusoe*]. Dir. Luis Buñuel. Perf. Dan O'Herlihy, Jaime Fernandez. 1952.

Alkon, Paul. *Defoe and Fictional Time*. Athens: U of Georgia P, 1979.

American Psychiatric Association. *Diagnostic and Statistical Manual of Mental Disorders*. 4th ed. Washington: Amer. Psychiatric Assn., 1994.

Aravamudan, Srinivas. *Tropicopolitans: Colonialism and Agency, 1688–1804*. Durham: Duke UP, 1999.

Armstrong, Nancy, and Leonard Tennenhouse. "The Interior Difference: A Brief Genealogy of Dreams, 1650–1717." *Eighteenth-Century Studies* 23 (1990): 458–78.

Atkinson, Geoffroy. *The Extraordinary Voyage in French Literature*. 1920–22. 2 vols. New York: Franklin, 1969.

Aubin, Penelope. *The Strange Adventures of the Count de Vinevil and His Family*. *Popular Fiction by Women 1660–1730: An Anthology*. Ed. Paula R. Backscheider and John J. Richetti. New York: Oxford UP, 1996. 113–51.

Ayers, Robert. "*Robinson Crusoe*: 'Allusive Allegorick History.'" *PMLA* 82 (1967): 399–407.

Bachelard, Gaston. *The Poetics of Space*. Trans. Maria Jolas. Boston: Beacon, 1969.

Bachstrom, Johann Friedrich. *Das Land der Inquiraner*. Frankfurt, 1736.

Backscheider, Paula R. *A Being More Intense: A Study of the Prose Works of Bunyan, Swift, and Defoe*. New York: AMS, 1984.

———. *Daniel Defoe: His Life*. Baltimore: Johns Hopkins UP, 1989.

———. "The Novel's Gendered Space." *Revising Women: Eighteenth-Century "Women's Fiction" and Social Engagement*. Ed. Backscheider. Baltimore: Johns Hopkins UP, 2000. 1–30.

Baker, Henry. *Universal Spectator* 466 (10 Sept. 1737): n. pag.

Bakhtin, Mikhail. *The Dialogic Imagination*. Ed. Michael Holquist. Trans. Caryl Emerson and Holquist. Austin: U of Texas P, 1981.

Ballard, J. G. *Concrete Island*. New York: Farrar, 1973.

Barbauld, Anna Letetia. "Defoe." *The British Novelists*. Ed. Barbauld. Vol. 16. London: Rivington, 1810. i–vii.

Barthes, Roland. *S/Z*. Trans. Richard Howard. New York: Hill, 1974.

Baskerville, John D. "Free Jazz: A Reflection of Black Power Ideology." *Journal of Black Studies* 24 (1994): 484–97.

Bastian, Frank. *Defoe's Early Life*. London: Macmillan, 1981.

Battestin, Martin C., with Ruthe R. Battestin. *Henry Fielding: A Life*. London: Routledge, 1989.

Bawerk, Böhm. *The Positive Theory of Capital*. Trans. William Smart. New York: Stechert, 1923.

Beattie, James. "On Fable and Romance. Dissertations Moral and Critical." Rogers, *Defoe* 59–60.

Beckett, Samuel. *Endgame*. Lawall and Mack 2455–87.

Behn, Aphra. *Oroonoko*. Ed. Joanna Lipking. Norton Critical Edition. New York: Norton, 1997.

Bell, Daniel. *The Cultural Contradictions of Capitalism*. New York: Basic, 1996.

Bell, Ian. *Defoe's Fiction*. London: Helm, 1985.

Bender, John. *Imagining the Penitentiary*. Chicago: U of Chicago P, 1987.

Benjamin, Walter. "The Storyteller." Trans. Harry Zohn. *Illuminations*. Ed. Hannah Arendt. New York: Schocken, 1969. 83–109.

Bernier, François. "A New Division of the Earth, according to the Different Species or Races of Men Who Inhabit It." *Memoirs Read before the Anthropological Society of London, 1863–4*. Vol. 1. Trans. T. Bendyshe. London: Longman, 1865. 361–62.

Bewick, Thomas. *Memoir of Thomas Bewick, Written by Himself 1822–28*. London: Lane, 1924.

Bhabha, Homi K. "Of Mimicry and Man: Ambivalence and Colonial Discourse." *The Location of Culture*. New York: Routledge, 1994. 85–92.

Bioy Casares, Adolfo. *The Invention of Morel*. Trans. Ruth L. C. Simms. New York: New York Rev., 2003.

Bishop, Elizabeth. "Crusoe in England." *Complete Poems 1927–1979*. New York: Farrar, 1983. 162–66.

Blackburn, Timothy C. "Friday's Religion: Its Nature and Importance in *Robinson Crusoe*." *Eighteenth-Century Studies* 18 (1985): 360–82.

Blackwell, Jeannine. "An Island of Her Own: Heroines of the German Robinsonades from 1720 to 1800." *German Quarterly* 58 (1985): 5–26.

Blaim, Artur. *Early English Utopian Fiction: A Study of a Literary Genre*. Lublin, 1984.

———. "The Text and Genre Pattern: More's *Utopia* and the Structure of Early Utopian Fiction." *Essays in Poetics* 6 (1981): 18–53.

Blair, Hugh. *Lectures on Rhetoric and Belles Lettres*. 1783. Rogers, *Defoe* 60–61.

Blanchot, Maurice. "Le journal intime et le récit." *Le livre à venir*. Paris: Gallimard, 1959. 271–79.

Blewett, David. *Defoe and the Art of Fiction*. Toronto: U of Toronto P, 1979.

———. *The Illustrations of* Robinson Crusoe. Gerards Cross: Smythe, 1995.

The Blue Lagoon. Dir. Randall Keiser. Columbia Pictures, 1980.

Bluestone, George. *Novels into Film*. Berkeley: U of California P, 1957.

Blumenbach, Johann Friedrich. *The Anthropological Treatises of Johann Friedrich Blumenbach*. Trans. and ed. Thomas Benyshe. London: Longman, 1785.

Boardman, Michael M. *Defoe and the Uses of Narrative*. New Brunswick: Rutgers UP, 1983.

Bohls, Elizabeth A. *Women Travel Writers and the Language of Landscape Aesthetics 1716–1818*. Cambridge: Cambridge UP, 1995.

Bond, Donald, ed. *The Spectator*. 5 vols. Oxford: Clarendon, 1987.

Bordieu, Pierre. *The Field of Cultural Production*. New York: Columbia UP, 1993.

Boucher, Philip P. *Cannibal Encounters: Europeans and Island Caribs, 1492–1763*. Baltimore: Johns Hopkins UP, 1992.

Boyle, Frank. *Swift as Nemesis: Modernity and Its Satirist*. Stanford: Stanford UP, 2000.

Bradley, Richard. *A Philosophical Account of the Works of Nature*. London: Mears, 1721.

Braverman, Richard. *Plots and Counterplots: Sexual Politics and the Body Politic in English Literature, 1660–1730*. Cambridge: Cambridge UP, 1993.

Brigham, Clarence E. "Bibliography of the American Editions of *Robinson Crusoe* to 1830." *Proceedings of the American Antiquarian Society* 67 (1958): 137–83.

Brophy, Elizabeth Bergen. *Women's Lives and the Eighteenth-Century English Novel*. Tampa: U of South Florida P, 1991.

Brüggemann, Fritz. *Utopie und Robinsonade*. Weimar: Dunker, 1914.

Buffon, Georges Louis Leclerc. *Natural History: General and Particular*. 1749. Trans. William Smellie. 35 vols. London: Cadell and Davies, 1812.

Bunyan, John. *Pilgrim's Progress*. Ed. N. H. Keeble. Oxford World Classics. New York: Oxford UP, 1998.

———. *Pilgrim's Progress*. Ed. Roger Sharrock. Harmondsworth: Penguin, 1987.

———. *The Pilgrim's Progress, from This World to That Which Is to Come: The Second Part*. Ed. James Blanton Wharey and Roger Sharrock. Oxford: Clarendon, 1960.

Burnham, Michelle. Introduction. Winkfield [ed. Burnham] 159–92.

Campe, Joachim Heinrich. *Robinson der Jüngere*. Hamburg, 1779.

Carson, James. "Narrative Cross-Dressing and the Critique of Authorship in the Novels of Richardson." *Writing the Female Voice: Essays on Epistolary Literature*. Ed. Elizabeth C. Goldsmith. Boston: Northeastern UP, 1989. 95–113.

Carter, Angela. "Master." *Fireworks: Nine Profane Pieces*. New York: Harper, 1981. 78–87.

Casas, Bartolomé de las. *A Short Account of the Destruction of the Indies*. Ed. and trans. Nigel Griffin. Introd. Anthony Pagden. London: Penguin, 1992.

Cast Away. Dir. Robert Zemeckis. Twentieth Century Fox and Dreamworks, 2000.

Certeau, Michel de. "Writing vs. Time: History and Anthropology in the Writings of Lafitau." *Yale French Studies* 59 (1980): 37–64.

Cervantes, Miguel de. *Don Quixote*. Trans. J. M. Cohen. London: Penguin, 1950.

Chalmers, Alan. "Film, Censorship, and the 'Corrupt Original' of *Gulliver's Travels*." Mayer, *Fiction* 70–87.

Chalmers, George. *Life of Daniel Defoe*. 1785. Rev. and enl. ed. London, 1790.

Claeys, Gregory, and Lyman Tower Sargent. "On the Frontiers of Utopia: Satires and Robinsonades." *Utopia: The Search for the Ideal Society in the Western World.* Ed. Roland Schaer, Claeys, and Sargent. New York: New York Public Lib., 2000. 180–83.

Clarkson, Thomas. *An Essay on the Slavery and Commerce of the Human Species, Particularly the African.* Philadelphia: Cruikshank, 1787.

Clowes, Edith W. "The Robinson Myth Reread in Postcolonial and Postcommunist Modes." *Critique: Studies in Contemporary Fiction* 36 (1995): 145–59.

Coetzee, J. M. *Foe.* New York: Viking, 1987.

Colley, Linda. *Britons: The Forging of a Nation.* New Haven: Yale UP, 1992.

Columbus, Robert. "Conscious Artistry in *Moll Flanders.*" *SEL* 3 (1963): 415–32.

The Compleat Geographer; or, The Chorography and Topography of All the Known Parts of the Earth. 4th ed. London: Knapton, 1723. N. pag.

"Complexion." *The Encyclopedia Britannica.* 3rd. ed. 1797.

Congreve, William. *Incognita.* The Mourning Bride, *Poems and Miscellanies.* Ed. Bonamy Dobrée. Vol. 2. London: Oxford UP, n.d. 1–74.

Conrad, Joseph. *Heart of Darkness.* Ed. Robert Kimbrough. Norton Critical Edition. 3rd ed. New York: Norton, 1988.

Cottom, Daniel. *Cannibals and Philosophers: Bodies of Enlightenment.* Baltimore: Johns Hopkins UP, 2001.

Cowper, William. "Verses Supposed to be Written by Alexander Selkirk during His Stay in the Island of Juan Fernandez." *The Poems.* By Cowper. Ed. J. C. Bailey. London: Methuen, 1905. 218.

Craig, Edward. Introduction. *The Life and Strange Surprising Adventures of Robinson Crusoe of York.* By Daniel Defoe. London: Basilisk, 1979. 7–42.

Crane, Ronald S. *Critical and Historical Principles of Literary History.* Chicago: Chicago UP, 1971.

Croft, Herbert. *Love and Madness.* London, 1786.

Crusoe. Dir. Caleb Deschanel. Perf. Aidan Quinn, Hepburn Graham, Ade Sapara. 1988.

Damrosch, Leopold, Jr. *God's Plot and Man's Stories: Studies in the Fictional Imagination from Milton to Fielding.* Chicago: U of Chicago P, 1985.

Daubenton, Marguerite. *Zelia in the Desert.* London, 1789. Trans. of *Zélie dans le désert.* Paris, 1786–87.

Day, Geoffrey. *From Novel to Novel.* London: Routledge, 1987.

Defoe, Daniel. *Aventures de Robinson Crusoe.* Paris: Fournier, 1840.

———. *Captain Singleton.* London, 1720.

———. *Colonel Jack.* Ed. Samuel Holt Monk. Oxford: Oxford UP, 1965.

———. *The Consolidator.* London, 1705.

———. *An Essay on the History and Reality of Apparitions.* London, 1727.

———. *An Essay upon Projects.* London, 1697.

———. *The Farther Adventures of Robinson Crusoe.* 1719. Introd. G. H. Maynadier. Boston: Old Corner Bookstore–Harvard UP, 1903.

————. *History of the Union between England and Scotland*. London, 1709.

————. *A Hymn to the Pillory*. London, 1703.

————. A Journal of the Plague Year: *Authoritative Text, Backgrounds, Contexts, Criticism*. Ed. Paula R. Backscheider. Norton Critical Edition. New York: Norton, 1992.

————. *Das Leben und die gantz ungemeine Begesbenheiten des* Robinson Crusoe. 6th ed. Leipzig, 1720.

————. *Moll Flanders*. Ed. G. A. Starr. Oxford: Oxford UP, 1981.

————. *A New Voyage round the World by a Course Never Sailed Before*. 1724. Ed. George A. Aitkin. London: Dent, 1902.

————. *The Political History of the Devil, as Well Ancient as Modern: In Two Parts*. London, 1726.

————. *Robinson Crusoe*. Ed. Michael Shinagel. Norton Critical Edition. 2nd ed. New York: Norton, 1994.

————. *Serious Reflections during the Life and Surprising Adventures of Robinson Crusoe*. Introd. G. H. Maynadier. Boston: Old Corner Bookstore–Harvard UP, 1903.

————. *The Shortest Way with the Dissenters*. London, 1703.

————. The True-Born Englishman *and Other Writings*. Ed. P. N. Furbank and W. R. Owens. New York: Penguin, 1997.

————. *Vindication of the Press*. London, 1718.

De la Mare, Walter. *Desert Islands and Robinson Crusoe*. London: Faber, 1930.

Deloria, Philip J. *Playing Indian*. New Haven: Yale UP, 1998.

Denby, David. "The Current Cinema." *New Yorker* 20 Dec. 2000: 108–09.

Doody, Margaret. *The True Story of the Novel*. New Brunswick: Rutgers UP, 1996.

Dostoevsky, Fyodor. *Notes from the Underground*. Lawall and Mack 1301–79.

Dunlop, John. *The History of Fiction*. Vol. 3. London: Longman, 1814.

During, Simon, ed. *The Cultural Studies Reader*. London: Routledge, 1993.

Earle, Peter. *The World of Defoe*. London: Weidenfeld, 1976.

Eco, Umberto. *The Island of the Day Before*. Trans. William Weaver. New York: Harcourt, 1995.

Ehrenpreis, Irvin. *The "Types Approach" to Literature*. New York: King's Crown, 1945.

Electronic Text Center. Robinson Crusoe. Univ. of Virginia. 3 Oct. 2004 <http://etext.lib.Virginia.edu/toc/modeng/public/DefCru1.html>. Rector and Visitors of the U of Virginia, 2000.

Elliot, Robert C. *The Shape of Utopia: Studies in a Literary Genre*. Chicago: U of Chicago P, 1970.

Encyclopedia Britannica. 3rd ed. 18 vols. Edinburgh: Bell, 1797.

Endo, Shusaku. *Silence*. 1969. Trans. William Johnston. New York: Taplinger, 1980.

The Erotic Adventures of Robinson Crusoe. Dir. Ken Dixon. Prod. Dick Randall. Spectacular Trading, 1972.

Fabian, Johannes. *Time and the Other: How Anthropology Makes Its Object*. New York: Columbia UP, 1983.

Fairchild, Hoxie Neale. *The Noble Savage: A Study in Romantic Naturalism*. New York: Russell, 1928.

Fausett, David. Introduction. Smeeks ix–lvi.

———. *The Strange Surprizing Sources of* Robinson Crusoe. Amsterdam: Rodopi, 1994.

Figuerola, Carmen. "The Robinson Myth in Jean-Richard Bloch's *Le Robinson juif*." *Robinson Crusoe: Myths and Metamorphoses*. Ed. Lieve Spaas and Brian Stimpson. New York: St. Martin's, 1996. 157–64.

Flynn, Carol Houlihan. *The Body in Swift and Defoe*. Cambridge: Cambridge UP, 1990.

———. "Consumptive Fictions: Cannibalism and Defoe." Defoe, *Robinson Crusoe* 423–32.

Foigny, Gabriel de. *The Southern Land, Known*. Trans. and ed. David Fausett. Syracuse: Syracuse UP, 1993.

Forster, E. M. *Aspects of the Novel*. 1927. New York: Harcourt, 1954.

Foucault, Michel. *The Order of Things: An Archaeology of the Human Sciences*. New York: Pantheon, 1970.

———. "What Is an Author?" *The Foucault Reader*. Ed. Paul Rabinow. New York: Pantheon, 1984. 101–20.

Frank, Andre Gunder. *ReOrient: Global Economy in the Asian Age*. Berkeley: U of California P, 1997.

Franklin, Benjamin. *Autobiography*. Writings 1305–1469.

———. "A Dissertation on Liberty and Necessity, Pleasure and Pain." *Writings* 57–71.

———. *Writings*. New York: Lib. of America, 1987.

Frohock, Richard. "Violence and Awe: The Foundations of Government in Aphra Behn's New World Settings." *Eighteenth-Century Fiction* 8 (1996): 437–52.

Furbank, P. N., and W. R. Owens. *A Critical Bibliography of Daniel Defoe*. London: Pickering, 1998.

———. *Defoe De-Attributions*. London: Hambleton, 1994.

Gall, Michel. *La vie sexuelle de Robinson Crusoë*. Paris: J'ai Lu, 1986.

Garnier, Charles G. T., ed. *Voyages imaginaire, songes, visions, et romans cabalistiques*. 36 vols. Amsterdam, 1787–89.

Garrett, Leah. "The Jewish Robinson Crusoe." *Comparative Literature* 54. 3 (2002): 215–28.

Genette, Gérard. *Fiction and Diction*. Trans. Catherine Porter. Ithaca: Cornell UP, 1993.

George, Jean Craighead. *Julie of the Wolves*. New York: Harper, 1972.

Gildon, Charles. *The Life and Strange Surprising Adventures of Mr. D— De F—, of London, Hosier, in a Dialogue between Him, Robinson Crusoe, and His Man Friday*. London, 1719.

———. *The Life and Strange Surprizing Adventures of Mr. D— De F—*. Robinson Crusoe *Examin'd and Criticis'd*. Ed. Paul Dottin. London: Dent, 1923. 63–128.

———. *The Life and Strange Surprizing Adventures of Mr. D—De F—*. Excerpt. Defoe, *Robinson Crusoe* 257–61.

Giraudoux, Jean. *Suzanne et la pacifique*. Paris: Émile-Paul, 1921.

Golding, William. *Lord of the Flies*. Ed. James R. Baker and Arthur P. Ziegler, Jr. New York: Perigee, 1988.

———. *Pincher Martin: The Two Lives of Christopher Martin*. San Diego: Harcourt, 1984.

Goldmann, Lucien. *Pour une sociologie du roman*. Paris: Gallimard, 1964.

Goldsmith, Oliver. *An History of the Earth and Animated Nature in Four Volumes*. Philadelphia: Carey, 1795.

Gove, Philip Babcock. *The Imaginary Voyage in Prose Fiction: A History of Its Criticism and a Guide for Its Study, with an Annotated Checklist of 215 Imaginary Voyages from 1700 to 1800*. New York: Columbia UP, 1941.

Graham, Maria. *Journal of a Voyage to Brazil*. London: Longman, 1824.

Green, Martin. *The Robinson Crusoe Story*. University Park: Pennsylvania State UP, 1990.

———. *Seven Types of Adventure Tale: An Etiology of a Major Genre*. University Park: Pennsylvania State UP, 1991.

Greenblatt, Stephen. *Marvelous Possessions: The Wonder of the New World*. Chicago: U of Chicago P, 1996.

Greene, Jody. "The Genre of Piracy." Unpublished essay. 1998.

Habermas, Jürgen. "Modernity: An Unfinished Project." Trans. Shierry Nicholsen. *Critical Theory: The Essential Readings*. Ed. David Ingram and Julia Simon-Ingram. New York: Paragon, 1991. 342–56.

Haken, Johann Christian Ludwig. *Bibliothek der Robinsone*. 5 vols. Berlin: Unger, 1805–08.

Hakluyt, Richard. *The Principal Navigations, Voyages, Traffiques and Discoveries of the English Nation*. 1598–1600. 12 vols. Glasgow: MacLehose, 1904.

Hamilton, Virginia. *The Planet of Junior Brown*. New York: Macmillan, 1971.

Hannaford, Ivan. *Race: The History of an Idea in the West*. Washington: Woodrow Wilson Center Press; Baltimore: Johns Hopkins UP, 1996.

Harris, W. C. "Whitman's *Leaves of Grass* and the Writing of a New American Bible." *Walt Whitman Quarterly Review* 16 (1999): 172–90.

Haywood, Eliza. *Love in Excess*. Ed. David Oakleaf. Peterborough, Ont.: Broadview, 1994.

Heilbrun, Carolyn G. *Writing a Woman's Life*. New York: Ballantine, 1988.

Herrmann, Claudine. *The Tongue Snatchers*. Lincoln: U of Nebraska P, 1989.

Hobbes, Thomas. *Leviathan*. Ed. C. B. MacPherson. Harmondsworth: Penguin, 1985.

Hoffman, Margit. "The J. A. Ahlstrand Collection of Robinsonades at the Royal Library in Stockholm." *Otium et Negotium: Studies in Onomatology and Library Science*. Stockholm: Acta Bibliothecae Regiae Stockholmiensis, 1973. 142–50.

Hopes, Jeffrey. "Real and Imaginary Stories: *Robinson Crusoe* and the *Serious Reflections*." *Eighteenth-Century Fiction* 8 (1996): 313–28.

Hulme, Peter. *Colonial Encounters: Europe and the Native Caribbean, 1492–1797*. New York: Methuen, 1986.

Hulme, Peter, and Neil Whitehead, eds. *Wild Majesty: Encounters with Caribs from Columbus to the Present Day*. Oxford: Clarendon, 1992.

Hume, Robert. "Historical Scholarship: Its Aims and Limits." *Review of English Studies* ns 53 (2002): 399–422.

Hunter, J. Paul. *Before Novels: The Cultural Contexts of Eighteenth-Century English Fiction*. New York: Norton, 1990.

———. *The Reluctant Pilgrim: Defoe's Emblematic Method and Quest for Form in* Robinson Crusoe. Baltimore: Johns Hopkins UP, 1966.

Hurlimann, Bettina. *Three Centuries of Children's Books in Europe*. Cleveland: World, 1968.

Hutcheon, Linda. *Modelling the Postmodern, Parody and Politics: A Poetics of Postmodernism, History, Theory, Fiction*. New York: Routledge, 1988.

———. *A Theory of Parody: The Teaching of Twentieth-Century Art Forms*. New York: Methuen, 1985.

Hutchins, Henry. Robinson Crusoe *and Its Printing, 1719–1731: A Bibliographical Study*. New York: Columbia UP, 1925.

James, Eustace Anthony. *Daniel Defoe's Many Voices: A Rhetorical Study of Prose Style and Literary Method*. Amsterdam: Rodopi, 1972.

Jarvis, Carol. *Physical Examination and Health Assessment*. Philadelphia: Saunders, 1996.

Johnson, Samuel. Excerpt. Defoe, *Robinson Crusoe* 264.

Jooma, Minaz. "Robinson Crusoe Inc(corporates): Domestic Economy, Incest, and the Trope of Cannibalism." *Lit* 8 (1997): 61–81.

Journal des scavans. Paris, 1720. 503–05.

Joyce, James. Excerpt. Defoe, *Robinson Crusoe* 320–23.

Kafka, Franz. *The Metamorphosis*. Lawall and Mack 1996–2030.

Kahn, Madeleine. *Narrative Transvestism: Rhetoric and Gender in the Eighteenth-Century English Novel*. Ithaca: Cornell UP, 1991.

Kay, Carol. *Political Constructions*. Ithaca: Cornell UP, 1988.

King, Stephen. "Survivor Type." *Skeleton Crew*. New York: Putnam, 1985. 407–26.

Knox, Robert. "Autobiography." Knox, *Historical Relation* [ed. Ryan] xxix–xxxvi.

——— *An Historical Relation of Ceylon*. Manchester: Ayer, 1977.

———. *An Historical Relation of Ceylon*. Ed. James Ryan. Glasgow: MacLehose, 1911.

———. *An Historical Relation of the Island Ceylon in the East Indies*. Introd. H. A. I. Goonetileke. New Delhi: Navrang, 1983.

Koonce, Howard L. "Mull's Muddle: Defoe's Use of Irony in *Moll Flanders*." *ELH* 30 (1963): 277–88.

Krakauer, Jon. *Into Thin Air: A Personal Account of the Mount Everest Disaster*. New York: Vintage, 1999.

Kupperman, Karen Ordahl. "Presentment of Civility: English Reading of American Self-Presentation in the Early Years of Colonization." *William and Mary Quarterly* 64 (1997): 193–228.

Lach, Donald, and Edwin J. van Kley. *Trade, Missions, Literature. A Century of Advance.* Vol. 3 of *Asia in the Making of Europe.* Ed. Lach. Chicago: U of Chicago P, 1993.

Lawall, Sarah, and Maynard Mack, eds. *The Norton Anthology of World Literature.* 2nd ed. New York: Norton, 2002.

Leavis, F. R. *The Great Tradition.* London: Chatto, 1950.

Le Clerc, Jean. *Bibliotheque ancienne et moderne.* 29 vols. Amsterdam, 1721.

Le Comte, Louis. *Memoirs and Observations Topographical, Physical, Mathematical, Natural, Civil, and Ecclesiastical, Made in a Late Journey through the Empire of China.* London, 1697.

Léry, Jean de. *History of a Voyage to the Land of Brazil.* Trans. and introd. Janet Whatley. Berkeley: U of California P, 1990.

Lestringant, Frank. *Cannibals: The Discovery and Representation of the Cannibal from Columbus to Jules Verne.* Trans. Rosemary Morris. Berkeley: U of California P, 1997.

Levine, Joseph M. *Humanism and History: Origins of Modern English Historiography.* Ithaca: Cornell UP, 1987.

Liu, Lydia H. "Robinson Crusoe's Earthenware Pot." *Critical Inquiry* 25 (1999): 728–57.

Locke, John. *Two Treatises of Government.* 1690. Cambridge: Cambridge UP, 1988.

London, April. *Women and Property in the Eighteenth-Century English Novel.* New York: Cambridge UP, 1999.

The Longman Anthology of British Literature. Ed. David Damrosch. 2nd ed. Vol. 1. New York: Longman, 2003.

Longueville, Peter. *The Hermit; or, The Unparalle[le]d Sufferings and Surprising Adventures of Mr. Philip Quarll.* 1727. New York: Garland, 1972.

Lost in Space. Dir. Stephen Hopkins. New Line Cinema, 1998.

Love, W. DeLoss. *Samson Occom and the Christian Indians of New England.* Introd. Margaret Connell Szasz. 1899. Syracuse: Syracuse UP, 2000.

Lovett, Charles, and Robert Lovett. Robinson Crusoe: *A Bibliographical Checklist of English Long Editions, 1719–1979.* New York: Greenwood, 1991.

Lyotard, Jean-François. "Answering the Question: What Is Postmodernism?" *The Postmodern Condition: A Report on Knowledge.* Trans. Geoff Bennington and Brian Massumi. Minneapolis: U of Minnesota P, 1984.

Macherey, Pierre. *A Theory of Literary Production.* Trans. Geoffrey Wall. London: Routledge, 1978.

The Making of Cast Away. Dir. Thomas C. Grane. Perf. Tom Hanks, Helen Hunt, Robert Zemeckis, William Broyles, Jr. *Cast Away.* Spec. ed. DVD. Twentieth Century Fox, 2001.

Mancall, Mark. *Russia and China: Their Diplomatic Relations to 1728.* Cambridge: Harvard UP, 1971.

Man Friday. Dir. Jack Gold. Perf. Peter O'Toole, Richard Roundtree. UAV, 1975.

Marin, Louis. *Utopics: Spatial Play*. Trans. Robert A. Vollrath. Atlantic Highlands: Humanities, 1984.

Markley, Robert. "'I Have Now Done with My Island, and All Manner of Discourse about It': Crusoe's *Farther Adventures* and the Unwritten History of the Novel." *Blackwell Companion to the Eighteenth-Century Novel*. Ed. Paula R. Backscheider and Catherine Ingrassia. Oxford: Blackwell, forthcoming.

———. "'So Inexhaustible a Treasure of Gold': Defoe, Credit, and the Romance of the South Seas." *Eighteenth-Century Life* 18 (1994): 148–67.

Marryat, Frederick. *Masterman Ready; or, The Wreck of the Pacific*. 1841. New York: Harper, 1928.

Martell, Yann. *Life of Pi: A Novel*. New York: Harcourt, 2001.

Martin, Charles. *Passages from Friday*. [Omaha]: Abbattoir, 1983.

Marx, Karl. "Crusoe and Capitalism." Excerpt. Defoe, *Robinson Crusoe* 274–77.

Maslen, Keith I. "Edition Quantities for *Robinson Crusoe*, 1719." *Library* 24 (1969): 145–50.

———. "The Printers of *Robinson Crusoe*." *Library* 7 (1952): 124–31.

Mayer, Robert, ed. *Eighteenth-Century Fiction on Screen*. Cambridge: Cambridge UP, 2002.

———. *History and the Early English Novel: Matters of Fact from Bacon to Defoe*. Cambridge: Cambridge UP, 1997.

———. "Three Cinematic Robinsonades." Mayer, *Eighteenth-Century Fiction* 35–51.

Mazella, David. "Some Implications of Curricular Change at the University of Houston." *Profession 1998*. New York: MLA, 1998. 89–104.

Mazer, Harry. *The Island Keeper*. New York: Laurel-Leaf, 1981.

McBurney, William Harlin. *Check List of English Prose Fiction, 1700–1739*. Cambridge: Harvard UP, 1960.

McCarthy, Keely. "'Reducing them to Civilitie': Religious Conversions and Cultural Transformations in Protestant Missionary Narratives, 1690–1790." Diss. U of Maryland, 2000. *DAI* 61 (2001): 9982812.

McFarlane, Brian. *Novel to Film: An Introduction to the Theory of Adaptation*. Oxford: Clarendon P, 1996.

McKeon, Michael. "Defoe and the Naturalization of Desire: *Robinson Crusoe*." Defoe, *Robinson Crusoe* 402–23.

———. *The Origins of the English Novel 1600–1740*. Baltimore: Johns Hopkins UP, 1987.

McKillop, Alan D. *Masters of English Fiction*. Lawrence: U of Kansas P, 1956.

Michaels, Walter Benn. "The Gold Standard and the Logic of Naturalism." *Representations* 9 (1985): 105–32.

Miller, Nancy K. "'I's' in Drag: The Sex of Recollection." *Eighteenth Century: Theory and Interpretation* 22 (1981): 47–57.

Mish, Charles C. *English Prose Fiction, 1661–1700*. Charlottesville: Bib. Soc. of the U of Virginia, 1952.

Miskolcze, Robin. "Transatlantic Touchstone: The Shipwrecked Woman in British and Early American Literature." *Prose Studies* 22 (1999): 41–56.

Mitchell, John. "An Essay upon the Causes of the Different Colours of People in Different Climates." *Philosophical Transactions* 43 (1744): 102–50.

Moore, John Robert. *A Checklist of the Writings of Daniel Defoe.* 2nd ed. Hamden: Archon, 1971.

———. *Daniel Defoe, Citizen of the Modern World.* Chicago: U of Chicago P, 1958.

Neill, Anna. "Crusoe's Farther Adventures: Discovery, Trade, and the Law of Nations." *Eighteenth Century: Theory and Interpretation* 38 (1997): 213–30.

Nerlich, Michael. *Ideology of Adventure: Studies in Modern Consciousness, 1100–1750.* Vol. 2. Minneapolis: U of Minnesota P, 1987.

Novak, Maximillian E. "Defoe." *New Cambridge Bibliography of English Literature.* Ed. George Watson. Vol. 2. Cambridge: Cambridge UP, 1969–77. 880–917.

———. *Daniel Defoe: Master of Fictions.* Oxford: Oxford UP, 2001.

———. *Defoe and the Nature of Man.* Oxford: Oxford UP, 1963.

———. *Economics and the Fiction of Daniel Defoe.* Berkeley: U of California P, 1962.

———. "Friday; or, The Power of Naming." *Augustan Subjects: Essays in Honor of Martin C. Battestin.* Newark: U of Delaware P, 1997. 110–22.

———. *Realism, Myth, and History in Defoe's Fiction.* Lincoln: U of Nebraska P, 1983.

O'Brien, Robert C. *Z for Zachariah.* New York: Atheneum, 1974.

Occom, Samson. *A Sermon upon the Execution of Moses Paul, an Indian.* New Haven, 1772.

O'Dell, Scott. *Island of the Blue Dolphins.* Boston: Houghton, 1960.

———. "Newbery Award Acceptance Speech." *The Horn Book* 37.4 (1961): 311–16.

———. *Sarah Bishop.* Boston: Houghton, 1980.

———. *The Serpent Never Sleeps: A Novel of Jamestown and Pocahontas.* Boston: Houghton, 1987.

Oxford Anthology of English Literature. Ed. Frank Kermode and John Hollander. New York: Oxford UP, 1973.

Paltock, Robert. *The Life and Adventures of Peter Wilkins, a Cornish Man.* London: Robinson, 1751.

Parker, Gillian. "Crusoe through the Looking-Glass." *The English Novel and the Movies.* Ed. Michael Klein and Parker. New York: Ungar, 1981. 14–27.

Pearson, Jacqueline. *Women's Reading in Britain, 1750–1835: A Dangerous Recreation.* New York: Cambridge UP, 1999.

Peterson, Spiro. *Daniel Defoe: A Reference Guide, 1719–1724.* Boston: Hall, 1987.

Pitman, Henry. *A Relation of the Great Sufferings and Strange Adventures of Henry Pitman.* 1689. *An English Garner.* Ed. Edward Arber. Vol. 2. London: Constable, 1909. 431–76. 12 vols.

Poe, Edgar Allan. "Descent into the Maelstrom." 1841. *Tales of Mystery and Imagination.* London: Dent, 1912. 243–58. Nov. 1994. *Electronic Text Center*, Univ. of Virginia. 12 Aug. 2004 <http://etext.lib.Virginia.edu>. Path: Collection; English; Online Holdings; Modern English Collection; Browse by Author's Last Name.

The Police. "Message in a Bottle." *Reggatta de Blanc.* A&M, 1979.

Pomeranz, Kenneth. *The Great Divergence: Europe, China, and the Making of the Modern World Economy*. Princeton: Princeton UP, 2000.

Pope, Alexander. Excerpt. Defoe, *Robinson Crusoe* 261.

Preston, Cathy Lynn, and Michael J. Preston, eds. *The Other Print Tradition: Essays on Chapbooks, Broadsides, and Related Ephemera*. New York: Garland, 1995.

Preston, Michael J. "Rethinking Folklore, Rethinking Literature: Looking at *Robinson Crusoe* and *Gulliver's Travels* as Folktales, a Chapbook-Inspired Inquiry." Preston and Preston 19–73.

Reeve, Clara. *The Progress of Romance*. New York: Facsimile Text Soc., 1930.

Retamar, Roberto Fernández. *"Caliban" and Other Essays*. Trans. Edward Baker. Minneapolis: U of Minnesota P, 1989.

Reynolds, David S. *Walt Whitman's America*. New York: Knopf, 1995.

Richardson, Leon Burr, ed. *An Indian Preacher in England*. Hanover: Dartmouth, 1933.

Richetti, John J. *Defoe's Narratives*. Oxford: Oxford UP, 1975.

Robertson, J. G. *A History of German Literature*. Edinburgh: Blackwood, 1966.

Rogers, Pat, ed. *Daniel Defoe: The Critical Heritage*. London: Routledge, 1972.

———. *Robinson Crusoe*. Unwin Critical Library. Gen. ed. Claude Rawson. London: Allen, 1979.

Rogers, Woodes. "Account of Alexander Selkirk's Solitary Life on Juan Fernandez Island for Four Years and Four Months." Excerpt. Defoe, *Robinson Crusoe* 230–35.

Rousseau, Jean-Jacques. *Émile*. Trans. Barbara Foxley. London: Dent, 1993.

———. Of the Social Contract *and* Discourse on Political Economy. Trans. Charles R. Sherover. New York: Harper, 1984.

———. "Rousseau on *Robinson Crusoe*: 1762." Rogers, *Daniel Defoe* 52–53.

———. "A Treatise on Natural Education." Excerpt. Defoe, *Robinson Crusoe* 262–64.

Ryan, James. Editor's Preface. Knox, *Historical Relation*, ed. Ryan ix–xxiv.

Said, Edward W. "Invention, Memory, and Place." *Critical Inquiry* 26 (2000): 175–92.

Saint-Exupéry, Antoine de. *The Little Prince*. Trans. Katherine Woods. New York: Harcourt, 1943.

"Savagery." *The Oxford English Dictionary*. 2nd ed. 1989.

Sayre, Gordon. "Communion in Captivity: Torture, Martyrdom, and Gender in New France and New England." *Finding Colonial Americas: Essays Honoring J. A. Leo Lemay*. Ed. Carla Mulford and David S. Shields. Newark: U of Delaware P, 2001. 50–63.

———. *Les Sauvages Américains: Representations of Native Americans in French and English Colonial Literature*. Chapel Hill: U of North Carolina P, 1997.

Schonhorn, Manuel. *Defoe's Politics: Parliament, Power, Kingship and* Robinson Crusoe. Cambridge: Cambridge UP, 1991.

Sedgwick, Eve Kosofsky. *Between Men: English Literature and Male Homosocial Desire*. New York: Columbia UP, 1985.

Séguin, Alfred. *The Black Crusoe*. Freeport: Books for Libs., 1972. Trans. of *Robinson Noir*. 1877.

Seidel, Michael. "Crusoe in Exile." *PMLA* 96 (1981): 363–74.

———. *Robinson Crusoe: Island Myths and the Novel*. Boston: Hall, 1991.

Shakespeare, William. *The Tempest*. London: Arden, 1998.

Sharpe, Jenny. "The Original Paradise." *Transitions* 62 (1993): 48–57.

Sherman, Sandra. *Finance and Fictionality in the Early Eighteenth Century*. Cambridge: Cambridge UP, 1996.

Shiels, Robert. "Daniel Defoe." Rogers, *Daniel Defoe* 49–51.

Shinagel, Michael. *Defoe and Gentility*. Cambridge: Harvard UP, 1968.

Sill, Geoffrey. *The Cure of the Passions and the Origins of the English Novel*. Cambridge: Cambridge UP, 2001.

———. *Defoe and the Idea of Fiction*. Newark: U of Delaware P, 1983.

Sinyard, Neil. *Filming Literature: The Art of Screen Adaptation*. New York: St. Martin's, 1986.

Six Days Seven Nights. Dir. Ivan Reitman. Buena Vista, 1998.

Smeeks, Hendrik. *The Mighty Kingdom of Krinke Kesmes*. Trans. Robert-H. Leek. Introd. David Fausett. Amsterdam: Rodopi, 1995.

Spark, Muriel. *Robinson*. London: Macmillan, 1958.

Spence, Jonathan D. *The Chan's Great Continent: China in Western Minds*. New York: Norton, 1998.

Spencer, Jane. *The Rise of the Woman Novelist: From Aphra Behn to Jane Austen*. New York: Blackwell, 1986.

Spivak, Gayatri Chakravorty. "Can the Subaltern Speak?" *The Postcolonial Studies Reader*. Ed. Bill Ashcroft, Gareth Griffiths, and Helen Tiffin. New York: Routledge, 1995. 24–28.

Starr, George A. *Defoe and Casuistry*. Princeton: Princeton UP, 1971.

———. *Defoe and Spiritual Autobiography*. Princeton: Princeton UP, 1965.

Stauffer, Donald A. *The Art of Biography in Eighteenth-Century England*. Princeton: Princeton UP, 1941.

Steele, Richard. "On Alexander Selkirk." Defoe, *Robinson Crusoe* 235–38.

Stephen, Leslie. "Defoe's Novels." *Hours in a Library*. Vol. 1. London: Smith, 1874. 1–78.

Stevenson, Robert Louis. *Treasure Island*. New York: Modern Lib., 2001.

Stoler, John. *Daniel Defoe: An Annotated Bibliography of Modern Criticism, 1900–1980*. New York: Garland, 1984.

Sutherland, James. *Daniel Defoe: A Critical Study*. Cambridge: Harvard UP, 1971.

———. *Defoe*. 2nd ed. London: Methuen, 1950.

Svilpis, Janis. "Bourgeois Solitude in *Robinson Crusoe*." *English Studies in Canada* 22 (1996): 35–43.

Swept Away. Dir. Guy Ritchie. Columbia Pictures, 2002.

Swept Away by an Unusual Destiny in the Blue Sea of August. Dir. Lina Wertmüller. 1974.

Swift, Jonathan. *Gulliver's Travels*. Norton Critical Edition. Ed. Albert J. Rivero. New York: Norton, 2002.

Tocqueville, Alexis de. *Democracy in America*. Ed. Phillips Bradley. 2 vols. New York: Knopf, 1945.

Todd, Janet. *The Sign of Angellica: Women, Writing, and Fiction, 1660–1800*. New York: Columbia UP, 1989.

Tournier, Michel. *Friday; or, The Other Island*. Trans. Norman Denny. 1967. Baltimore: Johns Hopkins UP, 1997. Trans. of *Vendredi ou les limbes du Pacifique*. 1967.

Tucker, Nicholas. *The Child and the Book: A Psychological and Literary Exploration*. Cambridge: Cambridge UP, 1981.

Tufail, Abu Bakr Ibn. *The History of* Hayy Ibn Yaqzan. Trans. Simon Oakley. London: Chapman, 1929.

Turley, Hans. "Protestant Evangelism, British Imperialism, and Crusoian Identity." *The New Imperial History: Culture, Identity and Modernity in Britain and the Empire, 1660–1836*. Ed. Kathleen Wilson. Cambridge: Cambridge UP, 2004.

———. *Rum, Sodomy, and the Lash: Piracy, Sexuality, and Masculine Identity*. New York: New York UP, 1999.

Ullrich, Hermann. *Robinson und Robinsonaden. Bibliographie, Geschichte, Kritik*. Weimar: Felber, 1898.

Vaughan, Alden T. "From White Man to Redskin: Changing Anglo-American Perceptions of the American Indian." *American Historical Review* 87 (1982): 917–53.

Vergil. *Aeneid*. Trans. Robert Fitzgerald. New York: Random, 1983.

Verne, Jules. *The Mysterious Island*. New York: Airmont, 1965.

Vickers, Ilsa. *Defoe and the New Sciences*. Cambridge: Cambridge UP, 1996.

Voltaire, Francois-Marie Arouet. *Candide*. Mineola: Dover, 1991.

Walcott, Derek. *Collected Poems 1948–1984*. New York: Farrar, 1986.

———. "Crusoe's Island." *Collected Poems* 68–72.

———. "Crusoe's Journal." Lawall and Mack 2956–58.

———. "The Figure of Crusoe." 1965. *Critical Perspectives on Derek Walcott*. Ed. Robert D. Hamner. Washington: Three Continents, 1993. 33–40.

———. "An Interview with Derek Walcott." Interview with Edward Hirsch. *Conversations with Derek Walcott*. Ed. William Baer. Jackson: U of Mississippi P, 1996. 50–63.

———. "The Muse of History." *What the Twilight Says*. New York: Farrar, 1998. 36–64.

———. Remembrance *and* Pantomime. New York: Farrar, 1980.

Warner, William B. *Licensing Entertainment: The Elevation of Novel Reading in Britain, 1684–1750*. Berkeley: U of California P, 1998.

Watt, Ian. "Defoe as Novelist." *Pelican Guide to English Literature*. Ed. Boris Ford. Vol. 4. Harmondsworth: Penguin, 1957. 203–17.

———. *Myths of Modern Individualism: Faust, Don Quixote, Don Juan, Robinson Crusoe*. Cambridge: Cambridge UP, 1996.

———. *The Rise of the Novel: Studies in Defoe, Richardson, and Fielding*. 1957. 6th ed. Berkeley: U of California P, 1967.

———. "*Robinson Crusoe* as a Myth." Defoe, *Robinson Crusoe* 288–306.

Weber, Max. *The Protestant Ethic and the Spirit of Capitalism*. New York: Scribner's, 1958.

Wheeler, Roxann. "The Complexion of Desire: Racial Ideology and Mid-Eighteenth-Century British Novels." *Eighteenth-Century Studies* 32 (1999): 309–32.

———. *The Complexion of Race*. Philadelphia: U of Pennsylvania P, 2000.

———. "'My Savage,' 'My Man': Racial Multiplicity in *Robinson Crusoe*." *ELH* 62 (1995): 821–61.

White, Hayden. *Tropics of Discourse: Essays in Cultural Criticism*. Baltimore: Johns Hopkins UP, 1978.

Whitman, Walt. *Complete Poetry and Collected Prose*. New York: Lib. of America, 1982.

———. "Democratic Vistas." *Complete Poetry* 929–94.

———. "Elias Hicks." *Complete Poetry* 1221–44.

———. "The Federal Constitution." *Complete Poetry* 1318–19.

———. "Preface to 1855 Edition of *Leaves of Grass*." *Complete Poetry* 5–26.

———. "Song of Myself." *Complete Poetry* 27–88.

Wiesel, Elie. *Night*. 1960. New York: Bantam, 1982.

Winkfield, Unca Eliza [pseud.]. *The Female American; or, The Adventures of Unca Eliza Winkfield*. Ed. Michelle Burnham. Peterborough, Ont.: Broadview, 2001.

———. *The Female American*. 1767. New York: Garland, 1974.

Wolves of the Sea (also known as *Jungle Island*). Dir. Elmer Clifton. Guaranteed, 1938.

Wood, William. *New Englands Prospect*. 1634. New York: Franklin, 1967.

Woolf, Virginia. "Robinson Crusoe." Excerpt. Defoe, *Robinson Crusoe* 283–88.

———. *The Essays*. Ed. Andrew McNeillie. Vol. 4. London: Hogarth, 1986–94.

Wright-St. Clair, Rex E. *Doctors Monro: A Medical Saga*. London: Wellcome Hist. Medical Lib., 1964.

Wyss, Johann David. *The Swiss Family Robinson*. Ed. John Seelye. New York: Oxford UP, 1994.

———. *Swiss Family Robinson*. Illus. Fritz Uredel. Garden City: Delux, 1954.

Yolen, Jane. *Children of the Wolf*. New York: Viking, 1984.

Yorinks, Arthur. *Hey, Al*. Illus. Richard Egielski. New York: Farrar, 1986.

Zagrodnik, Karen. "Voyages of the Unknown, Voyages of the Self: Women in Early Eighteenth-Century Travel Writings." Diss. Auburn U, 1998.

Zimmerman, Everett. *Defoe and the Novel*. Berkeley: U of California P, 1975.

INDEX

Modern Language Association of America

Approaches to Teaching World Literature

Joseph Gibaldi, series editor

Achebe's Things Fall Apart. Ed. Bernth Lindfors. 1991.

Arthurian Tradition. Ed. Maureen Fries and Jeanie Watson. 1992.

Atwood's The Handmaid's Tale *and Other Works.* Ed. Sharon R. Wilson, Thomas B. Friedman, and Shannon Hengen. 1996.

Austen's Emma. Ed. Marcia McClintock Folsom. 2004.

Austen's Pride and Prejudice. Ed. Marcia McClintock Folsom. 1993.

Balzac's Old Goriot. Ed. Michal Peled Ginsburg. 2000.

Baudelaire's Flowers of Evil. Ed. Laurence M. Porter. 2000.

Beckett's Waiting for Godot. Ed. June Schlueter and Enoch Brater. 1991.

Beowulf. Ed. Jess B. Bessinger, Jr., and Robert F. Yeager. 1984.

Blake's Songs of Innocence and of Experience. Ed. Robert F. Gleckner and Mark L. Greenberg. 1989.

Boccaccio's Decameron. Ed. James H. McGregor. 2000.

British Women Poets of the Romantic Period. Ed. Stephen C. Behrendt and Harriet Kramer Linkin. 1997.

Brontë's Jane Eyre. Ed. Diane Long Hoeveler and Beth Lau. 1993.

Byron's Poetry. Ed. Frederick W. Shilstone. 1991.

Camus's The Plague. Ed. Steven G. Kellman. 1985.

Cather's My Ántonia. Ed. Susan J. Rosowski. 1989.

Cervantes' Don Quixote. Ed. Richard Bjornson. 1984.

Chaucer's Canterbury Tales. Ed. Joseph Gibaldi. 1980.

Chopin's The Awakening. Ed. Bernard Koloski. 1988.

Coleridge's Poetry and Prose. Ed. Richard E. Matlak. 1991.

Conrad's "Heart of Darkness" and "The Secret Sharer." Ed. Hunt Hawkins and Brian W. Shaffer. 2002.

Dante's Divine Comedy. Ed. Carole Slade. 1982.

Defoe's Robinson Crusoe. Ed. Maximillian E. Novak and Carl Fisher. 2005.

Dickens' David Copperfield. Ed. Richard J. Dunn. 1984.

Dickinson's Poetry. Ed. Robin Riley Fast and Christine Mack Gordon. 1989.

Narrative of the Life of Frederick Douglass. Ed. James C. Hall. 1999.

Eliot's Middlemarch. Ed. Kathleen Blake. 1990.

Eliot's Poetry and Plays. Ed. Jewel Spears Brooker. 1988.

Shorter Elizabethan Poetry. Ed. Patrick Cheney and Anne Lake Prescott. 2000.

Ellison's Invisible Man. Ed. Susan Resneck Parr and Pancho Savery. 1989.

English Renaissance Drama. Ed. Karen Bamford and Alexander Leggatt. 2002.

Works of Louise Erdrich. Ed. Gregg Sarris, Connie A. Jacobs, and James R. Giles. 2004.

Dramas of Euripides. Ed. Robin Mitchell-Boyask. 2002.

Faulkner's The Sound and the Fury. Ed. Stephen Hahn and Arthur F. Kinney. 1996.

Flaubert's Madame Bovary. Ed. Laurence M. Porter and Eugene F. Gray. 1995.

García Márquez's One Hundred Years of Solitude. Ed. María Elena de Valdés and Mario J. Valdés. 1990.

Gilman's "The Yellow Wall-Paper" and Herland. Ed. Denise D. Knight and Cynthia J. Davis.

Goethe's Faust. Ed. Douglas J. McMillan. 1987.

Gothic Fiction: The British and American Traditions. Ed. Diane Long Hoeveler and Tamar Heller. 2003.

Hebrew Bible as Literature in Translation. Ed. Barry N. Olshen and Yael S. Feldman. 1989.

Homer's Iliad *and* Odyssey. Ed. Kostas Myrsiades. 1987.

Ibsen's A Doll House. Ed. Yvonne Shafer. 1985.

Works of Samuel Johnson. Ed. David R. Anderson and Gwin J. Kolb. 1993.

Joyce's Ulysses. Ed. Kathleen McCormick and Erwin R. Steinberg. 1993.

Kafka's Short Fiction. Ed. Richard T. Gray. 1995.

Keats's Poetry. Ed. Walter H. Evert and Jack W. Rhodes. 1991.

Kingston's The Woman Warrior. Ed. Shirley Geok-lin Lim. 1991.

Lafayette's The Princess of Clèves. Ed. Faith E. Beasley and Katharine Ann Jensen. 1998.

Works of D. H. Lawrence. Ed. M. Elizabeth Sargent and Garry Watson. 2001.

Lessing's The Golden Notebook. Ed. Carey Kaplan and Ellen Cronan Rose. 1989.

Mann's Death in Venice *and Other Short Fiction.* Ed. Jeffrey B. Berlin. 1992.

Medieval English Drama. Ed. Richard K. Emmerson. 1990.

Melville's Moby-Dick. Ed. Martin Bickman. 1985.

Metaphysical Poets. Ed. Sidney Gottlieb. 1990.

Miller's Death of a Salesman. Ed. Matthew C. Roudané. 1995.

Milton's Paradise Lost. Ed. Galbraith M. Crump. 1986.

Molière's Tartuffe *and Other Plays.* Ed. James F. Gaines and Michael S. Koppisch. 1995.

Momaday's The Way to Rainy Mountain. Ed. Kenneth M. Roemer. 1988.

Montaigne's Essays. Ed. Patrick Henry. 1994.

Novels of Toni Morrison. Ed. Nellie Y. McKay and Kathryn Earle. 1997.

Murasaki Shikibu's The Tale of Genji. Ed. Edward Kamens. 1993.

Pope's Poetry. Ed. Wallace Jackson and R. Paul Yoder. 1993.

Proust's Fiction and Criticism. Ed. Elyane Dezon-Jones and Inge Crosman Wimmers. 2003.

Rousseau's Confessions *and* Reveries of the Solitary Walker. Ed. John C. O'Neal and Ourida Mostefai. 2003.

Shakespeare's Hamlet. Ed. Bernice W. Kliman. 2001.

Shakespeare's King Lear. Ed. Robert H. Ray. 1986.

Shakespeare's Romeo and Juliet. Ed. Maurice Hunt. 2000.

Shakespeare's The Tempest *and Other Late Romances.* Ed. Maurice Hunt. 1992.

Shelley's Frankenstein. Ed. Stephen C. Behrendt. 1990.

Shelley's Poetry. Ed. Spencer Hall. 1990.

Sir Gawain and the Green Knight. Ed. Miriam Youngerman Miller and
    Jane Chance. 1986.

Spenser's Faerie Queene. Ed. David Lee Miller and Alexander Dunlop. 1994.

Stendhal's The Red and the Black. Ed. Dean de la Motte and Stirling Haig. 1999.

Sterne's Tristram Shandy. Ed. Melvyn New. 1989.

Stowe's Uncle Tom's Cabin. Ed. Elizabeth Ammons and Susan Belasco. 2000.

Swift's Gulliver's Travels. Ed. Edward J. Rielly. 1988.

Thoreau's Walden *and Other Works*. Ed. Richard J. Schneider. 1996.

Tolstoy's Anna Karenina. Ed. Liza Knapp and Amy Mandelker. 2003.

Vergil's Aeneid. Ed. William S. Anderson and Lorina N. Quartarone. 2002.

Voltaire's Candide. Ed. Renée Waldinger. 1987.

Whitman's Leaves of Grass. Ed. Donald D. Kummings. 1990.

Woolf's To the Lighthouse. Ed. Beth Rigel Daugherty and Mary Beth Pringle. 2001.

Wordsworth's Poetry. Ed. Spencer Hall, with Jonathan Ramsey. 1986.

Wright's Native Son. Ed. James A. Miller. 1997.